PARLIAMENT IN THE
GERMAN POLITICAL SYSTEM

The Bundestag in session. (Courtesy of Presse- und Informationsamt der Bundesregierung.)

PARLIAMENT
IN THE
German Political
System

By Gerhard Loewenberg

CORNELL UNIVERSITY PRESS
ITHACA, NEW YORK

Library of Congress Catalog Card Number: 66–23776

PRINTED IN THE UNITED STATES OF AMERICA

BY KINGSPORT PRESS, INC.

ILLUSTRATIONS PRINTED BY ARTCRAFT OF ITHACA

To my mother
and the memory
of my father

Preface

NO political institution is more clearly the creature of custom and convention than is a parliament. The precedents which the oldest parliaments of the world have developed, and which the newest have quickly borrowed, are evidence that parliaments depend heavily on tradition for their characteristic norms of procedure and patterns of organization. The study of any parliament therefore poses questions about its institutional origins. Consequently, after a brief introductory chapter, my analysis of the German Bundestag begins with an examination of the continuities and discontinuities of the German parliamentary tradition (Chapter II).

But a parliament is more than the product of a tradition. At any given moment, it consists of a group of members whose training and skills interact with inherited rules and structures. Chapter III deals with the Members of the German Parliament, their backgrounds, the process by which they are selected, and their parliamentary performances. Chapter IV considers the structure in which they act—both its formal, inherited elements and its informal responses to a rapidly changing political environment.

A parliament is related to other institutions in the political system and acts with them in carrying out the basic political functions. The second half of the book thus examines the role of the Bundestag in the performance of three major political functions: the selection of executive personnel (Chapter V), the making of rules (Chapter VI), and communication between the Government and the public (Chapter VII). The conclusion summarizes the chief consequences for the German political system of the particular relationship which exists between the structure of the Bundestag and the functions it performs. That relationship is a major theme of the book.

As indicated in the introductory chapter, the study of parliamentary institutions outside the United States and Great Britain enters on *terra incognita*. I have therefore set out in considerable detail the evidence I have gathered, both because it is not readily available and because I wanted to allow readers to consider the data for themselves and, quite possibly, to reach conclusions different from mine. This will explain, even if it does not entirely excuse, the length of the book.

Any study of a foreign political system raises questions of the translation of terms. I have used English equivalents drawn largely from the vocabulary of the House of Commons (e.g., whip, parliamentary party) because they correspond with familiar usage and are therefore more intelligible than literal translations would be (e.g., parliamentary business manager, faction). To avoid any possible confusion, however, I have given the German names of each major office or title the first time its English equivalent appears. I have used "Government" in the Continental European sense as an equivalent for "Cabinet," and have occasionally employed "caucus" as an equivalent for the full meeting of the parliamentary party. In the text I have also used some familiar American equivalents for the names of various Bundestag committees.

The sources for this book consist not only of the parliamentary documents, newspapers, and works of German political scientists which are cited in the footnotes, but also of information supplied by Members of Parliament and their staffs, and by ministerial officials— information which, in most cases, cannot be individually attributed. The willingness of many people to answer my questions candidly and extensively, and to make confidential documents available to me, has added decisively to my understanding of the institution, and I am glad to acknowledge the interested and helpful responses which I received.

This book would not have been possible without the cooperation of innumerable members of the staff of the Bundestag. I am grateful to the Director, Hans Trossmann, and to the Chief of the Research Division, Dr. Kurt Wernicke, for permitting me to work in the Bundeshaus for more than a year. I want especially to acknowledge the assistance of Dr. Gerhard Zwoch, who made the splendid resources of the Bundestag library available to me, and to thank the librarians, Berta Himme, Friederike Kloska, Ilsemarie Querner, and Anni Storbeck, for their unfailing help. I also owe many kindnesses to Kurt Homfeld, who permitted me to work in the parliamentary newspaper archives over a period of several months. Above all, I am deeply indebted to Werner Blischke, head of the Office of Legal Research, who generously placed his extraordinary knowledge of the German Parliament at my disposal at every stage of my work, and whose careful reading of the manuscript saved me from countless errors.

In Bonn I also enjoyed the help of many members of the staffs of the parliamentary parties, and of various parliamentary journalists. I profited especially from the friendly willingness of Dr. Ulrich Dübber, formerly RIAS correspondent in Bonn, to share with me his exceptionally well informed views on German politics.

At various points in my research, I had valuable help from a large number of scholars in this country and abroad. I am indebted for their interest and advice to Professor Gerard Braunthal of the University of Massachusetts, Professor Ernst Fraenkel of the Free University of Berlin, Professor Carl J. Friedrich of Harvard University, Dr. Wolfgang Kralewski of the University of Heidelberg, Professor Karl Loewenstein of Amherst College, Dr. Charles Naef of Colgate University, Dr. Eberhard Pikart of the Theodor Heuss Archiv, Professor Ulrich Scheuner of the University of Bonn, and Professor Rudolf Wildenmann of the Wirtschaftshochschule in Mannheim. From the beginning of my research to the end, I was especially fortunate to have the help, encouragement, and skillful criticism of the late Professor Otto Kirchheimer. I would also like to thank Professor Lewis Bowman of the University of Virginia for initiating me into the mysteries of data coding and analysis which proved of decisive value in handling the statistical material throughout the book.

The manuscript profited greatly from the meticulous and sensitive reading of Professor A. R. L. Gurland of the Technische Hochschule of Darmstadt. He generously applied his mastery of parliamentary sociology to the improvement of Chapter III, and made me aware of various problems of translation. Professor Steven Muller of Cornell University read the entire manuscript and made a number of important suggestions which have immeasurably improved the organization and clarity of the book. I am also grateful to the editors of the Cornell University Press for their interest in the manuscript from an early stage, and for their valuable editorial suggestions.

My friends and colleagues at Mount Holyoke College have given me moral support and stimulation throughout the phases of my work. The research librarians, Kathleen Cole and Nancy Devine, cheerfully and efficiently responded to my endless stream of requests for esoteric volumes on interlibrary loan, and supplied answers to the greatest variety of desperate questions.

My interest in the subject was first aroused during eight months of study at the University of Bonn in 1957–1958 under the auspices of a Fulbright Research Grant. A sabbatical leave from Mount Holyoke College and a grant from the Rockefeller Foundation permitted me to spend an uninterrupted year of research in Bonn in 1961–1962. I am deeply grateful to Dr. Gerald Freund of the Rockefeller Foundation for his confidence in my work. A Faculty Research Grant from the Social Science Research Council freed me from my teaching responsibilities during the fall semester, 1964–1965, enabling me to complete the writing of the manuscript, and permitted me to make a brief visit to Bonn during the summer of 1965 to bring my material up to date. I am also glad to acknowledge a supplementary grant from the Tona Shepherd Estate, and the help of Inter Nationes, Bonn, in supplying research materials.

Whatever merit this book may have as a study in comparative government is largely the result of my training at Cornell University, and is due particularly to my teacher, Professor Mario Einaudi, who taught me, by his example, what I know of standards of scholarship.

From the beginning, my wife Ina collaborated in every aspect of the work of this book. Most specifically, she spent the leisure time of more than one year in collecting and coding the biographical and performance data on Members of Parliament on which quantitative analyses throughout the book are based. She has also been the most severe and valuable critic both of the style and the logic of the entire presentation as it developed through numerous drafts.

This partial attempt to correct the misleading impression that this book is the work of one individual is of course an acknowledgment of debts, not an effort to spread the blame for the shortcomings which remain.

GERHARD LOEWENBERG

South Hadley, Massachusetts
April 7, 1966

Contents

Tables

Charts

Plates

Abbreviations

POLITICAL PARTIES

BP	Bayernpartei (Bavarian Party)
CDU/CSU	Christlich-Demokratische Union/Christlich-Soziale Union (Christian Democratic Union/Christian Social Union)
DFU	Deutsche Friedensunion (German Peace Union)
DP	Deutsche Partei (German Party)
DRP	Deutsche Reichspartei (German Reich Party)
FDP	Freie Demokratische Partei (Free Democratic Party)
FU	Föderalistische Union (Federal Union)
GB/BHE	Gesamtdeutscher Block/Block der Heimatvertriebenen und Entrechteten (All-German Bloc/Bloc of Refugees and Expellees)
GDP	Gesamtdeutsche Partei (All-German Party)
KPD	Kommunistische Partei Deutschlands (Communist Party of Germany)
NPD	Nationaldemokratische Partei Deutschlands (National Democratic Party of Germany)
SPD	Sozialdemokratische Partei Deutschlands (Social Democratic Party of Germany)
SSW	Südschleswigsche Wählervereinigung (South Schleswig Electoral League)
WAV	Wirtschaftliche Aufbauvereinigung (Economic Reconstruction League)
Z	Zentrum (Center Party)

PARLIAMENT IN THE
GERMAN POLITICAL SYSTEM

Introduction:
The Study of Parliaments

ASSERTIONS about the decline of parliament have been repeated with such confidence and frequency in this century that parliament has generally been dismissed as an unworthy subject for political study. As a result, the decline of parliament has become a dogma, subject to neither verification, refutation, nor qualification. Because of insufficient evidence to the contrary, the decline has been alleged to be not only true, but the whole truth.

Yet the conclusion that parliaments are in decline as institutions of government has never been based on careful inquiry into the function of parliaments in their presumed golden age, nor into their subsequent performance. In most cases, it has been merely the expression of nineteenth-century liberal prejudices on the adaptation of parliamentary institutions to twentieth-century democratic society. Such prejudices have prompted regrets about the declining intellectual ability of members, about the divisive effects of ideology and class-bound parties, about the rise in the temperature of parliamentary controversy, and about the multiplication of special interests in parliament. These developments have undoubtedly taken place, but they are the consequences of democratization. Unquestionably they have challenged the existing institutional framework of parliament, and the existing conventions and usages governing traditional parliamentary behavior. But this only means that the institution of parliament, like other political institutions, is subject to change in the process of political modernization. Instead of studying this change, observers have too often written it off as "decline."

Negative judgments on the transformation of parliaments also express the disappointment of the liberal faith that parliamentary institutions were a panacea for all the ills of the old autocracies. As soon as it became apparent that parliaments in France, Germany, and Italy, for

example, had taken on a national coloration, that they had not automatically introduced a British style into the politics of these states, and
that, worse still, they were quite consistent with elements of autocracy
and corruption, unqualified despair replaced what had been unrestrained hope.

The spectacular growth and development of executive institutions,
in contrast to the apparent rigidity of traditional parliamentary structures, may further explain the greater fascination which the cabinet,
presidency, and bureaucracy have held for students of political institutions. The proliferation of interest groups, and the intensification of
party organization, may explain the tendency to concentrate on groups
and parties to the exclusion of the parliamentary framework within
which they operate. But it should be perfectly obvious by now that
parliaments have survived the repeated prophecies of their demise,
have in fact vastly multiplied with the increase of independent states
and international political communities, and have performed political
functions of greatly varying significance in different political systems.
The role of parliament differs so clearly from one country to another,
and within particular countries over time, as to defy any general
conclusions about the institution. A far closer look at existing parliaments is needed before the last word can justifiably be spoken on
them.

The structure of parliaments has enabled them, at one time or
another, to play a role in the recruitment of executive personnel, in
lawmaking, in political communication between governors and the
governed, in the integration of interests, and in the legitimation of
policy. The study of parliaments is therefore not only the examination
of one of the oldest surviving political institutions of the Western
world, but it also leads necessarily into a consideration of the performance of some of the most important functions of the political system.

Parliament has occupied a particularly critical place in Germany.
Toward the end of the last century, it provided the chief access to
government for those large sections of the population whose entry into
politics marked the transformation of the old autocracy into a modern
democratic state. In the first third of this century, the failure of the
political system to achieve a balance between governmental authority
and popular participation was in large part due to the failure of the
German Parliament to perform necessary political functions. In the
sixty years of its existence on a national stage, it had not developed

adequate norms and procedures by which the conflicting demands of interest groups could be reconciled. It had not become a satisfactory source of executive personnel. It had not won the prestige necessary to supply legitimacy for a political system which could no longer rely on the belief in the divine right of kings. The failure of the Parliament helped to create the institutional vacuum on which totalitarianism thrived, and on which it built its own characteristic combination of mass participation and authority.

There was no question about the need for a national parliament in the postwar German political system. No institution received so little attention from the constitutional draftsmen. None was so generally taken for granted. A clear connection was assumed between the fate of parliament and the fate of German democracy. In fact, the awareness of the congenital weaknesses of German parliaments prompted widespread fears of a repetition of the disastrous history of the institution. Neither professional nor political observers in 1949 anticipated the sharply different development which parliament took in the postwar period.

An inquiry into the performance of parliament in the German political system after 1949 therefore has special fascination. In a nation which never knew a golden age of parliament, it is fatuous to speak of the decline of the institution, and therefore obviously important to examine its actual place. In a nation whose problems of political development have had such dire effect on the world, an examination of what has been a critical political institution has special importance. Finally, the particular combination of tradition and change which characterizes the evolution of the German Parliament offers exceptional insights into sources of institutional stability, and into causes of institutional adaptation to the dynamics of the political system.

Tradition and Change

T H E development of German parliaments has been closely con-
nected with German unification. By the standards of Western
Europe, both developments came remarkably late; but by the standards of other parts of the continent, it is notable that they came at all.
The name "Reichstag", to be sure, has a venerable history. The imperial diets which bore that name from the Middle Ages onward were
irregularly convened assemblies of the realm, and were composed of
delegates of the politically independent principalities and the estates
into which the nation was divided. As such, the Reichstage did not
represent the nation in any modern sense. Their members had no
discretion to go beyond the fixed instructions given them by their
principals. Rather than representative deliberative assemblies, the
Reichstage were congresses of ambassadors which, in the absence of a
central governing power, had no fixed jurisdiction.

THE SOURCES OF PARLIAMENTARY TRADITION

The provincial diets were of greater importance for the development of a parliamentary tradition. But the effectiveness of these bodies
also suffered from the divisions of the nation. The antagonism among
the different classes these parliaments represented weakened them
decisively in the various contests with their princes. Nevertheless,
according to the historian Carsten, these regional parliaments "preserved the spirit of constitutional government and liberty in the age of
absolute monarchy." [1] They were strongest in the states of the southwest, where an expansion of the suffrage in the early nineteenth

[1] F. L. Carsten, *Princes and Parliaments in Germany, From the Fifteenth to the
Eighteenth Century* (Oxford: Clarendon Press, 1959), p. 444.

century gave them a popular basis and made them training grounds for the first generation of German parliamentarians.

This was the extent of the German parliamentary tradition a scant hundred years before the present incarnation of parliamentary institutions in the Federal Republic of Germany. Among the various German political traditions, parliamentarism was vastly overshadowed by absolutism and monarchy. Carsten finds that "the tendency to denigrate the German Estates and to side with the princes, who tried to suppress them, persists to the present day." [2] When, in the revolutionary year 1848, a genuine all-German parliament convened, which, by including Austria, represented a larger proportion of German-speaking peoples than any subsequent parliament, its objectives were premature by the German calendar of political development. Meeting in Frankfurt as both legislative and constituent assembly, it drafted a constitution for a German national state in which the central government would be responsible to a popularly elected parliament. But, required as it was to address itself simultaneously to the problem of national unification and the problem of drafting a constitution, it experienced divisions of unusual complexity and severity. Despite the extraordinary caliber of its members, their lack of parliamentary experience proved a major obstacle to success, since the Frankfurt assembly began its work without an adequate appreciation of organizational and procedural prerequisites. Although it had been called into being by revolutionary uprisings throughout the country, and was elected by a universal franchise, its slow-moving work was not sustained by a national public. After a year of deliberations, it succumbed to the military forces available to the major German princes who opposed its aims.

Failure came because the parliament of 1848 had not been preceded either by national unification or by national representative institutions. Nevertheless, it marked the beginning of a genuine parliamentary development which, despite its sharp discontinuities, can be traced to the present day. It was in the Frankfurt Assembly that the parliamentary caucus first made its appearance among like-minded Members meeting in the cafés of the city, that political parties first formed to create popular support for the assembly's work, that parliamentary procedure first developed under the guidance of the notable student of Western European practices, Robert von Mohl, and that constitutional provisions for a national parliament based on universal suffrage

[2] *Ibid.*, p. 434.

were first drafted.[3] Between the failure of 1848 and the year 1871, the indispensable conditions for successful national unification and institutional development were created in the distinctive autocratic political environment of Prussia.

Constitutional Position of Parliament

Revolutionary events in Prussia had caused the Monarch to respond to long-standing demands for a constitution by promulgating a document which provided for a bicameral assembly to share with the King the power to enact legislation and appropriations. Monarchical prerogatives in the command of the armed forces, the appointment and dismissal of ministers, and the control of administration were not diminished. In the first chamber, a house of lords, members served by inheritance or by royal appointment. In the second, a house of representatives, the franchise was based on a division of the electorate into three classes which were equal only in the tax revenues derived from each and were, accordingly, grossly unequal in numbers. Since each class received equal representation in the chamber regardless of its numbers, the system assured that the House would have majorities equally as obedient to the Monarch as those in the other house. The overrepresentation of the highest income groups—at first landowners, and later industrialists as well—gave two-thirds of the seats to that fifth of the population paying the highest taxes, and discouraged the participation of the remainder of the electorate.[4]

---

[3] See Ludwig Bergsträsser, *Die Entwicklung des Parlamentarismus in Deutschland* (Schloss Laupheim Württ.: Ulrich Steiner Verlag, 1954), pp. 9–10; Wilhelm Treue, *Parlamentarismus in Deutschland, Entstehung und Entwicklung* (Bonn: Schriftenreihe der Bundeszentrale für Heimatsdienst, No. 54, 1961), pp. 12–16.

[4] In 1912, while voter participation in the Reichstag elections was 84.9%, only 32.8% participated in the elections for the Prussian House of Representatives. (Cited by Werner Frauendienst, "Zeitalter des persönlichen Regiments Wilhelms II," in *Das Parlament*, Sept. 28, 1960, p. 7. This issue of *Das Parlament* has been reprinted as Ernst Deuerlein, ed., *Der Reichstag: Aufsätze, Protokolle, und Darstellungen zur Geschichte der parlamentarischen Vertretung des deutschen Volkes* [Schriftenreihe der Bundeszentrale für Heimatsdienst, No. 58, 1963]; see p. 69.) In 1913, the percentage of the electorate in the three classes was I, 4.43%; II, 15.76%; III, 79.81% (cited by Herman Finer, *Theory and Practice of Modern Government,* rev. ed. [New York: Holt, 1949], p. 229). The Prussian Constitution of January 31, 1850, and the executive order promulgating the electoral system of May 30, 1849, can be found in *Quellen zum Staatsrecht der Neuzeit* (Tübingen: Matthiesen, 1949), I, 209–33.

These circumstances deeply affected the development of parliamentary institutions. First, that they were a gift of the King undermined the self-confidence of their members, notably in the conflict over military expenditures in 1862 in which the Government took the position that the King's business had to go on even in the absence of appropriations. Second, the fantastically unrepresentative electoral system discouraged popular support for the new institution (the survival of the system in Prussia until 1918 seriously undermined the popular basis of the later national government as well). Finally, the introduction of a parliamentary assembly into an autocratic system of long standing created a separation between the old and the new institutions, rather than the close parliamentary relationship existing in Great Britain.

These facts received a most influential justification in the constitutional theory of the conservative jurist, Friedrich Julius Stahl. Sharply contrasting the German system with the parliamentary system of government, Stahl wrote that in the German constitutional monarchy "the king has the right and the power to govern, by himself," that the ministers are responsible to the king, not to parliament, and that parliament is limited to giving its consent to new legislation and appropriations, and to the right of petition. In such a system—which, according to Stahl, alone corresponded to German traditions and requirements—parliament was confined to a peripheral role in the legislative process, and the Monarch was not answerable to the chambers nor subject to their influence. Rather, a sharp separation of personnel and powers divided the King and his Government from the representatives of the people, and, according to Stahl, the constitution obliged both sides to maintain their distance.[5] Until 1918, this theory provided the concepts in which parliamentarism was discussed in Germany, affecting its supporters and critics alike. Its vocabulary continues to exert influence to this day.

[5] Friedrich Julius Stahl, *Die Philosophie des Rechts*, Vol. II, *Rechts- und Staatslehre auf der Grundlage christlicher Weltanschauung*, 3rd ed. (Tübingen and Leipzig: Mohr, 1856), Pt. II, pp. 383–423, esp. p. 393. Cf. Dieter Grosser, *Grundlagen und Struktur der Staatslehre Friedrich Julius Stahls* (Cologne and Opladen: Westdeutscher Verlag, 1963), pp. 113–25; Friedrich Glum, *Das parlamentarische Regierungssystem in Deutschland, Grossbritannien, und Frankreich* (Munich and Berlin: C. H. Beck'sche Verlagshandlung, 1950), pp. 45–9; Bergsträsser, *op. cit.*, p. 11; Treue, *op. cit.*, pp. 16–31.

Parliamentary Procedure

The rules and organization adopted by the Prussian House of Representatives had a germinal effect on German parliamentary procedure. The model was British, as it had come to be understood on the Continent through the exposition of Bentham and the adaptation of British procedure found in French and especially Belgian practice. In his *Essay on Political Tactics,* published in 1816,[6] Bentham had made a unique attempt to describe British procedure, as it had historically developed to that time, in a logical and systematic manner. His analysis of the main provisions in terms of their utility in promoting rational legislative decisions assumed that the Parliament was a separate branch in the system of government whose rules facilitated the performance of its distinctive legislative functions. Precisely because this view failed to take account of the evolution of a cabinet system of government, it made British practice appear more relevant to the needs of the Prussian chamber than might otherwise have been the case. Bentham stressed publicity of proceedings, impartiality of the presiding officer, separation of the stages of deliberation from proposition through three readings to a vote, and free and extemporaneous debate.

When these principles found their way into French and Belgian practice, they were amended to take account of the ascendancy of the Government over Parliament which existed in those countries, as it did in Prussia. Among the notable Continental additions was a curtailed legislative procedure for cases of urgency (which Bentham found "terrible" when it was adopted in France), a system of specialized committees to examine bills, the privilege of members of the Government and their assistants to be heard at any time in the Parliament and its committees, and the right of Members to address questions to the Government and to debate the reply in the form of an interpellation. The Benthamite principles, and some aspects of their Continental reception, gained the admiration of Robert von Mohl, the chairman of the Committee on Rules in the Frankfurt Assembly, and through his influence and that of others, they substantially became the basis for the rules of procedure of the Prussian House. The most important French-Belgian element in the procedure of the Prussian chamber was

[6] John Bowring, ed., *The Works of Jeremy Bentham* (Edinburgh: Tait, 1848), II, 299–373.

the provision for specialized committees which prepared important bills for debate in the House.[7]

Parliamentary Parties

Neither Bentham's principles nor French and Belgian experience took account of the procedural problems raised by the existence of modern political parties in parliament. But by the middle of the 1860's parliamentary parties had become so important in the Prussian chamber that the appointment of committees could no longer be made without them.[8] Particularly the smaller ones among them could not hope for fair representation in the committees by means of the formal system of making appointments through the sections (*Abteilungen*) into which the House was divided by lot, nor could they hope for adequate participation in debate so long as speakers were recognized in the order in which they entered their names on a speakers list.

As a result, an informal Council of Seniors, consisting of the party leaders, began to make the arrangements which were of interest to the parties—notably the committee appointments, the order of speakers in debate, and later the determination of the size of committees and their chairmen. Membership in party groups correspondingly gained in importance. Although the Council of Seniors was not formally recognized in the Rules until after the First World War, it played an organizational role of immense importance even in this early period. It replaced some aspects of the formal organization, such as the sections, restricted others, such as the discretion of the President, and marked the beginning of a process of adapting the rules of a nineteenth-century legislature composed of individual Representatives to the requirements of a multiparty parliament.[9]

Meanwhile, the formal procedure was slightly revised in 1862 and became the basis of the procedure adopted in 1867 by the Reichstag of the North German Confederation. The main changes made at that

[7] Carl J. Friedrich, *Constitutional Government and Democracy*, rev. ed. (Boston: Ginn, 1950), pp. 306–9 and n. 7, p. 636; Josef Redlich, *The Procedure of the House of Commons, A Study of Its History and Present Form*, trans. by A. Ernest Steinthal (London: Archibald Constable & Co., 1909), Vol. III, Bk. III, Ch. I–II; Bruno Dechamps, *Macht und Arbeit der Ausschüsse* (Meisenheim am Glan: Westculturverlag Anton Hain, 1954), pp. 55–7.

[8] Dechamps, *op. cit.*, pp. 58, 132–4.

[9] Hans Trossman, "Reichstag und Bundestag—Organisation und Arbeitsweise," in *Das Parlament*, Sept. 28, 1960, p. 15, or Ernst Deuerlein, *op. cit.*, pp. 129–30.

time provided for a clear distinction between three readings in the legislative process, with the committee stage coming between the general first and the detailed second readings, and for the reservation of one day a week for private members' bills. In this form, the Rules became the inheritance of the first Reichstag of a unified German state in 1871.[10] They were the product of twenty years of legislative experience under constitutional monarchy, and were, suitably enough, the basis for the following forty-seven years during which parliament remained confined within the same system.

THE IMPERIAL REICHSTAG

National Institutions

The unification of 1871 nevertheless had a profound influence on parliamentary development. In the first place, it placed a representative assembly on a national stage with national attention and national issues. Second, it made this assembly the popular element in a mixed constitution, basing it on a remarkably progressive universal manhood suffrage which was designed by Bismarck to insure the widest possible representation of political views. But third, it put beside the Reichstag, sharply separated from it by a prohibition of dual membership, the Bundesrat, composed of instructed representatives from the *Länder*.

This institution expressed the incompleteness of a unification which had proceeded by force. Presuming collectively to constitute the federal executive, the Bundesrat in fact rapidly lost control over the burgeoning federal bureaucracy developing under the Imperial Chancellor. The Chancellor, ordinarily also Minister-President of Prussia, was, as such, responsible to a King who still claimed to govern by divine right. This Chancellor was, naturally, the dominant figure in the Bundesrat. Neither he nor his colleagues in the Bundesrat could be touched or held accountable by the popularly elected national Reichstag.[11] In this artfully constructed chaos which characterized the constitutional system of the German Empire, the chances of a parlia-

[10] The development of the Rules of Procedure is conveniently given in the *Synoptische Darstellung der Geschäftsordnung des Deutschen Bundestages und ihrer Vorläufer*, prepared by the Wissenschaftliche Abteilung, Deutscher Bundestag (Bonn, 1961).

[11] This relationship is clearly described by Walter J. Shepard, "Tendencies Toward Ministerial Responsibility in Germany," *The American Political Science Review*, V (1911), 57–69.

mentary relationship between central government and Reichstag were doomed, and the Reichstag was condemned to be the only democratically representative element in an essentially authoritarian pattern. Again the representative assembly was given a share in the legislative process, but again it was sharply separated from the executive.

National Politics

During the half century of the Empire, the industrialization of the economy and the urbanization of the population effectively nationalized German politics. The problems presented by the industrial revolution determined the importance of the Reichstag in the new system of government. The national budget increased tenfold between 1872 and 1913, the national bureaucracy doubled between 1861 and 1891, and the population grew 50 per cent between 1881 and 1911, the urban component rising from 41 to 60 per cent of the total. The need for basic national legislation grew accordingly; tariff, tax, agricultural, labor, and social security legislation of fundamental importance was enacted, not to speak of the civil and criminal codes, large parts of which are in effect to the present day. The legislative role of the Reichstag had a corresponding importance. Since no bill could become law without its approval, the ability of the Government to make policy, if not its tenure in office, depended on Reichstag approval.[12]

National Parties

Bismarck, during the nineteen years of his tenure, sought to secure the support of the Reichstag by direct negotiation with the party groups whose growing importance in that body was a direct result of the establishment of universal suffrage. Appearing first in the Frankfurt Assembly to agree on parliamentary tactics, strengthened then in the Prussian chamber through their control of committee appointments, these groups now became closely related to the electoral organizations which were growing in the country to appeal to the new, large, national electorate on the basis of programs containing general political and philosophical principles. The parliamentary caucuses, first inspired by parliamentary tactical considerations, were now at-

---

[12] My interpretation of the role of the Reichstag during the Empire owes much to Eberhard Pikart and especially to his important article, "Die rolle der Parteien im deutschen konstitutionellen System vor 1914," *Zeitschrift für Politik*, IX n.f. (1962), 12–32.

tached to extraparliamentary organizations and inspired by electoral considerations. The resulting party system had the curious characteristics which resulted from the juxtaposition of an advanced universal suffrage and a traditional monarchical government for which the parties had no responsibility. Under no compulsion to make the practical compromises which government requires, parties espoused programs based on a combination of tenaciously held principles and commitments to special economic interests. Under no compulsion to build governing majorities, parliamentary groups multiplied and prompted the multiplication of national parties. The electoral system permitting a second ballot runoff lessened the risk of divided appeals on the first ballot. The many-sided sectional, ideological, religious, and economic differences in the incompletely unified nation gained full expression in the party system. Under the influence of a rigid class society, party organization was in the hands of the existing elites, except in the Socialist and Center parties, where a new political elite was forming, narrow in its own way. The rank-and-file voter whose support was sought at the polls was not at first drawn actively into politics.

Under these conditions, Bismarck's tactics were to maintain close personal relations with party leaders controlling a Reichstag majority. He depended first on the National Liberal party, later shifting alliances to the Conservatives. With the help of these allies, he obtained legislation directed against the newer, less tractable parties, first against the Catholic Center party and then against the Social Democratic party, with only short-run success in either case. The "Kulturkampf" against the first party and the anti-Socialist legislation against the second were promoted with such fervor that they left a permanent effect on political attitudes. The concept that parties supporting the Chancellor supported the state, while those opposing him were in rebellion, stems from this time. Bismarck's maneuvers to divide the parties opposing him contributed to the multiplication of liberal parties. Although he was occasionally successful in appeals to the voters on behalf of the parties supporting him, the price of these tactics was a deepening distrust between parliamentary party leaders and the Government for which they bore no responsibility.[13]

[13] Thomas Nipperdey, *Die Organisation der deutschen Parteien vor 1918* (Düsseldorf: Droste Verlag, 1961), esp. pp. 9–41, 158–74, 196–200, 209–17, 261–4, 284–92, 381–6, 393–6.

Executive-Legislative Relations

Neither Bismarck's successors in the Chancellorship, nor, certainly, the new Emperor who fancied himself the real head of the Government, was able to build the necessary Reichstag majorities with Bismarck's highly personal methods. In the years following Bismarck's period in office, his two main political adversaries, the Center and the Socialists, were successively the largest parties in the Reichstag. (The Socialists achieved this position in 1912 despite the operation against them of a silent gerrymander: no redistricting of Reichstag constituencies took place between 1871 and 1918 to take account of the rapid growth of the urban bastions of Social Democracy.) Futhermore, a generation after the introduction of the universal suffrage, the parties began to develop into mass voter organizations attracting wide political participation. Meanwhile, the economic transformation of society brought forth with increasing strength the claims of special interests with which the parties had to deal.

Both developments increased the complexity of deliberations in the Reichstag. The party groups were less and less the docile following of traditional leaders, but self-assertive representatives of local, regional, and national interests. In confronting them, the Government was compelled to make greater concessions in the negotiations within the legislative committees which were established *ad hoc* by the Reichstag for all important legislation. The enduring practice was developed at this time that the Government would be represented in the committees by a large number of officials competent to make the necessary compromises on legislation, and willing to supply extensive information on matters of administration. Since their deliberations were confidential, the committees became the most important bodies in the legislative process. Only in privacy could Members of different parties reach agreements with each other, and with the Government.[14] Although little legislation was initiated by Members of the Reichstag, little legislation passed it without considerable change, and the administration of legislation was subject to its surveillance. Through the parties and the press, an interested electorate could follow the discussions in the public sessions of the House. Interested groups could seek

[14] Adolf Neumann-Hofer, "Die Wirksamkeit der Kommissionen in den Parlamenten," *Zeitschrift für Politik,* IV (1911), 51–85.

to influence the results.[15] But the Reichstag's decisions were increasingly taken in private—a practice that posed a distinct threat to the popular basis of the institution, as some of its more perceptive members realized even at the time.[16]

Bülow, the first Chancellor of the new century, consciously based his Government on a particular group of parties in the Reichstag, thereby acknowledging his need of a definite majority in the House. When this support failed in 1909, he took the consequences and resigned.[17] How far the position of the Government had come from being independent of Parliament and responsible only to the Emperor, as the constitution said, was suddenly but briefly illuminated by the lightning flash of the *"Daily Telegraph* Affair" of 1908. In response to the publication in England of an interview with the Emperor in which he expressed some highly personal foreign policy views, a united Reichstag conducted an interpellation debate in which the Government was called to account.[18] But the constitutional means for dismissing the Government were lacking, nor did they follow. Despite much talk of the need for "parliamentarization" of government, public indifference, the division of parties along interest-group lines, and the lack of a theoretical understanding of the parliamentary system combined as obstacles to constitutional reform. Although the Government had become dependent on the Reichstag for support of its program, it did not depend on the confidence of the Reichstag for its tenure in office. For example, an adverse vote against Bülow's successor, Bethmann-Hollweg, in the "Zabern Affair" in 1913, did not produce his resignation.[19]

In most cases, those who urged "parliamentarization" of government envisaged Reichstag influence on the appointment and dismissal of Governments, not government by a Cabinet chosen from among members of a Reichstag majority. In the middle of the previous century, von Mohl had written, in defense of a genuine parliamentary system, that he could not see why the "higher political view and the general direction of the power of the state would not come just as easily to a

[15] Pikart, *op. cit.*, pp. 23, 25.
[16] Hellmuth von Gerlach, *Das Parlament* (Frankfurt: Rütten und Loening, 1907), p. 50.
[17] Glum, *op. cit.*, p. 56.
[18] *Verhandlungen des deutschen Reichstages*, XII. Legislaturperiode, Nov. 10–11, 1908, pp. 5373–5439.
[19] Frauendienst, in Deuerlein, *op. cit.*, p. 73.

man experienced in parliamentary affairs and controversies, as to an official trained in the chancellery." [20] He had warned that the German system created a dangerous dualism between a Government having the power and an assembly limited to criticism and participation in legislation.[21] But after forty years under the Bismarckian constitution, even the meaning of parliamentary government had become uncertain.[22]

Procedural Innovation

Instead, a national representative assembly had developed which was divided into a multiplicity of modern political parties with dogmatic programs and active organizations in the country, placing the Members under pressure from a politicized electorate. The sharp differences among the parliamentary parties, unsoftened by the hope for office or responsibility for government, generated tactics of obstruction and disorder, endless procedural disputes, the destruction of existing parliamentary conventions, and even wholesale abstention to deny quorums. To meet these unaccustomed challenges to order, the Reichstag, in the first generation of its existence, adopted one set of procedural reforms. They were similar to those adopted a generation earlier by the House of Commons and admired by the Austrian jurist, Josef Redlich; [23] but while in England they strengthened the governing majority, in Germany they could only improve order among minorities. The ability of the President to deal with disorderly Members and with obstruction was strengthened. He obtained power to exclude Members from the sessions, to exercise discretion in accepting points of order, and to deny quorum calls if he, in agreement with the Members who served as Secretaries (Schriftführer), found them unjustified. A new procedure to facilitate voting, patterned after the "divisions" of the House of Commons, had been introduced in the Reichstag's first decade. Abuses of recorded votes were diminished by

[20] "Das Repräsentativsystem, seine Mängel und die Heilmittel" (1852), reprinted in Staatsrecht, Völkerrecht, und Politik (Tübingen: Verlag der H. Lauppschen Buchhandlung, 1860), I, 427.

[21] Ibid., p. 394.

[22] Pikart, op. cit., pp. 18–19. Cf. Reinhard J. Lamer, Der englische Parlamentarismus in der deutschen politischen Theorie im Zeitalter Bismarcks, 1857–1890 (Lübeck: Matthiesen, 1963).

[23] See his introduction to The Procedure of the House of Commons, pp. xxiii–xxvii.

the introduction of voting cards in 1902.[24] But weak attendance at its sessions enabled the larger parties to obstruct business by withdrawing their Representatives and causing the loss of a quorum. Under this pressure, the Government finally yielded to the Reichstag's long insistence on compensation for its Members.

Changes in Parliamentary Recruitment

For Bismarck, the constitutionally anchored prohibition against salaries for Members was a crucial counterweight to the universal suffrage. He expected that it would reduce the representation of the lower classes, and limit the length of Reichstag sessions.[25] Furthermore, it corresponded with the liberal-conservative conception of Reichstag membership as an avocation of the socially dominant classes, so well illustrated by the National Assembly of 1848. Fifty-five per cent of its Members were government officials and 38 per cent were drawn from the free professions, notably law.[26] However, the denial of parliamentary salaries had quite different consequences in the context of the social changes attending industrialization in the latter part of the nineteenth century. To be sure, it gave special advantages to candidates having independent sources of income, large business owners as well as landed aristocrats. But while 40 per cent of the Members were from the nobility in the first Bismarckian Reichstag, the figure was only 12 per cent at the end of the Empire. Owners of large business enterprises made up 6 per cent of the membership in the last decade of the nineteenth century, but by 1912 their representation had been halved. Because they could have leave to hold parliamentary mandates while continuing to draw their salaries and retain pension and seniority rights, Government officials were particularly favored; they made up 27 per cent of the first Imperial Reichstag, but their number, too, was reduced—to 12 per cent of the total—by 1912.

Those practicing professions which could be successfully combined with parliamentary activity, notably lawyers and writers, found no great obstacles in the absence of parliamentary salary; lawyers made

[24] Julius Hatschek, *Das Parlamentsrecht des deutschen Reiches* (Berlin and Leipzig: G. J. Göschen'sche Verlagshandlung, 1915), pp. 62–83.

[25] Theodor Eschenburg, *Der Sold des Politikers* (Stuttgart: Seewald Verlag, 1959), pp. 53–9.

[26] Karl Demeter, "Die soziale Schichtung des deutschen Parlaments seit 1848; ein Spiegelbild der Strukturwandlung des Volkes," *Vierteljahresschrift für Sozial und Wirtschaftsgeschichte*, XXXIX (1952), 1–29.

up a steady 10 per cent of the membership throughout the existence of the Empire. Because men from all other social and occupational backgrounds required special financial assistance to enter the Reichstag, the practice of parties and interest groups maintaining their representatives developed early, first among parties of the left and soon thereafter among the economic interest groups which multiplied with the advance of industrialization. Furthermore, politicians sought "double mandates," combining unpaid Reichstag positions with paid Landtag mandates. Both tendencies promoted professionalism in politics. By 1912, 24 per cent of Reichstag Members were party or interest group employees.

The introduction, in 1906, of payment of RM 3000 annually to Members, in the form of compensation for expenses rather than the constitutionally prohibited salary, did little to slow this trend in the composition of Parliament. Cunningly devised so that one-third of the amount would be withheld until the conclusion of the session, this compensation recognized, rather than caused, the decline of the political amateur drawn from the social elites. It provided a source of funds to the Social Democrats who promptly taxed their Members' pay to permit redistribution within the party. By deductions for absence, it created an inducement to regular attendance, discouraging organized abstention as a means of obstruction. But it did little to diminish the financial barrier to a parliamentary career. Such a barrier, far from maintaining the Reichstag as the preserve of the old privileged classes, merely meant that the new classes, forming as a result of industrialization, and every bit as class-conscious as the old, gained parliamentary representation through a new type of representative who was the product of political mass organization.[27]

Constitutional Crisis

Access to ministerial positions was still not possible for these professional politicians, however; and they could only endeavor to influence the Government by means of the legislative and appropriations powers of the Reichstag, and by means of public debate. To facilitate debate, another set of procedural reforms was enacted in 1912—a slow response to the famous interpellation of 1908. Against the Government's

[27] Peter Molt, *Der Reichstag vor der improvisierten Revolution* (Cologne and Opladen: Westdeutscher Verlag, 1963), pp. 38–48, 76–9, 155, 161–5, 193, 326–55.

constitutional doubts, the Reichstag asserted the right to follow an interpellation with a motion and a vote on the Government's reply. It also introduced the procedure of oral questions addressed to the Government, with supplementaries, on the model of the House of Commons' question period.[28] Although the stenographic record reports "hilarity and 'bravo' on the Right" when a government official refused to reply to the first question asked under the new rules—it was on foreign economic policy—the opposition parties made active use of the new instrument.[29]

By the time the First World War brought its normal activity to an end, the Reichstag created by Bismarck had succeeded in expanding its influence and asserting its independence in the system of government. But it never escaped the ambiguous position which Bismarck had given it, open to the political divisions of the electorate on the one hand, and, on the other, shut out from participation in the Government. Caught in a vicious circle, its lack of responsibility for government and exposure to increasingly complex interest-group pressures deepened its partisan divisions, which, in turn, made it incapable of governing. Whatever may have been accomplished in the imperial half century to establish a popularly elected representative legislature on the national political scene, that institution had received inadequate experience for the responsibilities that suddenly fell on it when the autocracy collapsed in October and November of 1918.

Out of public view, the transition to parliamentary government began over a year before the end of the war. In July, 1917, the leaders of the center parties in the Reichstag began regular, confidential meetings to arrive at a common position on an armistice and on other major policy questions. The Government, its authority weakening, gave this interparty committee running reports on the state of hostilities. Some members of the committee received appointment to ministerial positions. This constellation of center parties—presaging the Wei-

[28] *Geschäftsordnung des Reichstages*, pars. 31, 33. *Verhandlungen des deutschen Reichstages*, XIII. Legislaturperiode, May 3, 1912, pp. 1653–74, and May 8, 1912, pp. 1747 ff.

[29] *Ibid.*, May 14, 1912, p. 1960. Of 742 questions asked in the Reichstag between 1912 and 1918, the Social Democrats alone asked one-third of the total. The Conservatives refused, on the other hand, to participate in the new procedure until 1917 (*ibid.*, Sachregister, CCXCVI, 9184–9; CCCIV, 6303–20. E. G. Hoppe, "Die kleine Anfrage im deutschen Reichstage" [unpublished doctoral dissertation, University of Kiel, 1930], pp. 51–9, 72).

mar coalition—the experience of negotiation among the parliamentary leaders on major policy issues, and the close contact with the Cabinet, all laid the basis for the new political system. But although the interparty committee exercised a veto over the formation of Governments in the last year of the war, its leaders did not themselves take power until it was foisted on them by the abdication of the supreme military command and the flight of the Emperor, at the moment of an externally imposed defeat. By then time had run out for gradual reforms.[30]

THE REICHSTAG IN THE WEIMAR REPUBLIC

Constitutional Provisions

Although the new constitutional order foresaw a parliamentary system, it also perpetuated the fateful dualism of Government and Parliament. The new Weimar Constitution established a popularly elected presidency as a substitute for the widely mourned monarchy, in an effort to create a fixed star in the constitutional firmament, a counterweight, in the words of its chief draftsman, to the parties and the Parliament. Fears of a French-style assembly regime, admiration for the stable British parliamentary system, nostalgia for the monarchy, and the absence of a theory of parliamentary government free of monarchism, combined to produce the Weimar presidency. Amidst the disorders which had compelled the Constituent Assembly to meet in Weimar rather than Berlin, few doubts were expressed about the need to equip the President with substantial powers. The expectation was that, in normal times, the President and the Parliament, presumed to have a common constituency in the national electorate, would exist in harmony on the basis of "reciprocal respect." [31]

[30] The process of "parliamentarization" in the last two decades of the Empire is traced by Werner Frauendienst, "Demokratisierung des deutschen Konstitutionalismus in der Zeit Wilhelms II," *Zeitschrift für die gesamte Staatswissenschaft*, CXIII (1957), 721 ff. The development during the war is summarized by Rudolf Morsey, "Der Reichstag im ersten Weltkrieg, 1914–1918," in Deuerlein, *op. cit.*, pp. 75–84. The documentation of the interparty committee, and the last Government under the Empire, recently published, reveals the transition from the imperial to the Weimar political system in fascinating detail (Erich Matthias and Rudolph Morsey, eds., *Der Interfraktionelle Ausschuss 1917/18* [2 vols.], and *Die Regierung des Prinzen Max von Baden* [Düsseldorf: Droste Verlag, 1959, 1962]).

[31] Friedrich Glum, *op. cit.*, Ch. VII.

Party Behavior

What this constitutional structure failed to take into account was the behavior of the parties. Instead of responding to the opportunities for party government, they responded to opportunities for the centralization of party organization given by a new electoral system, and to the temptation to sharpen party programs in the crisis atmosphere of the postwar period. Building on the tendencies of the prewar years, the parties evolved further in the direction of doctrinaire mass organizations, failing to adapt adequately to the new constitution which made it possible for them to serve as sources of governmental leadership, and as policy-making organizations. The system of multiple parties hardened and promoted political division, formed obstacles to political integration, and prevented the Reichstag from playing the new governmental role which the constitution had opened for it.[32]

The electoral system of proportional representation enshrined in the new constitution gave even the smallest minorities and the newest formations their proportional quota of seats in the Reichstag. In the form adopted, the system divided the nation into only thirty-five constituencies and provided a national constituency for pooling "unused votes," thus placing the power of nomination into the hands of party leaders at the intermediate and national levels. The autonomy of the local organization, previously a source of individual differences within the parliamentary parties, was destroyed. In the first years of the Republic, party membership grew markedly. It is estimated that by 1920 15 per cent of the voters—a total of four to four-and-a-half million persons—were party members. This measure of mass organization, and the attendant development of party bureaucracies, created a new locus of power within the parties, above the local organization, outside of, and able to dominate, the parliamentary caucus. In some parties, like the Center party, and the German National People's party in 1928, the leadership of the parliamentary group was separated from the leadership of the party outside Parliament. Even where this did not occur, tensions developed between the parliamentary representatives and the party organizations, and in notable instances the parlia-

[32] Karl Dietrich Bracher, *Die Auflösung der Weimarer Republik*, 2d ed. (Stuttgart: Ring Verlag, 1957), pp. 28–37; Gerhard A. Ritter, *Deutscher und Britischer Parlamentarismus, ein verfassungsgeschichtlicher Vergleich* (Tübingen: J. C. B. Mohr Verlag, 1962), pp. 39–49.

mentary group was instructed by party congresses or executives.[33] The composition of the Reichstag corresponded to this development, with an increase in the number of Members who were party or interest-group employes, and a decline in Members who were popular local figures or were drawn from the free professions.[34]

The parliamentary groups themselves were more thoroughly or-ganized, whether under their own or under extra-parliamentary leader-ship. Voting discipline was so great that, on the average for all parties between 1924 and 1932, over 90 per cent of the Members voted with the majority of their group.[35] The caucus not only determined the vote, but selected the speaker to defend the party viewpoint, frequently giving him detailed instructions. It decided upon motions to be intro-duced, on committee appointments and tactics, and on the question of confidence in the Government.[36] Instances occurred of caucuses de-ciding to vote against Cabinets in which their own members partici-pated, even against the advice of their Ministers, and it happened that an SPD Chancellor, obedient to the decision of his parliamentary group, voted against his own Cabinet proposals in the Reichstag.[37]

Parliamentary Immobilisme

With a dozen such party groups consistently represented in it, some of them in opposition to the constitutional system itself, it was difficult for the Reichstag either to create Governments, to legislate, or to appeal to the electorate for a decision. Governing coalitions were made and unmade with great frequency in private negotiation among party leaders, not as the result of parliamentary votes of confidence or censure. When no agreement was possible on Members of the Reichs-tag to compose the Cabinet, compromise candidates were drawn from the outside, even from outside of party politics. Only eight of the twenty Cabinets during the Weimar Republic had the support of the Reichstag majority; the remainder were minority governments "tol-erated" by the House.[38]

The composition of Reichstag committees by an automatic calcula-

[33] Nipperdey, *op. cit.*, 396–406; Bracher, *op. cit.*, pp. 77–83.
[34] Demeter, *op. cit.*, pp. 1–29.
[35] Heinz Markmann, *Das Abstimmungsverhalten der Parteifraktionen in deutsch-en Parlamenten* (Meisenheim am Glan: Verlag Anton Hain, 1955), pp. 74–5.
[36] Walter Lambach, *Die Herrschaft der Fünfhundert* (Hamburg and Berlin: Hanseatische Verlagsanstalt, 1926), p. 96.
[37] Bracher, *op. cit.*, p. 35.   [38] Glum, *op. cit.*, Ch. IX.

tion of party strengths, and the selection of chairmen according to a comparable formula, caused paralysis in the work of some important committees. The Judiciary Committee, for example, twice refused to work under the chairman imposed on it, once when he was a Communist, once when he was a National Socialist.[39]

The use of procedure to obstruct took the forms of filibustering, endless quorum calls, and disorder. With some success the problem was met by revisions of the Rules, as it had been dealt with in the Imperial Reichstag, strengthening the power of the President of the Reichstag to maintain order, and limiting the speaking time to one hour.[40] In other cases, informal alterations were made in practice. Because of the flood of interpellations brought by the parties, they were no longer separately treated, but combined with substantive questions, especially with appropriations measures, thereby, however, destroying their distinctive purpose.[41] Likewise, the unrestrained use of oral questions, by the successors to those antiparliamentary parties which had found them ridiculous when instituted under the Empire, led to the practice of answering them in writing and thereby robbing them of their special publicity value. Paradoxically, the very parties which had promoted the institution of the question period in the final years of the Empire as a parliamentary instrument, voted for its abandonment within the first two years of the Weimar Republic, as a measure to defend parliamentary order.[42] The absence of procedural consensus indicated the weakness of the commitment to the institution of parliament.

Procedural changes were not adequate to enable the Parliament to

---

[39] Theodor Heuss, "Der Parlaments-Ausschuss," *Jahrbuch für politische Forschung*, I (1933), 136–7.

[40] *Geschäftsordnung des Reichstages*, par. 87, par. 90 and 91 as amended December 11, 1929, and February 9, 1931; Lambach, *op. cit.*, pp. 107, 112.

[41] Of 237 interpellations introduced between 1923 and 1928, only one led to a vote of censure on the Government (May 6, 1926) and only four were discussed separately; 118 were never reached (P. Thamm, "Die gegenwärtige Handhabung der Interpellation im Deutschen Reichstag" [unpublished doctoral dissertation, University of Kiel, 1930], pp. 71, 77, 85–94, 121–8).

[42] Of 2,901 questions asked between 1919 and 1922, the two conservative parties initiated nearly half. After the 1922 Rules' change, the total number declined markedly, to an average of a hundred between 1923 and 1926, and less than 30 annually thereafter, none of which were orally answered. For the statistics see Hoppe, *op. cit.*, pp. 71–3. For the debate on the Rules' change, see *Verhandlungen des deutschen Reichstages*, I. Wahlperiode, (November 23, 1922), pp. 9085–93.

perform its functions of creating Governments and deciding policy questions. In the first major domestic crisis, the inflation of 1922, the Reichstag delegated its lawmaking power to the Cabinet by means of a vote which in effect temporarily changed the Constitution.

This act of abdication contributed to the unfavorable popular comparison between parliamentary government incapacitated by partisan rivalry, and the recollection of the unity of the Imperial Government. Ignorance of the prerequisites of parliamentary government was equally great among the voters, the party leaders, and many of the constitutional lawyers. A spate of sometimes learned, sometimes popular treatises on the disintegration of the state under the influence of parliament and parties, in part cynically inspired by reactionary groups, in part merely confused or nostalgic, undermined confidence in the possibilities of parliamentary government in intellectual and official circles. These attacks persisted even during the five relatively tranquil years between the end of the economic crisis of 1922–1923 and the advent of the depression.[43]

When the world economic collapse of 1929–1930 confronted the Cabinet with a succession of serious policy problems, all of the weaknesses of the parliamentary system of the past ten years combined to obstruct action. After overthrowing the Government of Chancellor Müller in 1930, on a minor issue of increasing unemployment benefits, the Reichstag was unable either to form a new governing majority, or to allow a minority Government to take emergency measures. An ill-advised appeal to the electorate for a decision, in the midst of severe economic dislocations, produced a threefold increase in the strength of the radical parties of the totalitarian left and right, the National Socialists winning 107 seats where they had had 12, and the Communists increasing their strength from 54 to 77. Against this large antiparliamentary minority, only a great coalition of the remaining parties could have made parliamentary government possible. But this coalition was as unlikely in the moment of crisis as it had been earlier. Although parliamentary government was thereby doomed, the possibilities of constitutional government were not yet exhausted. The dualism of the constitutional system left the alternative of a presiden-

---

[43] The most invidious academic attack on the parliamentary system came from a noted legal scholar of the period, Carl Schmitt. See especially his *Geistesgeschichtliche Lage des heutigen Parlamentarismus* (Berlin: Duncker & Humblot, 1st edition, 1925). See also Bracher, *op. cit.*, pp. 37–47; Glum, *op. cit.*, Ch. VIII.

tial emergency regime, an alternative which helped to deter the formation of a parliamentary coalition because it offered the party leaders an escape from responsibility. At least the more conservative of them, nostalgic for authoritarianism, were not sorry to take it. The Reichstag, meeting only 41 times in 1931 and a mere 13 times in 1932, had, in effect, abdicated three years before Hitler came to power.[44]

The Inheritance

The chief elements of the German parliamentary tradition had taken shape during its longest period of uninterrupted development, between 1871 and 1914. On the eve of the First World War, the Reichstag performed substantial functions in the political system. Its membership contained authoritative spokesmen of major economic interests who bargained with each other and with the Government, in the process of writing the legislation for the new industrial society. If the Reichstag did not create the Governments, governing without it was impossible. But in the period of intensified conflict among parties and interest groups after the First World War, the institution formed in the governmental system of the Empire proved unsuited to the constitutional system of the Republic. Above all, it could not adequately supply the executive personnel required by a parliamentary government, form stable governing coalitions, negotiate settlements to the severe economic conflicts of the period, and provide the new regime with legitimacy. Disciplined political parties increasingly controlled their parliamentary representatives. The constant and direct intervention of highly organized interest groups made it difficult for the parties to reconcile their conflicting demands. The parties' desire to gain tactical electoral advantages overwhelmed their ability to negotiate policy decisions, paralyzing both parliamentary processes and governmental power. A fatal schism between the Reichstag of the parties, unable to act, and the problems of society, requiring urgent action, isolated Parliament from the public, undermined the electoral support of the parliamentary parties, and finally opened the way for the antiparliamentary movements and the Reichstag's unlamented demise. In this sense, the Weimar period added nothing to the German parliamentary tradition except a lesson on its inadequacies.

[44] Glum, *op. cit.*, pp. 232–45; Bracher, *op. cit.*, pp. 47–63. See also Werner Conze, in E. Matthias and R. Morsey, *Das Ende der Parteien* (Düsseldorf: Droste Verlag, 1960), pp. 3–8.

In the tragic interregnum between 1930 and 1933, presidential emergency powers, unused since the first five postwar years, became the legal basis of government, and the conservative ex-General who occupied the presidency, himself the product of the inability of the parties to present adequate political leadership in the first presidential election of 1925, was the sole source of authority. Cut off from Parliament, from most parties and interest groups, this Government became increasingly unrepresentative of the major forces in society, both in its composition and in its policies. Five elections in 1932, a caricature of the democratic appeal to the electorate, were abortive attempts to gain popular support for this form of presidential government. These elections only illustrated the growing radicalism among the voters. They included, in addition to two Reichstag elections which gave Nazis and Communists together a majority in the House, a two-ballot presidential election which returned Hindenburg, who had been supported, in their desperation, by all parties except the radical extremes. Landtag elections in four-fifths of the country gave additional evidence of Nazi strength. A last, frantic effort to restore authoritarian government of the pre-World War I variety failed with the ludicrous spectacle of the Government of the conservative aristocrat, Franz von Papen, which possessed no visible support outside of the narrow group surrounding President Hindenburg. In the final caricature of democracy, Hindenburg sought recourse to a Government possessing popular approval, and invested Hitler as Chancellor on the basis of his leadership of the largest party in the Reichstag. The radical changes which thereupon transformed conservative presidential government into totalitarian dictatorship demonstrated the weakness of traditional authoritarianism against the potency of a dictatorship capable of mobilizing the masses.[45]

THE RECONSTRUCTION OF PARLIAMENT

The Nature of the Commitment

The traumatic experience of Nazism effectively destroyed the appeal of the authoritarian alternatives with which parliamentary government had had to compete previously for public support. After 1918,

[45] The definitive study of the final phase is Bracher, *op. cit.*, Pt. II, and Karl Dietrich Bracher, Wolfgang Sauer, and Gerhard Schulz, *Die nationalsozialistische Machtergreifung* (Cologne and Opladen: Westdeutscher Verlag, 1960).

Parliament had been unable to replace the monarchy as the source of legitimacy for the political system. After 1945, there was at least a negative commitment to parliamentary government: *pas de mieux*, it was the only viable alternative to the systems which had brought unmistakable disaster. "We see no other way than that of a parliamentary democracy based on the experience of the free peoples of the West," Hermann Ehlers, a widely respected Bundestag President, could honestly say several years later.[46] But a negative commitment did not, of course, assure the previously elusive combination of governmental authority and popular participation expressed through parliamentary institutions. It assured only a concerted effort by political leaders to re-establish parliamentary institutions, and to give them greater influence within the political system.

Members

The catastrophe of Nazism had, however, destroyed many of the resources needed for the re-establishment of Parliament. Custom, tradition, and continuity, the psychological prerequisites of political institutions, were among the most important victims of the "thousand years" of destruction which separated 1933 from 1945. Few Members of the prewar Reichstag, accustomed to its norms of behavior, were available to serve in the Bundestag. When the first Bundestag convened on September 7, 1949, more than sixteen years had passed since Hitler's accession to power, and nearly twenty years since the Reichstag had, in effect, abdicated to presidential dictatorship. Between the generation of parliamentarians of 1930 and that of 1949, there existed the deep schism of totalitarian experience, which left no politician untouched. The old Reichstag building, symbolically, lay in ruins, the victim first of arson, then of the battle of Berlin. The ranks of the Members of the last free Reichstage were decimated by twelve years of persecution which brought exile, concentration camps, and death. Of 498 Reichstag and Landtag Members in democratic parties before Hitler's accession, 195 did not survive; and another 121 went into exile, many never to return. In all, 416 Members experienced Gestapo arrest, and 327 spent time in concentration camps.[47] Among the 402 Members

[46] "Die Fundamente des Parlaments" (radio address, Dec., 1951), reprinted in Friedrich Schramm, ed., *Um dem Vaterland zu Dienen* (Cologne: Schmidt, 1955), p. 7.
[47] Walter Hammer, *Hohes Haus in Henkers Hand* (Frankfurt: Europäische Verlagsanstalt, 1956), pp. 9, 123–5.

of the first Bundestag, only 61 had parliamentary experience on any level before 1933, fewer than one-third of these in the Reichstag. Although these included some prominent men, such as the former Reichstag President Paul Löbe and the leader of the SPD, Kurt Schumacher, their number was very small, and their own personal experience of limited importance to the new institution.

Rules and Powers

The German parliamentary tradition was therefore transmitted to the Bundestag indirectly. That part of it which was available in written rules of procedure and constitutional provisions was taken over largely intact. No question was raised about their relevance to postwar political circumstances. The provisions of the Basic Law establishing the Bundestag were largely copied from the Weimar Constitution. They created a popularly elected representative assembly with a four year term.[48] The Rules of Procedure adopted by the House closely followed the Rules of the Weimar Reichstag.[49] The weakness of the political system of Weimar was attributed not to the structure of Parliament, but to its place in the political system. The

[48] *Basic Law,* art. 38–49. For the drafting of these provisions, see Klaus-Berto von Doemming, Rudolf Werner Füsslein, and Werner Matz, "Die Entstehungsgeschichte der Artikel des Grundgesetzes," in Gerhard Leibholz and Hermann von Mangoldt, eds., *Jahrbuch des öffentlichen Rechts* (Tübingen: J. C. B. Mohr, 1951), I n.f., 346–79.

The dates of the first five terms of the Bundestag were as follows:

Term	Date of first meeting
1st Bundestag	September 7, 1949
2nd Bundestag	October 6, 1953
3rd Bundestag	October 15, 1957
4th Bundestag	October 17, 1961
5th Bundestag	October 19, 1965

Under the provisions of the Basic Law (art. 39), the term of the Bundestag ends four years after its first meeting, unless it has been dissolved prior to that date. Dissolution is possible only under limited circumstances (see n. 50, *infra*) and none of the first four Bundestage were dissolved.

Elections must be held within the last quarter-year of a parliamentary term, or, at latest, 60 days after dissolution. The electoral law specifies that the Federal President sets the date of the election; by custom he follows the recommendation of the Cabinet. A newly elected House convenes at latest 30 days after its election, but not prior to the end of the previous term.

[49] The main changes were those required by the altered relationship between Government and Parliament (H. G. Ritzel, "Parlamentarische Geschäftsordnungen im Reichstag und im Bundestag," in Deuerlein, *op. cit.*, pp. 145 ff.). See also *Synoptische Darstellung der Geschäftsordnung des deutschen Bundestages.*

chief constitutional innovations, as far as Parliament was concerned, were therefore designed to increase its importance in the system. The appointment of the Chancellor was specifically assigned to the Bundestag, which was to act by election. No escape from parliamentary to presidential government was permitted under the Basic Law. Parliament could dismiss the Chancellor if a majority of its Members could agree on a substitute. Parliament could only be dissolved if it had failed to give the Chancellor a vote of confidence he had requested. However, the power of dissolution, to be exercised by the Federal President on the Chancellor's recommendation, lapsed if a majority of the Members of the Bundestag elected a new Chancellor, and in any case the power ended 21 days after the failure of the confidence vote.[50] Thus the Bundestag inherited a formal structure which had developed within the weak and divided parliaments of Prussia and the Empire, while at the same time assuming constitutional powers and obligations greater than those of any of its predecessors.

Recruitment

Less perceptibly, the Bundestag also inherited a pattern of recruitment of parliamentary personnel by which members of the leading regional, denominational, and occupational groups had traditionally been attracted to the House to represent these groups in Parliament. While changes in the electoral system, and in the class system, reduced the number of parties in Parliament, with profound effects for its political organization, traditional concepts of representation preserved the interest-group composition of the House.

Experience

When, however, it came to the multitude of informal arrangements which characteristically exist in any parliament, there was a sharp discontinuity between German parliamentary traditions and the Bundestag. Of the members of the first Bundestag, 185—nearly half of the total—had had parliamentary experience on the local level between 1945 and 1949.[51] The director of the parliamentary staff, Hans Tross-

[50] *Basic Law,* art. 63, 67, 68, 81. Parliament may also be dissolved by the Federal President if, at the beginning of its term, it is unable to elect a Chancellor by an absolute majority vote.

[51] Emil Obermann, *Alter und Konstanz von Fraktionen* (Meisenheim am Glan: Verlag Anton Hain, 1956), pp. 104–5. For an analysis of the political experience of the Members of the second Bundestag, see Martin Virchow, "Die zusammen-

mann, had been initiated into parliamentary organization in the Bizonal Economic Council, a nonparliamentary assembly, not directly
elected, which had narrow policy-making powers in the British and
American zones of occupation between 1947 and 1949. Experience in
the *Länder* parliaments created under Allied military government, and
in the Bizonal Economic Council, therefore far outweighed Weimar
experience as a formative influence on the informal structure of the
new federal Parliament.

The model for the committee system, for example, as distinguished
from the method of appointing committees, was that of the Bizonal
Economic Council rather than of the Reichstag. It was there that
experience with the complexity of postwar domestic problems, which
seemed to demand a high degree of expertise in deliberation, had been
gathered. There the political consequences which undue specialization
and fragmentation of authority could have for an elected parliament
were not apparent. As a result, the Bundestag created 39 narrowly
specialized standing committees within the first two years of its existence, which contrasted sharply with the 17 more-general standing
committees of the Weimar Reichstag. Furthermore, each committee
was equipped with a small staff consisting of a professional assistant
and a secretarial office, for the express purpose of keeping records of
committee discussions.[52] The organization of the parliamentary parties
soon reflected the growth of specialization and staff among the committees. The resulting complexity of the decision-making process seriously impinged on the time available for the plenary sessions of the
House. Thus, new practices developed within old forms.

SYMBOLS OF CHANGE

Name

The symbols of Parliament give the most vivid evidence of the
interplay between tradition and change which has shaped the Bundestag. The name of the institution itself is something of an innovation. It was first adopted by a preliminary constitutional drafting
committee, on the inconspicuous precedent of the federal assembly

setzung der Bundestagsfraktionen," in Wolfgang Hirsch-Weber and Klaus Schütz,
Wähler und Gewählte, Eine Untersuchung der Bundestagswahlen 1953 (Berlin
and Frankfurt: Verlag Franz Vahlen, 1957), Pt. V.

[52] Dechamps, *op. cit.*, pp. 61–76.

which existed under the German Confederation after 1815. Presumably this return to early nineteenth-century usage was meant to convey the federal basis of the new governmental institutions. The Parliamentary Council later considered the name *Volkstag* (People's Assembly) as an alternative. Proponents argued that a new age should assign a new name to its institutions. They also guessed, rightly it later turned out, that the public would confuse "Bundestag" with "Bundesrat," the name for the federal council representing the *Länder*. But the desire for something traditional proved too strong. On the other hand, the venerable name "Reichstag" did not survive the Reich. Only one member of the Parliamentary Council, a conservative, advocated its use. To the others, it seemed inappropriate for what they regarded as a provisional political institution which would govern only a portion of the former Reich.[53] Furthermore, Hitler had compromised the name "Reichstag" by retaining it for the assembly of party hacks which he convened at irregular intervals to give ceremonial acclamation to his policy pronouncements. For a society which had had its fill of evocative political symbols, the colorless name Bundestag (Federal Assembly) was satisfactory.

Location

The Bundeshaus (Federal Building) in which Parliament works reflects in striking fashion the relationship between past and present. A visitor entering the chamber is struck by the evidence of modernity rather than tradition, of improvisation rather than continuity.

The location of Parliament was originally determined by light and transient causes. Amidst the widespread destruction still present in 1948, such a small thing as the existence, intact, of a teachers' training college on the outskirts of the university town of Bonn, which had an auditorium capable of housing a constituent assembly, was a compelling consideration in locating what was regarded as a provisional capital.[54]

[53] *Parlamentarischer Rat, Verhandlungen des Hauptausschusses* (Bonn: Bonner Universitätsbuchdruckerei Gebr. Scheur, 1948–49), Feb. 9 and May 5, 1949, pp. 628–9, 751, respectively; *Parlamentarischer Rat, Stenographischer Bericht* (Bonn: Bonner Universitätsbuchdruckerei Gebr. Scheur, 1949), May 6, 1949, p. 182.

[54] Hermann Wandersleb, "Die Bestimmung der vorläufigen Bundeshauptstadt Bonn," in Wandersleb, ed., *Recht-Staat-Wirtschaft* (Stuttgart and Cologne: W. Kohlhammer Verlag, 1950), II, 131–44; *Parlamentarischer Rat, Stenographischer Bericht*, May 10, 1949, pp. 264–6; Peter H. Merkl, *The Origin of the West*

Political Architecture

While the auditorium, which was the original attraction, could house the seventy members of the Parliamentary Council which drafted the Basic Law, it was wholly inadequate for a national parliament. The college buildings, constructed in the contemporary style of 1930, were therefore quickly in need of additions, which were designed in similar style. The work, which included the building of an entirely new parliamentary chamber, was rapidly done during the summer of 1949. The architect hired by the government of North Rhine–Westphalia, which owned the original buildings, suffered under a variety of extraneous influences. Among these, the desire to emulate the traditional Reichstag chamber was in most respects a very remote consideration.

As the Ministry of Reconstruction of North Rhine–Westphalia saw it, prudence required the new parliamentary chamber to be suitable for such alternative functions as concert, lecture, or banquet hall, looking to the day when Berlin would replace the provisional capital. Economy dictated that it also be large enough to house the quadrennial meeting of the 800-member Federal Assembly, which would convene for the first time soon after the first meeting of Parliament, in order to elect the Federal President. Although an exploration of various alternatives had persuaded the architect of the advantages of a semicircular chamber with the Cabinet sitting among the other members of the House, and all Representatives speaking from their seats, this design was less suitable for the alternative uses to which the House might be put than was the large auditorium design complete with podium and stage. It failed to receive the support of the Government of North Rhine–Westphalia for economic reasons, and of the President of the Parliamentary Council, Konrad Adenauer, because it was not traditional. Tradition therefore prevailed in the seating arrangement. Practical considerations prevailed in prescribing the di-

---

German Republic (New York: Oxford University Press, 1963), p. 64. In addition to such practical considerations, other influences were at work in the determination of Bonn as the provisional capital. The intensity of the pressures involved is indicated by the charge, made by the magazine, *Der Spiegel*, and subsequently the subject of a Bundestag investigating committee, that Members had been bribed to vote in favor of Bonn (see *Der Spiegel* [1950], no. 39; *Dt. Btag.*, 1. W.P. 89. Sitz., Oct., 5, 1950, pp. 3329 ff; Drs. I, 2274; 148. Sitz., June 7, 1951, pp. 5897 ff, and 149. Sitz., June 8, 1951, pp. 5961 ff.).

mensions, and the architect, referring to the character of the original college buildings, prevailed on questions of style. His desire to build in a modern idiom expressed a rejection of tradition. "I think it is right," he said, "that this new beginning have a bright, simple, contemporary house, open to the world." [55]

The Chamber

For the reasons given above, the Bundestag meets in a huge auditorium, bounded on two sides by glass walls which add to the impression of spaciousness. In area it is the largest parliamentary chamber in the world today, over half again as large as the United States House of Representatives, well over twice the size of the French National Assembly, and over four times the size of the British House of Commons.[56] Despite an increasing awareness of its shortcomings, this chamber has been conserved by a general reluctance to perfect that which is officially temporary, and by an inability in any case to agree on a substitute.

Over half a century before the Bundeshaus came into being, the prize-winning architect of a new Reichstag building had noted, in an essay prominently printed in the parliamentary handbooks of the time, that "an enlargement of the chamber was precluded in the new layout, because the existing dimensions (half the size of today's chamber) have already attained the outside limit of audibility." [57] A modern public address system does not compensate the Bundestag for ignorance or rejection of this experience, since intelligibility in parliamentary debate is not merely a question of audibility. The most striking characteristic of the present chamber is the vastness of the perspectives which it opens on all sides to distract from the corporate sense of the meeting. Its 518 seats, each with desk, in blocs of six or eight, conveniently never more than two abreast, are spread out with disintegrating effect in a square area 115 feet on each side. Some seats,

[55] Wera Meyer-Waldeck, "Das Bundesparlament in Bonn," *Architektur und Wohnform*, Vol. LVIII, no. 5 (June, 1950), pp. 99–109. When the seating arrangement in the chamber came under increasing criticism, the architect, Hans Schwippert, produced documentary evidence that the plan he executed was not his first choice, that it had been adopted for political, not architectural, reasons.

[56] Kurt Peschel, "Sitzungssäle der grossen Parlamente," *Das Parlament*, March 15, 1961, p. 12; published in an English version as "Council Chambers of the Great Parliaments," *Parliamentary Affairs*, XIV (1961), 518–33.

[57] Paul Wallot, "Das Reichstaghaus," *Reichstags Handbuch*, llte Legislaturperiode (Berlin, 1903), pp. 383–4.

in the rear corners under the visitors' balconies, are nearly 90 feet from the speaker's rostrum. They are on a level only imperceptibly higher than that of the other sixteen rows which stretch ahead, yet the room itself is 28 feet high.

Although those responsible for the blueprints of 1949 lacked experience with the work of parliament, and therefore found it easy to abandon the traditional spatial characteristics of parliamentary chambers, they did observe the traditional seating arrangement of German parliaments. The seats for members of the Government were placed to confront those of the other Representatives, and were raised thirty inches above the level of the rest of the House and enclosed in a five-foot-high wall which compels Members to stand on tiptoe when they want to confer with Ministers. This had been the arrangement of the Reichstag, originating in the provincial assemblies of the nineteenth century and earlier, in which a nonparliamentary separation of personnel existed between the bureaucracy of the king and the representatives of the people. The origin of the arrangement also explains the failure to distinguish between parliamentary Ministers and civil servants in admission to the Government bench. Its sixty seats, placed to the right of the presiding officer, are variously occupied by Ministers and federal officials; the comparably elevated Bundesrat seats to his left are available to the elected or appointed officials of the *Länder*, who, ostensibly, constituted the federal executive during the second Empire. Today they are little used, an architectural vestige of the past.

The aesthetic qualities of the chamber do little to contribute to that "sense of crowd and urgency . . . of the importance of much that is said, . . . [of] great matters . . . being decided, there and then, by the House," which Churchill wanted to see preserved in the atmosphere of the House of Commons. On the contrary, the scene which the Bundestag chamber presents to the hundreds of school children brought in an organized stream to Bonn to witness the proceedings, and to the occasionally much larger television audience, is disappointingly drab. An attendance of a hundred or two hundred Members, which would be considered substantial in most other chambers, is lost in the great spaces of the Bundestag chamber. The long distance between the rostrum and the Members' seats positively invites inattention. The comings and goings of officials on the Government bench, of speakers making their long way to the rostrum, and of Members occupying and relinquishing the front rows as their interest in a subject dictates, contribute an impression of chaos. The largest symbol in the room is a stout, stylized German eagle on the center of the front wall, which has been widely satirized as a representation of the economic miracle. Deliberate efforts to add dignity to the scene, by the appearance of the presiding officer in white tie and tails, preceded by a dramatic announcement of his entrance and a rising of all present, and the introduction in 1956 of an ornate uniform for the pages, consisting of red vest, gold buttons, white tie, and midnight blue tails, cannot elicit the reverence which traditional symbols might evoke.

IMPROVISATION

Low-lying buildings supplying office space have grown on either side of the chamber, and an eight-story office building stands on one end. In the lengthening corridors of these obviously temporary structures, offices for Members, committees, party caucuses, and the parliamentary administration developed as need arose, as staff and organization grew. But space always lagged substantially behind the need for it. After four terms of architectural improvisation, half of the Members still had to share an office, committees met in rooms barely seating their full membership, and a library containing 400,000 volumes had a reading room seating only two dozen people.

The buildings, like the name of the institution, reflect the uncertain beginnings of the Parliament which they house and the severance of this institution from its prewar predecessors. The continuing controversy surrounding the buildings expresses in architectural terms the evolution of the functions of Parliament and its Members in the postwar political system.

Westminster Style

The sprawling complex of structures, which still bears the marks of the school out of which it grew, has attracted bitter criticism from those compelled to work in it. No group of parliamentarians dislike their house more, and proposals for its basic reconstruction have gone through two major phases. The first occurred between 1957 and 1961, under the leadership of Bundestag President Eugen Gerstenmaier, who was then motivated by the desire to enhance Parliament's public performance. To facilitate debate between members of the governing majority and members of the Opposition, he wanted to eliminate the optical illusion of a separation between Government and the parliamentary majority. His model was the House of Commons: "The closer we get to the English system," he said, "the better." [58] His basic idea was to rearrange the seats in order to have Members of the governing party, including the members of the Cabinet, facing those of the parties in opposition, on two confronting tiers of seats, Westminster style. "This Chamber," he said, drawing an allusion that was frequently repeated, "has the character of a lecture hall, to which we are fully accustomed from kindergarten, through elementary and high school, up to the University. . . . This chamber artificially banishes a real chance for greater discussion." [59]

Gerstenmaier's proposal had support from the leaders of the two major parties, and from Members who had served in the Council of Europe.[60] There, as SPD whip Karl Mommer put it, "one speaks from one's place, surrounded by one's colleagues, and, because one does not then lecture, as one must here, but speaks to one's colleagues face to face, a different tone is developed. . . . Which of us in 1949 would have had this chamber built in this way," he asked, "had he been consulted beforehand and had he had a chance to look around in the world, to see how parliamentary chambers look and should look?" [61]

But although Gersteinmaier's plan had influential supporters, widespread opposition to it developed on four different grounds, reflecting a variety of views of Parliament, and eventually causing deadlock on the proposal. The controversy cut across party lines except in the case of the Free Democrats who, considering themselves the third party, united in resisting the division of the house into two sides. "The two-party system does not exist here," its floor leader pointed out. "Whether it shall ever exist is for the voter, not for the architect to decide." [62]

Among many Members in all parties, there was a reluctance to make moves which might place in question the provisional nature of the arrangements in Bonn. One of the oldest Members of the House, a veteran of the Reichstag, wrote that "so long as one fights for reunification with all the means at one's disposal and regards Berlin as the only possible capital of a united Germany, one cannot justify replacing the

---

[58] Quoted in *Die Welt*, Nov. 30, 1957.
[59] *Dt. Btag.*, 3. W.P., 147. Sitz., March 8, 1961, pp. 8302–3.
[60] *Ibid.*, p. 8304.   [61] *Ibid.*, p. 8306.   [62] *Ibid.*, p. 8302.

tolerable provisional arrangement in the Bundeshaus in Bonn with a more definitive arrangement." [63]

Among many backbenchers there was skepticism coupled with hidden fear about the effect of architectural changes. One Member cynically observed that he was reminded of the discussion of a church council which had concluded: "God's spirit does not reign in our House; let us therefore rebuild it." [64] Another justified his reluctance to make changes by the considerations of modesty and economy.[65] Many were still sensitive to the public criticisms of wastefulness which had arisen when the chamber was first built in 1949 in the depths of postwar poverty. Many had private offices provided by interest groups. Others devoted only a small part of their time to parliamentary business. A sufficient number of backbenchers feared for their desks and seats so that provision for a seat and desk for each Member was ultimately included in all remodeling proposals that were seriously advanced. Others undoubtedly looked with apprehension on the loss of the lectern, a requisite of the accustomed lecture style.

Opposition also came from the Government. Although its members were not prepared to say so openly, its spokesmen in the relevant parliamentary committees refused to accept any arrangement which did not illustrate the constitutional separation between Government and Parliament and which, incidentally, might deprive Ministers of the convenient proximity of their departmental civil servants.

After four years of public discussion in the press, and private negotiation in the Bundestag's steering committee, a number of compromise proposals were made, some of them providing for quite grotesque seating arrangements.[66] But the term of Parliament ran out before any of them could be implemented.[67] For a moment it seemed as if the only parliamentary architecture supported by sufficient native tradition lay in the ruins of the Reichstag in Berlin. For while no agreement had been reached on the chamber in Bonn, a decision had been taken to reconstruct the Reichstag in the old capital, even though the function which that building might serve outside the territorial limits of the Federal Republic was for the time being unclear.[68] Meanwhile, in Bonn, the arbitrary provisional arrangements continued, in the absence of agreement on a replacement.

[63] Quoted in Alfred Rapp, "Der Bundestag sitzt nicht eng genug," *FAZ*, March 16, 1960.   [64] *Dt. Btag.*, 3. W.P., 147. Sitz., March 8, 1961, p. 8307.
[65] *Ibid.*, p. 8301.   [66] *Die Welt*, March 8, 1961.   [67] *Ibid.*, May 31, 1961.
[68] *Das Parlament*, Sept. 28, 1960, p. 20; *Die Welt*, Nov. 12, 1963.

Office Style

When the Bundestag elected in 1961 convened, the architectural discussion entered its second stage. The important new factor was a dawning recognition that neither foreign models nor remote German precedents, but the needs arising from growing parliamentary experience, should guide the reconstruction. This indicated the necessity for a much more thorough reconsideration of the physical conditions under which Members worked.[69] Backbenchers who had been reluctant about a renovation limited to the style of the chamber became more interested. Meanwhile, the prospect of a capital in Berlin had been diminished by the erection of the wall, and there was correspondingly a greater readiness to find a more satisfactory arrangement in Bonn. Furthermore, the erection of ever more handsome quarters for Government ministries, and the impressive parliament buildings encountered by parliamentary leaders traveling in newly independent states, combined to arouse their envy.

A year after shelving plans for the renovation of the chamber, the Bundestag Executive Committee began consideration of a DM 110-million ($27.5-million) parliamentary building project. As adopted by the committee after two more years of discussion, it included a twenty-five-story building which would provide offices for every Member of the Bundestag, meeting rooms for its committees, and adequate space for staffs. Separate buildings would house the offices of the parliamentary parties and their working groups, the presidential offices, and the meeting chamber.[70]

The plan drew criticism equal to its scale: Chancellor Ludwig Erhard found it extravagant, a charge widely echoed in the press. The FDP and others raised the sensitive issue of the implication which the plan had for the eventual restoration of Berlin as the nation's capital.[71] The city of Bonn hesitated to give approval for the intrusion of new buildings onto a favorite park and recreation area.

Again it was the final year of the parliamentary term before a decision was reached. The proposal then presented, again guided by

[69] The change in the atmosphere of discussion was expressed in a well-received talk on "A Parliament House for the Times," given by one of the most respected Members, Adolf Arndt, to a group of his colleagues, and later published (see "Das zeitgerechte Parlamentsgebäude," lecture, June 27, 1962; Bonn: Interparlamentarische Arbeitsgemeinschaft, 1962).

[70] Die Welt, April 29, 1964; Das Parlament, July 10, 1963, p. 3.

[71] Die Welt, June 9, 16, 17–18, 1964.

President Gerstenmaier, and supported by the Executive and the Appropriations committees, was skillfully designed to win the Members' support. The high-rise building, with its promise of vastly improving the working conditions of the Representatives, would be the first to be erected. The first-year building appropriation was only DM 12 million ($3 million) toward an eventual cost of DM 48.5 million ($12.1 million).

Some Members tried to make the start of the project palatable to themselves, and to the public, by claiming that the tall structure could subsequently be stopped at any height, that the initial appropriation was not a commitment to construct the whole building. After a somewhat disingenuous debate, the appropriation was adopted, and the start was given.[72] When the fifth Bundestag convened in 1965, real estate negotiations with the city of Bonn had been successfully completed, and the President could promise Members that they would have more satisfactory working conditions by the second half of their term.[73]

Gerstenmaier, who had earlier been the foremost advocate of the reconstruction of the chamber, now favored the office building because it took account of the manner in which the work of the Bundestag was actually done.

One can regret the fact [he said] that German parliamentarism has, in these fifteen years, developed in such a way, that it takes place predominantly in the working groups of the parliamentary parties, in the committees . . . and in the individual work of the Members, . . . because this means the shift of the work of Parliament, out of its public sessions, and, thereby, naturally, out of public view.

"But," he added, reflecting on his own efforts, "this is something which the President of this House and its Executive Committee cannot change with the means available to them." [74]

Factors of Postwar Development

The architectural problems which have occupied the Bundestag reflect the antimonies of its existence: the uncertainties of its beginnings in a "provisional" state, yet its survival through a longer period

[72] *Dt. Btag.*, 4. W.P., 164. Sitz., Feb. 17, 1965, pp. 8130–52.
[73] *Dt. Btag.*, 5. W.P., 1. Sitz., Oct. 19, 1965, p. 4. *Die Welt*, Oct. 20, 1965.
[74] *Dt. Btag.*, 4. W.P., 164 Sitz., Feb. 17, 1965, p. 8141.

of democratic development than Germany has ever known; its inheritance of a century-old parliamentary tradition affecting the recruitment of its Members, its formal structure, and its rules of procedure, yet the sharp discontinuities of this tradition, permitting informal norms and organizations to grow easily in response to current influences; the customs and conventions derived from the ideological politics of a multiparty system, yet the realities of the issue-politics of a few large parties; the public conception of parliamentary government in terms of the political vocabulary of the Empire, yet the performance of parliament in an entirely different political system. As the following chapters will show, these conflicting influences of tradition and change have shaped the structure and functions of the postwar German parliament.

The parliamentary tradition which the Bundestag inherits is the product of a political system substantially different from the one which exists today. Molded largely in the period before the First World War, stunted in its further development by the intervening decades of turbulent political and social change which undermined parliamentary institutions, it is a tradition which has the force of long standing but lacks relevance at many points to the existing political system. Like all political institutions, the performance of the Bundestag varies with the issues of the moment, the demands of interest groups, the configuration of party power, and the abilities of particular Members. But it stands more exposed to these changeable factors than its century-old tradition would suggest.

The construction of a new twenty-five-story parliament building reflects the direction which the postwar development of the institution has taken: among Members, specialization and expertise over amateurism and common sense; procedurally, the subordination of public to private deliberation; in the performance of political functions, concentration on the details of lawmaking over promotion of public political discourse. The unsettled controversy over the shape of the chamber suggests the most baffling challenge: that of establishing a relationship between Bundestag and public which will permit this Parliament to perform the oldest and most distinctive function of the institution—representation—in the context of a modern political system.

III

Members

TWO major influences on the political behavior of members of parliament may be usefully distinguished: those due to their social background, and those due to the specific norms of behavior of the institution of parliament. In this chapter and the next, we will examine these two sets of influences in turn, with attention to their consequences for the performance of the Bundestag in the German political system.

A Model of Parliamentary Recruitment

The social composition of parliaments varies strikingly from one political society to another, while it appears to show considerable stability within a political society over time. The analysis offered in this chapter is based on the hypothesis that the recruitment of members of parliament is affected by a number of related and relatively stable variables. These include public orientations toward members of parliament, the material and psychological rewards and conditions of the mandate, the organization and membership structure of the political parties, their ideological commitments and their dependence on related interest groups, the pattern of interparty competition, and the requirements of the electoral law.

This chapter will first consider the content of these variables in Germany. Second, it will closely examine the social composition of the Bundestag, both for evidence of the influence of these variables and for the effect which this composition has on parliamentary performance. Third, in the final section, the chapter will deal with the relationship between parliamentary recruitment, the composition of parliament, and the functions performed by the Bundestag in the German political system.

Public Attitudes Toward Representatives and Representation

Public orientations toward members of parliament are part of the political culture. Composed of conceptions of what parliamentary representatives do, as well as feelings and judgments about their performance, these orientations do not necessarily rest on accurate perceptions of parliament. Because the development of parliamentary institutions, and of their functions in the political system, has been uneven and discontinuous in Germany, it is not surprising that there should be a lag between public images of members of parliament, and the political roles which members actually play. In fact, a number of attitudes exist side by side in Germany, not well reconciled with each other—the residues, apparently, of the distinct phases through which German parliamentary development has gone in modern times.

But although these attitudes do not necessarily take into account all the roles which parliamentary representatives actually play, they have a reality of their own. For they may affect parliamentary recruitment, helping to determine who will seek the mandate and who will be selected. They may affect the relationship between the Member and his constituency. The influence of the diverse attitudes toward members of parliament may be partly responsible for the great diversity which exists in the social backgrounds and political skills of Members of the Bundestag. It may account for the presence of some Members in the House whose motivations and qualifications are better related to past than to present functions of parliament. It may help to explain the variety which exists in the roles which different Members play in the Bundestag.

Among the traditional conceptions of the parliamentary representative still very much alive today is that originating in eighteenth- and nineteenth-century European liberalism, of the gentleman Member motivated by feelings of *noblesse oblige,* a political amateur whose public standing rests on the recognition and economic security he has obtained in private life. In this view, membership in parliament is an avocation pursued by free individuals, each supposedly animated by his own conception of the public good. As an ideal type, the free and independent representative replaced the instructed delegate of class or region who made up the medieval parliaments. Edmund Burke gave one of the earliest and most noble expressions of this view of the Member, and the French Constitution of 1791 gave it the first legal expression. Its provisions found their way, via the Belgian Constitution of 1831, into the constitution drafted by the German National Assembly in 1849, and from there into each of its successors.[1] Despite some reflections on the lack of realism of this view and of the perils of constitutional hypocrisy,[2] it easily prevailed in the Parliamentary Council of 1948–1949, and stands in Article 38 of the Basic Law of the Federal Republic of Germany as testimony to the tenaciousness of the liberal conception of the member of Parliament:

The Members of the German Bundestag [it reads] . . . are representatives of the whole people, are not bound by orders and instructions, and are subject only to their conscience.

That modern political parties and interest groups substantially affect the "independence" of Members, and that a modern parliamentary career imposes obstacles to the simultaneous pursuit of a private occupation are realities which have long received recognition in Germany, the birthplace of the mass party. But this recognition was generally accompanied by hope for the survival of the politics of the "notables." Max Weber wrote fifty years ago that the chief prerequisite for the development of a parliament capable of exercising significant power in Germany was the growth of a class of professional parliamentarians who would "exercise the mandate not as an occasional sideline but as the main content of [their] life's work, fully equipped with an office, assistance, and all sources of information." Weber appreciated the strong objection which existed and still exists to the "professional politician." "One may love this figure or hate him," Weber wrote, "but he is essential from the purely technical point of view."[3] At the same time, he hoped for the recruitment of a class of professionals who would live "for" rather than "off" politics, a class of financially independent gentlemen and members of the free professions chiefly distinguished from the "notables" of the liberal conception by their full-time devotion to politics. One of the foremost expo-

[1] See Klemens Kremer, *Der Abgeordnete* (Munich: Isar Verlag, 1953), pp. 11–13.

[2] Klaus-Berto von Doemming, Rudolf Werner Füsslein, and Werner Matz, "Die Entstehungsgeschichte der Artikel des Grundgesetzes," in Gerhard Leibholz and Hermann von Mangoldt, eds., *Jahrbuch des öffentlichen Rechts* (Tübingen: J. C. B. Mohr, 1951), I n.f., 353–5.

[3] "Parlament und Regierung im neugeordneten Deutschland" (May, 1918), reprinted in Max Weber, *Gesammelte politische Schriften*, 2nd ed., Johannes Winckelmann, ed. (Tübingen: J. C. B. Mohr, 1958), p. 352.

nents of the liberal conception today, Dolf Sternberger, editorial writer for the *Frankfurter Allgemeine Zeitung* and Professor of Political Science at Heidelberg, realized early in the experience of the Bundestag that "politics today is carried on to a good extent by those people who cannot afford it personally but only on the strength of their organizations." He concluded that "they do not represent the people, because the majority of the people do not belong to these organizations, neither to the interest groups nor, certainly, to the political parties." In an essay on "Professional Politicians and Politicians' Professions" he recalled the time when "politics was carried on by certain classes" and contrasted it with politics today "carried on by certain organizations" created on behalf of the classes previously excluded from politics. He warned that "a rebellion of the unorganized exists in latent form," calling it "the critical problem of representative democracy, at least with us." [4] Although this warning contained a sophisticated appreciation of the perils of political alienation, its implicit point of departure was a preference for the liberal conception of the representation of individuals by individuals.

The hold which this liberal view has had on intellectuals is echoed by newspapers and prominent political leaders, including Bundestag President Eugen Gerstenmaier. It expresses itself frequently and popularly in condemnation of the professional politician, who is regarded as a man lacking private accomplishments, living off the public purse, voting as he is told, and representing the narrow interests of his guild rather than the interests of the public. The implied comparison is either to the gentleman politician of a bygone age or, in a population not yet fully convinced of the merits of parliamentary representation in any form, to a more efficient system of government which dispenses with such appurtenances as members of parliament altogether.

The liberal ideal, and the frustrations which it inspires, exists elsewhere in Western Europe, as well as in the United States. But in Germany it competes with an entirely different conception of the parliamentary representative, at once older and yet more realizable today. This is the modern version of that medieval concept of the Member as an instructed delegate of his class, which the liberal con-

---

[4] "Berufs-Politiker und Politiker-Berufe," *Die Gegenwart*, V (1950), 9, reprinted in Ossip K. Flechtheim, *Die deutschen Parteien seit 1945* (Berlin: Carl Heymanns Verlag, 1955), p. 62. See also Sternberger's lecture, "Das allgemeine Beste," reprinted in *FAZ*, Sept. 20, 1961, p. 11.

ception sought to replace, and which the United States never knew. A concept of representation accompanies it which requires a representative to belong to the group he seeks to represent. When the King of Prussia addressed the Parliament he had called in 1847, he clearly told its members that they *were* "the estates of the realm."

You, Gentlemen, are . . . representatives and protectors of your *own* rights [he told them], the rights of the estates.

And he added,

I would not have called you here, had I entertained the slightest doubt that you would want to interpret your calling differently, and had a desire for the role of so-called representatives of the people.[5]

Harking back to a system of representation whose prerequisites were even then disappearing, this traditional view nevertheless gained new application in the second Empire. Now the principals were no longer the medieval estates, but the economic and social groups, organized in the wake of industrialization, seeking to defend their interests against the Government by deputizing parliamentary spokesmen. In a Parliament constitutionally cut off from the exercise of executive functions, it was pointless for Members to express general views on governmental policy. But since parliamentary approval was required for the enactment of legislation and appropriations, and since the rapidly changing economic and social order required many new laws and much public expenditure, Members could be quite effective in the defense of special interests. Thus the concept of the Member as interest representative assumed a new form. Even the claims of the newly enfranchised classes could best be advanced by Members so conceived. The Social Democratic Members of the Reichstag regarded themselves as agents for the working class, in quite the same manner as right wing Members acted as agents of particular agricultural or business interests. Only the Catholic Center party cut across interest lines, since its denominational concerns superseded narrower interests and its success depended on its ability to include Members of various economic and social groupings. But in spite of this exception, the parliamentary party system suffered the disintegrating effects of interest representation unrestrained by governmental responsibility. When the constitutional barriers to parliamentary government came down with the advent of the Weimar Republic, majority government proved nearly impossible,

[5] Quoted by Peter Molt, *Der Reichstag vor der improvisierten Revolution* (Cologne and Opladen: Westdeutscher Verlag, 1963), p. 327. Emphasis supplied.

Plate I. A view of the Bundeshaus on the Rhine. (Courtesy of Presse- und Informationsamt der Bundesregierung.)

Plate II. A side view of the Bundestag chamber. A Member standing at the microphone in the front row is requesting permission to interrupt the speaker with a question. (Courtesy of Presse- und Informationsamt der Bundesregierung.)

even before the rise of radical political movements, because the parties were so accustomed to emphasizing their separation from each other, and Members were so accustomed to regarding themselves, and to being regarded, exclusively as instructed delegates of special interests.

Just as the concept of the Member as interest representative survived, and handicapped the change in the constitutional position of Parliament during the Weimar Republic, it appears to be surviving the profound changes in the party system which occurred after World War II. The party as a coalition of various interests, on the model of the Center party, has replaced the narrower party associated with a single dominant interest, in the case of the Christian Democratic Union, and to a lesser extent, in the case of the Social Democrats. This survival of the concept of interest representation, in the face of other changes, is encouraged by the proportional element in the electoral system which almost invites the parties to make nominations according to interest quotas, by the efforts of certain politically oriented economic and social groups to have their accustomed representatives in Parliament, and by the specialized committee system in the Bundestag which welcomes that expertise in Members which frequently only the interests can supply.

The difficulties of this view of the Member are the difficulties of all theories of interest representation: the problem of fair recognition of all interests, and of reconciliation among them. The persistence of this conception of the member of parliament in influential economic and social groups may contribute to public cynicism toward parliament as an assemblage of selfish interests which disregard the general interest.[6]

---

[6] A national opinion poll reveals a gradual change in public conceptions of the motivation of Members of Parliament. To the question, "Do you believe that the Representatives in Bonn primarily represent the interests of the population, or do they have other interests, which are more important to them?", the replies were as follows:

	1951	1952	1953	1954	1955	1956	1958
Interests of the population	25%	33%	39%	39%	42%	38%	41%
Personal, private interests	32%	26%	20%	17%	19%	19%	17%
Interests of the party	14%	14%	13%	10%	8%	8%	8%
Other interests	11%	9%	8%	12%	8%	9%	10%
Don't know	23%	22%	24%	25%	24%	28%	25%

E. P. and E. N. Neumann, eds., *Jahrbuch der öffentlichen Meinung* (Allensbach: Institut für Demoskopie), I (1947–55), 163; II (1957), 177; III (1958–64), 262.

Like the liberal conception, it readily leads, in the German environment, to the disparagement both of the individual Member and of the institution of parliament.

A third general conception can be distinguished in the view that the member of parliament is a government official. In a society noted for the early developent of a modern bureaucracy, government is still widely regarded as a purely administrative matter. From this it is an easy step to the conclusion that administrators are the best-qualified occupants of any governmental position, and that the parliamentary mandate is a type of administrative office. Some public employees, up to the highest ranks, have traditionally sat in German parliaments. Instead of being hindered by laws on incompatibility, as in Britain, France, and the United States, they have been helped by election laws and civil service regulations which have granted them parliamentary eligibility either while in service, as during the Weimar Republic, or, as today, by granting them leave with full salaries while they campaign and the payment of retirement pensions while they hold parliamentary seats. Present laws guarantee retention of seniority and pension rights to civil servants in Parliament and reinstatement in active service at the end of their parliamentary tenure. In some German states today, as during the Weimar Republic, civil servants are even permitted to receive promotions during their term in Parliament. Popular admiration for the skills of government officials and the relevance of these skills to any form of political activity, and sometimes the Government's appreciation of the advantage of having some of its civil servants in the other branch, have overcome any conceivable objection that having executive personnel in Parliament violates the separation of powers.[7] Many constitutional commentaries find it necessary to explain that Members of Parliament are not formally officials.[8] But the public frequently misses the distinction and its judgments of Members are often based on criteria derived from bureaucratic organization: hours worked, volume of work accomplished, "efficiency," discretion in the dissemination of information, discipline, observance of hierarchy, and professional qualifications. To the extent that performance falls

[7] Theodor Eschenburg, *Der Sold des Politikers* (Stuttgart: Seewald Verlag, 1959), pp. 45–55; Peter Molt, *op. cit.*, pp. 139–156.

[8] See for example Hermann von Mangoldt and Friedrich Klein, *Das Bonner Grundgesetz*, 2d ed. (Berlin and Frankfurt: Verlag Franz Vahlen, 1957–61), p. 888; Theodor Eschenburg, *Staat und Gesellschaft in Deutschland* (Stuttgart: Curt E. Schwab Verlag, 1956), p. 503.

short by these standards, the reaction of the informed public is to disparage Parliament and its Members.[9] This response manifests itself in attacks on poor attendance on the floor, criticism of the length of debate and the slow pace of legislation, and dismay at the educational background of some of the Members. Such criticism is regularly found in the press.

These various conceptions of the parliamentary representative are expressions of more general attitudes found in the German political culture. In their comparative study of "political attitudes and democracy in five nations", Almond and Verba found that in Germany alone, confidence in administrators exceeds confidence in legislators. They also offer evidence that Germans find relatively little satisfaction in voting, and exhibit a relatively low level of trust toward each other on political matters.[10] These attitudes help to explain the general distrust of the parliamentary representative, which is evident in each of the three conceptions of him which we have distinguished. They also help to explain the preference for the administrative type, and for the direct representation of interests by Members belonging to each of the major groups in society.

These attitudes toward the Representative and representation constitute one set of influences on the recruitment process. By attracting

[9] Public regard for the ability of Members of Parliament has generally risen since 1949. To the question, "Do you believe that one must have great ability to become a Bundestag Representative in Bonn?" the replies were as follows:

	1951	1952	1953	1954	1955	1956	1958	1959	1960	1961
Yes	39%	44%	46%	49%	46%	46%	45%	58%	53%	61%
No	40%	38%	31%	34%	39%	37%	35%	27%	30%	22%
Undecided	21%	18%	23%	17%	15%	17%	20%	15%	17%	17%

But a breakdown of the responses given to this question in 1958 reveals that the respect for the ability of Members varies inversely with the educational level of the respondent:

	Public school (Volksschule)	Vocational high school (Mittlere Reife)	Academic high school (Gymnasium)
Yes	47%	40%	32%
No	32%	44%	56%
Undecided	21%	16%	12%

E. P. and E. N. Neumann, *op. cit.*, I, 162; II, 176; III, 263.

[10] Gabriel A. Almond and Sidney Verba, *The Civic Culture, Political Attitudes and Democracy in Five Nations* (Princeton: Princeton University Press, 1963), pp. 119–20, 151–3, 185–6, 203, 225–7.

some to a parliamentary career and deterring others, by affecting party choice in the nominating process and, to a lesser extent, voter choice in the election, they may help to determine who the Member of Parliament will be. Furthermore, through the expectations they create about the Member, they may affect other variables determining recruitment, such as the material and psychological conditions under which Members of Parliament work.

Financial Rewards of the Mandate

The emoluments of the parliamentary mandate still bear the marks of Bismarck's calculated rejection of salaries for Representatives. By keeping the material compensations of office to a minimum, Bismarck sought to exclude certain social classes from Parliament. The effects of his approach are still being felt. The prohibition against the payment of salaries to Members, contained in the Constitution of 1871 itself, was modestly amended in 1906 to permit the payment of an expense allowance. The amended text of that time still governs the language in which the payment of Members is discussed:

Members of the Reichstag may receive no salary as such [the 1906 provision declared]. They receive a compensation as provided by law.[11]

Although the Weimar Constitution dropped the prohibitory clause, it retained the provision for a compensation which Professor Gerhard Anschütz, the leading constitutional authority at that time, sharply contrasted with a parliamentary salary.

Membership in the Reichstag [continues] to be an honorary position whose occupant is not paid just for the fact of holding the office but . . . who has a claim to compensation for the expenses which arise from the exercise of his office.[12]

The Basic Law finally made a break with the past, to the extent of providing that compensation of Members should be "appropriate, adequate to ensure their independence." [13] But although the President of the Bundestag, in defense of a proposed increase in the schedule of

---

[11] At Bismarck's insistence, Article 32 of the Constitution of 1871 originally read: "The Members of the Reichstag may not as such receive any salary (or compensation)."

[12] Gerhard Anschütz, *Die Verfassung des Deutschen Reichs vom 11. August 1919* (Bad Homburg: Hermann Gentner Verlag, 1960; photo-offset reproduction of the 14th ed., 1933), p. 239.   [13] Art. 48, sec. 3.

compensation, referred to this provision as "the renunciation of the idea of a parliament of *notables*," [14] the history of postwar efforts to improve the material conditions of the mandate indicates the survival of both Bismarckian and nineteenth-century liberal opposition to the concept of the paid representative.

The compensation (*Entschädigung*)—the word "salary" (*Gehalt*) is still studiously avoided—which began at a modest level of RM 3,000 annually in 1906, reached a high during the Weimar Republic of RM 9,000 in 1927, to which RM 20 per day was added for every committee session attended on days when the House was not regularly in session. [15] When the Bundestag set the amount for the first time in the postwar period, it hesitated to implement the more permissive constitutional provision openly. It set the basic compensation at DM 7,200 annually, the last level prevailing in the Weimar Reichstag after a cut taken during the depression in 1930. However, a complicated schedule of sessional and expense allowances, contained in inconspicuous implementing regulations promulgated a year later, effectively tripled this amount, leaving Members nearly 50 per cent better off than their predecessors had been at the highest compensation level reached in the Reichstag, taking account of the rise in the cost of living. [16]

Three successive increases since that time, in 1954, 1958, and 1964, have each prompted heated public controversy in which traditional objections to salaries for Members of Parliament have reappeared. [17] In arguing for the most recent increase, Bundestag President Gerstenmaier acknowledged that on this question, "Bismarck has these days won some entirely new allies and imitators. . . . The public debate in recent days has shown me," he added, "that it is not good to ignore these reproaches and objections [to increased compensation]." But in refuting the critics on behalf of the House, Gerstenmaier still did not

[14] *Dt. Btag*, 3. W.P., 23. Sitz., April 18, 1958, p. 1247.

[15] Law on the Compensation of Members of the Reichstag of April 25, 1927, *RGBl.* II, 323. The basic compensation was defined in terms of the ministerial salary, at the rate of 25% of that salary.

[16] Law of June 15, 1950, on Compensation of Members of the Bundestag, *BGBl.* I, p. 215, and the implementing orders of June 20, 1950, Nov. 28, 1951, Sept. 11, 1952, and March 5, 1953, published in *Bundesanzeiger*, nos. 119 of 1950, 3 of 1952, 180 of 1952, and 47 of 1953, and reprinted in *Amtliches Handbuch des Deutschen Bundestages*, 2. Wahlperiode, 1953, pp. 96–104.

[17] For an unusually sympathetic journalistic examination of the problem of Members' salaries, see Volkmar Hoffmann, "Applaus für die Diätenkämpfer," *Frankfurter Rundschau*, March 11, 1964.

clearly argue for a salary appropriate to the job. The new levels, he said, were in many cases barely sufficient to enable Members to engage substitutes for themselves in their private occupations, or to compensate them for the loss of occupational earnings. Although, in view of the heavy demands which the mandate makes on an individual's time, he rejected the idea that compensation was merely an honorarium, he also argued in favor of retaining the traditional tax-free status of the compensation to distinguish it from a regular salary. In denying that it was an honorarium—yet insisting that it was not a salary but at most only a compensation for loss of private earnings—even the staunchest advocate of payment for Members clearly labored under the burden of the heritage of Bismarck's unsalaried Parliament.[18]

It is not surprising, therefore, that efforts have been made to remove the question from public scrutiny. The law of 1958 related the rate of compensation to ministerial salaries, fixing it at 22.5 per cent of the ministerial level. The sessional allowance was transformed into a fixed amount, no longer dependent on the number of meetings attended, although penalties for absences were retained. This change, designed to discourage the propensity to schedule unnecessary meetings, had the effect of raising the basic compensation without appearing to do so. In 1964 the level of this allowance, as well as that for office expenses, was removed from the law on Members' compensation and made subject to annual determination in the Bundestag budget. Thus the Bundestag has sought to escape the embarrassment of conspicuously determining the compensation of its own Members, by relating it in part to civil service salaries, and in part to annual determination within the general appropriations procedure. Attempts to hide the level of compensation have not, however, diminished public interest and sensitivity on the issue, nor, of course, helped to change public attitudes.

Compensation has risen to levels exceeding prewar standards, and is presently within the broad range existing in Western Europe.[19] At the

[18] *Dt. Btag.*, 4. W.P., 112. Sitz., Feb. 7, 1964, pp. 5156–62.

[19] The highest rate of compensation for Members of Parliament exists in Italy, where total compensation, after a recent increase, is the equivalent of DM 63,000 annually, well above the German level. The underworked members of the French Parliament receive DM 57,600 annually, but this amount is subject to income tax, bringing it close to the German level in effect. British MP's, after their recent increase, receive the equivalent of DM 36,400 annually, partly taxed, which is in effect somewhat below German levels. In the Benelux countries and Scandinavia,

beginning of the fifth term of the Bundestag, the figure for compensation stood at DM 16,320 ($4,080) annually, the sessional and office allowance was DM 19,200 ($4,800), and the average travel allowance, which varies with the distance between the Member's constituency and the capital, was DM 8,750 ($2,188) a total of DM 44,270 ($11,068) per year, tax free, for the average Representative.[20] To this a number of important services are added. Members are entitled to the free use of federal bus and railroad facilities, and, in the Bundeshaus, to unlimited use of the telephone, including long distance, and teletype. Ironically, in view of the generosity of these provisions, there is no franking privilege. Having existed briefly, and in limited fashion, for the Reichstag of the North German Federation, it was abolished in 1869 because the Government feared its abuse, and has never reappeared. This may in part explain the relatively small flow of correspondence between Members and their constituents.

If one excludes reimbursement for travel expenses from a comparison—despite its magnitude, the rise in travel expense merely reflects the change in the customary mode of travel from railroads to automobiles—the rise in the compensation of Members is not as steady nor as substantial as it appears. To be sure, in terms of constant Marks, compensation today exceeds the original level fourfold, is over twice the highest level attained in the Weimar Republic, and has risen 50 per cent since 1950. (See Table 1.) However, the increase is far less impressive when compared to the rise in the per capita real income of the rest of the population. By this standard—necessarily approximate, in view of the statistical problems of calculating it—the compensation of the Member of Parliament rose relatively faster than did average incomes between 1927 and 1950, but it has lagged considerably behind since that time. (See Table 1, col. 4.) Only if the rising value of his tax exemption is taken into account has the Representative approximately held his own over the past four decades. Although the compensation

parliamentary salaries are between one-third and one-half what they are in Germany. For two comparisons, see *The Financial Times*, May 18, 1963, and the *FAZ*, March 18, 1964. Since then, the British and Italian increases have occurred, the former in November, 1964, the latter in October, 1965.

[20] Law on the Compensation of Members of the Bundestag of March 25, 1964, *BGBl.* I, p. 230, reprinted in *Amtliches Handbuch des Deutschen Bundestages*, 4. Wahlperiode, 5. Nachtrag, 1964, pp. 97–101a. The average travel allowance is calculated from the total appropriation of DM 4,509,852 for 517 Members, given in the *Bundeshaushaltsplan*, 1965, Einzelplan 0201, Tit. 302. During 1966, two cost-of-living increases for all public servants raised the basic annual compensation of Members to DM 17,640 ($4,410). *Die Welt*, January 13, 1966.

Table 1. The development of parliamentary compensation in Germany

Year	Compensation paid to Members of Parliament (excluding travel expenses)			Parliamentary compensation in relation to national income (as % of 1927) (Col. 4)[a]
	In current Marks (Col. 1)	In constant Marks (at 1964 prices) (Col. 2)	In constant Marks (as % of 1927) (Col. 3)	
1906	3,000	8,940	56	59
1927 [b]	9,000	15,930	100	100
1950 [c]	18,200	22,740	142	138
1964 [d]	35,520	35,520	223	81

[a] The values given in Col. 4 must be regarded as rough approximations, in view of the limitations of the statistical sources employed (see below).

[b] Figures for 1927 do not include RM 20 per diem paid for attendance at committee meetings held while the Reichstag was not in session.

[c] Figures for 1950 include basic monthly compensation of DM 600 per Member, plus DM 300, the maximum expenses allowable under the implementing regulations which went into effect in 1951 and which nearly every Member received. They also include the flat DM 200 allowance for travel in the constituency, an item subsequently included under general expenses and therefore not regarded as "travel" for purposes of comparison here, and finally, an average monthly per diem compensation of DM 417. They do not include mileage expenses for automobile travel, which added an average of 25 per cent to the compensation of Members.

[d] Figures for 1964, as those for 1950, do not include mileage expenses for automobile travel, which presently add an average of 20 per cent to the compensation of Members. The exclusion of expenses for automobile travel permits a fairer comparison between prewar and postwar compensation, since the free rail pass was far more heavily used before the war.

Sources: National income and cost of living statistics were differently calculated in the pre- and post-war periods, and are altogether less reliable for the earlier dates. National income statistics for the prewar period are from *Das deutsche Volkseinkommen vor und nach dem Kriege* (Berlin: Statistisches Reichsamt, Verlag von Reimar Hobbing, 1932), pp. 32, 60. For the postwar period these statistics are from *Statistisches Jahrbuch für die Bundesrepublik Deutschland, 1965* (Wiesbaden: Statistisches Bundesamt, Verlag W. Kohlhammer, 1965), p. 552. Index figures measuring the purchasing power of the Mark were provided by the Statistisches Bundesamt through the courtesy of Walter Greiner of the Research Division of the Bundestag staff. On a scale where 1913 = 100, 1906 = 88, 1927 = 147.9, 1949 = 208.9, 1964 = 262.1.

of Members, by whatever name it is called, constitutes a salary sufficient to be attractive to some, it does not compare favorably with
business and professional incomes in a prosperous society. Most Members regard it as only a partial source of income.

A survey which the parliamentary parties made prior to the most
recent increase revealed that only 27 per cent of Members live on their
parliamentary compensation alone; these included 40 per cent of SPD
Members, 20 per cent of the others.[21] In view of its purpose, the survey
undoubtedly exaggerates the number of Members wholly dependent
on parliamentary pay. However, it indicates, even by understatement,
the extent to which the level of remuneration has attracted men and
women to the Bundestag who have supplementary sources of income
or can obtain them in office.

The debates on the ill-fated proposal for a pension for Members
reveals even more clearly the survival of hostility to paid professionalism in Parliament. A spokesman for the Free Democrats emphasized
that his party

happens to take the position that being a Representative is not a profession
and that parliamentary allowances represent neither payments nor recognition for accomplishments possibly achieved. Rather, it is a matter of
compensation for expenses associated with holding a mandate.[22]

A minority of Members in other parties, prominently led by Bundestag
Vice-President Carlo Schmid, supported the idea of a parliamentary
pension which, as Schmid pointed out, exists in most of Western
Europe and in the United States, but the proposal died in committee
after arousing a storm of newspaper criticism.

Working Conditions

The average Member of the Bundestag works under Spartan conditions. Under the duress of arrangements regarded as temporary when
made in 1949, but not easily improved so long as both capital and
political system are officially only provisional, the working conditions
for Representatives in the Federal Building are primitive. Half the
Members—quite naturally, the backbenchers—share their one-room
offices with a colleague. Most of these same Members rely on a
stenographic pool for their only secretarial assistance. Only officers of

[21] *Frankfurter Rundschau,* March 11, 1964.
[22] *Dt. Btag.,* 3. W.P., 101. Sitz., Feb. 12, 1960, p. 5442.

the House, including committee chairmen, have their own assistants and secretaries. The Research Division of the Bundestag has a staff of only seventeen hard-pressed officials available to do reference work for Members. The remainder of the staff is occupied with the maintenance of the library, the newspaper collection, and the parliamentary archives.

The condition of the Research Department is typical of the entire parliamentary staff, which largely performs housekeeping functions. This is due in part to the extraordinary prestige of the executive bureaucracy, whose relatively long history and high reputation make a parliamentary bureaucracy, performing research and reference services, appear like an unnecessary duplication. Because there has been no alternation of the major parties in Government, the development of a parliamentary staff has become something of a partisan issue between the governing party, which has adequate access to the executive departments, and the Opposition, which does not. To the extent that positions for research assistants exist on the parliamentary staff, it has been difficult to recruit trained personnel for them in competition with the far greater and better known opportunities available in the ministries for those embarking on a career in public administration. Rivalry between the executive and the parliamentary bureaucracy on questions of equivalent rank, exchange appointments, and training opportunities, have kept their personnel largely separate.

Through its legislative and appropriations powers, the Bundestag theoretically had the power to create an adequate staff for itself. But many Members, and not only those in the majority party, had their own reasons for dragging their feet. Some, with civil service backgrounds, opposed the creation of a parliamentary bureaucracy out of pride in the adequacy of the executive establishment. Although some Members were favorably impressed by the Legislative Reference Service of the United States Congress which they had studied firsthand on leader-exchange visits to the United States, a negative reaction was more typical. "In the United States," one Representative concluded,

the Government obviously cannot rely on so highly developed a bureaucracy as we have. I cannot therefore see any point in our developing our own Bureaucracy to compete with the bureaucracy of the Government.[23]

[23] *Dt. Btag.*, 1. W.P., 119. Sitz., Feb. 21, 1951, p. 4562. On the proposal, and its opponents, see *Die Neue Zeitung*, Aug. 11, 1950, and Dec. 2, 1950. The idea of a complete reference service has reappeared in discussion, but it has not been implemented (see for example *Freie Demokratische Korrespondenz*, Jan. 31, 1956,

A proposal for a staff of forty research assistants, at an eventual annual cost of DM 800,000 (then the equivalent of $190,475), was defeated in 1951, and no similarly ambitious project was subsequently considered.

The Bundestag hesitated not only out of deference to the executive bureaucracy, but out of a fondness for and familiarity with party bureaucracy. The party leaders in Parliament were far more anxious to obtain appropriations to enable them to appoint a staff of assistants for each parliamentary party separately than they were to develop a staff for the House as a whole.[24] The annual appropriation to the parliamentary parties for the support of their offices in the Bundestag contained, for the first time in 1955, an item of DM 225,000 (the equivalent then of $53,571) "for the appointment of research assistants by the parliamentary parties." After this special item was, for a number of years, combined with the regular appropriation for the party groups, an additional item of DM 468,900 ($117,225) appeared in the 1963 budget as an "increase for the legislative reference service (*Gesetzgebungsdienst*) of the parliamentary parties." By 1965, this amount was DM 781,500 ($195,375), the equivalent of the projected cost of the parliamentary reference service rejected fourteen years earlier. The total appropriation for the parliamentary parties in that year was DM 3,123,200 ($780,800), a ninefold increase in fifteen years.[25]

But this assistance, primarily available to the parliamentary party

Oct. 9, 1958, and Oct. 17, 1961; *Stuttgarter Zeitung*, April 11, 1957; *Frankfurter Neue Presse*, April 12, 1957; *FAZ*, Apr. 25, 1957; *DZ*, Nov. 15, 1958). See also the account of the failure to develop an adequate reference service in the *Frankfurter Rundschau*, March 26, 1964. With a total of just over 800 employees, the parliamentary staff is today about twice the size of its Weimar counterpart. The committee and parliamentary party staffs are entirely new. The report of an expert commission under the President of the Federal Accounting Office on the "Organization of the Administration of the Bundestag," presented in February, 1952, came to the conclusion that the parliamentary staff should be organized like that of a minor ministry. For the critical response in the Bundestag, see *Dt. Btag.*, 1. W.P., 225. Sitz., July 17, 1952, pp. 10096–104.

[24] Eberhard Pikart, "Probleme der deutschen Parlamentspraxis, Ein Beitrag zur Diskussion um den 'Parlamentarischen Hilfsdienst,'" *Zeitschrift für Politik*, IX n.f. (1962), 201–11; Kurt Kleinrahm, "Gesetzgebungshilfsdienst für deutsche Parlamente?," *Archiv des öffentlichen Rechts*, LXXIX (1953–54), 137–57; Karl Heinz Mattern, "Zum Begriff des Bundestagsbeamten," *Die öffentliche Verwaltung* (1953), pp. 7–9.

[25] *Bundeshaushaltsplan*, 1950, Einzelplan 0201, Tit. 301; *Ibid.*, 1955, 1963, 1965. *Dt. Btag.*, 2. W.P., 86. Sitz., June 14, 1955, pp. 4732–4. See also pp. 156–7, *infra*.

leaders, in addition to the assistance available to committee chairmen and officers of the House, still leaves the average backbencher, especially on the opposition side, relatively helpless. Reflecting on thirteen years of experience in the Bundestag, Adolf Arndt, one of its hardest working Members, observed that his working conditions appeared to rest on the assumption that

the Representative should spend his time like a clerk, filing legal texts, arranging parliamentary reports, opening correspondence, filling up his waste paper basket, and, at best, drafting proposals and letters by hand and licking stamps for them.

Arndt noted that "the problem of obtaining information . . . is the distinctive problem of the Representative of today, differentiating him from the Representative of the past" and he warned that in his present state of helplessness, "the Representative is being replaced by the agent of the interest group, because the interest group commands better sources of information." [26]

The parliamentary parties, which have contributed to the diversion of staff resources from the Bundestag as a whole to its party organizations, also divert some of their Members' individual compensation to finance party work. The tradition that the parties of the left must take care of their own Members by modest subventions developed before there was any compensation for Representatives, as a kind of redistribution of wealth within the party. With the advent of compensation, it seemed obvious to these parties to finance their parliamentary work by taxing a part of the compensation of their Members in Parliament. This practice spread from left to right and survived into the postwar period despite the advent of direct appropriations to the parliamentary parties for the support of their organizations. The disbursing office of the Bundestag withholds a party tax from the compensation of Members, varying with each party, and ranging from the nominal amount of DM 30 ($7.50) monthly in the CDU/CSU to DM 272 ($68) monthly, one-fifth of each Member's basic compensation, in the SPD.[27] In addition, deductions are made in each party for the support

[26] Adolf Arndt, "Das zeitgerechte Parlamentsgebäude" (lecture, June 27, 1962; Bonn: Interparlamentarische Arbeitsgemeinschaft).

[27] Eschenburg, *Der Sold des Politikers*, pp. 56–7, 80–2; see also Eschenburg's article, "Ist der Bundestag zu teuer?" *Die Zeit* (U.S. ed.), Feb. 21, 1964, p. 1. In his justification for the most recent increase in compensation, Gerstenmaier chastised the parties for taxing their Members as follows:

"There is no point in legally protecting the Members' compensation against

of their state and local organizations. The emoluments of office therefore escape the control of the Member to some extent, and are dispensed instead by the party in the form of salaries to its parliamentary leaders and the employees who serve them.

The salaries and working conditions of Members of the Bundestag are an obstacle to a parliamentary career for many individuals. They are also sources of vast differences in status between leaders and backbenchers, and between Members wholly dependent on the compensation and services provided, and those who can supplement them through interest-group support, the continuation of private incomes, or, in the case of civil servants in the Bundestag, the continuation of government salaries. In theory, the amenities of office are based on the assumption that the mandate is a free man's avocation. In practice, Members depend on the support of the party organizations within Parliament and the economic and governmental bureaucracies outside. These arrangements favor not the political amateur of the liberal conception, but the professional politician.

Working Schedule

The theory that the Bundestag must attract political amateurs influences another aspect of parliamentary working conditions, the time-

---

taxation by the Government, if instead the parties or party groups, and one or another of these well-meaning private organizations, tax their Members in a manner that makes the Government's tax rates at times seem really harmless by comparison. [*Laughter and applause.*]. . . . And so, ladies and gentlemen—all of you from left to right—I don't want to look at anyone here too directly . . . [*laughter*] because one's field of vision wouldn't be broad enough. But it just goes too far, when I see by the expenditure record of one Bundestag Member—you see, I have been given some pretty good material, and I have much more which I cannot present here—monthly party contributions alone of 502 Marks. [*Interjections from the SPD.*] Don't get excited. [*More interjections.*] What is it? Too little? Or too much? [*Interjections from the SPD.*] Too little! Well then, ladies and gentlemen, then I would like above all to say to *this* side of the House: you have fought for one hundred years against exploitation. [*Loud laughter and applause.*] But watch out! I know parties on the other side of whom the same thing is true. [*More laughter.*] But you, who have fought particularly against exploitation, I can only ask: Have you grown tired in the second century? [*Laughter.*] Now, ladies and gentlemen, in my naiveté I am assuming that these 502 Marks monthly represent an amount . . . at the upper limit of what Members of the Bundestag have demanded of them by the parties . . . and by other well-meaning and useful organizations. . . . This—quite seriously—cannot go on! At any rate, the improvement proposed by the present bill is not meant for the party coffers." (*Dt. Btag.*, 4. W.P., 112. Sitz., Feb. 7, 1964, pp. 5159–60.)

table of the House. The sessions of the Imperial Reichstag in the last century took place at first during a concentrated three-months' period each year. As the volume of work increased, an average of nearly one hundred sessions took place annually during the first decade of this century, and this rate continued throughout the Weimar Republic, but half of the year was still free of sessions.[28] Although everyone agrees that the work of Parliament has become still far more demanding of time, there has been extensive experimentation with the schedule in the postwar period to discover ways to permit a majority of Members to give the House only a part of their time. In the first four years, weeks of sessions alternated with "free" weeks which, however, tended to be full of caucus and committee meetings. A three-week rhythm in which every third week was free of sessions was tried during the next four year, withouts providing any regular blocks of free time for Members.

One should not delude oneself [an SPD leader concluded]. The continuation of the present work schedule will necessarily lead to an ever greater alienation of the Members from their professions and to the creation ot professional politicians.[29]

On his re-election to the presidency of the Bundestag in 1957, Gerstenmaier also warned his colleagues that failure to revise the schedule would make it impossible for Members to spend time in their constituencies and their professions.[30] Thereupon, a four-week schedule was introduced, with the relatively infrequent plenary sessions occurring during two weeks every month, and additional caucus and committee sessions during a third week, with every fourth week free of all meetings. In addition, five months of the year are parliamentary holidays, three in summer from about July 1 to October 1, and two constituting the recesses at Christmas, Easter, and Whitsun. But this timetable, which was in effect for the subsequent seven years, produced a very uneven distribution of work for Members willing to devote their full time, and yet very irregular free time for those

[28] Peter Molt, *op. cit.*, p. 312; Karl Gutzler, "Wie die Parlamente tagen," *Das Parlament*, Dec. 7, 1960.

[29] H. G. Ritzel, "Parlamentsreform," *SPD Pressedienst*, P/XII/244, Oct. 24, 1957.

[30] *Dt. Btag.*, 3. W.P., 1. Sitz., Oct. 15, 1957, pp. 6 ff. See also his radio address of September 18, 1957, reprinted in the *Bulletin des Presse und Informationsamts*, no. 175 (Sept. 20, 1957), p. 1618.

anxious to pursue private occupations. It included an average of only forty plenary sessions a year, less than half the number already taking place at the turn of the century, but the average session was twice as long. One Member found that the "constant change in the rhythm of work has been among the most irritating troubles."

Parliaments with very old traditions [he added] work according to firm, tested rules. They begin regularly at a definite time. . . . They hardly ever change the times or periods of meetings. . . . The foreign parliaments which are proud of their traditions on the whole assume the full application of their Members to their parliamentary work. This is not the least of the reasons explaining the high number of lawyers in the parliaments of the western world. In Germany, the fiction is still maintained that a Member really harnessed to his parliamentary work can successfully practice a profession beyond that. This fiction has determined the past efforts to fit the rhythm of parliamentary work to the possibility of such a practice of one's career.[31]

In 1964, the fiction was abandoned so far as the timetable was concerned, in the wake of a new schedule designed to increase the number of public sessions of the House and to distribute them more evenly over the month. Although the fourth week of each month was still theoretically left free, there were only two free weeks outside of the regular holidays between Christmas, 1964, and July, 1965.

If the schedule has harrassed the full-time Member, it has not really permitted the part-time Representative to pursue his career without neglecting his parliamentary duties. Instead, the large proportion of part-timers leaves a disproportionate share of the work to the professional politicians who are always on the scene, and to the interest representatives, who manage to be in the right committee meeting at the right time. Insiders do not take the attendance problem seriously so far as it concerns the plenary sessions, since large attendance at open sessions is uncommon in any free parliament; but public criticism of absenteeism is widespread. In committee sessions, however, the attendance problem is so great that all parties quietly allow any Member to substitute for any other, in spite of the existence of a complete set of official alternates for every committee. This contributes to a shifting committee composition that depends on the subject under

[31] Rudolf Vogel, "Weniger Gesetze, bessere Gesetze, ein neuer Arbeitsrythmus für den Bundestag," *Deutsche Korrespondenz*, Nov. 16, 1957.

consideration, and increases the influence of Members with the greatest material interest in a subject, and of Government officials whose numbers frequently equal those of Members in attendance.

The parliamentary timetable is certainly not alone responsible for this large-scale neglect of parliamentary obligations. But the assumption that the duties of the Member must be arranged to permit the simultaneous practice of private occupations invites the membership of part-timers, who are more often representatives of special interests than they are independent gentlemen of the liberal conception. At the same time, it does nothing to prevent the dominance of a small group of full-time professional politicians.

Incentives and Disincentives

The material conditions of the mandate make it acceptable mainly to those who have alternative sources of income. It is also acceptable to those having occupations in which income continues, or possibly even increases, during service in Parliament. Owners of large farms fit the first category, lawyers in private practice the second. Businessmen, unless they have large investment incomes, are generally able to enter the Bundestag only at considerable financial sacrifice, unless, of course, they serve very large firms willing to retain them in the Bundestag. University professors continue to receive full salaries while they sit in Parliament, but their lecture obligations may require them to commute over considerable distances once or twice weekly. Most other professions are more difficult to reconcile with a parliamentary career.

But employees of those economic or social organizations which are prepared to support their own parliamentary representatives, in the German tradition of interest representation, are, by contrast, in an advantageous position. Labor unions, refugee and veterans' organizations, agricultural associations, a few large business organizations like the Federation of German Industry, and some church and civic groups are the leading examples of organizations with such political objectives.[32] The mandate is also attractive for those party members who are

---

[32] For a brief discussion of the major political interest groups, see Gerard Braunthal, *The Federation of German Industry in Politics* (Ithaca: Cornell University Press, 1965), pp. ix-xi, 3–22. Cf. Arnold J. Heidenheimer, *The Governments of Germany* (New York: Crowell, 1961), pp. 79–84; Wolfgang Hirsch-Weber, "Some Remarks on Interest Groups in the German Federal Republic," in

able to draw a combination of political salaries, because in addition to their seat in Parliament, they serve on boards of directors of public corporations, or industries subject to "co-determination," or hold newspaper licenses, as nominees of their party. Both types of "organization men" in the Bundestag have the special advantage that they can supplement the skimpy staff and the office services available to the ordinary Member with the facilities which their sponsoring organizations possess.

Civil servants, including schoolteachers, and other public employees constitute another reservoir of those who can contemplate a parliamentary career. By law, they are entitled to full salary as candidates, and to between one-third and three-fourths of their salaries, depending on seniority, as pensions, while in "retirement" as Members of Parliament. Elective local government officials such as mayors and county commissioners retain their positions and full salaries while in the Bundestag, but at the price of holding two demanding jobs. Civil servants are entitled to re-employment in the same or equivalent positions upon their return, with parliamentary service counting toward their seniority and pension rights.[33] The law reflects the traditional German conception of the public official as a versatile member of government qualified to serve in legislative as well as executive capacities. Relatively few career officials actually avail themselves of a leave of absence for a term in the Bundestag. Those who enjoy the special advantage which the law offers to civil servants in Parliament are primarily schoolteachers, local government employees and members of various public bodies, senior officials who hold political ap-

---

H. W. Ehrmann, ed., *Interest Groups on Four Continents* (Pittsburgh: University of Pittsburgh Press, 1958), pp. 96–116. The best general treatment is Rupert Breitling, *Die Verbände in der Bundesrepublik* (Meisenheim am Glan: Verlag Anton Hain, 1955).

[33] Gesetz über die Rechtsstellung der in den deutschen Bundestag Gewählten Angehörigen des öffentlichen Dienstes, August 4, 1953, *BGBl.* I, p. 777, and the Rundschreiben des Bundesministeriums des Innern, "Beurlaubung der Angehörigen des öffentlichen Dienstes zur Vorbereitung ihrer Wahl zum Deutschen Bundestag," June 27, 1953, *GMBl.*, pp. 223. For a history of the development of the status of civil servants as Members of Parliament, see K. Schumann, "Die Entwicklung der Rechtsstellung des Beamten als Abgeordneter," *Zeitschrift für Beamtenrecht*, X (1962), 97–104. Allied efforts to establish the ineligibility of civil servants for parliament encountered insuperable obstacles in the contrary German tradition. The chief German concession resulting from the controversy was the requirement of temporary "retirement" for civil servants upon their election.

pointments, and politicians who have briefly served as officials at one point or another in their careers, as many did in the early occupation period. Some elected members of local legislatures, on the municipal or, rarely, *Land* level, also seek Bundestag seats. They do not, of course, enjoy the special financial advantages of public employees since they are not legally officials, but they can improve their lot by an accumulation of elective positions.

It is just this category of interest-group and public employees, and party beneficiaries, able not only to afford a parliamentary career but having a professional interest in it, who most offend the liberal conception of what a member of parliament should be. By contrast, in the few private occupations which are compatible with a parliamentary career, interest in politics is less likely. Since the days of the Empire, the parliamentary mandate has failed to attract the most ambitious, because it offered no advancement to executive office. "Since the parliaments have been impotent," Weber wrote half a century ago, "no man with the qualities of a leader would enter parliament permanently." [34] In a population accustomed to thinking of a bureaucratic rather than a parliamentary executive, it has only slowly dawned that the Cabinet is today very largely appointed from the Bundestag. But at around twenty, the number of executive appointments from Parliament is still very small, compared, for example, to seventy to one hundred Cabinet appointments from the House of Commons in Great Britain. For those members of private professions with limited political interests on the other hand, the large number of seats in state and local parliaments comprise alternatives which offer the advantage of demanding far less time and travel than a Bundestag mandate.

Other public positions more attractive than any seat in a parliament compete for the services of those who have political interests. In a society acutely conscious of pension rights, the traditionally prestigious and financially secure civil service, and appointive positions in *Land* and local government and in the foreign service, offer great inducements. Full-time employment in trade unions or other interest groups has similar economic advantages. A seat in the Bundestag is sometimes merely a way station to advancement in private occupations or in the sponsoring interest group, or is a means of gaining

[34] Max Weber, "Politik als Beruf," Oct., 1919, reprinted in *Gesammelte Politische Schriften, op. cit.*, p. 529.

sufficient political prominence to warrant special ambassadorial or civil service appointment, or a portfolio in a *Land* Government.

Finally, a very general political apathy operates as a disincentive to parliamentary candidacy across all social and occupational classifications. Undoubtedly the consequence of the experience with totalitarianism, this reluctance to engage actively in politics to the extent of running for office is a marked characteristic of the German political culture. In their cross-cultural survey, Almond and Verba found that the willingness to be active in community affairs is far lower in Germany than in the United States and Great Britain, and lower even than in Mexico. Although the propensity to participate varies directly with educational and occupational levels, the contrasts between the political cultures surveyed are more striking than the differences within any one of them.[35] There is some evidence that political apathy is declining in Germany, but if the expressed willingness to join a political party is taken as an index of active political involvement, no clear changes are indicated for the future. A recent survey shows only 5 per cent of young people planning definitely to affiliate with a political party—no clear gain over present proportions.[36] With party membership so low, candidates for Parliament must be drawn from a particularly small minority of political activists in the society. How candidates are selected from this small group of those who are available is obviously important, and we turn next to a consideration of this variable in the recruitment process.

The Electoral System

The nomination of candidates for the Bundestag is surprisingly decentralized.[37] The party organizations in 248 single-member constit-

---

[35] Almond and Verba, *op. cit.*, pp. 168–71, 176–7.

[36] Based on an EMNID survey, cited in a government report on the status of youth (*Dt. Btag.*, 4. W.P., Drs. 3515, pp. 28–31).

[37] There are relatively few restrictions on eligibility to the Bundestag. To be eligible, a candidate must be twenty-five years old on election day, and have been a German citizen for at least one year. Persons who have lost their civil rights by sentence of a court, or who are ineligible to vote because of mental disability, are disqualified (*BGBl.* I, 383, par. 16). Certain offices are incompatible with membership in the Bundestag: the federal presidency, membership on the Federal Constitutional Court, and the Federal Audit Office (*Basic Law*, par. 55, 94; *BGBl.* I, 765, par. 12). Judges are, like other public employees, except university teachers and elective officials, temporarily retired upon accepting a Bundestag mandate

uencies nominate their district candidates. In addition, party conventions in each of the ten *Länder* comprising the federation select lists of nominees for an equal number of seats which are filled by proportional representation. Voters vote separately for the district candidates and for the *Land* lists. Since the same candidate may be nominated in a constituency and on a list, there is incentive for the constituency and *Land* organizations of the parties to try to coordinate their efforts. Nomination is therefore in local hands at two levels of government.

The outcome of the election for the strength of the parties in the Bundestag is unrelated to the decisions of the voters in the various constituency contests. Only half of the 496 seats in the Bundestag (not counting twenty-two Representatives from Berlin) [38] are filled by plurality vote in the constituencies. The other half are distributed among the party lists according to a complex formula which assures each party a total number of seats in Parliament corresponding to the proportion of the *national* vote its *Land* lists have won altogether. Parties carrying insufficient constituencies to win their proportional quota of seats receive compensation in the form of seats for their candidates on *Land* lists. Success in the constituencies correspondingly

---

(See n. 33, *supra*). Although members of the Bundesrat, and members of *Land* Cabinets generally, are not barred from membership in the Bundestag by the Basic Law or other federal regulations, membership in both Houses is generally regarded as violating the principles of the bicameral system. After extensive study, the Bundesrat has taken the position that membership in the Bundestag is incompatible with a seat in the Bundesrat except for a brief transitional period enabling the affected individual to decide. This tolerant position continues to permit *Land* ministers to grace their party's list of Bundestag nominees, and to accept election to the Bundestag for a brief period of time, without losing their Bundesrat seat, as SPD Chancellor-candidate Brandt did, for example, in 1961 and 1965. (Bundesrat, *Sitzungsbericht*, 274. Sitz., Nov. 6, 1964).

[38] Twenty-two special representatives from Berlin are elected by its House of Representatives by proportional representation among the party groups. Their exceptional method of selection, and the denial to these Berlin Members of a vote on some questions in the public sessions of the House, is due to that city's legal status as territory under four-power occupation, not formally a *Land* in the Federal Republic of Germany. That status is jealously guarded by the western Allies and the German Federal Government because it is the legal basis for the Allied presence in Berlin. The Berlin Members are full participants in the work of the Bundestag, unrestricted except that their votes, although tabulated, formally do not count on the second and third readings of bills, on decrees, and on the election of the Chancellor. Several of their number have become Ministers; one, Krone, was for six years chairman of the CDU/CSU parliamentary party (see Elmer Plischke, "Integrating Berlin and the Federal Republic of Germany," *The Journal of Politics*, XXVII [1965], esp. 41–50).

reduces the number of list seats a party obtains. For the list seats which a party wins, its candidates are declared elected in the order of precedence in which they appear on the list.[39]

[39] Following are the main features of the electoral system: Voters cast separate votes, on a single ballot, for the constituency contest, among the individual candidates, and for the *Land* contest, among the party lists. Plurality decides the constituency contest. For the *Land* contests, a count is first made of the total votes cast for all the *Land* lists of each party throughout the Federation, counting only the lists of those parties which have received at least five per cent of the national vote, or have won at least three constituencies. Seats are then distributed among the parties, according to a mathematical formula devised in the last century by the Belgian mathematician, d'Hondt, whose name is still attached to the system. Seats are awarded to each party, in turn, so that the average number of votes cast, per seat won, will in the end be as nearly equal as possible among all parties. The seats given each party are then distributed by the same formula among its various *Land* lists, in proportion to the vote cast for each of them. As a result, proportionality is achieved not only among parties, but among the *Länder*, on the basis of votes cast, not population. But from the seats assigned to each *Land* list, the number of seats won by the same party in the constituencies of that *Land* is subtracted, so that constituency victories do not become additions to a party's proportional share of seats, but part of that share.

The only exception is for parties which win a greater number of constituencies than their proportional share of seats in a *Land*. They may retain these "superproportional mandates," and an equivalent number of seats is added to the Bundestag for distribution among the other party lists in the *Land*. There were two of these extra seats in 1949, three each in 1953 and 1957, and five in 1961. With two exceptions, they were won by the CDU because of its sweep of the rural, increasingly underpopulated Schleswig-Holstein constituencies.

The 1956 amendment to the electoral law provided for a non-partisan Boundaries Commission, on the British model, to propose revisions of constituency boundaries after each election, taking account of shifts in population. Although of importance, considering the high mobility of the German population, over- and underrepresentation of constituencies has only a limited effect on the outcome of elections because of the assignment of seats among the parties on the basis of votes cast. Nevertheless, as long as the "silent gerrymander" was permitted to work, the CDU had the advantage of a handful of "superproportional" victories in underpopulated rural constituencies. The Government ignored the first recommendation of the Boundaries Commission, which was made before the 1961 elections, and the CDU reaped the advantage of five seats it would not otherwise have had. However, after the Federal Constitutional Court clearly implied in 1963 that further failure to redistrict might cause it to declare the next elections invalid, the Government presented a redistricting plan proposed by the Commission, and the Bundestag adopted it, with some changes. For the committee report and the debate, see *Dt. Btag.*, 4. W.P., 101. Sitz., Dec. 11, 1963, pp. 4682–91, and Drs. IV, 1729. See also Theodor Eschenburg, "Die nächsten Wahlen sind ungültig . . ." *Die Zeit* (U.S. ed.), Aug. 2, 1963, p. 4.

For an excellent analysis of the electoral system in all its complexity, see U. W. Kitzinger, "The West German Electoral Law," *Parliamentary Affairs*, XI (1958), pp. 220–38; and, by the same author, *German Electoral Politics, A Study of the*

The object of the electoral system is to achieve a compromise between the highly centralized list system of proportional representation, in effect during the Weimar Republic, and the system of single-member constituency elections with second-ballot runoffs, in effect throughout the Empire. It therefore fits squarely into the German electoral tradition. The present modification of proportional representation was an effort to restore some contact between Representative and constituency, which was absent during the Weimar period, and regarded generally as one of its weaknesses. Single-member constituencies became part of the electoral system of most of the new *Land* Parliaments when local government was restored in 1946. The first federal election law also included this feature, under the influence of *Land* leaders who saw it as a means of influencing national elections. Their interest happened to correspond with that of the Allied Military Government, which was anxious to see the excesses of the Weimar system of proportionality avoided, and which gave these *Land* leaders encouragement and tactical assistance.

But the support for proportionality in the distribution of seats among the parties was very strong. In 1949, as today, only the CDU/CSU was receptive to a system of simple majority election in single-member constituencies. The smaller parties could readily calculate their total defeat under such a system, and held out for proportional representation. They were joined by the Social Democrats, who were uncertain of their prospects under a simple majority system, and who, in doubt about present advantages, remained loyal instead to the principle of proportionality which had delivered them in 1919 from the inequities of a badly gerrymandered two-ballot majority system which had painfully underrepresented them during the later years of the Empire. In view of this alignment of parties, there was agreement on only one restriction on the proportional distribution of seats in 1949: the exclusion of parties receiving less than 5 per cent of the vote in any *Land* from their proportional share. This clause had the advantage of being at once justified on the sound principle of barring splinter parties, and on the attractive expedient of distributing the potential seats of the disqualified parties among the larger parties. Strengthened in the 1953 and 1956 revisions of the electoral law to the

---

1957 Campaign (Oxford: Clarendon Press, 1960), Ch. II. An English translation of the main provisions of the electoral law is contained in Steven Muller ed., *Documents on European Government* (New York: Macmillan, 1963), pp. 245–56.

point of now requiring 5 per cent of the national vote or, alternatively, victories in three constituencies, to enable a party to qualify for its proportional share of the seats, this clause has been strikingly successful in reducing the number of parties in the Bundestag.[40]

The Bargaining Agents in the Nominating Process

Although candidates are locally selected under this electoral system, the outcome of the election for the parties is determined by the division of the national vote among the party lists. Because of the large number of names on these lists, their appeal to the voter does not depend on the candidates they contain, but on the party label. Even the fate of the local candidate is largely determined by the vote cast for these lists. Many of the constituency candidates are actually elected on the basis of having a second nomination on the list. In any case, most voters automatically pick the local candidate of the party whose list they endorse, thus even making their local choice by party rather than personality. Therefore, like their British counterparts, the local party nominating bodies in Germany are under little compulsion to consider the electoral appeal of potential candidates. They are primarily responsive to the pressures generated by the local party activists.

The party organizations which exercise such remarkable power in the nominating process are the products of an exceptionally narrow membership unrepresentative of the electorate. On the average, only 3 per cent of the voters are enrolled in one or another of the parties. The proportion of voters of each party who are also party members ranges downward from about 6 per cent in the case of the SPD to about 2 per cent for the CDU/CSU and the FDP.[41] Furthermore, the party membership is not a significant source of financial support for the parties, except in the SPD. In 1964, that party collected DM 15.1 million ($3.8 million) in dues, comprising 34 per cent of its income in that year, but the CDU collected only DM 3.1 million ($775,000), making up only

[40] The drafting of the first federal electoral law by the Parliamentary Council is well described by John Ford Golay, *The Founding of the Federal Republic of Germany* (Chicago: University of Chicago Press, 1958), pp. 138–47.

[41] The most recent party membership figures are: CDU, 285,052; CSU, 70,000 (est.); FDP, 80,000 (est.); SPD, 648,415 (*Die Welt*, March 29, 1965; *Jahrbuch der Sozialdemokratischen Partei Deutschlands*, 1962–63 (Bonn: Neuer Vorwärts Verlag, 1964), p. 342; Thomas Ellwein, *Das Regierungssystem der Bundesrepublik Deutschland* (Cologne and Opladen: Westdeutscher Verlag, 1963), pp. 75–6.

4.5 per cent of its income. Until 1958, the parties on the right depended heavily on associations of business contributors, who thereby gained substantial influence on nominations, among other things. A decision of the Constitutional Court in that year, invalidating the tax deductibility of contributions to political parties, caused the parties to turn to public funds for support. Voting themselves DM 5 million ($1.25 million) in the Bundestag in 1959, for "political education," they twice raised that figure, over SPD opposition, and in both 1964 and 1965 received DM 38 million ($9.5 million) from the federal treasury. In the campaign of 1965, furthermore, the parties voluntarily agreed to limit certain specified election expenditures to DM 46.5 million ($11.6 million), divided approximately equally among themselves. Although reliance on public subsidy and voluntary restraint freed them to some extent from financial pressure, large contributors continued to be influential. Their power assumed new importance after the Constitutional Court decided in 1966 that the public subsidy of parties was unconstitutional, at least as it had been practiced.[42]

Weak in membership and in their own financial resources, especially on the right, the party organizations are therefore particularly responsive, in exercising their nominating power, to those interest groups which can effectively mobilize political support. As Heinz Josef Varain observed in his study of nomination procedure in Schleswig-Hol-

[42] Income and expenditures for 1964 and 1965 were reported by the party treasurers in testimony before the Federal Constitutional Court on the question of the constitutionality of federal subsidy of political parties (*FAZ, Die Welt,* June 23, 1965, April 20, 1966). For the federal appropriations, see *Bundeshaushaltsplan,* 1959, Einzelplan 06, Tit. 620; *Ibid.,* 1962, Einzelplan 06, Tit. 612; *Ibid.,* 1964, Einzelplan 06, Tit. 612, and the debate on this appropriation, *Dt. Btag.,* 4. W.P., 122. Sitz., April 15, 1964, pp. 5746–51, 5754, 5755–61, 5777–82. Also, *Bundeshaushaltsplan,* 1965, Einzelplan 06, Tit. 612. For the inter-party agreement on campaign expenditures, see *Die Welt,* Jan. 11, 1965. For a general account of party finance in Germany, see Ulrich Duebber and Gerard Braunthal, "West Germany," in Richard Rose and Arnold J. Heidenheimer eds., "Comparative Political Finance," *The Journal of Politics,* XXV (1963), 774–89. See also Ulrich Dübber, *Parteifinanzierung in Deutschland* (Cologne and Opladen: Westdeutscher Verlag, 1962), pp. 75–84; Ulrich Dübber, "Zur öffentlichen Finanzierung politischer Parteien," *Die Neue Gesellschaft,* XI (1964), 105–11; Theodor Eschenburg, *Probleme der modernen Parteifinanzierung* (Tübingen: J. C. B. Mohr, 1961), *passim;* Rupert Breitling, "Das Geld in der deutschen Parteipolitik," *Politische Vierteljahresschrift,* II (1961), 348–63; Nevil Johnson, "State Finance for Political Parties in Western Germany," *Parliamentary Affairs,* XVIII (1965), 279–292. For the 1966 Court decision, see *Die Welt,* July 20 and 23, 1966.

stein, "the parties' lack of cohesive mass support confronts the interest groups' lack of politically legitimate decision-making power." [43] The bargaining process between the parties and the interest groups takes place on two levels: that of the single-member constituency, and that of the *Land*.

The framework is provided by an election law which regulates nominating procedure in some detail. Parties which have previously had at least five members in the Bundestag or a Landtag may nominate constituency candidates simply on the signature of their *Land* Executive Committee. Candidates of parties unrepresented in the federal or in a state parliament, or independent candidates, require two hundred signatures; few independents have presented themselves and none have been elected since 1949. But having bestowed on the parties a near monopoly over nominations, the law attempts to impose on them the obligation to employ democratic procedure. It requires that parties must make their nominations for the single-member constituencies by secret ballot taken at a meeting of party members in the constituency, or by their elected delegates. The second method is the more practicable, and is almost always employed. The militants in local party organizations jealously defend their legal prerogative to select candidates against interference from higher party councils. Although the law permits the *Land* Executive Committee of a party to request reconsideration of a constituency nomination, that request is almost never openly made for fear of arousing the resistance of the constituency party, which, under the law, has the final word in any case. But the autonomy of the local party is secure only if it can get its candidate elected without outside support. If its seat is safe for the party, as is the case with the CSU in most of Bavaria, or with the CDU and the SPD in their areas of strength, the constituency party can effectively control the nomination. But if a local candidate requires "reinsurance" through a second nomination on the *Land* list, which the law permits, the *Land* organization has a very effective source of influence upon the constituency in the bargaining over nominations. The law provides that a convention elected directly or indirectly by party members within each *Land* must nominate, by secret ballot, the party's list of candidates for the seats which are distributed to achieve

[43] Heinz Josef Varain, *Parteien und Verbände,* Eine Studie über ihren Aufbau, ihre Verflechtung, und ihr Wirken in Schleswig-Holstein, 1945–1958 (Cologne and Opladen: Westdeutscher Verlag, 1964), p. 116.

proportionality.[44] The constituencies make their nominations before the conventions meet, but unless the seat is safe for their party, their leaders are likely to negotiate with party leaders in neighboring regions, and with their *Land* headquarters, before they select their candidates, to assure the inclusion of their local nominee on the *Land* list.

Reinsurance is important, especially for candidates of the smaller parties, which have almost no chance to win the necessary constituency plurality. (See Table 2.) With the consolidation of party strength, the CDU/CSU and SPD, as the largest among a declining number of parties, won an ever-increasing share of the constituencies, the Free Democrats were gradually denied any local victories, and the German party succeeded only as long as it had stand-down agreements with the CDU. After 1957, all constituencies were won by the two largest parties, with a disproportionate share going to the CDU/CSU as the larger of the two. In *Länder* where the strength of one of these parties was concentrated, it won all the constituencies. This the CDU did in Schleswig-Holstein in 1953 and 1957, the CSU in Bavaria in 1957, and the SPD in Hamburg in 1961, and in Bremen since 1949. In the 1961 and 1965 elections nearly two-thirds of the CDU/CSU Members of the Bundestag but less than one-half of the SPD Representatives were elected in single-member constituencies. For the nominees of the other parties, local candidacy has been hopeless and the only real chance for election has come by nomination on the *Land* list. The structural characteristics of the parties reinforce the tendencies toward local autonomy in the CDU/CSU and centralization in the SPD, which the voting patterns produce.

The Interests of the Constituency Parties

Naturally, the constituency organization is anxious to reward its candidate for his effort on behalf of the local party by holding out some possibility of victory. It is equally anxious to be represented in the Bundestag by one of its own. It is therefore common practice, and in some *Länder* even a party rule, to give constituency candidates

[44] For the relevant legal provisions on the nominating procedure, see Bundeswahlgesetz, May 7, 1956, *BGBl.* I, p. 383 ff., pars. 19, 21, 22, 28. Parties not represented in the Bundestag or a Landtag by at least five Members must submit the signatures of one-tenth of 1% of the eligible voters in the *Land*, up to a maximum of 2,000, in support of their lists of nominees.

Table 2. Proportion of mandates won in single-member constituencies

Party	Election years	Total number of seats won [a]	Proportion of party's seats won in single-member constituencies [b] (in per cent)	Proportion of all single-member constituencies won by party [c] (in per cent)
CDU/CSU	1949	139	83	47
	1953	243	71	71
	1957	270	72	79
	1961	242	64	63
	1965	245	63	62
SPD	1949	131	73	40
	1953	151	30	19
	1957	169	27	19
	1961	190	48	37
	1965	202	47	38
FDP	1949	52	23	5
	1953	48	29	6
	1957	41	2	0.4
	1961	67	0	0
	1965	49	0	0
DP	1949	17	29	2
	1953	15	67	4
	1957	17	35	2
	1961	0	0	0
	1965	0	0	0
BP	1949	17	65	5
	1953	0	0	0
	1957	0	0	0
	1961	0	0	0
	1965	0	0	0
Others	1949	46	7	1
	1953	30	3	0.4
	1957	0	0	0
	1961	0	0	0
	1965	0	0	0

[a] Excluding Members elected by the Berlin House of Representatives.

[b] Under the electoral law, approximately 60 per cent of all Bundestag seats were filled in single-member constituencies in 1949. Thereafter, the proportion was approximately 50 per cent.

[c] The number of single-member constituencies was 242 in 1949 and 1953, 247 n 1957 and 1961, and 248 in 1965.

preferential places on the list.[45] In the Bundestag elected in 1957, only 18 out of the 123 SPD Members elected from the lists had not also been district candidates. All but one of the Free Democrats, and all of the German party Members similarly had had both nominations. In the CDU/CSU, 52 Members elected as list candidates had not stood in constituencies, but since the party, with 270 mandates, had won 23

Table 3. Nomination patterns by party, 1957 (in per cent)

Nomination categories	*CDU* (n = 215)	*CSU* (n = 55)	*SPD* (n = 169)	*FDP* (n = 41)	*DP* (n = 17)	*Total* (n = 497)
Members nominated in single-member constituency only	39	71	6	0	12	27
Members nominated on *Land* list only	21	13	11	2	0	14
Members nominated in single-member constituency and on *Land* list	40	16	83	98	88	59

more seats than there were districts, it should be noted that of its 241 constituency nominees, 194 won their constituencies, another 24 won places from the lists on which they had had secondary nominations, and only 23 lost in the constituency without having a list nomination as reinsurance. In sum, only 71 of the 497 Members of the third Bundestag had not been constituency nominees. In the fourth Bundestag, only 51 Members had not run in constituencies. This is a measure of the degree of coordination between the constituency organizations, as primary selection agencies, and the *Land* organizations, which determine the lists. (See Table 3.)

If over 85 per cent of the Bundestag is composed of Members who are nominees of the local parties (even if most of them are list nominees also), it is obvious that the choice of candidates exercised by the constituencies substantially affects the recruitment of parliamentary Representatives. Among the criteria of selection which these

[45] Karlheinz Kaufmann, Helmut Kohl, and Peter Molt, *Kandidaturen zum Bundestag* (Cologne and Berlin: Kiepenheuer & Witsch, 1961), pp. 102, 133, 179, 197–8, 235.

local organizations employ, the presumption in favor of sitting Members is very important. Of 228 Bundestag Members elected in single-member constituencies in 1953 and still sitting at the end of the term, 174 were renominated in the same constituencies, only 43 were not renominated at all, and among these only about half, or 10 per cent of the total, had sought renomination. They were mainly CDU/CSU Members unexpectedly swept in by the 1953 landslide for that party. In 1965, 42 sitting Members in the constituencies, nearly the same number as eight years earlier, were not renominated. Dissatisfaction with a Member's attention to constituency errands was the main reason for the failure of renomination; the desire to replace an older with a younger candidate was a second factor, which was especially strong in the CDU in 1965. Altogether, 24 per cent of the Members who had been elected to the second Bundestag in single-member constituencies, and who were still sitting at the end of the term, failed of re-election in 1957. In the third Bundestag, a comparable proportion, 23 per cent of constituency Members still sitting at the term's end, were not re-elected in 1961.[46] (See Table 4.)

Members elected on the lists did not fare quite as well in renomination, a sign of the value which local attachments have for the candidates. Of 240 Members elected from the lists in the second Bundestag and still sitting at the end of the term (not counting the Members of the All-German Bloc which did not survive the next election), 41 were not renominated, about half of these against their will. In 1965, 40 Members who had been elected on the lists four years earlier were not renominated. Another 31, though renominated in 1957, received a lower place on the list than they had previously had, or a nomination in a different *Land* or constituency, and failed to be re-elected; eight years later, this total was similar. A large proportion of those who switched party affiliation during the parliamentary term were among the defeated. Altogether, 34 per cent of the list Representatives serving at the end of the term were not re-elected in 1957. The proportion varied sharply by party, from 18 per cent of the SPD group, to 37 per cent of the CDU Members, and 52 per cent of those originally elected on the FDP lists, a consequence of that party's split during the term.

---

[46] In this and the following paragraph, the statistics for 1957 are from U. W. Kitzinger, *German Electoral Politics*, pp. 63, 77; those for 1961 are calculated from the official election returns; those for 1965 are provisional, as given in *FAZ*, June 30, 1965.

Table 4. Re-election of Members of the third Bundestag to the fourth Bundestag, by types of constituencies (in per cent, based on Members serving throughout the third Bundestag)

Re-election record, 1961	Elected from constituency in 1957 (n = 226)	Elected from list in 1957			All Members elected in 1957 (n = 457)
		Without constituency nomination (n = 69)	With secondary constituency nomination (n = 162)	Total (n = 231)	
Re-elected to 4th Bundestag	77	67	80	76	76
Not re-elected to 4th Bundestag	23	33	20	24	24

With far less party switching during the subsequent parliamentary term, only 24 per cent of the Members who had been elected on the list in 1957 and were still sitting at term's end were not re-elected in 1961. But of those who had been nominated only on a list, one-third failed to make it, while among those who also had a constituency nomination, only one-fifth were unsuccessful. (See Table 4.)

The prominence of the local Member, and his influence in the constituency organization, may account for his somewhat greater ability to obtain renomination and re-election. But his success also varies by party. (See Table 5.) The SPD has a stronger propensity altogether

Table 5. Re-election of Members of the third Bundestag to the fourth Bundestag, by party (in per cent, based on Members serving throughout the third Bundestag)

Proportion re-elected, 1961	CDU (n = 201)	CSU (n = 52)	SPD (n = 153)	FDP (n = 36)
Of all Members elected, 1957	70	79	84	86
Of Members elected in single-member constituencies, 1957	73	85	83	— a
Of Members elected from list without constituency nomination, 1957	62	— a	83	0 b
Of Members elected from list with secondary constituency nomination, 1957	68	0 b	84	86

a Insignificant number of cases.

b No cases.

to renominate sitting Members than the CDU/CSU; with the Free Democrats the tendency has varied, depending on the state of party unity. In the CDU, Members elected in the constituencies are more successful than Members elected from the lists in winning re-election. There is hardly any difference between the two categories among the Social Democrats, most of whose candidates receive both nominations in any case. (See Table 3.)

Half the time, the incumbent Member faces a contest for the nomination in his constituency, but he obviously confronts his opponent from a position of strength. In order to maintain ties between Member and constituency from which both candidate and party gain advantages, most Members elected as list candidates serve as "step-member" either for the constituency which they lost or for another one, reducing the differences between the two categories of Members. Of the Representatives elected as list candidates in 1953, 25 won in constituencies four years later—which indicates a measure of both the attraction and the prospects of such a switch.[47]

When the incumbent has withdrawn or has been rejected, and a new candidate must be chosen, local considerations predominate in the deliberations of the constituency party. Nearly 80 per cent of Representatives elected in the constituencies in 1957 were residents of the district they had won.[48] But party members in a constituency comprise only a small proportion of the electorate, varying in their social characteristics from one party to another, and not necessarily representative of the local population. The interests which are strongest within the local party membership have the most direct influence on the nomination. Interests outside the party are influential insofar as they can offer the candidate needed organizational support.

The strong articulation of economic and social interests within the CDU/CSU, and the weaknesses of its party organization in many places, cause it to pay particular attention to the occupational and denominational identification of potential candidates. In rural areas, landowners and leaders of agricultural associations are likely nominees; in industrial regions, business owners, leaders of employers' or-

[47] U. W. Kitzinger, *German Electoral Politics*, p. 77; cf. Kaufmann, Kohl, and Molt, *op. cit.*, p. 76.
[48] U. W. Kitzinger, *German Electoral Politics*, p. 64. An example of a constituency nominating meeting is graphically described in Kaufmann, Kohl, and Molt, *op. cit.*, pp. 106–13.

ganizations, and employees of Catholic trade unions have great appeal.[49] The religious affiliation of CDU/CSU Members of Parliament corresponds closely to the religious composition of their constituencies. Of 121 CDU/CSU Catholics elected in the constituencies in 1957, 89 per cent represented districts in which Catholics constituted over two-fifths of the population, and in which they doubtless comprised a majority of CDU/CSU voters, and an even stronger majority of CDU/CSU party members. Of its 73 Protestant Members elected in the constituencies that year, 93 per cent won in districts which were over three-fifths Protestant.[50] The social and economic characteristics of CDU/CSU candidates reflect the interests which are best organized within the party, or best financed from the outside. Refugees, young people, women, small-business owners, Protestants, and government officials all have their own intraparty organization, pressing for the nomination of a candidate identified with them.[51]

Because the social composition of the SPD is narrower, party organization stronger, and party cohesion more dependent on the large proportion of members who are officeholders, different factors influence the selection of its candidates. Denominational considerations are absent, and party prominence and party loyalty are more important. Farm and business groups are only sparsely represented in the party membership, and few of the party's candidates belong to these groups. But trade union employees, party organizers, local government officials, and teachers constitute important components of the membership in most areas, and a large proportion of the party's candidates are therefore drawn from these ranks. The only groups extensively organized within the party are women and young people, who work for the nomination of one of their own as their counterparts do in the CDU/CSU.[52]

The FDP has a still far narrower social base. Its relatively small and ill-defined membership comes largely from business and professional groups. Because the party's prospects in the constituencies are extremely poor, it frequently has difficulty finding any candidates. In

[49] Kaufmann, Kohl, and Molt, *op. cit.*, pp. 199–200, 208, 213.

[50] U. W. Kitzinger, *German Electoral Politics*, p. 65.

[51] Kaufmann, Kohl, and Molt, *op. cit.*, pp. 162, 200, 201; Heinz Josef Varain, *op. cit.*, pp. 151–64; 184–92. Cf. by the same author, "Kandidaten und Abgeordnete in Schleswig-Holstein, 1947–1958," *Politische Vierteljahresschrift*, II (1961), 400–2.

[52] Kaufmann, Kohl, and Molt, *op. cit.*, pp. 111–12, 176–7, 200, 201, 208–13; Douglas A. Chalmers, *The Social Democratic Party of Germany* (New Haven: Yale University Press, 1964), p. 198.

Plate III. A rear view of the Bundestag chamber, showing the press, diplomatic, and visitors' galleries. (Courtesy of Presse- und Informationsamt der Bundesregierung.)

Plate IV. A close-up of the CDU/CSU and FDP front benches during a question hour. (Courtesy of Presse- und Informationsamt der Bundesregierung.)

1957 it made special efforts to nominate farm leaders, in order to make inroads on the farm vote. The tactic was largely unsuccessful because of the small impact which candidates make on voter choice. On the whole, the candidates of the FDP also represent its economic and social composition. Its small membership and weak organization promote the candidacy of financial contributors.[53]

As we have seen, in the selection of a constituency candidate, the appeal of the nominee to the voter is a secondary consideration. From the party's national or even regional point of view, the outcome of the election is not decided in the constituencies in any case, because the list victories compensate for constituency defeats and assure the party Bundestag representation fully corresponding to the proportion of the total vote cast nationally for its lists. There is scattered evidence that candidates with weak appeal in their constituencies can undermine the vote for a party's lists. In Baden-Württemberg in 1957, for example, the weakness of the FDP's local candidates appears to have hurt the vote for its lists.[54] But in general, the coattails' effect of local candidates is doubtful. Voters are strongly inclined to vote for the party rather than the candidate, especially in balloting among party lists. In the 1953 election, the first in which the law provided for a separate vote for constituency candidates and *Land* lists, only 2 to 3 per cent of the electorate split their vote because of a preference for a constituency candidate of a party other than the one whose *Land* list they endorsed. An opinion poll disclosed that even among voters who had made up their mind about the party they would vote for, only 36 per cent knew the name of its local candidate, and only 2 to 4 per cent of all voters gave the personal qualifications of the local candidate as a reason for their decision.[55] The pattern of vote splitting in 1957 and 1961 indicated a further decline in the tendency to split ballots for any reason.[56] A few conspicuous exceptions, such as Carlo Schmid, Eugen Gerstenmaier, or even a locally popular candidate like August Dres-

---

[53] Kaufmann, Kohl, and Molt, *op. cit.*, pp. 132–44, 185–7, 200–1, 208–13; Varain, *Parteien und Verbände*, p. 164.

[54] Kaufmann, Kohl, and Molt, *op. cit.*, p. 225.

[55] Wolfgang Hirsch-Weber and Klaus Schütz, *Wähler und Gewählte* (Berlin and Frankfurt: Verlag Franz Vahlen, 1957), pp. 299, 335–7, 340–5.

[56] Statistisches Bundesamt, *Statistik der Bundesrepublik Deutschland*, Vol. 200, no. 2, pp. 33, 38–41; Statistisches Bundesamt, "Wahl zum 4. Deutschen Bundestag am 17. September 1961," series A, pt. 8, no. 4 (Stuttgart and Mainz: W. Kohlhammer, 1964), p. 51; U. W. Kitzinger, *German Electoral Politics*, pp. 288–9; Kaufmann, Kohl, and Molt, *op. cit.*, 227–9.

bach, have pulled a vote 3 or 4 per cent greater than that cast for the list of their parties. A great number of lesser prominences outdraw their party by smaller amounts.

But from the constituency party's point of view, the electoral prospect of potential candidates is really important only if it determines whether the district has direct representation in the Bundestag. Therefore, in the relatively small number of marginal constituencies, the effect of a candidate on the local voter may be an important consideration. In these instances, national or *Land* leaders prominent within the party, or well-known local officials, especially mayors, are regarded as particularly attractive candidates. In some cases, efforts are made to find candidates who will appeal to the voter because of occupational or personal reputations. However, the number of marginal constituencies is small. In the election of 1957, for example, only 16 per cent of constituencies were won by margins of less than 10 per cent of the vote. In over half of these districts, furthermore, the winning candidate also had a safe place on the *Land* list of his party, which would have guaranteed him election in any case. Where the electoral outcome is at all uncertain, therefore, the constituency's best prospect of having a winning candidate consists of placing him safely on the *Land* list. This means taking into account his broad regional appeal and the various factors influencing the *Land* organization of the party.

The Interests of the Land Parties

On the *Land* level, a wider perspective prevails than in the constituencies. A balanced list, taking the major party interests within the region into account, is a foremost consideration, as is the parliamentary prominence of at least the leading candidates.[57] The most promising positions are normally filled by candidates who are already nominated in the constituencies. But those in hopeless constituencies can be given favorable positions on the list. Over 36 per cent of the Members elected to the Bundestag in 1957 had lost their constituencies. The composition of the *Land* lists therefore has a substantial influence on the prospective parliamentary delegation of the party, and permits a redress of the group interests reflected in the constituency nominations.

In composing the lists, representation of the various regions within

---

[57] Kaufmann, Kohl, and Molt, *op. cit.*, pp. 111–12, 198, 227–9, 236–7.

the *Land* is of first importance, especially in those *Länder* where historical sectional loyalties persist. In some, like North Rhine–Westphalia and Rhineland-Palatinate, for example, the CDU and SPD are still organized along traditional regional lines, and the *Land* organization of the party is merely a creature of the regional organizations. Places on the SPD list in these two *Länder* are filled by the regional organizations, each receiving a share of the promising places in proportion to the vote which the party won in that region at the last election. In the North Rhine–Westphalian SPD, the regional organizations in turn allow the constituency parties to select the actual candidates. Without usually permitting this degree of decentralization of the decision, all *Länder* parties give regional representation of candidates on the list careful consideration. This pattern reflects the tenacity with which traditional sectional loyalties have persisted within the parties and the extent to which the *Länder* are still artificial political units.[58]

In the process of nomination by regional standards, strong efforts are also made to achieve representation of the major economic and social groups within the party. A list of nominees almost invites efforts to achieve a balance of interests, as nominations in single-member constituencies cannot do. Furthermore, regional and national interest groups can more easily influence the *Land* than the district organizations of the parties. The first five names on the list receive special consideration, because they alone appear on the ballot. As the party's window dressing, they generally include prominent party leaders, at least one woman candidate, and, in the CDU/CSU, members of both denominations. They are usually not the effective candidates, however, since most of them will also have safe constituencies in which they accept election, passing the mandates won by the party list down to the candidates next in line. The real struggle is therefore for the places immediately below the top of the list, including all those positions which hold some promise of election according to the highly uncertain forecast of the proportion of the popular vote which the party will win, and the number of constituencies it will carry. Although the names of candidates in these positions will not even appear on the ballot, and the personal appeal of the candidate to the voters is therefore unimportant, the response of organized sections of the elec-

[58] *Ibid.*, pp. 86–7, 124–7, 164–5, 177–83; U. W. Kitzinger, *German Electoral Politics*, pp. 68–70.

torate to the list may depend in part on the recognition which these groups have received in the nominations. Since the vote cast for the list directly determines the number of seats the party will occupy in the Bundestag, appeal to groups capable of getting out the vote is an important matter at this level of nomination. The demands of refugee and veterans organizations, business and farm groups, and trade unions for the inclusion of some of their number on the list of candidates are not easily resisted, especially if these groups constitute parts of the party's potential electorate or financial contributors.[59]

To the extent that past or prospective parliamentary performance is a standard for the selection of candidates, the constituency organizations are chiefly concerned with the Member's performance of constituency errands and his representation of local interests. The *Land* party organizations must take a broader view. Their parochial interests are mainly served by their Representatives in *Land* politics. But insofar as the party's image, and the voter's response to it, is affected by its performance in the federal government and in the Bundestag, the *Land* organizations must consider the contribution which prospective candidates can make to the parliamentary party. Not only the defense of regional interests but also parliamentary performance by national standards is considered. In 1957, after the FDP in the Bundestag had split, the loyalty of candidates to party decisions in Parliament became an important consideration in that party. In all parties, there is concern that the parliamentary delegation have Members qualified to handle the major legislative subjects, and an adequate number of *ministrables.*[60]

Simultaneous consideration of all these factors obviously requires a balancing act of great skill. Preliminary discussion of the party list is therefore generally extensive, and takes place in consultation with the district organizations in the region. By the time the *Land* convention meets, the *Land* executive committees are ready to present a complete proposal, backed by the prestige which the executive commands, and the bargains which have been struck with the various local delegations to the convention regarding the inclusion of their candidates on the

[59] The influence on nominations in the CDU exercised by industrial groups through their financial contributions is examined in Gerard Braunthal, *op. cit.,* pp. 136–45.

[60] U. W. Kitzinger, *German Electoral Politics,* pp. 70–5; Kaufmann, Kohl, and Molt, *op. cit.,* pp. 86–7, 118–21, 134–7, 164, 170–1, 182–3, 189–90, 197–202.

list. Critical discussion of this proposal in the convention is common, but changes are rare, even though a secret vote may be taken on every name on the list. The chances for the executive proposal to prevail are so great, because a change in favor of even a single name will adversely affect all other candidacies, upsetting the carefully contrived balance. In the nomination of list candidates, the *Land* organizations or their regional subdivisions are therefore very powerful, although their success depends, especially in the loosely organized CDU, on their ability to take the interests of major groups within the party into account.[61]

The Interests of the National Parties

The national leaderships of the parties have no formal way to affect nominations. All attempts at "outside interference" are likely to elicit an equal and opposite reaction. Like all groups external to the nominating process, the influence of the national leaders depends on the extent to which they are active members of *Land* or local party organizations. Their proportion on some *Land* party executive committees is very high in the SPD, but in the CDU/CSU by contrast, officeholders in the *Land* Government dominate the *Land* executives.[62] In order to have the necessary base in local party organizations, most national leaders maintain candidacies in safe constituencies in spite of the burden of nursing the constituency. In the Bundestag elected in 1957, all but one of the members of the Cabinet held parliamentary seats in safe constituencies, and the frequency of constituency nomination and election was also markedly higher among parliamentary leaders than among backbenchers. (See Table 6.) But the national leaders are unable, judging by their frequently expressed complaints, to assure the nomination of other candidates whose services the parliamentary party requires as legislative experts, committee chairmen, or possible Cabinet members. The problem is greater in the CDU/CSU than in the more centralized SPD. The national leaders depend on the responsiveness of the *Land* executive committees to their needs, and these have many other concerns. The electoral fate of important members of the parliamentary parties is therefore often quite uncertain. In 1961, for example, the CDU/CSU lost four of its six most qualified Members in the fields of taxation and finance. Three of them failed to

[61] *Ibid.*, pp. 88–91, 122–4, 165–71, 180, 199.
[62] *Ibid.*, pp. 85, 123, 152–3, 172–3, 199.

be elected as list candidates and one, who had been chairman of the Finance Committee, failed to obtain any nomination.[63] However, attempts to revise the electoral law to give national leaders a direct part in the nominating process have been unsuccessful. Adenauer, in 1960, suggested the addition of a federal list of candidates for the seats which are proportionately distributed, in the expectation that the parlia-

Table 6. The relation of parliamentary position to constituency, third Bundestag

Constituency, 1957	Members of Cabinet (n=18) (in per cent)	Parliamentary leaders[a] (n=141) (in per cent)	Parliamentary backbenchers [a] (n=360) (in per cent)
Nominated in single-member constituency	100	91	83
Elected in single-member constituency	94	55	46
Elected from "safe" seat, list or single-member constituency [b]	94	75	61

[a] For definition, see Table 18.

[b] Defined as Members elected with a margin of 10 per cent or more of the total vote in single-member constituencies, or elected from *Land* lists among the top two-thirds of successful candidates.

mentary leaders would be able to nominate this list in each party. But the proposal, which had Weimar tradition on its side, made little headway against the interests of entrenched local leaders. That Adenauer advanced it at all indicates that the leader of the largest party felt a strong need to increase national influence on the recruitment of Members of Parliament.[64]

There is no assurance that the candidates of the constituencies and

[63] *Der Spiegel*, XV (Sept. 27, 1961), 34; *Die Zeit* (U.S. ed.), Oct. 11, 1963, p. 14.

[64] Kaufmann, Kohl, and Molt, p. 197. For an assessment that attributes somewhat greater power to the national leadership, see U. W. Kitzinger, *German Electoral Politics*, pp. 74–5; for Adenauer's proposal, see *Die Welt*, April 28, 1960, p. 4; for the need to give the federal party executive some power to "plan" the party's parliamentary group, see Hans Peters, "Zur Kandidatenaufstellung für freie demokratische Wahlen," in Theodor Maunz, ed., *Vom Bonner Grundgesetz zur Gesamtdeutschen Verfassung*, Festschrift zum 75. Geburtstag von Hans Nawiasky (Munich: Isar Verlag, 1956), p. 349.

the *Länder,* who are selected primarily in response to the demands of organized interests within the party and of outside contributors, will perform adequately as Members of the Bundestag. The electorate's judgment of candidates, insofar as it considers their parliamentary performance, is only a remote influence on the nominating agencies. The constituency parties judge parliamentary performance largely in terms of constituency advantage; the *Land* parties give it broader consideration, but they are sensitive to a multiplicity of conflicting interests in making their selection. In either case, the system of selection gives great advantages to the candidate advanced by an influential interest group within the party, by its financial contributors, or by an influential group of party leaders at the local level.

The Factors in the Recruitment Process

The chief variables in the recruitment process appear to have a systematic influence on the composition of the political class from which Members of the Bundestag are selected. Despite nostalgia for a parliament of "notables," none of the variables seem to favor the candidacy of political amateurs or of members of the free professions. The material conditions of the mandate and widely prevalent attitudes against active involvement in politics limit the attraction of a seat in Parliament to the politically organized few. The electoral system, the weakness of the parties financially and in terms of members, the dependence of the parties on interest-group support, and the legal framework of the electoral system all appear to favor the candidacy of that small minority of citizens who are party activists at the constituency or *Land* level. In addition, it seems to favor candidates enjoying the support of locally prominent interest groups, including those local government officials having an influential local political clientele. It might also leave room for the candidacy of men and women not previously active in party politics, if they have the support of an interest group with strong political influence in the party from which they seek nomination.

The recruitment process appears to produce Members who fit some of the expectations of the political culture. In favoring interest-group representatives and government officials, it creates a class of parliamentarians corresponding to public concepts of the Member of Parliament. But the recruitment process appears to take little account of recent political and constitutional changes in the position which Parliament occupies in the political system. Nothing in the process seems to assure that Members of Parliament will have the relevant political skills.

The effect of the influences on recruitment which we have identified can be determined by a closer examination of the composition of the Bundestag, contrasting it, where possible, with the composition of other parliaments subject to different influences on recruitment. We therefore turn next to an inspection of the age and seniority patterns in the House, and the religious, regional, educational, and occupational backgrounds of the Members. In order, eventually, to establish the relationship between parliamentary recruitment and the performance of Parliament in the political system, we will also consider the effect of social background on the roles which Members play in the House.

COMPOSITION

The third Bundestag, elected in September, 1957, is the main subject of the analysis which follows. The universe studied consists of all Members who took their seats at the first meeting of that Parliament on October 15, 1957. Although the two Parliaments elected since then exhibit small differences in composition, some of which are mentioned at relevant points below, they did not differ substantially in make-up from the Bundestag which sat from 1957 to 1961. In fact, available evidence indicates a considerable continuity in the social composition of the Bundestag throughout the postwar period.

Age and Seniority

When the third Bundestag first convened, the average age of its Members was 52.5 years. This was about the same as the average age of United States Representatives, but was slightly higher than that of the Bundestag's British, and substantially higher than its French and Italian, counterparts.[65] Thirteen per cent of its Members were 40 or younger, 30 per cent were between 41 and 50, 38 per cent were be-

---

[65] The average age of Members of the U.S. House of Representatives which convened in January, 1957, was 52.96 years; between 1953 and 1965, this was the highest average age. The lowest, 50.6 years, was reached in the House which convened in January, 1965. The average age of Senators is 5 to 7 years higher (*Congressional Quarterly Weekly Report,* Jan. 6, 1961, p. 15; Jan. 4, 1963, p. 22; Jan. 1, 1965, p. 25).

tween 51 and 60, and 19 per cent were 61 or older.[66] The efforts of party youth organizations to obtain places for their members on the *Land* lists apparently produced few successful candidacies. Only twenty-seven Members were 35 or below, and none of them had been a candidate on a list, although the organized youth groups concentrate their efforts on these lists.[67] The proportion of Members older than 60 was large, both by previous German standards, and by British, French, and Italian comparison. The average age had been 50 both in the Reichstag of 1928, the last before the crisis of the Weimar Republic, and in the Bundestag of 1949, the first national Parliament after the war.[68]

If the age of German Representatives is relatively high, this partly reflects the failure of the nonsocialist parties to give as much consideration to young candidates as, for example, the British Conservative party has given. In several *Länder,* the CDU regards "youth" as any age up to 40, setting that as the age limit for membership in the party's youth group. While the average age of Conservative members of the postwar House of Commons has ranged from 45 to 48, and that of Labour members has been between 50 and 55, the age relationship

[66] Unless otherwise noted, the statistics in this section are based mainly on an examination of the biographical data of the 519 Members of the third Bundestag, elected in 1957, as given in the official directory, the *Amtliches Handbuch des Deutschen Bundestages,* 3. Wahlperiode (Neue Darmstädter Verlagsanstalt, 1958). It is also based on the lists of committee memberships contained in that directory, as well as the stenographic reports of the debates held during the four year term of that House. The biographical data has the shortcomings that are associated with biographical materials supplied by elected representatives themselves for public scrutiny. It has been used critically, checked for internal consistency, and augmented wherever other information was available, notably from newspaper reports and personal sources. Fifty-six items of information drawn from the biographies, and from the records of electoral and parliamentary performance of each of the Members originally elected to that Bundestag, were coded, recorded on IBM punch cards, and analyzed with the use of an IBM counter-sorter and a Model 1620 computer. For the use of this equipment, I acknowledge, with appreciation, the cooperation of the Research Computing Center, University of Massachusetts, and the Mount Holyoke Political Studies Center. A useful survey of recent research on the memberships of the parliaments of France, Israel, the United Kingdom, the United States, and the Soviet Union, is contained in a special issue of the UNESCO *International Social Science Journal,* Vol. XIII, no. 4 (1961), entitled "The Parliamentary Profession," Jean Meynaud, ed. It includes an article by the editor on the problems of this type of research.

[67] U. W. Kitzinger, *German Electoral Politics,* p. 71.

[68] Otto Kirchheimer, "The Composition of the German Bundestag, 1950," *Western Political Quarterly,* III (1950), 591–2.

between Representatives of left and right has been just the reverse in the Bundestag.[69] The average age of CDU/CSU and FDP Members has ranged from 51 to 53.5, while SPD Members have been two years younger on the average.[70]

The relatively higher age of German Members may also be partly due to the absence of a social revolution after the war, of the kind which produced parliaments much younger than their prewar predecessors in the first postwar elections in Britain and France, and in the first Parliament under the new Italian Constitution in 1948. (See Table 7.) Furthermore, between 1949 and 1957, the age of Members of the Bundestag had crept up from levels already high as a result of continuity of membership from one electoral period to another. Such continuity is without precedent in Germany, or in France, in this century, and is exceeded only by the continuity of parliamentary membership in Great Britain. (See Table 8.) It is the consequence of the factors favoring incumbents in the system of nominations, and an expression of the institutional and political stability in postwar Germany, which has not been equaled since the Empire.

If this has meant an older House, it is also itself a contribution to the stability of the institution. Only 18 of the 402 Members of the first Bundestag had belonged to the pre-Hitler Reichstag, but 262 of these Members, 62 per cent of the total, went on to serve in the second Bundestag. That House, larger in size than its predecessor, had 46 per cent new Members; the third Bundestag was 34 per cent new, the fourth 25 per cent. In 1965, the first slight reversal occurred in the growing continuity of the House, as 26 per cent of the Members elected that year had no prior Bundestag experience. The average Member entering the fourth Bundestag in 1961 had nearly six years' previous service, and when the fifth Bundestag convened in 1965, the average Member had nearly seven years' previous service. While this does not yet equal tenure in the U.S. House of Representatives, whose average Member has had nine years of prior service when a new House convenes,[71] nor in the British House of Commons, whose average

[69] J. F. S. Ross, *Elections and Electors* (London: Eyre and Spottiswoode, 1955), p. 399; D. E. Butler, *The British General Election of 1955* (London: Macmillan, 1955), p. 40; D. E. Butler and Richard Rose, *The British General Election of 1959* (London: Macmillan, 1960), p. 125; D. E. Butler and Anthony King, *The British General Election of 1964* (London: Macmillan, 1965), p. 234.

[70] Taken from the official handbooks of each Bundestag.

[71] G. B. Galloway, *The Legislative Process in Congress* (New York: Crowell, 1953), p. 371.

Table 7. Distribution of age groups in Western European parliaments (in per cent of total membership)

Parliaments	Under 40 [a]	40–49 [a]	50 or over [a]
France			
Chamber of Deputies, 1936	20	38	42
National Assembly, 1946	43	35	22
National Assembly, 1956	17	43	40
Italy			
Chamber of Deputies, 1948	40	[b]	[b]
Chamber of Deputies, 1958	32	32	36
United Kingdom			
House of Commons, 1935	23	24	53
House of Commons, 1945	26	29	45
House of Commons, 1959	14	31	55
House of Commons, 1964	21	30	49
Germany			
Reichstag, 1928	17	36	47
Bundestag, 1949	14	35	51
Bundestag, 1957	13	30	58
Bundestag, 1961	13	27	60
Bundestag, 1965	15	30	55

[a] Because of the variety of standards used by the different authors on whom I have relied, the age ranges are not absolutely comparable to each other. For the French National Assembly of 1946, the House of Commons of 1935 and 1945, the Italian Chamber of Deputies, and the German Bundestag of 1957 and 1961, Column 1 includes Members through age 40, and Column 2 includes Members through age 50.

[b] No information available.

Sources: Figures for France, 1936 and 1956, from Mattei Dogan, "Changement de régime et changement de personnel," Association française de science politique, *L'établissement de la cinquième République, le référendum de septembre et les élections de novembre 1958* (Paris: Librairie Armand Colin, 1960), p. 270. Figures for France, 1946, from Maurice Duverger, *Political Parties,* 2d ed. (London: Methuen, 1959), p. 167. Figures for Italy from G. Sartori, "Parliamentarians in Italy," UNESCO, *International Social Science Journal,* XIII, no. 4 (1961), 586. Figures for the United Kingdom, 1935 and 1945, from J. F. S. Ross, *Elections and Electors* (London: Eyre & Spottiswoode, 1955), p. 394. Figures for the United Kingdom, 1959 and 1964, from D. E. Butler and Richard Rose, *The British General Election of 1959* (London: Macmillan, 1960), p. 125, and D. E. Butler and Anthony King, *The British General Election of 1964* (London: Macmillan, 1965), p. 234, respectively. Figures for Germany, 1928 and 1949 from Otto Kirchheimer, "The Composition of the German Bundestag, 1950," *Western Political Quarterly,* III (1950), 591–592. Figures for Germany for 1957 and 1961 from *Amtliches Handbuch des Deutschen Bundestages,* 3. Wahlperiode (Darmstadt: Neue Darmstädter Verlagsanstalt, 1958). *Ibid.,* 4. Wahlperiode. Figures for Germany for 1965 from *Die Welt,* September 24, 1965.

Table 8. Continuity of membership in Western European parliaments (in per cent of total membership)

Parliaments	New members	Years of previous membership		
		Up to 5	5–10	Over 10
Germany				
Reichstag, 1898	42	24	34 [a]	
Reichstag, Dec., 1924	14	54	16	16
Reichstag, Nov., 1932	9	61	13	17
Bundestag, 1949	96	0 (46) [b]	0	4 [c]
Bundestag, 1953	46	51	0	3 [c]
Bundestag, 1957	34	34	29	3 [c]
Bundestag, 1961	25	27	24	24
Bundestag, 1965	26	24	20	30 [d]
France				
Chamber of Deputies, 1919–1936 average	41			
Constituent Assembly, 1945	77			
National Assembly, 1945–1956 average	37			
National Assembly, 1956	29	16	14	41
National Assembly, 1958	61			
Italy				
Chamber of Deputies, 1948	54			
Chamber of Deputies, 1953	35			
Chamber of Deputies, 1958	36			
United Kingdom				
House of Commons, 1918–1935 average	29	31	18	22
House of Commons, 1945	51	12	15	22
House of Commons, 1950	21	41	11	27
House of Commons, 1959	16	16	29	39

[a] Combined figure for over 5 years of continuous previous service.

[b] Previous Reichstag or Landtag experience of any length before 1949.

[c] Previous Reichstag experience of any length before 1933.

[d] Among these, 71 Members, 14 per cent of the 5th Bundestag, have served continuously since 1949.

Sources: Figures for France for 1958, from Mattei Dogan, "Changement de régime et changement de personnel," *L'établissement de la cinquième République, le référendum de septembre et les élections de novembre 1958* (Paris: Librairie Armand Colin, 1960), pp. 270–72. Figures for 1919–1936 and 1945–1956 from Mattei Dogan, "Les Candidats et les Elus," in Association Française de Science Politique, *Les Elections du 2 Janvier 1956* (Paris: Librarie Armand Colin, 1957), pp. 447, 450–52. Figures for Italy from G. Sartori, "Parliamentarians in Italy," UNESCO,

Member has served more than eight,[72] it exceeds the continuity of membership in both prewar and postwar French Parliaments, in the Italian Chamber, and in the Reichstag of the Weimar Republic. (See Table 8.)

Seniority directly affects the position and activity of Members in the House. Between 1957 and 1961, only 6 per cent of Members in their first term spoke more than fifty times; but 8 per cent of those with one previous term spoke that often, and 13 per cent of those with two previous terms did so. A better measure of activity, in a Parliament whose main work is not done in public sessions, is the position which Members have achieved in the organizations of their parliamentary parties, or in the committee structure of the House. Of the new Members, one was a committee chairman and two were deputy chairmen, while among the second termers there were six chairmen and twelve deputy chairmen, and the third termers included nineteen chairmen and twelve deputy chairmen. Positions of leadership within the parliamentary parties were similarly occupied by the more senior Members. Nine Members in their first terms held positions of leadership within their parliamentary parties, against thirty-nine with one previous term and forty-two with two previous terms. The last group, with the highest seniority, included the President of the Bundestag, the three Vice-Presidents, eleven of the seventeen members of the Council of Elders, the important steering committee, and thirteen of the eighteen members of the Cabinet. The relationship between seniority and influence which these figures reveal indicate that if continuity of membership has contributed to the rising age of the House, it has also contributed to the establishment of institutional experience as an attribute of the parliamentary leadership, a stabilizing factor in the

---

International Social Science Journal, Vol. XIII, No. 4 (1961), p. 585. Figures for the United Kingdom for 1918–1950 from J. F. S. Ross, *Elections and Electors* (London: Eyre & Spottiswoode, 1955), p. 400. Figures for 1959 from Philip W. Buck, *Amateurs and Professionals in British Politics, 1918–1959* (Chicago: University of Chicago Press, 1963), p. 131. Figures for Germany for 1898 from Peter Molt, *Der Reichstag vor der improvisierten Revolution* (Cologne: Westdeutscher Verlag, 1963), pp. 320–21. Figures for 1924 and 1932 from Emil Obermann, *Alter und Konstanz von Fraktionen* (Meisenheim: Verlag Anton Hain, 1956), p. 106. Figure in parentheses for 1949 indicating previous experience in parliaments, given in Obermann, p. 105. Figures for 1953 and after derived from the *Amtliches Handbuch des Deutschen Bundestages,* and the files of the Bundestag secretariat.

[72] J. F. S. Ross, *op. cit.,* p. 402.

Table 9. Seniority and leadership in the Bundestag, 1957–1961
(in per cent of seniority categories)

Criteria of parliamentary leadership	New Members (n = 174)	Members elected to one previous term (n = 185)	Members elected to two previous terms (n = 160)
Participated over 50 times in debate	5.7	7.6	13.1
Committee chairmen	0.6	3.2	11.9
Deputy committee chairmen	1.1	6.5	7.5
Office in parliamentary party	5.2	21.0	26.2

development of the new institution. (See Table 9.) Meanwhile, the elections of 1961 and 1965 produced a reversal of the rising age trend in the House. While the average age of new Members was still high in comparison with that of Members entering the French and British

Table 10. Age of Members at first election to the French, British, and German parliaments (in per cent of total membership)

Parliaments	Under 40	40–49	50–59	60 and over
France				
National Assembly, 1958	34	34	23	9
United Kingdom				
House of Commons, 1950	44	39	17	0
Average, 1918–1959	37	33	23	7
Germany				
Bundestag, 1957	26	29	35	10

Sources: Figures for France from Mattei Dogan, "Changement de régime et changement de personnel," Association française de science politique, *L'établissement de la cinquième République, le référendum de septembre et les élections de novembre 1958* (Paris: Librairie Armand Colin, 1960), p. 271. Figures for the United Kingdom from J. F. S. Ross, *Elections and Electors* (London: Eyre & Spottiswoode, 1955), p. 388, and Philip W. Buck, *Amateurs and Professionals in British Politics, 1918–1959* (Chicago: University of Chicago Press, 1963), p. 112. Figures for Germany calculated from biographical sketches in *Amtliches Handbuch des Deutschen Bundestages, 3.* Wahlperiode (Neue Darmstädter Verlagsanstalt, 1958).

parliaments, or the United States House of Representatives,[73] at 49 years it was in 1961 one year below the average of entrants four years earlier. (See Table 10.) Its further decline in 1965 brought the average age of the House elected in that year down to 50.6 years, the lowest since 1953.[74]

Two Generations

Age groups have particular significance in Germany, because of the sharp differences which exist between the formative political experiences of the generations. The nation has been governed under four fundamentally different political systems within living memory. Among those entering Parliament after the war, a distinction of special importance existed between the group which had grown to political maturity under the Empire or the Weimar Republic, and, on the other hand, those who had reached that age during or after the Nazi regime. For the Members in the first group, the Nazi period disrupted any political careers. The severe persecution of all non-Nazi political activity left few alternatives: participation in Nazi politics, the abandonment of political activity, clandestine activity, emigration, or, for a few, survival in a concentration camp. For a decade and a half, during years of maturity, an open non-Nazi political career was closed to this generation, and the chances of survival for anyone who had had a conspicuous career of this kind before 1933 was considerably poorer than the chances for those who had not. Despite conspicuous exceptions, the largest proportion of the members of the older generation in the Bundestag had spent the formative years of their careers in private occupations.[75]

[73] The average age of new Members entering the House of Representatives was 43 in 1963 and 43.8 in 1965 (*Congressional Quarterly Weekly Report*, Jan. 4, 1963, p. 22; Jan. 1, 1965, p. 25).

[74] *Die Welt*, Sept. 24, 1965.

[75] Otto Kirchheimer reported that among the Members of the first Bundestag, 9 per cent had spent an extended period of time in concentration camps during the Nazi period, 8 per cent had suffered minor persecutions, 7 per cent had emigrated. 46 per cent of the Members had held minor positions as clerks, insurance agents, salesmen, and farmers, while 12 per cent held leading positions in business, agricultural organizations, or the academic world, and 2 per cent were government officials. But no information was available on 16 per cent (Kirchheimer, "The Composition of the German Bundestag, 1950," *op. cit.*, pp. 592–3). For a broader analysis, see Lewis J. Edinger, "Post-Totalitarian Leadership," *The American Political Science Review*, LIV (1960), 58–82, esp. 66–7, 69, 80; and, by the same author, "Continuity and Change in the Background of German Decision-Makers," *Western Political Quarterly*, XIV (1961), 17–36, esp. 20–22.

By contrast, the members of the younger generation, reaching maturity during or after the Nazi regime, had a far better opportunity to pursue a continuous political career. For a few, this began as a career in Nazi politics. Karl Loewenstein determined that 53 Members of the first Bundestag, or 13 per cent of the total, had been members of the Nazi party. In the House elected twelve years later, the Association of Victims of the Nazi Regime still found that 111 elected Members, 22 per cent of the total, had "served the Nazi state as officials, diplomats, jurists, or war economists." [76] However, neither Nazi party membership, nor public service of these types, necessarily corresponded to an active political career in Nazi Germany. Very few of those who conspicuously participated in National Socialist politics, in either generation, made a successful transition into postwar parliamentary politics. The political experience of the younger generation of Bundestag Members began with the disillusionment of the collapse of Nazism, and active experience began with Allied military government and the reviving institutions of German democracy. These experiences, formative for the younger Members, were merely transitional experiences for their elders.

Examination of the political training of Members of these two different age groups at comparable stages of their careers confirms the contrast between them. Taking as a dividing line the age of 50 at the time of the parliamentary election of 1957, those who were younger had been under twenty-five when the Weimar Republic disintegrated, too young to have embarked on a political career, while those who were older had been over twenty-five at that time, and had embarked on their careers. Among the younger generation of Members, there is far greater early experience in democratic elective office than among the older. Thirty-six per cent of this group had held elective municipal office, another 11 per cent had been elected to office in *Land* government, and, counting various regional elective offices, 58 per cent had served in elected positions before their entry into the Bundestag. Comparing the record of the older group of Members, at a comparable stage of their careers before the advent of Nazism, only 12 per cent had held elective municipal office, and only 24 per cent had held

[76] Karl Loewenstein, "The Government and Politics of Germany," in J. T. Shotwell, *Governments of Continental Europe*, rev. ed. (New York: Macmillan, 1952), p. 525, n. 10; *Die unbewältigte Gegenwart* (Frankfurt: Präsidium der Vereinigungen der Verfolgten des Naziregimes, 1962), pp. 24–9.

elective office of any kind at that time. The contrast between the generations in nonelective public activity is only slightly less great. In the pursuit of private occupations, on the other hand, the older generation considerably outdistanced the younger. (See Table 11.)

Table 11. Prior political experience of Bundestag Members, 1957: Contrast between generations (in per cent of each age group)

Political Experience	Older group [a] (prewar experience) (n = 299)	Younger group [b] (postwar experience) (n = 220)
Elected offices		
Municipal	12.4	36.4
Land	3.7	10.9
Other	8.3	10.8
Total	24.4	58.1
Non-elected political positions		
Party employee	6.7	12.8
Interest group employee	16.3	18.2
Government official	3.3	6.4
Other public employee	12.0	11.9
Combinations of above	1.7	1.7
Total	40.0	51.0
Private occupations [c]	82.7	58.7

[a] Members born in 1906 or earlier.
[b] Members born in 1907 or later.
[c] Totals exceed 100 per cent because of Member holding more than one of the above positions.

Although there are, of course, conspicuous exceptions, especially in the SPD, the average Member in the older group began his active political career after the war, following a lifetime spent in a private occupation. There is some variation among the parties in this respect. The average SPD Member of the older generation had been affiliated with that party even before 1933, but less than half of the older CDU Representatives (mainly its Catholic members) and only a small fraction of FDP Members had any prewar party affiliation. The generally small proportion who had held elective office was also slightly larger in the SPD than in the other parties. But for the average Member over fifty years of age, elective political experience was crowded into the brief period between 1945 and his entrance into the Bundestag, which came most likely in 1949, or in 1953. The average Member in the younger group, however, held elective office from an early point in his career, and held other political positions as well. Over two-fifths of this group had pursued no private occupations at all.

As a qualification for parliamentary success, the advantages which the younger generation enjoys, as a result of active political experience

Table 12. Bundestag seniority: Contrast between generations
(in per cent of each age group)

Bundestag Membership prior to 1957	Older group [a] (n = 299)	Younger group [b] (n = 220)
Two terms	41	20
One term	33	36
None	26	44

[a] Members born in 1906 or earlier.
[b] Members born in 1907 or later.

from an earlier age and in more continuous fashion, offset its disadvantages in Bundestag seniority (see Table 12), in age generally, and, perhaps, in the quality of its earliest political impressions. The rapid rise of Members under fifty to positions of leadership in the Bundestag

Table 13. Comparison of age groups in positions of parliamentary leadership in the Bundestag, 1957–1961 (in per cent of each age group)

Position	Older group [a] (n = 299)	Younger group [b] (n = 220)
Executive committee of parliamentary party	16.7	18.2
Chairmen or deputy chairmen of Bundestag committee	11.4	8.2
Bundestag presidium, Council of Elders, Executive Committee	11.4	10.9
In all parliamentary leadership positions [e]	27.8	26.4
Members of the Cabinet	4.7	1.8
Nonparticipants in debate	21.8	8.6

[a] Members born in 1906 or earlier.
[b] Members born in 1907 or later.
[e] This figure is less than the total of those given above because many Members simultaneously hold several leadership positions.

strongly suggests their special qualification. Except at the Cabinet level, these younger Members occupied high offices in the third Bundestag at the same rate as their older colleagues, and the proportion of silent Members, those who never participated in debate throughout the four-year term, was, among the younger members, considerably less than half of the proportion among older Members. (See Table 13.) The relationship between the generations in the Bundestag appears to arise from the severe shortage in relevant political skills, which is among the gravest consequences of the Nazi political persecutions.

Women in Parliament

Approximately 7 to 9 per cent of the Members of the Bundestag have been women in each of the five terms, a remarkably high propor-

Table 14. *Women in Western European parliaments and the U.S. Congress (in per cent of party groups and total membership)*

			Germany			
Party	*1928*	*1949*	*1953*	*1957*	*1961*	*1965*
CDU/CSU		7.9	7.6	7.9	7.2	6.0
SPD		10.0	13.5	12.2	10.3	8.8
FDP		3.8	5.8	7.0	6.0	4.0
Total	7.3	7.6	8.9	9.2	8.2	6.9

	United Kingdom		
Party	*1945*	*1959*	*1964*
Conserv.	0.5	3.3	3.6
Lab.	5.3	5.0	5.4
Lib.	8.3	0.0	0.0
Total	3.7	4.0	4.4

	France		
Party	*1945* [a]	*1956* [b]	*1958* [b]
MRP	5.7	— [c]	—
Socialist	4.5	—	—
Radical	0.0	—	—
Communist	11.5	—	—
Total	6.1	3.5	1.3

Table 14 (continued).

Italy ᵉ

Party	1948	1958
Christian-Democrat	5.2	3.7
Communist	15.3	7.1
Total	7.0	3.7

U.S. ᵈ

	1953	1965
Total	2.3	2.2

ᵃ Constituent Assembly.
ᵇ National Assembly.
ᶜ Chamber of Deputies.
ᵈ House and Senate.
ᵉ Dash indicates no information available.

Sources: Figures for Germany from Gabriele Bremme, *Die politische Rolle der Frau in Deutschland* (Göttingen: Vandenhoek & Ruprecht, 1956), pp. 140 ff., and from the *Amtliches Handbuch des Deutschen Bundestages,* 1953 ff. Figures for the United Kingdom from J. F. S. Ross, *Elections and Electors,* p. 255; D. E. Butler and Richard Rose, *The British General Election of 1959,* p. 126; D. E. Butler and Anthony King, *The British General Election of 1964,* p. 234. Figures for France from Association française de science politique, *L'établissement de la cinquième République,* pp. 272–273; Maurice Duverger, *The Political Role of Women* (Paris: UNESCO, 1955), p. 90. Figures for Italy from G. Sartori, "Parliamentarians in Italy," UNESCO, *International Social Science Journal,* Vol. XIII, no. 4 (1961), p. 586. Figures for the United States from G. B. Galloway, *The Legislative Process in Congress,* p. 355; *Congressional Quarterly Weekly Report,* Jan. 1, 1965, p. 25.

tion in comparison with Britain, France, or the United States. (See Table 14.) The membership of political parties, however, contains a smaller proportion of women in Germany than in Britain or the United States.[77] Furthermore, survey research indicates that women in

[77] Over 40 per cent of the individual members of the Labour Party, and over 50 per cent of the membership of the Conservative party has in recent years consisted of women (*Report of the 62nd Annual Conference of the Labour Party, 1963* [London: 1963], p. 47; J. Blondel, *Voters, Parties, and Leaders; The Social Fabric of British Politics* [London: Pelican Books, 1963], p. 91). In the United States, criteria for party membership are vague in comparison to Europe, and vary from state to state. Available evidence indicates that the rate of party affiliation shows no difference between men and women. In sharp contrast, women constitute between 10 and 20 per cent of the membership of the main parties in Germany

Germany have a less positive attitude toward political participation than women in Britain or the United States, although this is not true of women at the higher educational levels and shows signs of changing throughout the population.[78] The relatively high representation of women in the Bundestag, in spite of their relatively low participation in politics, seems to be a consequence of the preference given to candidates of organized groups within the parties in the selection process, and, particularly, of the balancing of group interests on the *Land* lists. The proportion of women candidates adopted on the lists is more than twice what it is in the constituencies. Furthermore, women are given a preference on the lists; a woman candidate tends to be included among the first five nominees whose names appear on the ballot.[79] As a result, in the election of 1957, 39 of 48 women elected to the Bundestag won as list candidates. In comparison with other Western European states, it is not the proportion of women candidates for Parliament which is striking, but their good chance of election. In Germany women have nearly as good a chance as men, while in Britain and France it is only one-third to one-half as good.[80]

Although women have been included among all parties in the Bundestag, the SPD has consistently had the highest proportion. Women also constitute a slightly larger proportion of its membership than they do that of the other parties, making up 18 per cent of the total SPD membership as compared with 14 per cent of the CDU.[81] The special

(F. A. von der Heydte and Karl Sacherl, *Soziologie der deutschen Parteien* [Munich: Isar Verlag, 1955], p. 289). The proportion in France is probably similar (see Maurice Duverger, *The Political Role of Women* [Paris: UNESCO, 1955], pp. 103–7). The most complete study of the role of women in German politics is Gabriele Bremme, *Die politische Rolle der Frau in Deutschland* (Göttingen: Vandenhoek & Ruprecht, 1956). On the membership of women in German parties, see especially pp. 147–212.

[78] Almond and Verba, *op. cit.*, pp. 387–400.

[79] The CDU/CSU included a woman among its top five candidates in eight of its 10 *Land* lists in 1957, and in nine of ten in 1961; the SPD included a woman in this position in 7 of 10 of its lists in 1957 and in 6 of 10 in 1961; the FDP, perhaps because it can hope to elect far fewer candidates from its lists and therefore has less room for maneuver in achieving a balanced ticket, included women in top places on 5 of 10 lists in 1957 and on 4 of 10 in 1961 (see also Duverger, *op. cit.*, p. 81; Bremme, *op. cit.*, pp. 144–5).

[80] Bremme, *op. cit.*, pp. 140–43; J. F. S. Ross, *op. cit.*, p. 258; Duverger, *op. cit.*, pp. 87–9.

[81] Bremme, *op. cit.*, pp. 154, 176–7; von der Heydte-Sacherl, *op. cit.*, p. 289. For many years, the SPD alone released detailed membership figures, and an indica-

consideration which the SPD gives to women candidates reflects the important role which woman's organizations play within the party and the historic association of the SPD with the cause of equal rights for women.[82] The party's support of women candidates is also due to an effort to improve its relatively weak appeal to women voters, who have disproportionately supported the CDU/CSU.[83]

In the House, women Members play an active part, exhibiting a special concern for the interests of women's groups. They occupy positions of leadership, especially in the executive committees of the parliamentary parties, out of proportion to their numbers. In the third Bundestag, sixteen women, one-third of the total, held among themselves a committee chairmanship, three deputy chairmanships, seven executive positions and three working group chairmanships or deputy chairmanships in the parties, four places on the executive committee of the House, and one place on the Council of Elders. One of them, Elisabeth Schwarzhaupt, was elected deputy chairman of the CDU/CSU caucus and, at the beginning of the next term, became the first woman to obtain ministerial office in the federal Cabinet, as the

---

tion of women's membership (see M. G. Lange, Gerhard Schulz, and Klaus Schütz, *Parteien in der Bundesrepublik* [Stuttgart: Ring Verlag, 1955], p. 186; *Jahrbuch der Sozialdemokratischen Partei Deutschlands 1962–63* [Bonn: Neuer Vorwärts Verlag, 1964], p. 344). The CDU issued its membership statistics for the first time at its 1965 conference (*Die Welt*, March 29, 1965).

[82] Lange, Schulz, and Schütz, *op. cit.*, pp. 184–7; von der Heydte-Sacherl, *op. cit.*, pp. 295–6. By comparison with the SPD, the women's organization in the CDU is relatively sketchy (Lange, Schulz, and Schütz, *op. cit.*, p. 136). A detailed study of the nominating process in Baden-Württemberg and Rhineland-Palatinate reveals that favorable placement of women candidates is an explicit objective of the SPD (Kaufmann, Kohl, and Molt, *op. cit.*, pp. 119, 183).

[83] Women outnumber men in the total electorate, but to an even greater extent among CDU/CSU voters, as the following table indicates:

	all voters		CDU/CSU voters		SPD voters	
	men	*women*	*men*	*women*	*men*	*women*
1953	46.0	54.0	41.5	58.5	50.4	49.6
1957	46.7	53.3	42.2	57.8	51.7	48.3
1961	46.7	53.3	41.6	58.4	51.3	48.7

Per cent of men and women among

See Erwin Faul *et al.*, *Wahlen und Wähler in Westdeutschland* (Villingen: Ring Verlag, 1960), pp. 148, 195, 233; Statistisches Bundesamt, "Wahl zum 4. Deutschen Bundestag am 17. September 1961," *op. cit.*, pp. 40–41.

result of concerted efforts of the Association of CDU Women. Another, Maria Probst, was elected as a Vice-President of the Bundestag at the beginning of its fifth term. Women also hold their own in debate; their proportion of nonparticipants corresponds to their proportion of the total membership. In committee work, they gravitate toward those fields of traditional interest to women, and to women's organizations. They made up 41 per cent of the Committee on Cultural Policy (education), and 35 per cent of the memberships of the committees on Family and Youth, and on Health. They were altogether absent from the committees on Economic Affairs, Small Business, and Transport, but they were strongly represented on the Judiciary Committee, and on the committees on Local Government and Public Welfare, Social Policy, and War Victims.

Religious Denominations

Consciousness of denominational representation in German politics is not so much an expression of some latter day "Kulturkampf," as it is the result of the emphasis which the CDU/CSU places on denominational parity. For that party, the representation of both Catholics and Protestants at all levels of its organization, and among its candidates, was for many years a matter of basic importance for the attainment of one of its original aims, that of gathering members of both religious groups within one party. In a society nearly evenly divided between Protestants and Catholics, it is also a formula which holds out the prospects of spectacular electoral success. Animated both by the ideal and the material attraction of the theme of Christian unity in politics, the CDU/CSU keeps alive an awareness of the denominational affiliation of candidates. The other parties try to evade it. Restricted by the historical association between liberalism and anticlericalism, on the one hand, and between social-democracy and Marxist atheism on the other, they insistently dismiss the religious affiliation of their candidates as irrelevant, just as the Christian Democrats stress it.

Only the nominees of the CDU/CSU, therefore, openly and without exception, reveal their religious ties. In the constituency nominations, as indicated before, the tendency is to choose a candidate of the same denomination as that of the majority of party members; in the list nominations, a strenuous effort is also made to achieve denominational proportions among the candidates which will be representative of the party membership in the area. The ratio of Catholics to Protestants is about three to two among both the party's membership and its elected representatives, although among its voters the proportion of Protestants has been somewhat higher, especially in those elections in which it has been generally most successful. The Members of the other two large parties are mostly Protestant, or, particularly in the SPD, without formal church affiliation. This reflects the greater proportion of Protestants among their voters. SPD voters are Protestant two to one, FDP voters nearly three to one.[84] (See Tables 15 and 16.)

Only in the parliamentary group of the CDU/CSU does religious affiliation therefore play an appreciable role. As in all parts of the party, careful efforts are made to reflect the religious composition of the party faithfully in its parliamentary leadership. The executive committee of the parliamentary group was 55 per cent Catholic and 45 per cent Protestant during the third Bundestag. This reflects a tendency to lean over backward to place Protestants in conspicuous party positions. The CDU/CSU also makes efforts to achieve denominational parity among its Members on those Bundestag committees, like the committees on education and on the family, whose jurisdictions are of special concern to the churches.

Regional Representation

The electoral system provides for regional representation. It assures the representation of the *Länder* in the Bundestag in direct proportion to the vote cast in each, and, due to the efforts of some parties, even the proportional representation of regions within the *Länder*. Consciousness of regional identity varies among the Representatives of different sections of the country, being strongest in the area of the south and southwest, where *Land* boundaries coincide most closely with historic political units. But nowhere is regional loyalty strong enough to provide much basis for concerted action on behalf of local interests across party lines.

The most conspicuous regional grouping within the Bundestag is the Bavarian CSU, a party separately organized both in the country and

[84] Faul *et al., op. cit.*, pp. 202–8, 234–7. Statistisches Bundesamt, "Wahl zum 4. Deutschen Bundestag am 17. September 1961," *op. cit.*, pp. 44–6. Of CDU party members, 62.3 per cent are Catholic, 36.7 per cent are Protestant, and 1 per cent belong to other religions, according to the report made to the 1965 party conference (*Die Welt,* March 29, 1965).

Table 15. Religious affiliation of Bundestag Members by parties (in per cent of each party group)

Religious affiliation	2nd Bundestag 1953				3rd Bundestag 1957				4th Bundestag 1961		
	CDU/CSU	SPD	FDP	DP	CDU/CSU	SPD	FDP	DP	CDU/CSU	SPD	FDP
Catholic	62	13	11	0	61	–[a]	19	0	61	17	21
Protestant	38	32	77	87	39	–	65	65	39	63	66
Other	0	2	0	0	0	–	0	0	0	0	0
None	0	33	2	13	0	–	0	0	0	1	0
Not obtainable	0	20	10	0	0	–	16	35	0	19	13

[a] Dash indicates adequate data not obtainable.

Sources: Figures on 2nd Bundestag from Wolfgang Hirsch-Weber and Klaus Schütz, Wähler und Gewählte, Eine Untersuchung der Bundestagswahlen 1953 (Berlin: Verlag Franz Vahlen, 1957), pp. 357, 367, 379, 384, 389, based on interviews, questionnaires, and published sources. Figures for 3rd Bundestag based on the biographies in the Amtliches Handbuch des Deutschen Bundestages, 3. Wahlperiode. Figures for 4th Bundestag from Kürschners Volkshandbuch, Deutscher Bundestag, 4. Wahlperiode (Neue Darmstädter Verlagsanstalt, 1962), p. 259; FAZ, Oct. 3, 1961; Die Welt, Oct. 13, 1961; Günter Triesch, "Struktur eines Parlaments," Die Politische Meinung, VI (1961), 5–6.

Table 16. Religious distribution of Bundestag membership
(in per cent of total membership, or of population)

Religious affiliation	Population, Federal Republic 1950	2nd Bundestag 1953	4th Bundestag 1961
Catholic	45	37	39
Protestant	51	43	52
Other	3	1	0
None	0	11	0
Not obtainable	1	8	9

Sources: See Table 15. Religious affiliation in the population from *Statistisches Jahrbuch für die Bundesrepublik Deutschland, 1958* (Wiesbaden: Kohlhammer, 1958), p. 41.

in the House. Within the CSU, local attachments are particularly strong, expressing themselves in a very close constituency control over nominations and in a tendency to nominate local "notables". Since the CSU swept all Bavarian constituencies in 1957, 87 per cent of its Members in the third Bundestag were constituency candidates, and most of these had been nominated in a constituency only. Because of their separate organization in the House, and the leadership of effective and ambitious politicians, they have vigorously defended the economic interests of their region, and the claims of their party to federal patronage.

The membership from the southwestern state of Baden-Württemberg is distinctive not as the result of its separate organization, but of the unusual proportion of parliamentary leaders it has supplied. Members of all parties from this part of the country occupied 17 per cent of the leading positions in the third Bundestag, but only 11 per cent of the backbenches. Their performance quite possibly reflects the effect which the long history of parliamentary institutions in this section of Germany has had on the recruitment of political personnel.

In the *Länder* of the north, members of the same party in each *Land* combine chiefly for the purpose of patronage, notably in the appointment of Ministers. The regional composition of the Cabinet, and of the party executive committees, is watched closely, more so in the CDU/CSU and the FDP than in the SPD. But on substantive questions of policy, economic and social interests, which do not coincide with *Land* boundaries, usually submerge regional differences.

Education

The education and occupational training of Members varies with their parties, reflecting the differences among the groups from which the various parties recruit their candidates. More than half the Members of the Bundestag have had higher education, an indication of the respect which formal education commands in Germany. The proportion has been rising steadily since the time of the Weimar Republic. But the figures vary sharply by party. Over three-fifths of CDU/CSU Members have had education at the university or the technical college level, but less than one-third of Social Democratic Members have attained it. In the SPD, half of the Members have had only a vocational apprenticeship, while this is true of only one-fourth of the parties to the right. In a society in which higher education has been accessible chiefly to the privileged few, this contrast, more than anything else, reflects the difference in the social origins of the Representatives of the different parties. It is duplicated in many respects in the French, Italian, and British parliaments. (See Table 17.)

Four kinds of training predominate among Members: law, business, agriculture, and skilled trades. The first is the most frequent training

Table 17. Education of members of Western European parliaments
(in per cent of categories at left)

Parliaments	Members with education at university or technical college level
Germany	
Bundestag, 1957	52
CDU/CSU	62
SPD	32
FDP	65
Parliamentary leaders [a]	60
Backbenchers [a]	46
Nonparticipants in debate	27
Members of Cabinet	94
Bundestag, 1953	47
Bundestag, 1949	41
Reichstag, 1928	37
United Kingdom	
House of Commons, 1959	55
Conservatives	62
Labour	44

Table 17 (continued).

Parliaments	Members with education at university or technical college level
France	
National Assembly, 1958	64
UNR	66
Moderates	64
Radical Socialists, RGR	70
MRP	65
Socialists	61
Communists	10
Italy	
Chamber of Deputies, 1948–1958	
average	70
Christian Democrats	83
Liberals	93
Social Democrats	73
Socialists	72
Communists	37

ᵃ For definition, see Table 18.

Sources: The figures for different parliaments are not entirely comparable. For the third Bundestag they are based on the biographies of Members in the *Amtliches Handbuch des Deutschen Bundestages.* For 1953 they are based on Wolfgang Hirsch-Weber and Klaus Schütz, *Wähler und Gewählte,* pp. 358, 369, 379, 385, 390. For 1949 and 1928 they include only Members with earned university degrees or teacher's certificates, a slightly different group from those with education at the college or university level. They are from Otto Kirchheimer, "The Composition of the German Bundestag," *Western Political Quarterly,* III (1950), 591–2. British figures, from D. E. Butler and Richard Rose, *The British General Election of 1959,* p. 128, are for Members with university education. French figures, from Mattei Dogan, "Changement de régime et changement de personnel," Association française de science politique, *L'établissement de la cinquième République,* pp. 264–65. The first parliament of the Fifth Republic had an unusually high proportion of university-educated Members because of the unusually small representation of Communists and Socialists, among whom university education is less common than among Members in parties to the right. The figures for Italy are for Members with University degrees, and are from G. Sartori, "Parliamentarians in Italy," UNESCO, *International Social Science Journal,* XIII, no. 4 (1961), 590.

of the college educated; the last is the most frequent preparation of those who took a vocational apprenticeship. Legal education and skilled trades each account for the training of roughly one-fifth of the

Table 18. *Training of Members of the Bundestag, 1957–1961, by party and parliamentary position*
(in per cent of categories at top of each column)

Training	All Members (n = 519)	CDU/ CSU (n = 223)	CSU only (n = 55)	SPD (n = 181)	FDP (n = 43)	Parliamentary leaders[a] (n = 141)	Backbenchers[a] (n = 360)	Government[b] (n = 43)	Nonparticipant (n = 84)	Debate[c]		
										Generalist (n = 31)	Specialist (n = 186)	Expert (n = 211)
Law	18.9	22.7	30.9	9.9	32.6	23.4	16.3	41.8	4.8	45.2	23.1	16.5
Business	15.0	13.3	7.3	15.5	20.9	14.1	15.8	11.6	17.8	16.1	15.1	13.2
Skilled trade	20.0	13.7	9.1	35.4	2.3	14.8	23.0	4.6	29.8	9.7	19.9	18.5
Agricultural management	9.4	12.2	18.2	2.2	16.3	9.2	10.0	4.6	9.5	0.0	5.9	14.2
Teaching (inc. university)	8.9	9.7	7.3	9.9	2.3	12.0	7.2	11.6	8.3	6.5	8.6	9.0
Science and engineering	4.6	4.7	3.6	3.3	4.7	2.8	3.8	13.9	3.6	3.2	3.8	6.2
Other	23.2	23.7	23.6	23.8	20.9	23.7	23.9	11.9	26.2	19.3	23.6	22.4

[a] Includes Committee chairmen and deputy chairmen, the President, Vice-Presidents, and members of the Executive Committee of the Bundestag; members of the Council of Elders; and the chairmen, deputy chairmen, members of the executive committees, as well as chairmen and deputy chairmen of the working groups of the parliamentary parties. The parties are represented in this leadership group in close proportion to their strength in the House.
[b] In order to include a sample of statistically significant size, this group is composed of all Members of the third Bundestag who then were, previously had been, or subsequently were appointed as members of the Cabinet.
[c] A "Generalist" is defined as a Member less than one-third of whose contributions were on any one subject; a "Specialist" is a Member one-third to two-thirds of whose contributions were on any one subject; and an "Expert" is a Member over two-thirds of whose contributions were on one subject.

membership, the former concentrated among CDU/CSU and FDP Members, the latter among those of the SPD. Either business or agricultural management has been the training of about a quarter of the House, with agriculture most heavily represented in the CSU and, because of special efforts in 1957 to attract farm votes, in the FDP. The Social Democratic Representatives, with a proportionate share of Members with business training but very few trained in agriculture, include the largest proportion of schoolteachers. (See Table 18.)

An examination of the educational background of Members, according to the positions which they occupy in the Bundestag, reveals the relevance of the type of training a Representative has had for his parliamentary performance. Members with higher education predominate in positions of leadership. In the third Bundestag, 94 per cent of the members of the Cabinet, 60 per cent of leaders at all levels in the House, but only 46 per cent of backbenchers were university or college educated. Among Members who never participated in debate throughout their terms, only 27 per cent had had higher education. Members trained in the law and as teachers made up a disproportionate share of the governmental and parliamentary leadership, while those who had learned skilled trades were disproportionately represented among the backbenchers.

Members with legal training were, in addition, distinguished by the frequency and the breadth of their participation in debate. Although making up less than 20 per cent of the House, they constituted less than 5 per cent of those who never spoke, but a conspicuous 45 per cent of those whose contributions were not concentrated in one or two areas but ranged over a variety of subjects. Those with skilled trades, however, were disproportionately represented among the nonparticipants in debate, making up nearly 30 per cent of this category although they too constituted just one-fifth of the House. Those among them who did speak tended to participate narrowly on one or two subjects. Members trained in law were, furthermore, heavily concentrated in the busiest and most important committees. Not surprisingly, they constituted 83 per cent of the membership of the Judiciary Committee, but they also made up 38 per cent of the Foreign Affairs Committee, 28 per cent of the Committee on Interior Affairs, whose jurisdiction includes government employment, and 36 per cent of the Finance Committee.

Occupation

The discrepancy between the importance, in the Bundestag, of men trained in law, and the limited numbers in which they enter the House, illustrates the contrast between the characteristics affecting recruitment and those affecting parliamentary performance. Candidates are selected less on the basis of their past training than on the basis of their present occupation, and the two do not necessarily correspond. Less than half the Members trained in the law were attorneys at the time of their entry into the Bundestag, and almost none of those trained in skilled trades were skilled workers upon their election. The Marxist hope for a parliament of workers is no more realized than the hope which Max Weber expressed that the professionals who were needed among the members of parliament would be lawyers. "In an age of the reign of jurists," he wrote, "the great lawyer is the only jurist who, in contrast to the government official, is trained in combat and in the effective defense of a position through combat." [85] Out of his preference for professional parliamentarians who would live "for" rather than "off" politics, Weber saw in the lawyer the one professional person who could get away from his occupation to devote himself to parliament, without thereby sacrificing his professional career.

But as Weber also knew, in German society, law as a profession does not have the prestige which caused De Tocqueville to regard lawyers as the aristocracy of American society. The startling proportion of lawyers in the United States Congress—steadily between 50 and 60 per cent of the membership—is the result not only of the lawyer's relative freedom to devote himself to politics without abandoning his career, especially if he is a member of a sizable firm, but also of the popular view that the lawyer's skills in advocacy and debate, developed in the adversary procedure of the courts, his experience in settling disputes, and his technical competence in matters of law, uniquely qualify him as a legislator. [86] By contrast, the German lawyer

[85] Weber, *Gesammelte Politische Schriften*, p. 352.
[86] See, for example, the excellent discussion of the reasons for the heavy proportion of lawyers in the U.S. Senate, in Donald R. Matthews, *U.S. Senators and Their World* (Chapel Hill: University of North Carolina Press, 1960), pp. 33–5.

possesses neither quite the same skills nor the same reputation, and political questions are less frequently regarded as matters of law than as matters of administration requiring the skills of the official. At best, in a status-conscious society, the attorney competes for parliamentary mandates with members of other occupations and professional groups.

In addition to lawyers in private practice, government officials and employees of interest groups or large business organizations frequently bring legal training to the Bundestag. The sensitivity of the electoral system to candidacies advanced by organized groups is, on the whole, an obstacle to the nomination of independent lawyers, and facilitates the nomination of interest-group or business representatives, whether or not they possess legal skills. The working conditions of the Member, insofar as he does not have organization support, are also a drawback for the independent lawyer, even if his practice permits him to accept a mandate. For these reasons, Members trained in the law are more likely to have regarded law as an entree into business, government service, or politics, than as a profession privately practiced, and their successful candidacy is more likely to have been due to their position in business, party, or government, than to their legal training. Their number depends on the propensity of interest groups and parties to select them as their representatives, rather than on the intrinsic relevance of their training for the work of Parliament.

As a result, the proportion of attorneys in the Bundestag is low by comparison not only with the United States Congress but with other European parliaments as well. At the turn of the century, attorneys were the leading occupational group in the parliaments of Britain, France, and Italy. (See Table 19.) Among the "notables" who dominated the parliamentary politics of the age, the special qualification of attorneys for the work of parliament was widely recognized. The rise of universal suffrage and of modern parties, first on the left and subsequently throughout the political spectrum, led to the replacement of the "notables" with career politicians, and consequently a steady decline in the number of attorneys in parliament. But in the German Parliament, attorneys never were a dominant occupational group. Except in the opposition parties, where together with journalists they made up the leadership before the First World War, attorneys were outnumbered by government officials and party and interest-group employees.[87] Members of the free professions, notably attorneys,

[87] Molt, *op. cit.*, Ch. X, esp. pp. 161–5.

Year	Germany Bundes-(Reichs-)tag		France National Assembly (Chamber of Deputies)		United Kingdom House of Commons		Italy Chamber of Deputies	United States	
	Law degree	Attorneys & notaries	Law degree	Attorneys, judges and notaries [a]	Called to bar	Practiced as barristers, advocates & solicitors	Lawyers	House Law degree	Senate Law degree
1848	50	16							
1871	42.5	12		32					
1890		5		31					
1893				27					
1910	20.9								
1912		9		29					
1924		4.4							
1928		3.3							
1936				20					
1918–35					22.8	18			
1929–38								56–65	61–75
1945				14	16.0	13.0			
1946				15			33		
1948							28		
1949		7.1							
1950				15	20.0	17.3			
1951					19.6	17.0		55	67
1953	17.1	7.3			19		24		
1955								56	63
1956				13					
1957	18.9	7.7	20						
1958				16			21	56	65
1961		7.5							

[a] Judges, who are included among lawyers only in the French parliament, made up 19 per cent of the total in 1951; without judges the proportion of lawyers for that year would be 12.5%.

Sources: Based on Heinz Braugsch, "Rechtsanwälte in den Parlamenten des In- und Auslandes," Anwaltsblatt, VII (1957), pp. 64–65. Supplemented, for France, by Mattei Dogan, "Changement de régime et changement de personnel," L'établissement de la cinquième République, pp. 264–69; Mattei Dogan, "L'origine sociale du personnel parlementaire français élu en 1951," Partis politiques et classes sociales en France, pp. 308–311; additional information on the United Kingdom from J. F. S. Ross, Elections and Electors, pp. 433–445; additional information for Germany from Wolfgang Hirsch-Weber and Klaus Schütz, Wähler und Gewählte, pp. 356–392, and Karl Demeter, "Die soziale Schichtung des deutschen Parlaments seit 1848," Vierteljahresschrift für Sozial und Wirtschaftsgeschichte, XXXIX (1952), 1–29, as well as from the biographies of Members in the Amtliches Handbuch des Deutschen Bundestages; additional information on Italy from G. Sartori, "Parliamentarians in Italy," UNESCO, International Social Science Journal, XIII (1961), 593.

were never attracted to the relatively powerless German Parliament of the Empire as they were to its prestigious Western European counterparts. This had been precisely Weber's point: only if parliament had power, he said, could it attract the politically talented lawyer.[88] But the early introduction of universal suffrage, giving large economic and political organizations control over the nominating process, and the late development of parliamentary influence combined to deter the formation of a class of parliamentarians drawn from the legal profession. Contrary to the trend in neighboring states, the proportion of attorneys is actually over twice as high in the Bundestag today as it was in the Reichstag before Hitler. Since this higher proportion of attorneys has existed in the Bundestag from the start, the explanation is not likely to be found in any gradual postwar development. It is probably neither a response to the increasing need for legal skills in the work of Parliament, nor a result of the growing "convergence" of the legal and political professions, which a recent study of American state legislatures offers as an explanation of the large proportion of lawyers found there.[89] In part, it may be due to the postwar dominance of parties of the center and the right, which have always had a relatively greater proportion of Members from the free professions than those of the left. Compared with the SPD, there are twice as many attorneys among CDU Bundestag Members, three times as many in the CSU, and nearly four times as many in the FDP. (See Table 20.) It may also be due to the reintroduction of single-member constituencies, for whom the attorney has the special attraction of being a local "notable" standing outside the competing interest groups. In the third Bundestag, 42.8 per cent of the attorneys had been elected in single-member constituencies without having had a safe place on the list, compared to 32.6 per cent of the House as a whole. But even with the increase since Weimar, the proportion of attorneys in the Bundestag is still below what it is in other European, let alone American, legislatures. (See Table 19.)

The factors in the recruitment process which favor the organization man have not only kept the number of attorneys low, but have likewise restricted the recruitment of members of other professions and occupations. Although over half the Members of the third Bundestag

[88] Weber, *op. cit.*, p. 352.

[89] Heinz Eulau and John D. Sprague, *Lawyers in Politics* (Indianapolis: Bobbs-Merrill, 1964), esp. Ch. V.

Table 20. Bundestag Members according to private occupations, 1957–1961

Comparative occupational backgrounds [a] (in per cent of total membership)				Occupation	All Members (n = 519) (in per cent)	CDU (n = 223) (in per cent)	CSU (n = 55) (in per cent)	SPD (n = 181) (in per cent)	FDP (n = 43) (in per cent)	Parliamentary — Leaders [b] (n = 141) (in per cent)	Backbenchers [b] (n = 360) (in per cent)	Debate [b] — Nonparticipants (n = 84) (in per cent)	Generalists (n = 31) (in per cent)	Specialists (n = 186) (in per cent)	Experts (n = 211) (in per cent)	Per cent of Experts in occupationally related subjects	Per cent of members of occupationally related committees	Per cent listing membership in occupationally related groups	Per cent indicating interest group employment	Per cent holding other elective office
U.K. 1951	France 1956	Italy 1948–58	Germany 1957																	
				Lawyers	6.6	7.2	10.9	3.9	14.0	8.5	6.1	0.0	6.4	9.7	6.2	66.7	58.6 [e]	20.6	2.9	29.4
				Teachers (inc. university)	5.2	4.9	1.8	8.3	0.0	4.3	5.8	5.7	0.0	6.5	4.3	8.3	20.7 [d]	3.7	3.7	18.5
				Writers, journalists	3.3	2.2	1.8	6.1	0.0	2.8	3.6	2.9	0.0	4.8	2.8	8.3	20.7 [e]	23.6	11.8	11.8
				Other	3.5	4.5	0.0	3.9	0.0	2.8	4.0	0.0	3.2	4.8	3.8			5.5	0.0	38.8
35.5	41.5	54.0	22.6	Total, professional	18.6	18.8	14.5	22.2	14.0	18.4	19.5	8.6	9.6	25.8	17.1	38.9		13.5	4.2	24.0
				Business manager	6.0	7.2	3.6	3.9	11.6	5.6	6.3	8.6	6.4	3.2	7.6		13.0 [f]	31.3	3.1	35.4
				Business owner	11.0	14.3	9.1	5.0	21.0	13.5	10.5	12.9	12.9	10.2	10.9		47.9 [f]	37.4	10.5	44.0
13.1	20.8	7.1	18.7	Total, business	17.0	21.5	12.7	8.9	32.6	19.1	16.8	21.5	19.3	13.4	18.5	42.5	38.6 [g]	35.2	7.9	41.0
5.3	10.3		10.6	Agriculture	10.4	13.4	20.0	1.1	18.6	6.4	12.5	17.1	0.0	3.8	15.6	68.7	62.0 [h]	66.7	0.0	39.0
6.4	6.1	6.4	4.4	Skilled trade	3.5	3.1	0.0	6.1	0.0	0.7	4.7	4.3	3.2	1.6	4.7		6.9 [i]	38.8	0.0	61.0
7.4	1.5	2.0	5.0	Others	4.0	4.9	5.4	3.9	0.0	5.0	3.9	8.6	0.0	3.8	3.8			52.3	9.5	23.8
67.7	80.2	69.5	61.2	Total, private occupations	53.5	61.7	52.6	42.2	65.2	49.6	57.3	60.1	32.1	48.4	59.7			35.4	4.7	35.0
32.2	19.8	30.5	38.8	Total, no private occupation	46.5	38.3	47.4	57.8	34.8	50.4	42.7	39.9	67.9	51.6	40.3				24.8	25.2

[a] Comparative statistics, at left, unlike statistics for Germany at right, include Members' occupations whether or not they were practiced at time mandate was held.

[b] For definition, see Table 18.

[c] Judiciary Committee.

[d] Committee on Cultural Policy and Publishing (Education).

[e] Committee on Cultural Policy and Publishing.

[f] Committee on Middle Class (Small Business).

[g] Committees on Finance, Economic Affairs, Middle Class (Small Business), and Transport.

[h] Committee on Agriculture.

[i] Committee on Labor.

identified themselves with a private occupation at the time of their membership, including businessmen, farmers, and skilled tradesmen, only some of them were actually practitioners of these occupations. A large proportion were in Parliament as representatives of their occupational organizations, to which they were bound by a variety of overt and covert ties, ranging from being outright employees of interest-groups to being part-time consultants and members on retainers.

Among those listing current activity in the free professions, in addition to the group of attorneys, there were teachers and journalists. These were more frequently found in the SPD, in contrast to the attorneys who existed in larger numbers in the parties to the right. The parliamentary mandate is particularly accessible to schoolteachers, because, as civil servants, they share the special advantages—job security and the payment of retirement pensions while on leave—enjoyed under the law by all public employees who serve in the Bundestag. University professors may hold on to their positions while in Parliament. Journalists and writers are frequently employed by interest groups to represent them. Including a sprinkling of physicians, engineers, social workers, and members of the clergy, nearly one-fifth of the House consisted of Members identifying themselves with the professions.

The number indicating occupations in business, agriculture, and the skilled trades was half again as large, making up nearly one-third of the Bundestag. Businessmen were especially numerous in the FDP and the CDU, and skilled tradesmen were prominent in the SPD. Members citing agricultural occupations were concentrated in the CSU, the nominees of rural Bavarian constituencies, and, in the third Bundestag, also in the FDP, which was trying to win farm votes. The uneven distribution of these occupational groups is a striking indication of the differing strengths of key economic groups in the respective parties. Nearly 80 per cent of all Members listing occupations as business managers or owners, and over 90 per cent of the farming Representatives, were in the CDU/CSU and in the FDP, while over 60 per cent of Members indicating skilled trades were in the SPD. (See Table 20.)

The performance of the Members indicating private occupations reveals their special interests. As a group, they occupied fewer than their share of positions of parliamentary leadership. Members listing agriculture and skilled trades made up 6.3 and 0.7 per cent of the front benches, respectively, but 12.2 and 4.7 per cent of the backbenches. Members identified with business and industry, however, posed an exception, playing important roles in the leadership of both the CDU and the FDP. The relatively narrow concern of Members indicating private occupations is also apparent from a study of their participation in debate. Although as many as 59 per cent of all Members spoke only ten times or less in the four-year term of the third Bundestag, this was true of 72 per cent of farm Representatives and Members from skilled trades, and 68 per cent of business owners. On the whole, a disproportionate number of Members associated with private occupations were among those who never spoke in debate, although Members in the professions constituted an exception here. Those who did speak, furthermore, tended to limit their participation to the subjects in which they had a special stake. Nearly half the farm Representatives spoke mainly or exclusively on agricultural subjects when they did speak, and nearly one-third of Members from industry and business limited themselves predominantly to those subjects.

The committee work of this group of Members also indicates its special concerns. While only 8 per cent of all Representatives indicated membership in agricultural organizations in their biographies, those who did made up 55 per cent of the Agriculture Committee; all told, 62 per cent of its members had agricultural backgrounds. Further, nearly two-thirds of its members came from the five most heavily agricultural *Länder* in Germany, whose total representation, however, made up less than half of the House as a whole. Although the committee interests of businessmen ranged more widely, they made up over three-fifths of the committee on small business, and nearly two-fifths of the four main committees dealing with questions affecting business. Over two-fifths of the members of the committee on education were school and university teachers and writers, and over one-third of the Committee on Family and Youth were women. Four of the six physicians in the House belonged to the Committee on Health, and all the members of the Bundestag indicating membership in veterans' interest groups belonged to the veterans' committee. Although business managers and owners comprised only 17 per cent of the House, they made up 38 per cent of the Committee on Transport; and though civil servants and public officials constituted only 16 per cent of all Members, they made up 41 per cent of the Interior Committee which has jurisdiction over civil service legislation and compensation.

Two factors prevent this gravitation of interest representatives to "their" committees from completely dominating Parliament's deliberations on the subjects of special concern to them. One is their uneven distribution among the parties. Since committee seats are assigned to the parties in proportion to their parliamentary strength, party coloration on the committees offsets interest coloration to some extent. The SPD members on the Agriculture Committee, for example, are only rarely representatives of farm groups, and the CDU members on the Labor Committee are not exclusively trade unionists. Second, the parties make an effort to attain some occupational breadth among their members on each committee, to save themselves from identification with unduly narrow interests. Because of its heterogeneity, the CDU/CSU particularly tries to have a representative cross-section of its membership on each committee, seeking to give a voice to all its organized factions—denominational, regional, and economic. But success varies with the pressure exerted by the interest groups.

The official biographies of Members give only a small clue to their organizational affiliations. Fourteen per cent of the Members of the House clearly indicate that they are professional interest-group employees, presumably assigned to represent their groups in the Bundestag, or, in a few cases, in several parliamentary bodies. The actual total is far larger. It includes labor union employees and Members engaged by small business associations. Agricultural and larger business organizations appear to prefer representation by Members engaged in these occupations. The ties of such Members to the organizations they represent are less apparent than the affiliations of interest-group employees. Over a third of the Members indicating private occupations hold other elective offices on top of their Bundestag mandate. The figure is especially high among Members associated with business, agriculture, and the skilled trades. This statistic is perhaps the clearest index of all that the profession of a large number of the Members indicating private occupations consists of representing their occupations in politics, rather than practicing these occupations in private.

These Members do not therefore fit the liberal conception of independent representatives recruited for their prominence in private occupations. The narrow interests which many of them display in their parliamentary activity does not warrant the favorable comparison between them and those Members lacking private occupations, who in the liberal view are so readily disparaged as professional politicians or as government and party bureaucrats. On the contrary, the important role of both government and party employees in German parliaments can be understood only when one recognizes the tendency of Members drawn from the private occupations to be interest representatives or semiprofessional politicians.

The eligibility of civil servants for election to Parliament, under very inviting conditions, is a distinctive characteristic of the German political system. Civil servants enjoy high social status as well as financial independence resulting from permanent appointment and a generous pension plan. With some exaggeration, the German Reichstag used to be contrasted as an assembly of officials to the French assembly of intellectuals and the American assembly of lawyers. Although the proportion of public employees of all kinds was as high as 50 per cent in the Frankfurt Assembly of 1848, it declined steadily with the appearance of private officials—interest-group representatives and party employees—in the course of the development of the Reichstag during the Empire. The proportion of public employees of all kinds in those years ranged between 10 and 27 per cent of the House, and it was 19 per cent of the Reichstag of 1928.

Among the Members of the third Bundestag, 9.5 per cent identified themselves as public employees, but only 3.9 per cent held the exalted ranks of the civil service (*Beamte*). Public employees included men and women with the greatest variety of experience in government positions, from elected local government officials, simultaneously holding their posts while serving in the Bundestag, to political leaders who had briefly held civil service jobs sometime during the postwar period and who were, under the law, temporarily retired from their positions and entitled to retirement pay. Very few genuine career civil servants were among them. If Members permanently retired from all types of public employment are included, 16 per cent of the House consisted of sometime public servants, and if one further adds those who served or had served as elected executives in state and federal cabinets, the group made up 23.7 per cent of the Bundestag. Counting school and university teachers, nearly one-third of the House could be said to consist of public employees. (See Table 21.) Indeed, such a statistic is frequently cited by interest groups to give the impression that the German Parliament is overrun by government officials.

This tabulation conceals, however, the most important occupational distinctions. Despite their legal status as government officials and the special economic advantages this gives them, schoolteachers, who may draw retirement pay while in the Bundestag, and university professors, who may continue to hold their chairs, must, by training and interests, be regarded as members of the free professions. Most other Members who are counted as public employees are in some sense interest representatives or politicians. Among those who have retired, some serve as representatives of civil service interest groups, or as spokesmen for the public corporations or local authorities for which they have worked. Among those who are in the temporarily retired status which the law provides for officials elected to the Bundestag, some have held government positions only very briefly in the past, and are today local or national party leaders. The remaining public employees hold, or have held, a great variety of governmental positions, some elected, some politically appointed, very few on a career basis. They include federal and *Land* cabinet ministers, mayors, school administrators, county officers, and members of public corporations and other administrative boards.

This heterogeneous group of Bundestag Members was represented in all parties. Of those still active in their public positions, or temporarily retired while in the House, 57 per cent were in the CDU/CSU, 39 per cent in the SPD, and 4 per cent in the FDP; the SPD had a larger share of all those who had held government positions at any time during the postwar period.

In view of the various capacities in which they have served, and the various parties with which they are affiliated, the Members who are or have been public employees are in no sense hidden allies of the Executive in Parliament. Those who represent civil service interests on the Committee on Interior Affairs, where they constitute two-fifths of the membership, do play a specialized, occupationally related role in the House. But generally, the participation of this group of Members is as various as are their true occupational backgrounds. Administrative experience may have imparted to these Members an executive view of politics, with its appreciation of efficiency, expert knowledge, and privacy of decision making, but this is a political style common to other groups of Members as well, including the large number whose backgrounds are in private bureaucracy.

By training, this group does show some common characteristics, notably a large number of Members with legal education and political experience. This equips them for an active role in the committees,

Table 21. Public employees in the Bundestag, 1957–1961
(in per cent of categories at top of each column)

Comparable occupational background		Public Employment	All Members (n = 519)	CDU (n = 223)	CSU (n = 55)	SPD (n = 181)
U.K. 1951	France 1956					
3.2	3.9	Career civil servants	6.4	6.7	14.5	3.9
		Active, in temporary retirement	3.9	4.5	7.3	2.2
		Other public employees	9.6	8.5	7.3	14.4
		Active, in temporary retirement	5.6	4.9	5.5	8.3
		Elective political executives (incl. Federal Cabinet)	7.7	9.0	9.1	5.1
		In office	3.7	5.4	7.3	0.0
		Teachers, professors	6.6	6.3	3.6	9.4
		Still practicing	5.2	4.9	1.8	8.3
		Total with postwar public employment (excl. teachers and prof.)	23.7	24.2	30.9	23.4
		Total with present public employment (excl. teachers and prof.)	13.2	14.8	20.1	10.3
		Total with present public employment (incl. teachers and prof.)	18.4	19.7	21.9	18.6

ᵃ For definition, see Table 18.

where they are particularly well prepared for the confrontation with federal officials defending Government bills. Both their committee positions and their participation in debate bear out the relevance of the training of these public employees for the work of the House. Although those among them who hold elective positions in local gov-

	Parliamentary		Debate [a]			
FDP (n = 43)	Leaders [a] (n = 141)	Back-benchers [a] (n = 360)	Nonpar-ticipants (n = 84)	Generalists (n = 31)	Spe-cialists (n = 186)	Experts (n = 211)
7.0	7.0	6.1	3.6	12.9	9.7	3.3
4.7	4.2	3.8	1.2	12.9	5.5	1.9
2.3	12.7	8.0	4.8	16.1	10.7	10.0
0.0	3.5	6.6	4.8	12.9	5.4	5.2
4.7	9.2	2.5	2.4	9.7	8.1	9.1
2.3	0.0	0.2	0.0	3.2	2.1	5.2
2.3	6.4	7.0	4.8	0.0	7.3	5.7
0.0	4.3	5.8	4.8	0.0	6.3	3.7
14.0	29.0	16.7	10.7	38.7	28.5	24.4
7.0	7.8	10.5	6.0	29.0	13.0	12.3
7.0	11.4	16.4	10.7	29.0	19.3	16.0

ernment simultaneously with their Bundestag mandate occupy relatively few positions of leadership in the House, the group of public employees as a whole is conspicuously represented in positions of leadership, both in committees and in the party organizations, out of proportion to its numbers. In part, this is due to the ability of these Members to devote themselves to parliamentary work, undistracted by the need to supplement their income by other occupations. In part, it is the result of the century-old German belief that the governmental skill of those who have been public employees is relevant to the work of Parliament.

The group of Members who come to the Bundestag neither to represent a private occupation, nor with the background of an executive or administrative position, but because of a career commitment to parliamentary politics itself, constitutes at once the most disparaged and most important part of the House. They are disparaged because these are the Members who live "off" politics, the professional politicians *par excellence* who most directly offend all of the attitudes in the political culture concerning parliamentary representation. The skills which these Members contribute to the work of Parliament is not readily appreciated by a culture accustomed to the administrative concept of a politics of expertise. Because their career is politics, these Members lack accomplishments in the more prestigious public and private pursuits, which, in the liberal view, are the standard for selecting parliamentary representatives. Finally, from the point of view of status representation, the mandate of these Members is not at all clear.

Two kinds of professionals in this sense nevertheless sit in the Bundestag: those who simultaneously hold several elective offices and therefore devote themselves to the national Parliament only part time, and those whose sole occupation is their Bundestag mandate. The distribution of Members with two or more elective positions shows a heavier concentration in the parties in opposition, which lack alternative forms of patronage, than in the governing party. While only 6 per cent of the Members of the House attempt to combine their Bundestag with a Landtag seat, nearly one-fourth of them try to reconcile some sort of municipal or county mandate with their duties in Bonn, although they do so quite obviously at the expense of their participation in the work and leadership of the national Parliament. Those who hold multiple mandates hold few positions of leadership in the Bundestag, and count over twice as many nonparticipants in debate as their proportion in the House warrants. But all together they make up little more than one-fifth of the group of professional politicians. (See Table 22.)

Those who devote themselves exclusively to the House, on the other hand, hold positions of leadership twice their proportionate share, are very active in debate, and extremely versatile in their participation. In

Table 22. *Professional politicians in the Bundestag, 1957–1961 (in per cent of categories at top of each column)*

Political Position	All Members (n = 519)	CDU (n = 223)	CSU (n = 55)	SPD (n = 181)	FDP (n = 43)	Parliamentary leaders[a] (n = 141)	Back-benchers[a] (n = 360)	Non-participants (n = 84)	Debate[a] Generalists (n = 31)	Specialists (n = 186)	Experts (n = 211)
Party employees	8.9	4.5	7.3	14.4	9.3	13.5	7.5	8.4	22.6	9.7	6.6
Members holding *Land* or other elective office [b]	4.8	2.2	5.5	7.2	9.3	3.5	5.6	10.7	6.4	3.2	3.3
Members holding no occupation beside Bundestag mandate	9.1	7.2	7.3	10.5	11.6	19.1	5.6	7.1	0.0	13.4	7.6
Total	22.8	13.9	20.1	32.1	30.2	36.1	18.7	26.2	29.0	26.3	17.5

a For definition, see Table 18.
b Includes only those Members holding no other political positions or private occupation.

one form or another, many of these Members are party employees, receiving compensation for their full-time service to the party organization in Parliament. Their pay, about which little is known, undoubtedly varies greatly with their position, their circumstances, and the party to which they belong. More important, their state of dependence on the party varies. There can be no comparison, for example, between the staff member who is a subordinate of the organization, and the party leader upon whose management, and policy decisions, the organization itself depends. Many of these leaders, nominally party employees, are dependent on the party in the financial sense only. It is they who control the party, rather than the other way around.

The proportion of professional politicians has tended to be greater among the parties of the left than among the "bourgeois" parties, whose origin is in the politics of the "notables". Avowed party employees still make up a greater proportion of the parliamentary group of the SPD than of the other parties. In this first of the modern German parties with a mass organization, the salaried staff member continues to play a greater role than in the other parties, which have a more rudimentary organization and fewer subsidiary enterprises, such as party newspapers, from which to recruit parliamentary candidates. The CDU/CSU and FDP, on the other hand, seem to have a considerable number of parliamentary leaders whose status as party employees is unclear, but who give no evidence of any alternative public or private employment. (See Table 22.) The proportion of party employees also varies according to the parties' position in Government or Opposition. The governing party has the political leadership of Chancellor and Ministers to supplement its parliamentary leadership, and the ministerial bureaucracy to provide it with a wide range of services. The opposition parties are, by comparison, far more dependent on their Members in the Bundestag. They have special need, therefore, of the Member who, as party employee, is fully committed to the party's service in the House. A substantial number of their parliamentary leaders are generally on the party payroll, in compensation for the full-time demand which the party makes on them.

The influence of the professional politicians in the Bundestag, particularly those of them who hold no other elective office, far exceeds their number. More than 84 per cent of party employees in the third

Bundestag were re-elected to the fourth, compared with 70 per cent of the membership as a whole, a measure both of the power of these professionals within their parties and their commitment to the House. To a great extent they are the product of modern party organization, and therefore difficult to reconcile with nineteenth-century concepts of parliamentary representation. But their importance in the Bundestag, judged by their performance in leadership, debate, and committee, indicates that they possess special qualifications for the work of a modern parliament which Representatives from the other occupational groups lack. Since their loyalty is to party rather than to a private occupation, their object is to reconcile conflicting economic and social interests in order to achieve a position on which the party can unite. Because their experience is in party organization rather than administration, their skill consists in negotiating cooperation among men of diverse views, rather than obedient performance from subordinates. If they have held previous elective office, as many members of this group have, especially at the municipal level, it has provided experience in electioneering and constituency contact. But neither municipal nor *Land* parliaments provide substantial policy-making experience, in view of the restricted jurisdictions of these bodies. Since they rise through the party organization, rather than through any particular occupational or social class, the professional politicians have economic and social backgrounds as varied as the composition of the different parties. In this sense they constitute a broadly representative parliamentary elite. But it is a managerial elite, whose members do not necessarily possess articulative and forensic skills or the capacity to innovate policy. To the extent that the Bundestag depends on this group for leadership, it acquires a managerial approach to politics which is one of the distinguishing characteristics of its style.

A Membership Typology

When the social and economic backgrounds, as well as the present occupations, of the Members of the Bundestag are examined closely, it becomes apparent that they only remotely resemble any of the ideal types which have developed in the German political culture. Few of them are the "notables" for whom the liberals are nostalgic; few actively practice the professions and occupations with which they identify, and few are career civil servants. Although Members can be found to fit any of these descriptions, the dominant type is an organization man, a representative of an organized economic or political group, who makes a career of representing its interests.

This becomes even more apparent from an examination of the overlapping membership of Bundestag Representatives in various occupational categories. Although three-fifths of the Members of the House identify themselves with a private occupation, and about one-half of all Members claim still to be practicing it, fewer than one-third of the Members have private occupations without holding additional elective or political positions. Those having political positions, aside from their Bundestag mandate, are almost certainly unable to concentrate on their private careers, and are in reality greatly involved with politics. (See Table 23, and Chart I.) Similarly, although 16 per cent of the Members identify themselves as public employees of one kind or another, very few of these are career civil servants. A large proportion of the Members in this category are either politically nominated local government officials who hold their positions by election, or politically appointed members of other public agencies, or retired officials acting as representatives of civil service or local government interest groups, or party leaders who have briefly held positions as officials at an earlier point in their careers. Only 7 per cent of the Members of the House are currently government employees—only half of these being civil servants—if one disregards those who have held this status at any point in their careers but do not hold it now, and those who combine it with elective office or private employment. (See Table 23.)

An empirical typology of the membership of the Bundestag must therefore distinguish not only between Members with backgrounds in private occupations, and those with backgrounds in public service, but within each of these categories, between those actually holding the occupations with which they choose to identify publicly, and those who are professional politicians or interest-group representatives. The proportions in each of these categories are difficult to establish with any degree of precision from the official biographical sketches available, because of a tendency to hide both interest representation and professional commitment to politics. If one regards Members who list affiliation with an occupationally related interest group in their official Bundestag biographies as being in some sense representatives of these interests in the House, and adds to this group those who indicate that

CHART I

OVERLAPPING MEMBERSHIP OF
BUNDESTAG REPRESENTATIVES
IN OCCUPATIONAL GROUPS

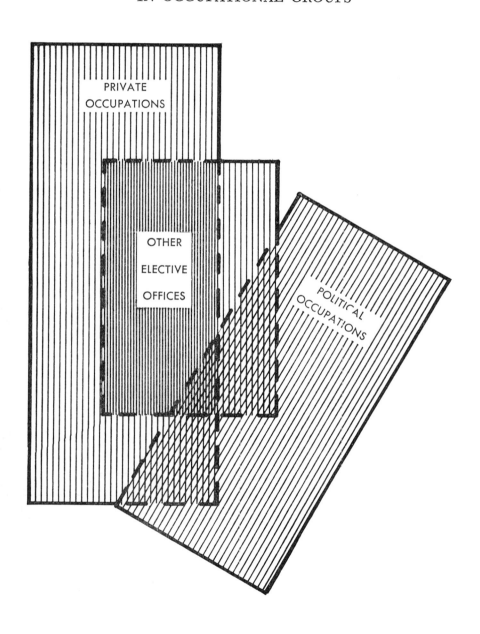

CHART II

COMPOSITION OF THE BUNDESTAG, 1957 – 1961
FOUR MAJOR TYPES OF MEMBERS
(indicating occupations)

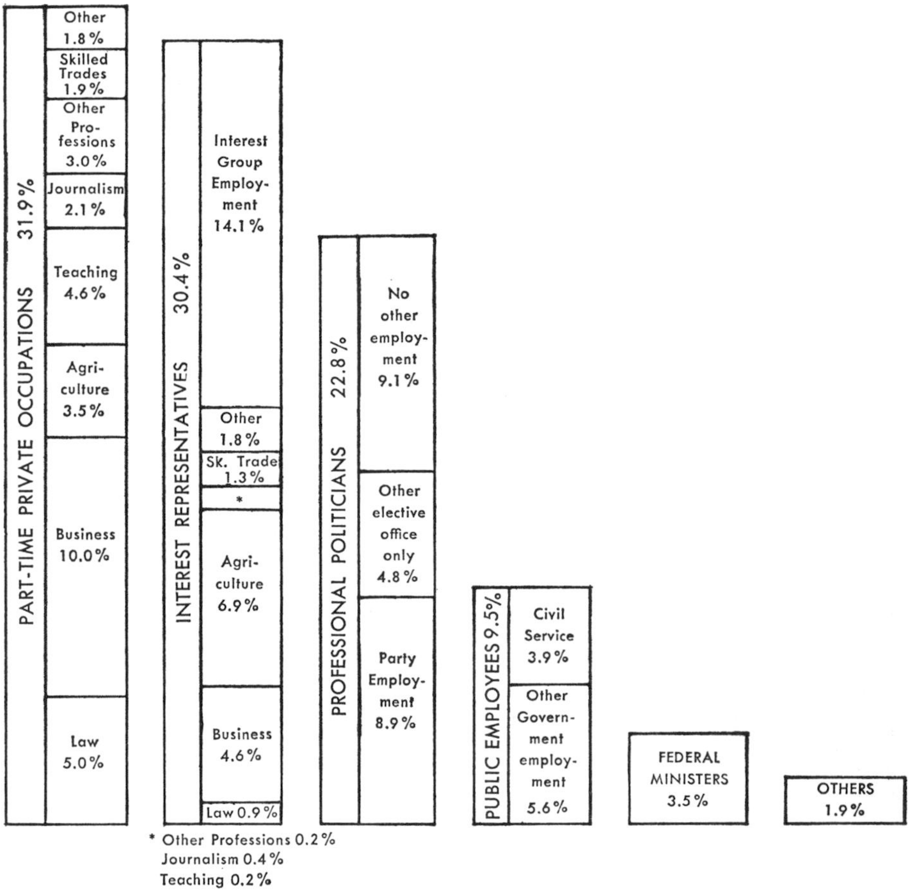

PART-TIME PRIVATE OCCUPATIONS 31.9%

- Other 1.8%
- Skilled Trades 1.9%
- Other Professions 3.0%
- Journalism 2.1%
- Teaching 4.6%
- Agriculture 3.5%
- Business 10.0%
- Law 5.0%

INTEREST REPRESENTATIVES 30.4%

- Interest Group Employment 14.1%
- Other 1.8%
- Sk. Trade 1.3%
- *
- Agriculture 6.9%
- Business 4.6%
- Law 0.9%

* Other Professions 0.2%
Journalism 0.4%
Teaching 0.2%

PROFESSIONAL POLITICIANS 22.8%

- No other employment 9.1%
- Other elective office only 4.8%
- Party Employment 8.9%

PUBLIC EMPLOYEES 9.5%

- Civil Service 3.9%
- Other Government employment 5.6%

FEDERAL MINISTERS 3.5%

OTHERS 1.9%

they are interest-group employees, then just over 30 per cent of the Members are interest representatives. Another 32 per cent have part-time private occupations. One-third of these hold elective positions, mostly in municipal government, on top of their Bundestag mandates, and are therefore likely to devote more than half of their time to politics rather than to their private careers. Others have covert ties to interest groups. Many of the Members in this category might therefore be classified as semiprofessional politicians, in Giovanni Sartori's terms,[90] although they enjoy the prestige associated with their respec-t've private occupations. If one counts as public employees those civil servants and other government officials who presently hold or are on leave from their positions, they constitute 9.5 per cent of the Bundes-tag, but this total includes some Members who might properly be counted in the fourth group, that of professional politicians. Including in that group those who are party employees, Members with more than one elective position but no other apparent employment, and a group of parliamentary leaders having no other apparent political or private occupation, the group of professional politicians makes up 22.8 per cent of the House.

Even if precise proportions among these occupational groups cannot be reliably established, these four types of Members can be identified in the Bundestag. (See Chart II and Table 24.) The *interest repre-sentatives*, strongest in the parties of the center and right, tend to have commercial backgrounds, particularly in business, agriculture, and the skilled trades, to have the lowest parliamentary experience of any of the groups, the lowest representation in parliamentary leadership, and the lowest and narrowest participation in debate. In contrast, among Members with *part-time private occupations*, professional back-grounds predominate, particularly law, and activity in party organiza-tion outside of Parliament is higher, although Bundestag seniority is not. However, a significantly higher proportion of these Members occupy positions of leadership, and the frequency and breadth of their participation in debate is also notable.

Members holding *public employment* include the highest propor-tion of those trained in the law. Although more of them are found among the backbenches than in parliamentary leadership, they are among the most active Members in debate and in the work of those

[90] G. Sartori, "Parliamentarians in Italy," UNESCO, *International Social Science Journal*, XIII (1961), p. 597.

Table 23. Overlapping membership of Bundestag Representatives in occupational groups, 1957 (in per cent of total membership)

Occupational group	Position held during postwar period	Position held while in Bundestag	Excluding Members with other political occupations	Excluding Members with other elective offices	Excluding Members with other private occupations	Excluding Members with other private and political occupations	Excluding Members with other political occupations and elective office	Excluding Members with other private occupations and elective office
Private occupations (details, Table 20)								
Professions								
Law	7.7	6.6	6.0	4.6			4.0	
Teaching incl. university	6.6	5.2	4.8	4.2			3.9	
Writer, journalist	4.4	3.3	2.5	2.9			2.1	
Other	3.8	3.5	3.3	2.1			2.1	
Total	22.6	18.6	16.6	13.8			12.1	
Business								
Salaried managers	7.5	6.0	5.4	3.9			3.5	
Owners, self-employed	11.1	11.0	9.2	6.2			4.8	
Total	18.7	17.0	14.6	10.1			8.3	
Agriculture	10.6	10.4	10.4	6.4			6.4	
Skilled trades	4.4	3.5	3.3	1.3			1.3	
Others	5.0	4.0	3.3	3.1			2.5	
Total, Private occupations	61.2	53.5	48.2	34.7			30.5	

Political occupations (details, Tables 21, 22)					
Interest-group employees	17.5	14.1	11.0	11.6	8.9
Party employees	9.2	8.7	6.0	7.3	4.8
Public employees	16.0	9.5	7.7	8.3	7.0
Combinations of above	2.3	0.2	0.2	0.2	0.2
Other (holding no private or other elective position)	9.1	9.1	9.1	9.1	9.1
Total, Political occupations	54.1	41.6	34.0	36.5	30.0
Other elective offices (details, Table 22)					
Municipal or district	32.2	22.7	17.3	8.3	3.5
Landtag	11.9	5.4	3.9	1.7	0.6
Combinations of above	12.7	1.5	1.2	1.0	0.6
Land cabinet	4.8	0.2	0.2	0.2	0.2
Total, other elective offices	61.6	29.8	22.6	11.2	4.8
Federal ministers	4.6	3.5	3.5	3.5	3.5
Not ascertainable		1.8	1.8	1.8	

committees with the broadest legal and administrative responsibilities in the House. (See Table 28, p. 198.) It is the *professional politicians* who clearly dominate the leadership. Although as a group they make up less than one-fourth of the House, counting a number of part-time Members who hold several elective positions, they supply half the committee chairmen and over half the membership of the important

Table 24. Four major types of Members in the Bundestag, 1957–1961
(in per cent of categories at left)

Positions in Bundestag	Part-time private occupations	Interest representatives	Professional politicians	Public employees
Total membership [a] (n=519)	31.9	30.4	22.8	9.5
Party				
CDU (n = 223)	35.0	40.0	13.9	9.4
CSU (n = 55)	20.0	38.2	20.0	12.7
SPD (n = 181)	33.0	20.4	32.0	10.5
FDP (n = 43)	27.9	37.2	30.2	4.7
Parliamentary				
Leaders[b] (n = 141)	31.9	23.4	36.1	7.8
Backbenchers [b] (n = 360)	33.6	34.7	18.6	10.5
Debate activity				
Nonparticipants (n = 84)	23.8	42.9	26.2	5.9
10 speeches or less (n = 223)	36.2	31.4	21.0	8.5
Over 50 speeches (n = 45)	26.7	13.3	24.4	13.3
Generalists [b] (n = 31)	22.6	19.3	29.0	25.8
Specialists [b] (n = 186)	33.3	24.2	26.3	10.8
Experts [b] (n = 211)	34.6	33.2	17.5	7.1
Parliamentary positions				
Committee Chmn. (n = 26)	23.1	23.1	50.0	3.8
Comm. Dep. Chmn. (n = 26)	50.0	23.1	21.8	3.8
C. of Elders (n = 22)	31.8	4.5	54.5	4.5
Parl. Pty. Exec. (n = 73)	28.7	23.3	37.0	11.0
Parl. Pty. Chmn. (n = 5)	0.0	0.0	100.0	0.0
Parl. Whips (n = 7)	0.0	0.0	85.8	14.2

[a] These columns do not add to 100% across the page, because of the exclusion of Cabinet ministers and a very small group of unclassified Members, together comprising 5.4% of the total membership.

[b] For definition, see Table 18.

Table 24 (continued). *Four major types of Members*

(*in per cent of categories at top of each column*)

Occupational and political backgrounds	Part-time private occupations (n = 166)	Interest representatives (n = 158)	Professional politicians (n = 118)	Public employees (n = 49)
Occupational training				
Law	24.0	10.8	17.7	26.6
Teaching (inc. univ.)	10.8	3.8	10.2	12.3
Agriculture	7.8	19.6	0.8	4.1
Business	15.0	18.4	14.4	12.3
Skilled trades	15.7	24.0	25.4	16.4
Science (inc. medicine)	10.2	2.5	0.0	4.1
Public Administration	0.0	1.3	5.9	8.2
Other or not ascertainable	16.4	19.6	25.4	16.2
Constituency				
Sing. member const., defeated on list	7.2	8.9	4.2	4.1
Sing. member const., also safe on list	10.2	12.7	19.5	10.2
Sing. member const., only nomination	27.8	29.8	17.8	32.8
Total, sing. member const.	45.2	51.4	41.5	47.1
Total, *Land* list	52.5	46.2	51.6	45.0
Marginally elected [c]	36.8	35.0	32.2	28.5
Membership on national party organizations				
Federal Executive	9.6	8.2	22.9	2.0
Land Executive	11.4	7.0	9.3	12.2
Federal committee	7.2	4.4	5.1	16.3
Land committee	7.2	3.8	4.2	10.2
Bundestag seniority				
No previous terms	41.0	32.3	28.0	40.8
One previous term	30.0	41.7	34.7	40.8
Two previous terms	28.9	26.0	37.3	18.4
Reelected to 4th Btag.	70.0	71.5	71.0	69.5
Age				
40 or below	16.2	7.6	12.7	24.4
41–50	31.3	31.6	23.7	32.7
51 or over	52.4	60.8	63.5	42.9

[c] Marginally elected is defined as election in a single-member constituency with a margin of less than 10% of the total vote over the nearest rival, or election on a list among the bottom third of candidates who were successful.

steering committee, the Council of Elders. Their participation in debate is marked by its breadth. Only in this group, and among the public employees, do "generalists" outnumber "specialists" and "experts." [91] Their activity in party organization and their seniority in the House exceed those of any other group. The wide variety in the educational background of these Members indicates the diverse social groups from which they have been recruited.

The fact that professional politicians are more frequently nominated both in constituencies and in safe places on the *Land* lists than are other Representatives is a measure of their influence within their parties. Apart from this advantage which the electoral system offers to the professional politicians, no clear correlation exists between types of Members and their constituencies. The electoral system appears to be equally advantageous to the candidacies of all the major types of Members which the recruitment process brings forth.

PARLIAMENTARY RECRUITMENT AND PARLIAMENTARY FUNCTIONS

The types of Members composing the Bundestag are the product of a process of parliamentary recruitment which is sensitive to many influences: the concepts of representation existing in the German political culture, the relationship between highly organized social and economic interest groups and political parties weak in membership and financial resources, the decentralized system of nominations, the method of proportional representation. But most of these influences, which determine what kinds of qualifications the Members of Parliament possess, are only remotely related to the functions which Parliament performs in the political system. Compared to the profound changes which have occurred in the constitutional position of Parliament since the Empire, the factors influencing recruitment have been relatively stable. This contrast reflects the lag between changes in the actual functions performed by Parliament, and the perception of these functions among the groups selecting the candidates. The criteria by which Members of the Bundestag are recruited still partially reflect the position which the Reichstag occupied in the political system of the Empire. The insistence of the major interest groups upon representation in the Bundestag by their own members or employees reflects the conception of a parliament whose chief function is the

[91] For a definition of how these terms are used, see Table 18, note c.

expression of group demands to an irresponsible administrative bureaucracy. The disparagement of professional politicians, and the
effort to conceal their identity by attributing to them various private
occupations or government careers, comes from a failure to recognize
that the Bundestag today is virtually the only source of the nation's
political leadership—that is, of Cabinet members—and plays a major
role in policy making and the control of administration.

The discrepancy between the qualifications for which candidates
are selected and the qualifications which enable them, once elected, to
participate effectively in the work of the House, produces the contrasts
which exist in the parliamentary performance of the different types of
Members. Ironically, the professional politician, who is least acceptable in the political culture, dominates the work of the Bundestag. The
product of modern party organization, he possesses the organizational
and managerial skills which are important within the large, heterogeneous parliamentary party groups in which the major policy decisions
are made. His relative freedom from narrow commitments to interest
groups or ideological positions gives him a special role as negotiator
among different views. His full-time commitment to the work of the
House and his exceptional ability to obtain re-election give him the
advantages of experience and seniority over most of his colleagues.

By comparison, the role of the interest representative is far narrower, confined to the specialized committees and party working
groups where the detailed legislative work is done. His contribution is
substantive expertise, and he serves as a channel of communication
with the interest groups. The Member whose background is in public
employment brings legal training and administrative-political experience which enables him to play an important part, particularly in the
legislative work of Parliament. Drawn mainly from the state and local
level, he also serves as an important point of contact between national
and local politics. The Members with part-time private occupations
are in many cases semiprofessional politicians, devoting the major
proportion of their time to politics, at least for the moment. They act
either as representatives of their occupational groups in both the
national and a local parliament, or as intermediaries between the
Bundestag leaders and the party rank and file.

The work of the Bundestag is very unevenly distributed among its
Members, depending on their skills and the proportion of time which
they are willing to devote to it. This contributes to the dominance of a

small group of what might be called professional parliamentarians, preponderantly but not exclusively drawn from among the professional politicians, whose style of work has become in large measure the style of the House. This style incorporates a typically professional *esprit de corps,* transcending party lines and productive of a significant body of informal procedural norms designed to facilitate agreements. It exhibits caution in policy innovation and willingness to compromise differences. It shows a penchant for organization, leading to a proliferation of legislative committees, working groups, interparty negotiating bodies, and party executive committees and inner executives, in which the decisions of the House are "prepared," and in which each type of Member contributes his special skill. This in turn produces a bureaucratization of the parliamentary process, with the characteristics of division of labor, hierarchy, and secrecy of decision making. The public sessions of the House consequently have a staged atmosphere. The professionals who manage them do not like to leave much to chance. Public discussion of the bargains they have negotiated in private only complicates their task, and they do not necessarily possess the skills of public speaking which parliamentary debate requires.

Although the professionalization of parliament is a widely observed phenomenon which has many causes,[92] the contribution made to it by the recruitment process in Germany has a special significance for the position which the Bundestag occupies in the political system. For the domination of the professional politician in the Bundestag occurs in spite of the lack of regard for him in the political culture. It is the consequence of the lack of qualification for parliamentary leadership, and therefore the narrower parliamentary roles played by the more highly esteemed types of Representatives which the recruitment process produces. Although among its Members the Bundestag has representatives of all the major politically organized groups in the country, it is led by that type of Representative who enjoys the least respect from the society in whose name Parliament presumes to act.

[92] "The Parliamentary Profession," UNESCO, *International Social Science Journal,* XIII (1961), esp. pp. 526–30, 595–9.

The Framework of Action

BEFORE he ever enters the House, the Member of Parliament has already been conditioned to certain norms of political behavior, already possesses a set of political skills, and already has obligations to various groups, all of which help to determine the role he will play as a Representative. In that sense, the composition of the House, the social background of its Members, their prior political experience, and the circumstances of their election constitute one set of determinants of the performance of the institution. But once he has entered the House, the Member undergoes a new process of politicization in which he becomes responsive to the specific norms of the institution of parliament itself. These norms are established by the organization and procedure of the House. Some are the explicit, formal, written rules of the Bundestag. Many are the implicit, informal, unwritten customs which exist in a parliament as in any stable group of persons. Together, they constitute the structure within which Members work. Having considered the recruitment process and the parliamentary membership it produces, we turn now to an examination of the institutional framework within which the Members act.

FORMAL AND INFORMAL STRUCTURE

The official organization of the Bundestag, and the formal Rules of Procedure by which its Members work, are the products of early German parliamentary development. They are today remarkably similar to the organization and procedure of the Reichstag before the first World War, and during the Weimar Republic. The similarity is notable because the Bundestag performs substantially different functions in the political system from its predecessors, and has an entirely different party composition. As a result, a body of informal procedural norms and an intricate, semiofficial party organization has developed, considerably altering and adapting the inherited formal structure. The architects of the new, informal structure are the professional parliamentarians who dominate much of the work of the House, and their style is evident in the result. Equally evident is the political occupancy of the House. Three large parties, subdivided to different extents into interest factions and specialized working groups, have replaced the smaller and more homogeneous parties which occupied the Imperial and Weimar Reichstage, producing an entirely new distribution of power. Finally, the new structure reflects changes in the functions performed by the Bundestag, particularly the increasing quantity and complexity of the legislative issues with which it deals.

Organization and procedure have not therefore remained rigidly unchanged in the face of changes in the substance of parliamentary politics. But few of the structural alterations which distinguish the Bundestag from its predecessors are overt, and few have been undertaken systematically. It is a general experience in parliaments of long standing that procedure consists of conventions developed in practice far more than of rules of order formally promulgated. However, this characteristic of parliamentary procedure corresponds much more closely to the Anglo-American than to the Continental European legal tradition.[1] While parliamentary procedure has been lovingly compiled by generations of clerks of the House of Commons, it has received very little attention in Germany, either from its practitioners or from the academic community. The first, and for fifty years the only work on German parliamentary procedure in this century, published by Julius Hatschek in 1915 and never completed, clearly indicated the importance of practice as the source of procedure. "The rules of procedure," Hatschek wrote, "depend for their existence, their origin, and their effectiveness, on parliamentary usage."[2] Hatschek recognized,

[1] A. V. Dicey, *Introduction to the Study of the Law of the Constitution,* 8th ed. (London: Macmillan, 1931), p. 27; Lord Campion, *An Introduction to the Procedure of the House of Commons,* 3d ed. (London: Macmillan, 1958), pp. 1–4.

[2] Julius Hatschek, *Das Parlamentsrecht des deutschen Reiches* (Berlin and Leipzig: G. J. Goschen'sche Verlagshandlung, 1915), p. 45. For an interesting recent German attempt to explain the role of practice in parliamentary procedure, see Klaus Friedrich Arndt, *Die parlamentarische Geschäftsordnungs-autonomie; Inhalt, Umfang, und Grenzen* (unpublished doctoral dissertation, University of Mainz, 1964), esp. p. 97.

furthermore, that usage is shaped by the behavior of the parliamentary parties and the functions which Parliament performs in the system of government. But for half a century after he wrote, no one in Germany followed Hatschek's lead. Without a compilation of existing procedure, its further development through precedents established in practice was severely handicapped. The actual procedure of the Bundestag, and its real organizational structure, are therefore not well perceived by the interested public, or even by the rank-and-file Member.[3]

The changes which have occurred, subtly and informally, have in many respects been the trade secrets of the parliamentary leaders who originated them. This has contributed to those leaders' mastery of the parliamentary scene. It has also permitted them to advance changes which serve their interests, and to avoid others. New precedents, elaborate party machinery, and tacit understandings have facilitated the decision-making process in Parliament, and, incidentally, strengthened the position of the leaders. Other structural changes are the product of a rampant specialization and division of labor, encouraged by the complexity of the issues the Bundestag faces, and by interest groups whose access to points of decision increases with the multiplication of specialized committees. This type of change has occurred despite the wariness of party leaders, who recognize it as a threat to their authority. It has intruded into the organization of the parties, impairing their cohesion, and multiplying the loci of power within them. Finally, there are aspects of parliamentary organization which have hardly changed. This is particularly true in those areas where the work of the Bundestag impinges on other political institutions, such as the Cabinet and the Bundesrat. Here the possibility of new constitutional relationships has been impaired by the tenacity of traditional organizational forms and procedures.

The unevenness and obscurity with which changes in the structure of the Bundestag have occurred have contributed to public mystification about its methods of work. They have also sharpened the distinc-

[3] The first comprehensive treatment of the procedure of the Bundestag is due to be published in 1966 by its staff Director. But while it takes account of practice, this work fails to include systematic citation of precedents, apparently out of the author's conviction that at this stage of its development, procedure should not be rigidly bound by precedents. Hans Trossmann, *Parlamentsrecht und Praxis des Deutschen Bundestages* (Bonn: Stollfuss-Verlag, 1966).

tion within the House between the role of those Members who perceive its organizational structure and can operate effectively within it, and those who do not.

To understand the actual framework in which the Members of the Bundestag act, it is necessary to examine the official organs of the House, its offices and committees, and also its political organization— the parliamentary parties, their factions, working groups, and executive committees. It is necessary to take account of the provisions in the formal Rules of Procedure, as well as the informal norms by which they are applied, elaborated, and, sometimes, set aside.

PRESIDING OFFICERS

Powers of the President

The presidency of the Bundestag is the highest office in the organization of the House. The Rules provide for the election of a president and an undetermined number of vice-presidents by an absolute majority of the Members of the House, or, failing that on two ballots, by a plurality on the third. The Rules charge the President with representing the Bundestag, preserving its dignity and its rights, furthering its work, chairing its sessions in a "fair and nonpartisan manner," and maintaining order. For these purposes, his powers under the Rules appear substantial.[4] He is an ex-officio member of all committees (par. 7, sec. 1), and chairman of the Council of Elders (*Ältestenrat*), a steering committee, and of the Executive Committee (*Vorstand*) charged with the administration of the House (pars. 6, 15). He opens, chairs, and closes the sessions of the House (par. 24), has discretion in recognizing points of order (par. 34) and in permitting speeches to be read (par. 37), and puts questions to a vote (pars. 50, 52). He determines the admissibility of oral questions for the question hour, and the acceptance of supplementary questions from other Members (*Richtlinien für die Fragestunde,* pars. 8, 15). He may call speakers to order (par. 40), withdraw recognition from them (par. 41), expel them from the session for up to thirty days (par. 42), suspend the session (par. 44), and exercise police powers within the House (par.

---

[4] *Geschäftsordnung des Deutschen Bundestages* (Bonn: Herausgegeben von der Verwaltung des Deutschen Bundestages, July, 1962). The relevant paragraphs are in each case noted in the text. An English translation of the Rules of Procedure is available in Hans Trossmann, *The German Bundestag, Organization and Operation* (Darmstadt: Neue Darmstädter Verlagsanstalt, 1965), pp. 72–156.

7). He transmits parliamentary questions, interpellations, and bills which have been enacted, to the Government (pars. 106, 110, 111, 123). He interprets the Rules of Procedure in case of dispute during a session (par. 128). He is administrative head of the parliamentary staff (par. 7). On top of these special powers, he is a regular Member possessing the right to speak and vote (par. 56).

As a matter of protocol, the President of the Bundestag stands second only to the President of the Republic. He has been clothed with the dignity to express his ceremonial and symbolic position as the personification of Parliament. His basic compensation is three times that of other Members, he has an official apartment, and he controls parliamentary expense accounts totaling DM 270,000 ($67,500) annually. A ritual has been developed to signify appropriate respect for him in the House. Upon announcement over a loudspeaker that the President is about to enter the chamber, all present rise, and as he makes his brief way from the wings to the chair, dressed in white tie and tails, a relatively austere Parliament has one of its few moments of spectacle. By custom he enjoys absolute freedom from personal criticism by the Members for his conduct of the meeting.[5]

This considerable array of formal powers and ceremonial trappings stands in obvious contrast to the original conception of the parliamentary presidency in the last century, a conception based on the weak French model, rather than on the far stronger British one. The office today, however, is the beneficiary of powers added during critical periods of obstruction to enable the President to maintain order. These include his right to expel Members and suspend sittings, first granted in 1895 and strengthened in 1922 and 1929 to permit expulsion without pay for periods up to—at present—30 days. They include also the President's discretion in acceptance of points of order, provided in 1902,[6] and his right to withdraw recognition from a speaker, added in 1929. The office has also been strengthened by the extension in 1922 of what was originally an annual term to a term covering the entire electoral period, and by the provision, introduced in 1951, which expands his electoral base by requiring an absolute majority vote for election on the first two ballots.

But despite these additions to the powers of the office as originally conceived, and despite the catalog of powers available to the President

[5] Hatschek, *op. cit.*, pp. 215–16.
[6] *Ibid.*, pp. 67–70.

under the Rules today and the studied care with which his dignity and prestige have been enhanced in recent years, presidential influence has in fact remained severely limited. This is simply the result of the control exercised over the office by the parliamentary parties. For the employment of many of his formal powers, the President requires the consensus of the parties, or the support of a majority. The exceptions are relatively unimportant. Where spontaneous decisions are required in the chair, on points of procedure, the President may give temporary rulings pending a final decision by a majority of the House. He has discretion in the acceptance of points of order and of supplementary oral questions from the floor, may call Members to order, or ultimately expel them, for using unparliamentary language or for other disruptive behavior; in case of disorder he may suspend the sitting. But the decline in the temperature of partisan controversy after the first term of the Bundestag has reduced the need to exercise these powers.[7] The others can be employed only with party support. In the appointment, promotion, dismissal, and supervision of the staff of the Bundestag and in the general administration of the House, the President must work closely with the Bundestag Executive Committee, in which the parties are proportionately represented. In chairing the sessions, he must follow agreements reached in the Council of Elders on the agenda, the order of recognition of the main speakers, and the format of the debate.[8] For this reason, the President's most important gain in German parliamentary history was his assumption of the chairmanship of the Council of Elders, which occurred when Count Ballestrem took that position in 1889. Until then, the influence of the Council had been exercised behind the President's back.[9] Since that time, presidential power has depended on presidential influence within the Council, where the parties are proportionately represented, primarily by their chief tacticians, and where decisions are reached by consensus.

[7] While there were 150 calls to order during the first term of the Bundestag, there were only 30 during the second term, 36 during the third, and only 13 during the fourth. For failing to heed the call to order, recognition to speak was withdrawn 35 times during the first Bundestag, but never again thereafter. Likewise, 15 Members were expelled in the first term, none in the second, one in the third (see the subject indexes to the debates, *Dt. Btag., Sachregister*, 1. W.P., pp. 171–4; 2. W.P., pp. 266–7; 3. W.P., pp. 170, 291). See also pp. 386–7, *infra*.
[8] Karl Josef Partsch, "Die Wahl des Parlamentspräsidenten," *Archiv des öffentlichen Rechts*, LXXXVI (1961), 5–6.
[9] Hatschek, *op. cit.*, p. 178.

Selection of the President

The influence of the parties on the presidency is apparent from the development of their role in his selection. The impartiality of the British Speaker was achieved by substantially removing the office from party choice, by granting the incumbent, once chosen by the majority in consultation with the Opposition, tenure in office unaffected by changes in the party composition of the House. The impartiality of the German presidency has been achieved by giving the parties their proportional share in the selection.

In the time of the Empire, the presidential function of representing the Reichstag to the Emperor meant, in the political atmosphere of that time, that the President had to come from a party supporting the Emperor's Government. Changes in the governing coalition could cause a change of President, incumbency averaging only three years. In the Weimar Republic, this consideration was of course eliminated, and although all presidential elections were contested, the nominee of the largest party in the Reichstag invariably won the office.[10] Paul Löbe of the SPD, who held the office with one brief interruption from 1920 to 1932, succeeded in gaining confidence from all except the radical Members of the House for his impartial discharge of presidential duties. But the accession of Hermann Göring as representative of the National Socialists, who had become the strongest party in 1932, demonstrated the extent to which the presidency could be used for partisan advantage.

The implicit custom of permitting the candidate of the largest party to hold the presidency has been further established in the Bundestag, with a developing practice of not contesting the election. In seven elections for a parliamentary president there have been only two contests, one resulting from a nomination made by the Communists during the first Bundestag, and one upon Eugen Gerstenmaier's first election in 1954. The latter was an instructive exception to the developing practice. The SPD objected to the failure of the CDU/CSU majority to clear its candidate with the other parties, explaining that "the strongest party names the President not for itself alone, but for the entire Parliament." [11] But instead of nominating its own candidate, the SPD cast one blank ballot, then voted for another CDU/CSU

[10] Partsch, *op. cit.*, pp. 14–18.

[11] *Dt. Btag.*, 2 W.P., 55. Sitz., Nov. 16, 1954, p. 2696. See also pp. 2694, 2697.

Member whom the FDP had nominated in similar protest. Subsequently, Gerstenmaier was re-elected in 1957, 1961, and 1965 without opposition.

Selection of Vice-Presidents

But combined with the custom of permitting the largest party to propose the President, and, upon consultation with the other parties, of electing him without opposition, is the expansion of the number of vice-presidencies to permit all parties to have their proportionate share of a "presidium." In chairing the sessions of the House, and in participating in the Council of Elders and the Executive Committee of the Bundestag, the vice-presidents perform functions equivalent to those of the President. However, as administrative head of the House, and as its representative spokesman, the President in practice supersedes the vice-presidents, and he exercises leadership in the determination of the policy of the chair. Nevertheless, the prestige of the vice-presidency, and the emoluments of the position—basic compensation 50 per cent above that of other Members, an elegant office suite, secretarial assistance—have made the position an attractive party prize. Although the office has existed in the Reichstag from the earliest times, to provide a substitute for the President in the chair,[12] the multiplication of the vice-presidencies to permit their proportional distribution among the parties was a development which took place in the Bundestag. Since the formal Rules left the number of positions open,[13] each House has been free to fit the number to the parties' demands for spoils.

The first Bundestag elected two, Carlo Schmid of the SPD, second strongest party in the House, and Hermann Schäfer, candidate of the FDP, the third in strength. The second Bundestag chose a third vice-president from the CSU, Richard Jaeger—a concession the CSU had won for itself during the negotiations on the formation of the Cabinet. Schmid was re-elected, but instead of Schäfer, Ludwig Schneider was presented by the FDP. How far the vice-presidencies had come to be regarded as party preserves became apparent when Schneider resigned from the FDP in a party split in 1956, and the Free Democrats responded by calling for his resignation as vice-president. Unable to compel it, since the vice-presidential term extended through

[12] Hatschek, *op. cit.*, pp. 201–3.
[13] *Geschäftsordnung, op. cit.*, par. 2.

the life of the Parliament, they reached an agreement with the other parties for the creation of a fourth vice-presidency, to which their member, Max Becker, was elected.[14] The issue came up again four years later when Viktor-Emmanuel Preusker of the German party, who had been elected as a fourth vice-president in the third Bundestag against SPD protest, left his party for the CDU in 1960. Refusing at first to resign the vice-presidency, he eventually did so, but not before the SPD had called for a new rule requiring resignation in such instances.[15] The choice of a fourth vice-president in 1958 had been controversial, with the Social Democrats and Free Democrats charging patronage as the chief motive, and the Christian Democratic–German party governing coalition stressing the objective need for a fourth presidential substitute during long sessions of the House.[16] In the Council of Elders, where attempts were regularly made to reach agreement among the parties on such elections, the Social Democrats privately raised the issue of proportionality, claiming unsuccessfully that if the German party, which had only 17 seats, were given a vice-presidency, the Social Democrats with 181 seats deserved a second one, even if the total were raised thereby to five. The CDU/CSU was committed to support a vice-presidency for Preusker as part of its coalition agreement with the German party, but it was unwilling to create a fifth position. On Preusker's resignation in September, 1960, no substitute for him was chosen for the final year of that Parliament's term.

But when the fourth Bundestag convened in October, 1961, the Social Democrats reasserted their claim to a second vice-president, should there be a total of four, and the issue was joined once again, with the partisan accents particularly strong. The CDU/CSU agreed to the election of four vice-presidents, in order to justify its desire to re-elect CSU Member Jaeger to a vice-presidency. With only three parties remaining in the House, and the President to be chosen from among the CDU/CSU, there could be no dispute that the SPD, with 203 seats, and the FDP with 67, were entitled to the first two vice-presidencies. By proportional representation, the CDU/CSU, with 251 seats, would be entitled to any third vice-presidency, the SPD to any fourth. In fairness, the governing party did not want to stop at three,

[14] *FAZ*, April 13, May 4, July 3, and July 5, 1956.
[15] *Ibid.*, Sept. 13, 1960; *Die Welt*, Oct. 5, 1960.
[16] *Dt. Btag.*, 3. W.P., 24. Sitz., April 23, 1958, p. 1304. *FAZ*, April 24, 1958.

which, counting the presidency, would have given it two of four positions in the "presidium." The FDP, with no interest in more than two vice-presidencies, was in favor of a reduction to that number. Thereupon the SPD, at least for tactical reasons, decided to adopt the FDP's position. It was, for the moment, prepared to spurn a second vice-presidency for itself, in order to promote a fight between the CDU/CSU and the FDP, the partners of the new, but shaky, governing coalition. Only after an interruption of the first session of the new House to allow further interparty discussions did the Free Democrats yield to their stronger partner's insistence on four vice-presidencies, whereupon the SPD, with a second vice-presidency to gain, yielded also. The election, as in previous cases, was by acclamation for the entire slate, instead of by ballot for each position. Once again there were four vice-presidents, with the partisan reasons for that number particularly evident.[17]

During the vice-presidential elections at the start of the fifth Bundestag, one Member demanded a separate vote for each of the four candidates who had been nominated for the four positions, but, on presidential urging, he did not insist on the secret ballot which the Rules provide for. The distribution of vice-presidents among the parties remained unchanged. However, the appointment of Richard Jaeger as Minister of Justice required the CSU to make a new choice. Its first nominee, Friedrich Zimmermann, withdrew after controversy concerning a case of perjury in which he had been involved. The party thereupon named Maria Probst, who was elected by acclamation as the first woman to hold a Bundestag vice-presidency.[18]

Partisanship and Impartiality

The subtle position of the presidential—and vice-presidential—office, between partisanship and impartiality, has other aspects beyond the selection of its occupants. The Imperial custom requiring Presidents to resign at least from their parliamentary party group, if not from their national party membership, was explicitly discontinued in

---

[17] *Dt. Btag.*, 4. W.P., 1. Sitz., Oct. 17, 1961, pp. 6–7.

[18] *Dt. Btag.*, 5. W.P., 1. Sitz., Oct. 19, 1965, pp. 4–5; *Ibid.*, 12. Sitz., Dec. 9, 1965. *Die Welt*, Nov. 10, Dec. 8, 9, 10, 1965. Although the Rules (par. 2) require a separate, secret ballot for the election of the President and each vice-president, in practice the vice-presidential elections have been by acclamation for the entire slate.

the intensely partisan atmosphere of the Weimar Republic.[19] But while Löbe, as Reichstag President, rarely spoke as a Member of the House, despite his activity within the SPD, Bundestag presidents and vice-presidents have done so, frequently on institutional questions and occasionally on substantive political issues as well. They have generally been prominent Members of their parties, active in party councils and election campaigns, and, occasionally, ambitious for other offices.[20] They regularly cast their votes as Members of the House. Although by no means recruited from the backbenches, like the British Speaker, they have not usually been the most contentious party politicians. The parties have tended to regard the presidential offices as the U.S. vice-presidency is often regarded, as sinecures, useful for distributing spoils among party factions, or, occasionally, for kicking an inconvenient politician upstairs. They have then attempted to control their nominees in the exercise of presidential power through the Council of Elders and the Bundestag Executive Committee.

Yet the many intrusions of partisanship on the presidential office have been reconciled with a high degree of impartiality in the exercise of presidential functions. The rotation in the chair of presidents and vice-presidents of different parties would tend to check any tendency toward partisanship in the conduct of the session. Except for the greater procedural authority of the officers with the greatest seniority, there is no discernible difference in the chairmanship of the various incumbents. The settlement of all controversial questions by interparty consensus in the Council of Elders further precludes the exercise of presidential power to partisan advantage. The role of the Council is so important that sessions of the House have been interrupted to obtain resolution of a procedural dispute by means of negotiation in the Council rather than by a ruling made by the Chair.[21] The administrative powers of the President and his personnel policies governing the Bundestag staff have been supervised by the Executive Committee, limiting the President to those decisions which the leaders of the parties—or at least the majority of them—will accept. When the President speaks for the House, his text is customarily cleared by the party leaders. A strict formula of proportional shares according to

[19] Partsch, *op. cit.*, p. 32.

[20] In 1965 Richard Jaeger resigned the vice-presidency, to which he had just been re-elected, to become Minister of Justice in the Federal Cabinet.

[21] See, for example, *Dt. Btag.*, 4. W.P., 132. Sitz., June 24, 1964, pp. 6457–9, 6467.

party strengths even governs the distribution of that part of the presidential expense account which pays for the junkets of Members abroad.

The powers which remain as the personal prerogatives of the President of the Bundestag can be employed only in a manner which is, and is seen to be, nonpartisan. Nominated and controlled in their official positions by their parties, actively involved in their parties but dependent for their official authority on nonpartisanship, the position of the presiding officers is a delicate one. Presidential influence has been highly personal, and the prestige of the office has been the residue of the success of some of its incumbents. That success has depended on the ability of Presidents to identify themselves in their official capacity with the institutional interests of the Bundestag, and to distinguish this role sharply from their involvements in their parties.

The Men

Erich Köhler, elected President in the first Bundestag on the strength of his experience as chairman of the far smaller, far less partisan Bizonal Economic Council, failed dramatically to adjust to the demands of his office. He lost the confidence of the Social Democrats early, and fell victim within the first year to personal attrition from exposure to partisan controversy. His successor, Hermann Ehlers, succeeded notably, both inside and outside the House, and was deeply mourned on his death after only four years in office. Eugen Gerstenmaier became President in a controversial election, but vindicated himself quickly and has more than anyone else put his personal imprint on the office through a long incumbency.

Only Carlo Schmid, a vice-president throughout the existence of the Bundestag, shares Gerstenmaier's personal prestige. Both men are able to make difficult procedural decisions in the chair and have them accepted, both are able to rule the sessions with an obvious personal authority, and both are recognized outside the House as representatives of the institution. Both men share an intellectual approach to politics which is free of the sharpest partisan overtones, a style which apparently lends itself to the difficult reconciliation of their partisan and nonpartisan roles. The other vice-presidents have had a shorter tenure than Schmid. The most colorful one, Thomas Dehler, a passionate partisan, often controversial within his own party, has occasionally suffered the hostility of his political opponents, although his conduct in the chair has been unexceptionable. Compared to Gerstenmaier and Schmid, none of the other vice-presidents has been as sure-footed on procedural questions, as well known outside the House, or has exercised as much discretion in the chair. Their conduct of meetings places greater reliance on the staff parliamentarians, who occupy a desk behind the President's chair, largely hidden from view, and on the Secretaries, two Members of the House from parties other than that of the presiding officer, who flank him on either side, keeping lists of speakers and assisting in decisions on the outcome of votes and the presence of a quorum.

The respect which Gerstenmaier and Schmid have won from the House enables them to confront the party leaders who face them on the floor, or in the Council of Elders, with some personal authority which effectively extends their prerogatives. Furthermore, they have found a response outside the House to their speeches on behalf of the institution of Parliament and its collective view on national issues. They have had some success in defending Parliament, its officers, or aspects of its functions, against narrow partisan attacks. Gerstenmaier has also played an active role in proposing parliamentary reforms. But the limit to personal presidential influence is the point where controversy within the Bundestag begins. At this point the authority of the President is quickly exhausted, for although he cannot be dismissed during the term of Parliament, he rules at the pleasure of the parties.

COMMITTEES OF THE HOUSE

The Relationship between Committees and the House

If the formal Rules overstate the position of the President, they considerably understate the importance of the committees in the organization of the Bundestag. Without establishing any particular committees, the Rules provide that there shall be standing, special, and investigating committees which shall be "organs of the Bundestag" to prepare subjects for its consideration (pars. 60–63). They are expressly limited to the consideration of subjects referred to them (par. 60, sec. 3), a stipulation dating back to the rules adopted by the National Assembly of 1848 which were based on the strict British subordination of committees to the House.[22] This principle of subordi-

[22] Bruno Dechamps, *Macht und Arbeit der Ausschüsse* (Meisenheim: Westkulturverlag Anton Hain, 1954), p. 57.

nation prevailed against an effort, made by the Social Democrats in 1951 when the Bundestag adopted its new Rules, to empower committees on behalf of the whole House to take legislative initiatives and to exercise certain controls over the Government in their own area of jurisdiction. The party's spokesman, Heinrich Ritzel, chairman of the Bundestag's Committee on Election Validation, Immunity and Rules, and veteran of the Weimar Reichstag, argued that the overburdened House was incapable of exercising all of its powers unless it delegated some of them to its committees. "We should take account of reality," he said, urging a permissive rule "in preparation for the future development which will come without any doubt." [23] Fear that the committees might escape the control of the House—specifically its majority—caused the parties in the governing coalition to reject the proposal.[24]

In practice, however, a considerable measure of committee autonomy has developed, fulfilling Ritzel's prophecy. The volume of legislation inspired by postwar issues, the need for specialization to master the complex subject matter, and the desire of interest representatives to remove the issues of concern to them to committees they could dominate, all contributed to this development. Although the Rules provide that, before referral to committee, bills will receive a first reading in the House, in which "the basic principles of the proposal are discussed," first readings have become increasingly rare in practice (par. 78). For lack of time, and because of the parties' desire to reserve their positions until committee negotiations begin, this stage is now usually passed *pro forma*. This means that parliamentary discussion begins in the committees—and among the specialists within each party—rather than in the House as a whole, and leaves the House primarily in command of committee referral in the initial stage of deliberation.

Committee Referral

The committees exercise a good deal of control over their own jurisdictions, and therefore over the question of which matters come before them. The Rules themselves provide for the automatic referral of certain topics: proposals affecting expenditure, except the budget and amendments to it, must go directly to the Appropriations Commit-

[23] *Dt. Btag.*, 1. W.P., 179. Sitz., Dec. 6, 1951, p. 7432.
[24] *Ibid.*, pp. 7433–4.

tee, a rule designed by the majority to deter irresponsible spending proposals (par. 96, sec. 2); citizens' petitions, and requests to lift the immunity of Members of the House, are likewise referred to the relevant committees without prior discussion (par. 112, sec. 1, and par. 114). Beyond these special cases, referral tends to be decided by a consensus among the interested committees, with majority vote in the House employed only as a last resort. The proliferation of standing committees in the Bizonal Economic Council, and the Council's loose and unprecedented practice of settling jurisdictional disputes among committees by referring subjects to several of them simultaneously, has carried over into the practice of the Bundestag. The provision of the Rules that multiple referral take place only in "special cases" (par. 79, sec. 1) remains a pious hope.

The committee chairmen themselves take the initiative in the question of referral. They express their jurisdictional demands through their assistants, who meet weekly at a staff conference. The resulting proposals on referral are taken to the Council of Elders for approval by the party leaders. These, in turn, have received the recommendations of their own party specialists. By means of trades and multiple referrals, it is generally possible to reach an agreement which will suit all the special committee interests. But tenacious differences can persist, especially if opposing interests expect that the contending committees would reach different conclusions because of their compositions or the identity of their chairmen. Only as a last resort is the issue settled on the floor, because the party leaders are well aware that party discipline may not hold on the question of referral, that the vote may reflect committee alignments.

The decision on referral merely determines which committee will have charge of reporting on a bill, and which others will also consider it. Ordinarily it carries no instructions, except on those relatively few partisan issues on which a first reading debate has outlined the respective party positions. Furthermore, so much material is referred to committees—not only alternative texts of bills, but Government reports, resolutions, and other "material for deliberation"—that most committees have a broad choice of subjects for discussion. Nothing prevents committees from completely rewriting the bills referred to them, and it is the committee version which the House considers in second reading. It has long been accepted in German parliamentary law that although they are organs of the House, committees are free to form their own judgments, unbound by instructions.[25] Nor are committees compelled to act promptly, although the Rules urge them to do so (par. 60, sec. 2). Complete failure to consider a bill referred to a committee usually occurs only during the final year of the parliamentary term when the pressure of business provides good excuses. Pigeonholing a bill without such justification is regarded as a denial of the constitutional right of Members to introduce bills, and is theoretically subject to judicial review.[26] But if the parliamentary leaders of all parties tacitly agree to leave a matter in limbo, even major legislative projects may die in committee.[27] And toward the end of a term committee chairmen can effectively defeat a bill merely by dragging their feet.

To some extent all committees act without waiting for referral of a specific subject. The Rules permit the Committee on Election Validation, Immunity, and Rules to take up matters within its jurisdiction on its own initiative (par. 130). Under an informal agreement reached in the Council of Elders, the Judiciary Committee may consider any bill which raises constitutional questions, whether it has been specifically referred to it or not. An amendment to the Basic Law, enacted at the time the Government assumed control over defense, specifically empowers the Defense Committee of the Bundestag to act as an investigating committee within its area of jurisdiction, and obliges it to conduct investigations on the demand of one-quarter of its members.[28] It, as well as the committees on Foreign Affairs, All-German and Berlin Questions, and Interior (on questions of internal security), in practice initiates deliberations within its subject area at its own discretion. Since all committees are entitled, under the Basic Law, to compel

[25] Hatschek, *op. cit.*, pp. 240–46.

[26] Hans Trossman, "Der Deutsche Bundestag," in *Kürschners Volkshandbuch, Deutscher Bundestag*, 4. Wahlperiode (Darmstadt: Neue Darmstädter Verlagsanstalt, 1962), p. 38. Also published, essentially unchanged, as a separate brochure by the same publisher, entitled *Der Deutsche Bundestag, Organisation und Arbeitsweise* (1963); English translation, *The German Bundestag, Organization and Operation* (1965). Both brochures contain the text of the Rules of Procedure.

[27] This was the case with the long delayed bill on political parties during the third Bundestag. The Government introduced a bill in December, 1959, (Drs. III, 1509) but it was never discussed in the Committee on Internal Affairs to which it was referred. A similar fate befell the bills on the same subject referred to a special committee during the fourth Bundestag (Drs. IV, 2853, 3112).

[28] *Basic Law,* art. 45a (2).

the attendance of ministers,[29] as is the whole House, most committees regularly interrogate the representatives of the Government within their subject area on the annual departmental appropriation, as well as on other problems of interest to the committee, whether specifically referred to them by the Bundestag or not.

Committee Meetings

The Appropriations Committee has attained the highest measure of committee autonomy. Not only does it have blanket permission to meet while the House is in session—something for which other committees require presidential approval in each case—but it has delegated power to act on Government expenditure in place of the House. Every annual appropriations bill contains provisions empowering the Committee to make binding decisions which the House has not been able to take for lack of time or information.[30] The House has retained a greater measure of control over the other committees. Under the schedule now in effect, they may meet only two days a week, and then only during hours when the House itself is not in session. The results of their deliberations are subject to the approval of the House in second and third readings. In that sense, the committees remain the agencies of the House. But the House is, in another sense, highly dependent on its committees, for the time they save it, the indispensable expertise they provide, and the private forum they offer for the negotiation of compromises.

The frequency of committee meetings is one measure of the proportion of parliamentary work which they do. After the exceptionally heavy volume of legislation during the first two terms, the average committee has settled down to about a hundred meetings during a four-year term, the equivalent of one meeting per week while the House is in session. But there are great variations within this average. The Appropriations and Judiciary committees are most hard-pressed, averaging over two hundred meetings in a four-year term, more than the House as a whole. Many sessions are day-long. Also very active, with a hundred to a hundred and fifty meetings quadrennially, are the committees on Agriculture, Defense, Economic Affairs, Social Policy,

[29] *Ibid.*, art. 43 (1).

[30] See, for example, the Haushaltsgesetz 1961, *BGBl.* II, p. 357, pars. 2(2), 10, 11, 18(2), 26(3); the general provisions are contained in the Reichshaushaltsordnung, *RGBl.* II (1923), p. 17.

Finance, Foreign Affairs, Transport–Post Office–and–Telecommunications, Interior, Labor, and Health, in that order.[31]

Committee Organization

In the manner in which they organize their work, the committees are completely independent of the House. They determine their own calendar of meetings and set their own agenda. Their chairmen and deputy chairmen together exercise great power over committee organization and procedure. In stating that they have the task of preparing and conducting the committee sessions, the Rules fail to do justice to the position of these chairmen. (par. 69, sec. 2). Subject formally to the decision of his committee, the chairman, in close consultation with the deputy chairman, takes the initiative in setting the time of meetings, determining the agenda, inviting experts to testify, appointing the reporter for each bill, conducting the meeting, and employing the committee assistant and secretariat. In the absence of specific rules of procedure for committees, the chairman's discretion in the conduct of what is a highly informal meeting is considerable. His influence on the pace of business can be very great. His control of the small staff is important in a Parliament whose Members have very little assistance. The appointment of the reporter may significantly affect the fate of a bill, although custom dictates that the reporter should not ordinarily be chosen from among proponents of a bill, and that his report must be objective, presenting both majority and minority viewpoints. In comparison to the ordinary committee member, the chairman and deputy chairman are in a dominating position. Although appointed by their party, their term covers the electoral period, and in practice their chances of continuous reappointment are great.

Committee Specialization

The decisions of the committees have the authority of expertise. The creation of thirty-nine standing committees by the first Bundestag greatly increased the degree of specialization in the committee structure by comparison to the Weimar Reichstag, which had fewer than

---

[31] *Bulletin des Presse-und Informationsamtes der Bundesregierung*, Oct. 25, 1961, pp. 200–1. The figures are for the third Bundestag, during which altogether 2432 committee meetings were held, a committee average of nearly 94. Less than 20 per cent of the total represents subcommittee meetings. During the first two Bundestage, with 50 per cent more committees, the total number of committee meetings was 5414 and 4210 respectively. During the fourth Bundestag, there were nearly 2,900 committee meetings, a committee average of 91.

half as many committees. The increase was due only in part to the increasing complexity of legislative work. It was also a response to the multiplication of organized interest groups each demanding a committee corresponding to its particular area of concern.[32] But this development created serious obstacles to the dispatch of legislative business, by introducing severe problems in defining committee jurisdictions, sharpening rivalries among committees and the interests associated with each, and producing unmanageable burdens for Members having multiple committee assignments. After eight years of such experience, a consensus among party leaders enabled the Council of Elders to reverse the trend toward committee proliferation by reducing the number of committees to twenty-six at the start of the third Bundestag in 1957.[33] From that point the number again rose slightly, in response to the creation of two new Cabinet ministries which immediately obtained committee counterparts in 1962. A renewed effort initiated by President Gerstenmaier to control the multiplication of committees resulted—after some hard bargaining both within and between the parties—in their reduction to twenty-three at the start of the fifth Bundestag in 1965.[34] Several committees dealing with postwar issues of declining importance were combined into one, as were a number of committees in the field of economic policy. Each effort to eliminate committees has had to face protest from interest groups anxious to retain "their" committees.[35]

[32] Dechamps, op. cit., pp. 62–6. Cf. Rupert Breitling, Die Verbände in der Bundesrepublik (Meisenheim: Verlag Anton Hain, 1955), pp. 128–34.

[33] Dt. Btag., 3. W.P., 5. Sitz., Nov. 28, 1957, p. 101, and Drs. 18.

[34] The following standing committees were established by the fifth Bundestag:

1. Election Validation, Immunity, and Rules
2. Petitions
3. Foreign Affairs
4. All-German and Berlin Questions
5. Defense
6. Interior
7. Damages of War and Persecution
8. Science, Cultural Policy, and Publishing
9. Local Government, Town and Country Planning, and Housing
10. Family and Youth
11. Health
12. Judiciary
13. Appropriations
14. Finance
15. Economic and Middle Class (Small Business) Affairs
16. Foreign Aid
17. Food, Agriculture, and Forestry
18. Social Policy
19. Labor
20. Transport
21. Post Office
22. Expellee and Refugee Affairs
23. Federal Property

In addition, there is a special committee on the Reform of the Criminal Code.

[35] See, for example, the view of the German Confederation of Government Officials, expressed in DZ, Nov. 2, 1957.

Special committees do not offer an effective way to bypass the standing committees. They are created only rarely, in part because the standing committees jealously guard their own jurisdictions, in part because Members are fully absorbed by their regular committee assignments. A special committee established during the fourth Bundestag in an effort to obtain passage of a bill on political parties, which had died in the Interior Committee during the previous term, failed to report out an acceptable measure. Another special committee, on the revision of the criminal code, did not complete its work, and had to be continued in the fifth Bundestag.

Committee Composition

In view of the dependence of the Bundestag on its regular committees, the manner of their composition is clearly a matter of greatest importance. Proportional representation of minorities is the guiding principle. It was the *raison d'être* of the Council of Seniors, created a century ago in the Prussian chamber to take over the appointment of committees from the sections (*Abteilungen*). Within the first decade of the existence of the Reichstag, the Council had agreed to distribute committee seats according to a mathematical calculation of proportionality, as the multiplication of party groups made a simpler distribution of seats by agreement among the parties too difficult.[36] The essentials of the system, developed at that time to suit the needs of a multiplicity of minority parties, have been retained. The number of places to which each parliamentary party is entitled is determined by the d'Hondt system of proportional representation, a formula slightly more favorable to the larger parties than that employed during the Weimar period. The only discretion required of the Council of Elders —successor to the Council of Seniors—pertains to the size of committees, and the determination of the minimum size a parliamentary party must have to be recognized as such and be entitled to committee representation at all. The final decision on both questions is made by the House on the Council's recommendation. On occasion it has been used to affect particular parties. In January, 1952, the minimum strength of the parliamentary party was raised from ten to the present figure of fifteen, thereby denying party status to the Communists and removing their Members from the committees.[37] In keeping with the

[36] Hatschek, *op. cit.*, pp. 185–8; 229–33.
[37] Emil Obermann, *Alter und Konstanz von Fraktionen* (Meisenheim: Verlag Anton Hain, 1956), p. 45.

spirit of committee representation, those committees which had had twenty-one members in the third Bundestag were increased in size at the beginning of the fourth, on the insistence of the Social Democrats and the Free Democrats and the acquiescence of the CDU/CSU, because the d'Hondt calculation based on the new party alignments in the House turned out to entitle the CDU/CSU to eleven seats on twenty-one-member committees, even though it lacked a majority in the House as a whole.[38]

Once party quotas are established, the actual appointments of committee members, as well as changes of appointment at any time, are made by the parliamentary parties and need merely be communicated to the President of the House. Likewise, committee chairmanships are distributed among the parties by proportional representation, and the parties fill the positions falling to them. Parties may choose the particular committees they wish to chair in the arithmetic order in which the chairmanships fall to them by the d'Hondt calculation, but they frequently make trades with each other. Although the Rules provide that committees appoint their chairmen "in accordance with the agreements reached in the Council of Elders" (par. 69), the attempt of a committee to reject the chairman designated by the party entitled to choose him is regarded as a violation of custom. This was demonstrated in 1957 when Adenauer failed to persuade the Members of his party to reject the appointment of Herbert Wehner, the Social Democrats' choice as chairman of the Committee on All-German and Berlin Questions.[39] The appointment of deputy chairmen is made on the basis of agreements among the parties reached in the Council of Elders, on the principle that the deputy should come from a party other than that of the chairman.

Party appointment of committee members and chairmen does not, however, place the committees under simple party control. The parliamentary parties themselves are complex organizations, in which power is, in part, distributed according to a pattern of subject specialization which parallels that of the committees. The relationship between the parties and the committees is not therefore one of simple one-way supervision, but one of reciprocal influence. This means that the proportional representation of the parties in the committees has lost much of the rationale which it had in a system of multiple, homogeneous

[38] Agreement of the Council of Elders, Nov. 7, 1961, reported in *Die Welt*, Nov. 8, 1961.

[39] *Die Welt*, Nov. 27, 28, 29, 1957.

parties, most of which possessed a high degree of unity in the interests they represented and in their policy objectives. Then proportionality among the parties meant the representation of the major interests according to their strength in the House, and it was justified as a recognition of the pattern of power. As a prominent Reichstag Member in the 1920's put it:

For every ruthless exclusion in one place, a group can take revenge at another, at least in the election campaign. Whoever is not in the committee, talks all the longer and more annoyingly in the House. Whoever fails to obtain any chairmanship, makes the life of all other chairmen all the more difficult. That is why the system of "just" participation has become established, which is after all also the principle of the electoral system. One places responsibility on every group, and thereby deprives them of some possibilities of extreme opposition. . . . "Do unto others," one says to oneself, and thinks of the results of the next election, which could perhaps transform the strength of today into the weakness of tomorrow.[40]

But the pattern of power in the Bundestag is substantially different. Only three parliamentary parties remain, none of them inclined to practice obstruction. They are clearly distinguished from each other throughout a parliamentary term by their participation either in the Government or in the Opposition. But as constituencies for purposes of representation on the committees, each party is too large and diverse. The proportional representation of the parties does not assure the proportional representation of the major interests within the parties. Nor does it assure the Government the control which it can expect on the basis of its parliamentary majority, since the governing parties may well be represented on some committees by Members having special interests at variance with those of the Government. For the same reason it does not permit the Opposition to hold the Government accountable for committee decisions.

The major interests within each parliamentary party seek influence on committee decisions by getting their Members appointed where they can be most effective. To the extent that they succeed, the major units represented in the committees are the intraparty interest groups. To that extent also, the system of party appointment of committees, designed to assure party influence on committee decisions in proportion to their strength, today allows the committee to escape from the

[40] Walter Lambach, *Die Herrschaft der Fünfhundert* (Hamburg and Berlin: Hanseatische Verlagsanstalt, 1926), p. 64.

control of the parties, as well as from the Government and the Opposition, and constitutes them as autonomous preserves of the major interest groups within their fields of jurisdiction. This development is a consequence of the changes which have occurred in the parliamentary parties as units of parliamentary organization.

PARLIAMENTARY PARTIES

The Consolidation of the Parties

Parliamentary parties were traditionally far smaller, and more numerous, than they are today. In the five Weimar Reichstage until 1930, there were, on the average, nine groups large enough to be recognized under the Rules, with an average membership of 54 Representatives each.[41] The picture in the Imperial Reichstag was very similar. In the postwar Bundestag the configuration has changed markedly. In the first House elected in 1949, there were still eight officially recognized party groups with an average membership of 52; in the second Bundestag of 1953 there were five groups with an average of 101 Members; in the third Bundestag of 1957, there were only four groups, averaging 130 Members each; in the fourth Bundestag of 1961, only three groups remained, the CDU/CSU with 251 members, the SPD with 203, and the FDP with 67—for an average of 174. The election of 1965 produced a continuation of this pattern. (See Table 25.) The dramatic change in the size of the parliamentary parties is in part merely the mechanical result of an altered electoral law which limits the splintering effect of proportional representation by excluding parties with less than 5 per cent of the national vote, or fewer than three victories in single-member constituencies, from their proportional share of seats.[42] It also reflects the success of the broad national appeal made first by the CDU/CSU and later by the SPD, and the decline in the attractiveness of such special-interest parties as the various expellee groups and the extremist neo-Nazi and Communist parties. Factors promoting this development include the licensing policies of the Allied military government, which aimed to prevent the

[41] Based on statistics in Obermann, *op. cit.*, pp. 23–31.

[42] The law of 1949 only required parties to obtain five per cent of the votes in a *Land*, or one victory in a single-member constituency, to be eligible for their proportional share of that *Land's* seats (see *BGBl.*, p. 21, par. 10[4, 5]). This was tightened to require five per cent nationally in the law of 1953 (*BGBl.* I, p. 470) and the law of 1956 (*BGBl.* I, p. 383, par. 6[4]).

appearance of narrow, special-interest parties;[43] the example of the Soviet zone of occupation, which destroyed the appeal of the Communists; and the provisions of the Basic Law, under which the leading neo-Nazi party and the Communist party were outlawed.[44] Profound sociological changes in postwar Germany contributed by diminishing class and regional differences. These developments not only reduced

Table 25. Party strengths in the Bundestag (number of seats after each election with additional representatives from Berlin indicated in parentheses)

Party	1949	1953	1957	1961	1965
CDU/CSU	139 (5)	244 (6)	270 (8)	242 (9)	245 (6)
SPD	131 (9)	151 (11)	169 (12)	190 (13)	202 (15)
FDP	52 (5)	48 (5)	41 (2)	67 (0)	49 (1)
GB/BHE a	– b	27	0	0	–
DP a	17	15	17	0	–
BP c	17	0	0	–	–
KPD	15	0	–	–	–
WAV	12	–	–	–	–
Z c	10	2	0	–	–
DRP d	5	0	0	0	0
SSW	1	0	0	–	–
Independent	3	–	–	–	–
Total	402 (19)	487 (22)	497 (22)	499 (22)	496 (22)

a In 1961, GDP.

b Indicates no candidates presented.

c In 1957, FU.

d In 1965, NPD.

the number of parties, with a corresponding growth in the size of those which remained, but they diminished the differences between the parties in comparison with the differences within them. The implications of these changes for Parliament were suggested by Gerstenmaier in the speech he made upon his re-election as Bundestag President in 1961. He noted that with only three parliamentary parties remaining in that Bundestag, each party had the need to "be ever roomier." But departing from his customary liberal emphasis on the need to strengthen the position of the individual Member, he added that it

[43] Richard M. Scammon, "Political Parties," in Edward H. Litchfield, ed., *Governing Postwar Germany* (Ithaca: Cornell University Press, 1953), p. 477.

[44] BVerfGE 2, 1; BVerfGE 5, 85.

was necessary for each party to "bring freedom and restraint into such harmony with one another" that, on the one hand, the independence of the Member "is fully respected but, on the other hand, the compelling parliamentary political necessities are taken into account." As he explained, "a parliamentary party which cannot arrive at a fairly unified viewpoint, is not of much use to the House. And a parliament, which cannot form adequate majorities, is incapable of acting." [45]

As the parliamentary parties have grown in size, encompassing an ever-increasing variety of interests, it has become far more difficult for them to perform the functions of organizing, expressing, and reconciling these interests in order to make the accustomed party unity possible. The difficulty is not a consequence only of their size and internal variety. It is the result also of the declining appeal of traditional ideologies, which served as important sources of cohesion in the past, and of the confrontation with more complicated and more numerous legislative issues, especially in the immediate postwar period. But at the same time as the difficulties have increased, the premium on party cohesion has increased also. As one of three parliamentary parties rather than one of eight or nine, each party has a greater incentive than ever before for mobilizing its Members in a disciplined fashion, because its prospect for affecting the formation of majorities, and thus the decisions of the House, has grown directly with its growth in size. Furthermore, in the new constitutional system, not only do important legislative decisions depend on majorities, with no escape possible to presidential emergency government, but the appointment of the Chancellor also depends on a majority vote in Parliament.

In response to the challenge, the party groups in Parliament have undergone structural changes, developing internal organizations far more complicated than anything known before the war. Interest groups have formed within them, working groups have been organized to obtain the advantages of division and specialization of labor, and research staffs have been hired. The party meeting, or caucus, inflated in size, has become an organ of ratification, and the function of producing party agreement has fallen to elected executive committees. These profound changes in the organization of the parliamentary parties has greatly affected the performance of the House, increasing the proportion of the decision-making process which takes place in the secrecy of party councils, stimulating specialization among Members,

[45] *Dt. Btag.*, 4, W.P., 1. Sitz., Oct. 17, 1961, p. 3.

and creating the need for a new breed of parliamentarian to act as broker among the specialists and interest representatives.

The Official Status of the Parties

The parliamentary party (*Fraktion*) has occupied a semiofficial position in the organization of Parliament since before the turn of the century. Tracing its ancestry to a period well before the existence of parliamentary government, the organization of the party group developed in entire independence of the Cabinet. Before they were formally recognized in the Rules, the administration of the Imperial Reichstag had placed meeting rooms and offices at the disposal of the parties in Parliament.[46] The party was the unit of representation in the committees, and through the Council of Seniors the party leaders arranged the agenda and the order of debate in the House.[47] Each party had its chairman and executive committee; some had rules and kept minutes. The Rules of the Weimar Reichstag [48] mentioned parliamentary parties for the first time, but merely defined them as "associations of at least 15 members" (par. 7). The Rules adopted by the Bundestag contained a more restrictive definition (Par. 10). An officially recognized parliamentary party today must consist of members of the same political party, unless the Bundestag specifically makes an exception. Opportunistic combinations of Members, hoping to gain the privileges of party status, are precluded. The minimum strength which a party must have is not set by the Rules, but has been placed at fifteen in a separate decision made by the House.[49]

For the first time, money is now appropriated to the parliamentary parties in support of their work. This subvention has grown by leaps and bounds, a measure of the expansion of the parties' activities and organization. From a total of DM 348,000 ($82,857) for eight parties in 1950, it has risen to DM 3,123,200 ($780,800), for the three remaining parties in 1965. This amount is distributed among the parties by

---

[46] Eberhard Pikart, "Die Rolle der Parteien im deutschen konstitutionellen System vor 1914," *Zeitschrift für Politik*, IX n.f. (1962), pp. 19–20.

[47] Hatschek, *op. cit.*, pp. 188–90.

[48] *Verhandlungen des Deutschen Reichstages*, 1. W.P., 280. Sitz., Dec. 12, 1922, p. 9278; *RGBl.* II (1923), p. 101.

[49] *Dt. Btag.*, 1. W.P., 185. Sitz., Jan. 16, 1952, p. 7894. See also *FAZ*, Jan. 18, 1952; *Die Welt*, Dec. 8, 1951. This decision has been repeated at the beginning of every parliamentary term (see, for example, *Dt. Btag.*, 4. W.P., 3. Sitz., Nov. 8, 1961, p. 12).

appropriating a basic sum of DM 72,000 ($18,000) annually to each, and adding DM 5580 ($1,395) per Member, giving the larger parties a great advantage. The title in the budget specifies that the amount is a "subsidy paid to the parliamentary parties for the maintenance of their offices as well as their staff of professional assistants."[50] Each party also secures an additional indirect subsidy by the deduction it makes from the parliamentary compensation of its Members. The CDU/CSU withholds DM 30 ($7.50) monthly—enough, with the subsidy, to permit the parliamentary party organization to break even. The FDP deducts DM 50 ($12.50). The SPD keeps DM 272 ($68), or 20 per cent of its Members' basic compensation—enough for a tidy profit which is contributed to the party's general fund.[51]

New Influences on Party Organization

Within the first two years of the existence of the Bundestag, a recognition of the inadequacies of the traditional party organization grew among the leaders of the main parties, and most acutely among their whips (*Parlamentarische Geschäftsführer*). In a privately prepared memorandum written in 1951, which illustrates the early awareness of the problem, the floor leader of the fifty-two-member FDP group, Fritz Oellers, described the breakdown of the party caucus as a place for achieving a party position on the issues.[52] Long meetings crowded with highly technical subjects had reduced attendance to 30 per cent of the group, consisting of the leadership and a number of specialists varying with the subject. Oellers pointed out a lack of coordination between the decisions of the caucus and the decision taken by its members in committees, between the party and its coalition partners, between the party and individual ministries, and between the party and the Cabinet. He proposed various organizational remedies, foremost among them the formation of five specialized

[50] See *Bundeshaushaltsplan*, 1961, Einzelplan 0201, Tit. 301. p. 12; *ibid.*, 1950, 1965.

[51] Ulrich Dübber, *Parteifinanzierung in Deutschland* (Cologne and Opladen: Westdeutscher Verlag, 1962), p. 25. The SPD reports a net income from the parliamentary party of DM 711,029 ($177,757) for 1963 (see *Jahrbuch der Sozialdemokratischen Partei Deutschlands*, 1962/63 [Bonn: Neuer Vorwärts Verlag, 1964], p. 377).

[52] "Gedanken und Vorschläge zur Reform der parlamentarischen Tätigkeit." I would like to thank Rudolf Wildenmann for making a photostatic copy of the memorandum available to me. He cites the document in *Macht und Konsens* (Frankfurt: Athenäum Verlag, 1963), pp. 106–9.

working groups of the parliamentary party to deliberate on the technicalities of issues and to recommend a party position to the caucus. The caucus, as a whole, would concern itself only with large questions of general political importance. The working groups would roughly parallel groups of committees of the Bundestag and consist of the party's Members on these committees. The executive committee of the parliamentary party would either refer subjects to the working groups or bring them directly to the caucus meeting. The executive would also supervise the attendance and work of the party's Members in the Bundestag committees. Generally, Oellers recommended an expansion of the role of the party whips and an increase in their staff. He also made proposals for facilitating the public sessions of the House, suggesting greater authority for the Council of Elders in fixing the agenda, and elimination of the reading of committee reports and, ordinarily, of first and third reading debates. He hoped thereby to make the second reading an occasion for genuine, spontaneous discussion receiving the attention of the Members and the public.

Oellers' memorandum expressed the desperation of a floor leader lacking the organizational instruments to provide the tactical leadership with which he was charged. By the beginning of the second parliamentary term, his proposals to remedy these organizational deficiencies, and similar proposals from other sources, appealed to the leaders of the larger coalition partner, the CDU/CSU, even more than to Oellers' own party. Three years later the SPD put comparable organizational changes into practice. However, Oellers' concern about the relationship among the coalition parties in the Bundestag, and between them and their leaders in the Cabinet, did not gain such quick acceptance. His proposal that parliamentary secretaries of state be appointed to maintain communication between parliamentary leaders and the Cabinet, and his request that ministries keep the governing parties in the Bundestag fully informed of their legislative plans, could not be realized by the parliamentary leaders alone. Under Adenauer's Chancellorship there was no inclination on the part of the Cabinet to adopt recommendations which might increase parliamentary influence on the Government. Nor was there any general awareness that the traditional relationship between Cabinet and Parliament was fundamentally changing because of the nearly exclusive recruitment of Cabinet Ministers from Parliament, and because of the essential stability of the governing coalition throughout the parliamentary term, which produced a clear distinction between governing and opposition parties in the House. Thus the internal organization of the parliamentary parties changed drastically in the early years of the Bundestag, but the relationship between the parties and the Cabinet continued to take place within traditional forms, with only occasional *ad hoc* adaptations.

CDU/CSU

Composition. The internal organization adopted by the three leading parliamentary parties varies in complexity with their size and the heterogeneity of their composition. The CDU/CSU encountered the greatest problems, requiring the most organizational ingenuity. Its caucus consists of members of two organizationally separate parties: the CDU, active in ten *Länder;* and the CSU in Bavaria, reflecting that state's traditional separatism in politics. One of the basic premises of the CDU/CSU is the need for the political association of all Christians, Protestant and Catholic, in spite of a tradition of their political separation. As the one leading non-Marxist party, the CDU/CSU has attracted the support of the entrepreneurs, the managers, the professional classes, and the farmers, and has deliberately sought working class support as well. As a result, the formulation of its economic policies is subject to unusually diverse pressures. Finally, it has been the leading Government party, generally obliged to support the policies of a coalition Government composed only in part of its own members. With its organization on the parliamentary level separate from the Cabinet and its parliamentary leaders different from its Cabinet leaders (and the demand for leadership personnel within the party therefore exceptionally great), it must provide the necessary coordination between the Cabinet and its parliamentary supporters. Meanwhile, old habits still cause ministers to regard themselves as executive officials who must keep Parliament at arm's length, even now that they owe their appointment to their position as leaders in the parliamentary party.

The heterogeneous composition of the parliamentary party, essentially unchanged since the second Bundestag, expresses itself in the formation of organized interest groups within the party. The CSU members form a separate *Land* group with its own chairman and deputy chairman, its own whip, and its own office staff. Its association with the CDU in the CDU/CSU has occurred in each Bundestag as the result of its express decision, and the approval of the House to the formation of a parliamentary party composed of organizationally separate extraparliamentary parties.[53] The union rests on an agreement stating conditions, which in 1957 included, as a substantive point, an undertaking to oppose any changes in the Basic Law "which the CSU must reject for federal reasons." Procedurally, the agreement contained an assurance that the chairman of the CSU group would be included in any discussions between the Chancellor and the CDU/CSU parliamentary leaders, that his name would appear alternatively with the name of the CDU/CSU chairman as signatory to resolutions introduced on behalf of the party in the Bundestag. The agreement also included an understanding that the CSU chairman would be made a deputy chairman of the CDU/CSU group, and that CSU Members would be proportionately represented in the executive committee and the working groups of the parliamentary party, as well as in the committees of the House and in the occupancy of their chairmanships.[54] The chief objective of the CSU group has been to advance the interests of its members in personnel questions, notably in the appointment of the Cabinet and the parliamentary committees and their chairmen. Its achievements can be seen, for example, in the appointment of a fixed quota of CSU members to each of the Bundestag committees. In the third Bundestag, there were generally three CSU members on each committee of twenty-nine, slightly in excess of the CSU's proportional strength. In the distribution of committee chairmanships, the CSU also received at least its full share: three chairmanships and four deputy chairmanships. More striking is the appointment of successive chairmen of the CSU parliamentary group to ministerial office, beginning with Franz Josef Strauss, chairman in the first Bundestag, and including Richard Stücklen, chairman in the second, Hermann Höcherl, chairman in the third, and Werner Dollinger, chairman in the first eighteen months of the fourth. After the return of Strauss to the chairmanship of the CSU in the Bundestag in

[53] *Dt. Btag.*, 4. W.P., 1. Sitz., Oct. 17, 1961, p. 1. In 1965 the SPD, for the first time, voted against the formation of a joint CDU/CSU parliamentary party (*Dt. Btag.*, 5. W.P., 1. Sitz., Oct. 19, 1965, p. 1).

[54] From an exchange of letters between Hermann Höcherl, then chairman of the CSU caucus, and Heinrich Krone, then chairman of the CDU caucus, dated November 26 and 28, 1957, respectively, cited in Jürgen Domes, *Mehrheitsfraktion und Bundesregierung* (Cologne and Opladen: Westdeutscherverlag, 1964), pp. 65–6.

1962, after his spectacular departure from the Cabinet in the "*Spiegel* affair*,*" it became clear that under ambitious leadership the group might also advance distinctive views on policy questions, even in the field of foreign affairs.

CDU Members from some other *Länder,* including North Rhine–Westphalia, Lower Saxony, Baden-Württemberg, and Rhineland-Palatinate, meet at regular intervals to discuss common interests, particularly personnel questions at the time a new Bundestag is organized, but they seldom take special policy positions, have no separate organization, and have not realized their potential for bridging other differences among party Members.

Interest groups. Economic interest is the basis of a number of groups within the party, of which the "labor group" is the most clearly organized.[55] It has its own executive and its own office, with a secretary and an assistant paid out of the parliamentary party's budget; it meets at least once a month, and has had between fifty-five and sixty-five members since the second Bundestag. It reserves the right to determine which Members may join it, and labor union membership is at least implicitly a qualification for belonging. The group is closely associated with the so-called Social Committees of the Christian Democratic Labor Movement, which represent the interests of labor within the party. These organizations expresses their views in regular conferences and in a monthly periodical. Within the parliamentary party, the labor group seeks to arrive at a common position on economic and social issues, and to win the caucus to it. Its ultimate sanction is to vote with the SPD in the House. Its implicit sanction is the appeal of its viewpoint to labor union members among potential CDU voters. Its tactic is to place its Members in influential positions in the Bundestag and in Government, especially in those offices dealing with social and economic policy. There is a tacit agreement that one of the deputy chairmen of the parliamentary party shall be a member of the labor group.

A second economic group of CDU/CSU Members is the "discussion

---

[55] The discussion of the economic groupings within the CDU/CSU caucus is based on the study by Domes, *op. cit.,* pp. 33–40. A detailed analysis of the backgrounds and parliamentary positions of the members of the labor group in the third and fourth Bundestage was published by the Deutsches Industrie Institut, Cologne, Sondermaterial no. 1 (1962), "Der 'linke Flügel' der CDU/CSU" (mimeographed). On the activities of the group during the fourth Bundestag, see *Die Zeit,* Jan. 12, 1962, p. 17; *ibid.* (U.S. ed.), July 19, 1963.

group on middle-class (small-business) affairs" which is associated, and shares offices, with a similar organization within the national party. Consisting of Members with a small-business background, but open to all members of the parliamentary party, its participants—a hard core of thirty but occasionally as many as eighty in the third Bundestag—meet fortnightly, after each party caucus, to coordinate views on questions before the parliamentary party, and to press personnel interests within Government and Parliament. Members pay dues to finance the group, although it also receives support from the budget of the parliamentary party. It too has an implicit claim on a deputy chairmanship.

A third economic faction, the "study group on food and agriculture," consists of Members—sixty to seventy in the third Bundestag—who share such definite interests that little organization is required to make the group effective within the party. It meets after each caucus of the party, claims one deputy chairmanship, and has exerted particular influence on the appointment of the Minister of Agriculture.

Other groups exist on a less organized basis. Of the fifty to fifty-five owners or managers of large businesses or trade organizations, about thirty-five met every six to eight weeks during the third Bundestag to discuss common interests. Thirty-two Members, cutting across all other group lines but united on the basis of their geographical origin in Eastern Germany and closely associated with the major interest group of the expellees, the Federation of Expellees, also met at irregular intervals. Still other groups have formed *ad hoc* to discuss particular legislative projects, like the Discussion Group on Problems of the Family, in the third Bundestag, and that on Problems of Foreign Aid, in the fourth, but these usually work as subcommittees within the jurisdiction of the legislative working groups of the parliamentary party.

The multiplicity of interests within the CDU/CSU is not exhausted by these formations. Although no parliamentary organization exists along denominational lines and the denominational issue has been declining in importance, continuing awareness of the need for representation of both Catholics and Protestants at all levels of the party justifies considering these as potential groups. Still other interests, rising and falling with the issues, have similar status.

The formation of groups on the parliamentary level is accepted as a legitimate expression of the heterogeneity of the party, and of the group basis of its extraparliamentary organization. The leading groups receive organizational and financial support from the parliamentary, the federal, or the *Land* organizations of the party. They contribute to the aggregation and expression of special viewpoints, and to the recruitment of the party's parliamentary personnel. However, nearly one-fourth of the Members avoid explicit association with any groups, and among these is found the core of the parliamentary leadership of the party. Numbering seventy-eight in the third Bundestag, they included the parliamentary party chairman, two of five deputy chairmen, eight of the thirty-one further members of the executive committee, two of the five chairmen of the working groups, six of the party's fifteen chairmen of Bundestag committees, and the party foremen (*Obleute*) in six further committees. This leading group, composed chiefly of professional politicians, therefore has the task of producing a unified party position. The formal organization of the parliamentary party is an instrument to that end.

Caucus. The essentials of this organization, in common with that in the other parliamentary parties, are the meeting of all the members of the parliamentary party or caucus, the executive committee (*Vorstand*), and the working groups (*Arbeitskreise*). The caucus, formally the ultimate authority, is a semipublic meeting which takes place at least once during every week that the Bundestag or its committees are in session, on the average five times monthly. Although the caucus nominally consists of all members of the CDU/CSU in the Bundestag, the average attendance is one-half to two-thirds of the membership, dropping off as the meeting, which tends to last nearly three hours, progresses. A handful of the party's Cabinet ministers take part, depending very much upon the subjects under discussion. In addition, attendance includes, in a nonvoting capacity, members of the parliamentary party's employed staff, "friendly" newspapermen including representatives of some of the largest German newspapers, senior civil servants who are party members, if the subject touches their ministries, occasionally party members of the Bundesrat or chairmen of the parliamentary parties in the Landtage, officials of the national party organization, and even representatives of interest groups. Although the meetings do not take place in public, their composition in itself assures that their proceedings will not remain secret. The newspapers publish extensive reports, the party issues press releases, and, in cases of great controversy, Members on opposing sides are likely to appeal directly to the public.

Minutes of the proceedings are kept, in which the discussion is summarized and important remarks are transcribed *verbatim*. Although not published, a dozen copies are mimeographed for the use of the parliamentary leaders and for office files, providing a record whose existence contributes to the formality of the meeting.

The character of the meeting—its size, frequency, lengthy agenda, and composition—and the diversity of interest among its Members limit its value as a deliberative assembly. It is a forum for the expression of views, an organ of ratification, and, occasionally, an electoral body. The success of the caucus in achieving a unified party position depends on the care with which its meetings are prepared. This is in part the task of the six working groups which function as committees of the parliamentary party. They were first established in the CDU/CSU after the 1953 elections, which saw party ranks in the Bundestag grow from 144 to 250 Members. Members of other parties viewed them critically at first, as undermining the work of the Bundestag committees.[56] By the next term, however, both the SPD and the FDP had created them also, demonstrating that they had become an organizational necessity.

Working Groups. In the CDU/CSU in the fifth Bundestag, there are working groups on General and Legal Questions, Economic Policy, Financial Policy, Social Policy, Foreign and Defense Policy, and Science and Publishing.[57] Each of the six is open to all Members, but in practice membership consists of the members of the Bundestag committees whose subjects it covers. Attendance varies with individual interests. Each working group has an executive consisting of its chairman, deputy chairman, and the chairmen or party foremen on the relevant Bundestag committees.[58] The chairmen of the groups are elected by the caucus, usually on a single slate and without discussion, on the recommendation of the parliamentary party's executive committee. Chairmen of Bundestag committees are almost never elected as chairmen of the working groups—an indication of the dispersion of

[56] For a good description of the organization of the CDU/CSU caucus, see "Die Kunst, eine Fraktion zu lenken," *DZ*, Dec. 28, 1957. Cf. Domes, *op. cit.*, pp. 40–46.

[57] For a discussion of the working groups, see Domes, *op. cit.*, pp. 40–43. For their organization at the start of the fifth Bundestag, see *Die Welt*, November 10, 1965.

[58] *Arbeitsordnung der CDU/CSU Bundestagsfraktion*, 2. Bundestag (mimeographed, n.d.), par. 4.

power within the party. One chairmanship, that of the group on foreign policy, has been continuously held by a single individual, the party's prominent foreign affairs spokesman, Ernst Majonica. In other positions, tenure has not been as great. The groups on legal and financial questions have tended to be chaired by experts in these fields who were, furthermore, past or potential ministers. Karl Weber, for example, a leading member of the German Bar Association, headed the working group on General and Legal Questions during the third and fourth Bundestage, until he became Minister of Justice; in the fifth Bundestag, Ernst Benda, who had just missed succeeding Weber in the Ministry, became the group's chairman. The group on Financial Policy has been chaired by Werner Dollinger, who later became Minister of Federal Property, by Franz Etzel, after he had been Finance Minister, and by Wolfgang Pohle, a prominent leader of business interests in the party. The chairmanships of the groups on Economic and Social Policy have been quite definitely reserved for leaders of the relevant interest groups. The chairmen of the first, Kurt Schmücker (later Minister of Economics), Peter Brand, and Alfred Burgemeister, have invariably been prominent businessmen and members of the "discussion group on middle-class (small-business) affairs"; the chairmen of the second, Peter Horn, Hans Schütz, Josef Stingl, have consistently been trade unionists and members of the labor group of the parliamentary party. This exemplifies the extent to which the working groups are led by Members identified with related interest and professional groups within the party. In many cases, the chairmanships have been stepping stones to higher office; at the very least, they have provided their incumbents with secure positions of influence.

The working groups, which meet weekly, are responsible for preparing recommendations on pending bills and other questions of parliamentary policy and tactics for the caucus. They make proposals regarding the party position in the relevant Bundestag committees, and, in some cases, prepare bills for submission to the Bundestag in the name of the party. *Ad hoc* committees are usually formed within them, and even between them, to deal with particular legislative projects. They hear interest representatives and confer with civil servants and ministers. One of their most important functions is to educate their members to a legislative specialty, which is for most Representatives the first step to achieving a position of influence within the party and the House. In the informality of the working group, the individual Member has the best chance to express himself, to exchange views, and to gain competence on a particular subject. Their chief weakness as policy-making bodies is their specialization. Although their membership cuts across the interest groups within the parliamentary party, their deliberations attract primarily the best informed, and therefore usually the most "interested" Members on the subject in question. Their conclusions may be correspondingly unrepresentative of the caucus. The limit to their one-sidedness is the possibility that their recommendations will be contested in the caucus, a likelihood which is great only if the "specialists" are not in complete agreement, or are not in agreement with the experts in the Government.

Executive Committee. To avoid the disintegrating consequences of this specialization, the working groups in the CDU/CSU are closely tied to the parliamentary party's executive committee. Subjects are referred to the working group by the executive committee, often with policy recommendations, and the chairmen of the working groups are ex-officio members of the executive committee. The executive tries to hold the reins, therefore, not only of the caucus as a whole, but of its working groups as well.

The executive committee consists of the chairman of the parliamentary party, four to six deputy chairmen, two or three whips, the six chairmen of the working groups, sixteen members elected by the caucus, and eight to twelve additional members co-opted by the remainder of the executive with the approval of the caucus. The entire body is chosen at the beginning of the parliamentary term, subject to a second election after one year.[59] A carefully balanced slate of nominations for the sixteen elected places is presented by the outgoing executive committee. Additional nominations, which may be made by any member of the parliamentary party, tend to double the number of candidates. Every Member casts sixteen votes in the resulting ballot, with a majority required to elect.[60] Although certain candidates will clearly be identifiable as spokesmen of particular groups, and the trading of votes among groups takes place, the election is also a popularity contest whose result will not guarantee group balance. The co-optation of the remaining Members of the executive committee, by those who are elected, is designed to achieve that balance.

[59] *Ibid.*, par. 5, 7.   [60] *Ibid.*, par. 7(3).

The integration of the parliamentary party through a system of group representation extends to the choice of the deputy chairmen. There is generally no contest for these positions, but instead an apportionment of them among the major regional, religious, and economic groups within the party. The chairman of the CSU group receives one place, representatives of the labor, farm, and business groups usually receive others, and considerations of denominational parity as well as the desire to include a woman, also govern the selection.[61] The number of deputy chairmanships has even been adapted to meet the needs of group balance. When the CSU Protestant leader, Werner Dollinger, entered the Cabinet in 1962, and was replaced as parliamentary leader of the party by a Catholic, Strauss, the prospect that three out of four deputy chairmen would be Catholic produced a search, openly discussed in the press, for a Protestant candidate for a fifth deputy chairmanship. A suitable candidate was found in Ernst Lemmer, who had just lost his Cabinet post, and he was duly elected.[62] For the sake of regional balance, a sixth deputy chairman was elected in 1965. In view of the method of their selection, the authority of the deputy chairmen is largely limited to serving as spokesmen for the groups they represent.

Chairman. The party's efforts to fill its two highest positions, that of chairman and that of whip, require a different recruitment formula than proportional representation and provide a test of its cohesion as a political organization. The only election contest for the chairmanship occurred in 1955 when Heinrich von Brentano, who had held the position from the beginning, became Foreign Minister. In a three-sided contest, Heinrich Krone, the incumbent whip, an old-time professional Center party politician and Reichstag Member during the Weimar Republic, defeated Kurt-Georg Kiesinger, Brentano's rival for the Foreign Ministry, and Karl Müller, a diversionary third candidate. Out of 250 Members of the parliamentary party, only 216 cast valid votes—a demonstration of incomplete participation by the member-

[61] The CSU has had a deputy chairman successively in Strauss, Stücklen, Höcherl, Dollinger, and Strauss. The business group has had Kunze, Burgemeister, Schmücker and Brand, successively, in the deputy chairmanship, covering most of the period since the beginning of the second Bundestag, with the exception of 1957–1960, and 1963–1964. The labor group has had deputy chairmen continuously in Albers, Arnold, Arndgen, and Blank; the agriculture group has had a deputy chairman in Struve since 1957.

[62] *Die Welt,* Jan. 22, and Feb. 13, 1963.

ship in even the most important decisions of the caucus. Krone won 122 votes to 83 for Kiesinger and 11 for Müller, hardly an overwhelming victory, despite the support which Krone had from Adenauer and the incumbent leadership. Krone was re-elected without opposition in 1957 with 203 out of 210 votes cast. When he was appointed to the Cabinet in 1961, at the same time that Brentano relinquished his Government post, the latter's resumption of the chairmanship was taken for granted. Brentano received 165 out of 179 votes cast, without an opponent.[63]

The real test occurred two years later, when Brentano's illness and subsequent death created the need for a successor. The emergence of a new leader, from the postwar political generation, without an open electoral contest, illustrates the qualifications which the position requires and the process by which it can be filled. The new chairman, Rainer Barzel, trained in law, had become prominent in the government of North Rhine–Westphalia where, as a protégé of the Minister-President and leader of the CDU labor wing, Karl Arnold, he had risen to one of the highest ranks in the civil service before he reached thirty. A political appointee, Barzel left his government post when Arnold's CDU Cabinet was overthrown in 1956, and served for a year as salaried party manager in North Rhine–Westphalia. On the strength of his position in the party, he was nominated as its candidate for the Bundestag in the rock-ribbed CDU constituency in which he lived; the incumbent, an old party stalwart, was given a promising place on the *Land* list. During his first term in the House, Barzel served on the important Economic Affairs Committee and as an alternate on the committees on Defense and on Cultural Policy. A fairly active participant in debate on a variety of economic and cultural subjects, and a sharp partisan intensely loyal to the party's Cabinet leaders, particularly the Chancellor, he was a spokesman for Catholic social policy and a blatant anticommunist. In keeping with the position of his mentor, Barzel joined the labor group in the parliamentary party on the basis of his membership in a Catholic labor union, although he had never come close to being a workingman. But he did not exclusively identify with any faction, winning respect from many sides, including the Chancellor. After his re-election in 1961, Adenauer charged him with the preparation of a report on the party's basic principles. This

[63] The contested election took place at the caucus of June 15, 1955 (see *Die Welt,* June 16, 1955, Nov. 6, 1957, and Nov. 25, 1961).

gained Barzel a place on the agenda of the party's national conference in 1962, although the synthetic quality of his disquisition hardly established him as an accomplished theoretician.

At the beginning of his second term in the House, he was elected to the executive committee of the parliamentary party, coming in tenth in the contest for sixteen places, with 139 out of 189 votes. When the Adenauer Cabinet was reorganized after the "*Spiegel* affair" in December, 1962, Barzel was appointed Minister for All-German Questions, a post which he relinquished within ten months, however, when Erhard became Chancellor. Refusing to accept another Government post after FDP leader Mende had successfully demanded his portfolio, Barzel returned to the parliamentary party as that rare hero in German politics, a Cabinet minister who had not clung to office. He was immediately elected deputy chairman of the party, this time receiving 131 out of 161 votes without opposition. Among his three colleagues as deputy chairmen, he alone enjoyed general support. One of them, Strauss, held the post as CSU chairman, one, Detlef Struve, represented the farm bloc, and the third, Josef Arndgen, was the representative of the labor group, and was, at the age of nearly seventy, ready to retire.

Barzel found himself in this advantageous position just after party chairman Brentano had been compelled to withdraw from the parliamentary scene because of serious illness. It was the consensus that Barzel would serve as acting chairman, a position in which he distinguished himself by his tactful, restrained conduct of the meeting, a preference for avoiding issues in order to preserve party unity, and an instinctive awareness of the group divisions within the party. Upon Brentano's death, a year later, he had no challenger for the chairmanship and was elected in his own right by 179 out of 189 votes cast.[64]

In his rapid rise to the chairmanship by the age of forty, Barzel had touched base with most of the major influence groups within the party, the party organization of the largest *Land* in the federation, the Catholic labor unions, the business representatives on the Bundestag Economic Affairs Committee, the party's ideologues, the parliamentary executive committee, and the Cabinet leadership. He had developed a professional touch in reconciling the conflicting claims of

[64] *Die Welt,* Dec. 4, 1963, and Dec. 2, 1964. After refusing to consider a Cabinet post, he was re-elected chairman without a contest at the start of the fifth Bundestag (*Die Welt,* Oct. 19, 1965).

the groups within the parliamentary party, and experience in managing its complex organization. He had demonstrated his capacity as a peacemaker during the difficult period of Brentano's illness, Erhard's accession, Adenauer's retirement, and Strauss's challenge. His assumption of the chairmanship demonstrated that the party could produce, and could recognize, the type of leader it needed in order to remain intact, and could permit him to emerge without a series of divisive votes.

Whip. The office of chief whip has changed hands only once, when, in 1955, Krone, its first occupant, obtained the chairmanship. At that time the full significance of the whip as the party's main parliamentary tactician was not yet apparent, because the development of informal norms of procedure out of the tactical relationships among the parties had not yet progressed very far. Under these circumstances, a small group of party leaders were able to select Krone's successor by employing sharp practices to avoid a genuine consultation of the party. Their choice was Will Rasner, a little-known thirty-five-year old newspaper man, only recently a party member, in his first term in the Bundestag. Apparently aware of his tactical gifts, a number of CDU Cabinet ministers strongly pushed Rasner for the post. At a special evening meeting of the caucus, called without warning, and attended by only ninety Members, the executive committee proposed a slate of five Members who were to undertake special assignments in various fields on behalf of the party. The proposal of Rasner as whip was presented as one of these special assignments, to camouflage the importance of the choice. A heated discussion ensued, nevertheless, in which the executive committee skillfully assuaged the misgivings of various Members about Rasner. In the end, the joint proposal received 60 affirmative and 5 negative votes, with 25 abstentions.[65] Rasner was never directly challenged again, as his skill and influence grew in the job. Intermittent appointments of additional whips to share the position never diminished his primacy.

Sources of Cohesion. The division of the CDU/CSU into special-interest groups is therefore reflected up to the highest councils of the parliamentary party, short of the chairmanship and the position of parliamentary whip. The executive's representative character makes it not only a heterogeneous body, but a sizable one as well. Among its forty members, another hierarchy exists. A "Council of Eleven," con-

[65] The caucus took place on July 6, 1955, from 8:00 to 8:45 P.M. Cf. *Der Spiegel*, July 20, 1955, p. 8.

Plate V. A special committee of the Bundestag on the reform of the criminal code hearing testimony in a closed session. (Courtesy of Presse- und Informationsamt der Bundesregierung.)

Plate VI. A meeting of the CDU/CSU parliamentary party. (Courtesy of Presse- und Informationsamt der Bundesregierung.)

sisting of the chairman, the deputy chairmen, the whip, and the chairmen of the working groups, provides the leadership within the large executive body. The Council meets privately, without any ministerial participation, in advance of each meeting of the executive committee, officially to prepare the agenda of the executive meeting but actually to discuss its contents as well.

The executive in turn meets regularly in advance of the caucus, taking the initiative in all major policy decisions. It refers subjects to the working groups together with a recommendation of the policy framework within which the matter is to be considered, hears reports from their chairmen, and prepares the meeting of the caucus by determining its agenda and formulating recommendations on all major questions. The importance of its decisions is illustrated by the presence at its meetings of a larger contingent of ministers, on the average, than that which attends the caucus itself. The demonstration of the executive's effectiveness is its ability to get its recommendations accepted by the caucus in 85 to 90 per cent of all cases.[66] This is also a sign of its sensitivity to the will of the membership.

The caucus itself serves largely to ratify the policy of the executive committee. The agenda of the meeting, prepared by the executive but not issued to the Members in advance, is liable to consist of so many separate items—nominally all questions before the Bundestag that week—that its accomplishment within the three hours available for the caucus places all discussion under great pressure of time. Although the meeting may be composed of one hundred and fifty to two hundred participants when it begins, only a perfunctory set of rules guides its procedure. They state, for example, that no quorum shall be necessary for taking decisions, and make the following provision for caucus deliberation:

> The discussion of the agenda takes place in such a manner, that on the reports of the rapporteurs of the working groups questions may be asked by non-members of the respective working groups and answered by the rapporteur. Thereafter the position of the caucus will be determined.[67]

The desultory discussion which takes place under these circumstances demoralizes backbench participation, limits attendance to begin with, and causes the meeting to peter out as the hours drone on

[66] Jürgen Domes, op. cit., p. 44. This is confirmed by the author's interviews with Members of the parliamentary party and its officials.

[67] Arbeitsordnung der CDU/CSU Bundestagsfraktion, 2. Bundestag (mimeographed, n.d.), par. 3.

and more and more Members leave. The position of the executive is certain to be defended by the experts who have prepared it in the working groups, placing any opposition to it at a disadvantage. Only when the experts are divided, or an issue is so general that expertise is not important, is it possible to persuade the caucus, or a considerable minority within it, of a view contrary to that of the executive. The practice in such cases is to stop short of a vote and to refer the matter back for further discussion in the executive, or in an *ad hoc* group of the interested members, in an attempt to develop a broader consensus. In these situations much depends on the chairman's support among Members not affiliated with any of the interest groups within the party, his ability to maintain a balance of power among the groups, and his skill in determining the sense of the meeting without resorting to a vote, which is regarded as a divisive procedure. In any case, by the time the caucus is prepared to vote at the end of a discussion of a particularly controversial subject, only a minority of its Members are likely to still be present.

The complex organization of the party provides the mechanism for maintaining cohesion, but not for exercising strong leadership. The hierarchy of the decision-making process assures the clearance of all policy proposals with the main interest groups within the party, and the formation of a consensus. It all but precludes decisions to which there is any substantial objection, producing stalemate more readily than the resolution of conflict.

The incentives and sanctions available to maintain discipline are varied but subtle. The rules of the caucus, although specifically repudiating compulsory voting discipline, oblige Members who are unwilling to accept the decision of the majority "to express their divergent viewpoint promptly to the caucus and its chairman." [68] The social pressure which this rule implies, and the knowledge that disunity will favor what is likely to be a united opposition, constitute some incentive for party dissidents to follow the party line. Respect for expertise and a general apathy among a large proportion of backbenchers make the development of dissent unlikely. Responsibility for governing

[68] *Ibid.*, par. 10. The rules (par. 8) also provide for a three-member Council of Elders within the parliamentary party. It was activated at the beginning of the fifth Bundestag, as an agency to mediate such differences among Members as seemed susceptible to quiet negotiation. Heinrich Krone, a Cabinet minister and former chairman of the parliamentary party, was named to head this Council. *Die Welt,* Nov. 24, 1965.

has at times also been an important unifying force for the party. Adenauer was able to exploit it with particular success to obtain united support for his policies, especially in foreign affairs, but in doing so he imposed discipline over the heads of the parliamentary leaders and weakened their position.

With the decline of Adenauer's influence and his retirement, the parliamentary leaders have had to rely more heavily on their own resources. The Chancellor and the Cabinet, no longer supplying unquestioned leadership in any field, have become another source of demands upon the parliamentary party, to be reconciled with the others. The relationship between Cabinet and parliamentary party, nowhere institutionalized, takes a great variety of forms, from the participation of civil servants in the party's working groups, to the presence of ministers in the meetings of its executive committee and caucus, to the constant informal conferences in person and by telephone between Members and ministers. The party chairman, in particular, plays a central role as mediator between the Cabinet and its parliamentary followers, a function which Krone and Barzel have both performed with particular skill. But while, for Krone, the objective of this mediation was to provide a coherent parliamentary majority for the Cabinet, for Barzel the aim has been to expand the influence of the parliamentary leaders over the Cabinet.

The chairman and whip, as the top leaders of the parliamentary party, control little patronage and few favors to enable them to compel support for their lead among their followers in the House. Ministerial portfolios are few, their redistribution rare, and their assignment not exclusively in the hands of the parliamentary leaders. Nevertheless, the Cabinet has been increasingly recruited from among the parliamentary party leadership, and the hope for office is unquestionably a source of cohesion among its more prominent Members. Choice parliamentary positions, especially on Bundestag committees, are assigned according to so many criteria that they cannot be used for specific disciplinary purposes. While a general concern for party cohesion governs the making of committee assignments, they are drawn up by a special committee on committees, representative of all sections of the party, at the beginning of the term, and only rarely altered in midsession. Parliamentary favors, such as inclusion on international junkets, are distributed by the working groups. Efforts to discipline Members by intervention in their constituencies are very difficult to undertake, due to the decentralization of the nominations procedure. This leaves small prizes, such as favorable office space and staff assistance, for the parliamentary whips to dispense, but they do not go far to effect discipline. The threat of expulsion from the party has been used only as a weapon of last resort, notably in the case of the maverick, Gerd Bucerius, a prominent publisher and Bundestag Member, who resigned from his seat and from the party after being censured for views expressed in his publications.

In policy making, the leadership must therefore operate largely within the consensus which it can produce after consulting all factions within the party. But in day-to-day tactics, which have decided significance for policy, the leaders have much more discretion. For in the execution of its decisions, the party must rely from moment to moment on the skill of the whips, who work closely with the chairman. They are its tactical leaders on the floor of the Bundestag; its representatives in procedural negotiations with the other parties, directly or through the Council of Elders; its contact men with the Cabinet, the national party organization, and with sister parties in the Landtage on questions of coordination and timing; its press spokesmen; and its chiefs of staff. The position of the whips differs from that of their counterparts in the House of Commons as does the German from the British parliamentary party organization. They lack the prestige, power, and sources of information which come with membership in the Cabinet, since they are officers of a parliamentary organization which is separate from the Government. But they perform some of the same functions "behind the chair" as their British counterparts, and have an even greater liberty to make arrangements which suit them.

The small but growing staff, which adds to the effectiveness of the organization, and therefore to the influence of the chairman and the whips, consisted of fifty-three employees in the CDU/CSU by the end of the fourth Bundestag. These party employees are paid out of the appropriation which the House makes to the parliamentary parties. About half of the staff members provide clerical help, but a group of nine are research assistants, one or two for each of the working groups, and one for the labor group. There are administrative assistants for the chairman, the head of the CSU group, and the parliamentary whips; and two press secretaries, an archivist, bookkeepers, and office workers.

The increasing power of the whips has never really been sanctioned by the caucus and has been a growing source of grumbling among the backbenchers. But the whips' influence is a direct expression of the cumbersomeness of the party's decision-making machinery, which leaves a power vacuum on questions requiring quick action. Without a basic reorganization of the party, a change in the system of checks and balances among the groups, and the development of new sources of influence for the other leaders, the restriction of the whips' power would only diminish the party's effectiveness in Parliament. For the organization and procedure of the Bundestag is by now so heavily dependent on the informal norms which have grown out of the post-war relationship of the parties with each other, that all parties require the tactical leadership of experts in the subtleties of the folkways of the Bundestag.

Relations between Parliamentary and Extraparliamentary Party. The parliamentary party not only performs important functions within the Bundestag, but also plays an important role in the national party organization. Containing a very large proportion of the CDU's most prominent leaders, and convening with great frequency, it is in a dominant position within the party structure. In fact, it antedates the national organization of the CDU by over a year. Not until the autumn of 1950 was a federation of CDU *Land* organizations established at the national level. It then developed under the effective control of the party leader who occupied the highest governmental position in the country at the time, Chancellor Adenauer, who was elected national party chairman, a post he held until 1966. From the start, parliamentary leaders held key positions in the party's extraparliamentary organization. The twenty-four members of the "inner executive" elected at the 1960 party Congress included thirteen Members of the Bundestag, for example, and among the fifty-nine members elected to the federal executive committee as a whole there were thirty-four Members of the Bundestag. Altogether, 55 per cent of the CDU Members of Parliament occupied leading party positions outside the House during the third Bundestag.[69]

This has protected the parliamentary party from outside dictation of the kind common during the Weimar Republic. But it has also placed on it the additional burden of supplying leadership for the party nationally. During the years of Adenauer's supremacy—between the

[69] Rudolf Wildenmann, *Partei und Fraktion* (Meisenheim: Verlag Anton Hain, 1955), pp. 154–60; Domes, *op. cit.*, pp. 46–7.

time he effectively subjugated the party's *Land* leaders in 1949–1950, and the party controversy over the party's presidential candidate in 1959—Adenauer supplied this leadership personally. But with the decline of Adenauer's power after 1959, the appearance of various centers of influence within the party produced serious challenges to party unity. The trend manifested itself in the assertion of power by some of the party's most ambitious leaders in the *Länder*, notably Strauss, who took over the chairmanship of the Bavarian CSU in 1961. It also showed in the unprecedented challenge to Adenauer demonstrated by the party congress in 1962, when it created a national party manager beside the national chairman. The separation between the Chancellorship and the party chairmanship, when Erhard succeeded Adenauer as head of Government, but not as national party leader, in 1963, threatened another division of power. When the two offices were again combined in one man, upon Erhard's election to the party chairmanship in 1966, it was at the price of an expansion of the party presidium to twelve members, ten of them Members of the Bundestag.[70] With the parliamentary party increasingly the meeting place of all the contending leaders of the national party, it has become the framework for intraparty controversies of all kinds, over questions of leadership, patronage, organization, electoral strategy, parliamentary tactics, and governmental policy. Thus the parliamentary party stands at the center of the entire party organization, free, without question, from control by extraparliamentary party bodies, but challenged to serve as an organ of integration for the party not only in the Bundestag, but everywhere else as well.

SPD

The SPD is, by comparison with the CDU/CSU, a far more homogeneous party. Although it was torn by dissent on important issues in the 1950's, and on questions of leadership more recently, the opposing positions were not taken by established groups within it. Differences have usually been expressions of old rivalries, of past issues or ideological positions, or of differing calculations about the momentary advantages of alternative party tactics. Some divisions of opinion have existed between different *Land* organizations of the party, or between the national and the local organizations, reflecting the fact that the party has been in power in some states and localities, while in opposi-

[70] *Die Welt,* March 15, 24, 1966.

tion in others as well as nationally. The labor union affiliations of Members have sometimes affected their views, especially on social welfare issues, but the unions have not generally spoken with one voice. However, none of these differences have produced organized interest groups. Furthermore, despite its extensive organization on *Land* and local levels, the national organization of the party is far more powerful than it is in the CDU, and acts as a unifying force.

Rather than the reconciliation of diverse interests within the party, the problem of the SPD in the Bundestag has been to take positions sufficiently broad to extend its traditional electoral appeal. While the CDU/CSU has from the start been a horizontal party, embracing a diversity of interests and cutting across traditional class lines, the SPD was in the past a party with a definite class appeal and associated with particular interests. In a multiparty system its electoral base had the advantage of stability. But with the reduction of the number of parties, its problem has been to extend that base. Confinement to the status of opposition has made the transformation difficult. The SPD has not had responsibility for national government, and has lacked access to official information and to government officials, placing it at a disadvantage, in comparison with the CDU, in the development of pragmatic new policies which could be identified with the national interest. On the other hand, it has not had to face the particular problem of coordinating the views of the parliamentary party with those of its leadership in Government.

Working Groups. For all these reasons, the organization of the SPD in the Bundestag has developed differently from that of the CDU/CSU. There are no separate interest groups within its parliamentary party, with their own meetings, officers and staffs, with the possible exception of those Members belonging to the same or similar labor union who act together on some issues *ad hoc*. There is greater emphasis on the working groups, of which there are eight, each with one or more research assistants and secretaries. These groups deal respectively with foreign policy, internal policy, economics, social policy, appropriations and finance, refugees and expellees, law, and security. Most are further subdivided into study groups corresponding to the jurisdiction of the Bundestag committees, so that the SPD has a group system largely paralleling that of the House itself.[71] The chair-

[71] The working groups of all three caucuses are listed in Trossmann, *op. cit.*, p. 47. For the SPD they are also reported, with their chairmen, in the party yearbook

man and deputy chairman of each working group, elected by the caucus, are in most cases either the chairman or the party's foreman (*Obmann*) in the main Bundestag committees within the purview of that working group. Personal rivalries create occasional exceptions. But by contrast to the CDU/CSU, the SPD feels less need to distribute the chairmanships in the Bundestag committees and the working groups among different Members and interests, and greater need to develop subject expertise among its Members. Even more than in the CDU/CSU, the chairmen enjoy considerable continuity in office.[72]

All bills, resolutions, and interpellations which the SPD introduces in the Bundestag receive their initial consideration in the working groups. Feeling itself cut off from the Government bureaucracy, the SPD relies for its expertise on its working groups to a greater extent than the other parties do. Neither confronted with so many internal divisions as the CDU/CSU, nor subject so directly to the initiatives of the Government, the SPD usually allows the policy-making process to originate in the working groups, rather than in the executive committee. The groups are not only subdivided into study groups, but all of their active members undertake a subspecialization within the subject covered by the group.[73]

Although each group is nominally open to all Members, invitations to its meetings go to the thirty to sixty Members of the Bundestag committees whose subject is within the group's jurisdiction. The actual work is done by a small core of regulars, among whom the chairman— who schedules the work, directs the staff, and leads the meetings—is by far the most influential. In the course of their work, the groups may invite outside party experts or the staffs of the national party committees for advice, receive written or oral testimony from specialists or interest groups, occasionally at public hearings, and draw upon *Länder* ministries which stand under Social Democratic leadership. By

---

(see *Jahrbuch der Sozialdemokratischen Partei Deutschlands,* 1956/57, p. 11; 1960/61, p. 181; 1962/63, p. 178. See also *Vorwärts,* Aug. 10, 1956 and Dec. 6, 1957). For a reference to the study groups, see *Die Welt,* Jan. 19, 1963.

[72] Seven changes occurred in the chairmanships of the eight working groups in the two parliamentary terms after their establishment. Two were caused by the death of their incumbents (Maier, Reitzner), two by the elevation of the individuals to higher offices (Schoettle, Erler), two by a voluntary curtailment of activities by the individuals involved (Deist, Arndt), and one by resignation from the Bundestag (Wittrock). At the beginning of the fifth Bundestag in 1965, all incumbent chairmen were re-elected (*Die Welt,* November 25, 1965).

[73] Karl Mommer in *Vorwärts,* Jan. 24, 1958.

the time a working group is ready to submit a parliamentary motion to the caucus for its consideration, it has not only formulated the position the party should take but has drafted the relevant resolution and nominated the speakers to defend it in the Bundestag. When the caucus has acted, it becomes the responsibility of the working group to see the measure through the parliamentary stages, and especially to supervise the committee stage. For new Members willing to work actively, the working groups offer the first opportunity to develop a specialty and make a name for themselves; for the less active, they offer an orientation to party policy in one area.

Executive Committee. As in the CDU/CSU, the executive committee of the party occupies a most important position. No matter comes before the caucus without first being considered in the executive, so that it is to the executive committee that the working groups report. The executive consists of the chairman, four deputy chairmen, the parliamentary whips, and sixteen additional members, all elected by the caucus.[74] The chairmen of the working groups are not ex-officio members of the executive, though in fact they usually are elected to it. They do, in any case, participate in its sessions without vote.

Within the executive, an "inner executive"—consisting of the chairman, the deputy chairmen, and the parliamentary whips—meets weekly, in advance of the session of the larger body, to discuss the major policy questions. When the executive committee meets, it receives the recommendations of this circle of leaders, and the specific proposals of the working groups. Since the executive is broadly representative of the main currents of opinion in the party, the reception it gives the recommendations made to it is very likely to indicate the reaction of the caucus. If recommendations are made to the caucus unanimously, they are likely to be accepted. It is the function of the executive committee to attempt to reconcile conflicting positions among the leaders or the specialists, or conflicts of views among working groups, to relate specific recommendations for parliamentary action to the general policy and interests of the party, and to anticipate any opposition among the rank and file. Often this requires that the recommendations of the working groups be modified or referred

[74] *Geschäftsordnung der Fraktion der SPD im Bundestag,* in the version adopted on Oct. 23, 1957, par. 10. Under a provision adopted in 1965, party members of the Bundestag presidium are *ex-officio* deputy chairmen of the parliamentary party (*Die Welt,* Oct. 20, 1965).

back for further consideration. As the intermediary between the caucus and its specialized working groups, a major function of the executive is to prepare the meetings of the caucus. Loyalty of the members of the executive to the decisions it takes, even if controversy has attended them, diminishes the likelihood of controversy on the floor of the caucus itself. But occasionally working groups do appeal the decisions of the executive to the caucus.

Caucus. The caucus is not entirely a perfunctory meeting. It is a somewhat more important decision-making body than its CDU/CSU counterpart, because it is smaller and more formally organized, because its working groups exercise more initiative, because it is not divided by organized factions, and because its decisions bind its members more effectively. The caucus, which meets weekly when the House or its committees are in session, has before it a mimeographed agenda prepared by the executive, and the text of all resolutions up for its consideration. A majority constitutes a quorum, and attendance is generally somewhat better than that, averaging between two-thirds and three-quarters of the nominal membership. Attendance of outsiders is limited to the research assistants of the parliamentary party and the national party organization, and to a half-dozen correspondents of the party press. Much less is reported of the meetings than of their CDU/CSU counterparts. Only brief minutes are kept, summarizing the decisions taken.

A heavy agenda must be disposed of in the three hours or so available for the meeting, including all of the issues before the Bundestag during the week and such time-consuming organizational matters as elections and the appointment of delegations to make foreign tours. Many items are dealt with in rapid fashion, with a brief report from the *rapporteur* of a working group, and a three- or four-sentence summary from the Member chosen to express the party's view in the Bundestag, indicating what he will say. There may be some short contributions from other Members. But in more than 90 per cent of all cases the pressure of time allows nothing more. Only if there is disagreement among the leaders or the experts, or if a general issue touches traditional sensitivities within the party, such as questions of defense and rearmament, or, finally, if definite interests within the party are at stake, notably those of labor unions in particular industries, does the discussion become lively, occupy an hour's time, and end in a vote. The division is hardly ever between a united executive and the rank and file; more likely, it is a division between two working groups, within one, or between a working group and the executive, which deliberation in the executive committee has failed to reconcile.

Election of Officers. The elections conducted by the party caucus have performed a different function from those in the CDU/CSU, where elections mainly allocate offices according to the proportional claims of the factions. Offices in the SPD are filled at the beginning of the term of the Bundestag, for a twelve-month period, and twice thereafter for eighteen-month terms. Particularly since 1957, these frequent elections have been actively contested. They have been the instrument by which the parliamentary party has established parliamentary service and distinction, in place of party seniority or prominence outside the Bundestag, as the qualifications for membership on the parliamentary executive committee. In that year, disappointed over the party's third straight defeat in the Bundestag elections, the parliamentary party rebelled against the tradition of electing the party's national deputy chairman as parliamentary deputy chairman. In a contested election, with 148 out of 181 Members voting, the party's most distinguished parliamentarians, Carlo Schmid, Herbert Wehner, and Fritz Erler, received 131, 110, and 101 votes respectively, winning the three deputy chairmanships, against only 72 votes for Wilhelm Mellies, the party's national deputy chairman. At the same time, seven new members were elected to the parliamentary executive committee, all of them prominent as Members of the House. Three of the nominees presented by the incumbent executive committee, as well as the only trade union official nominated, were defeated.[75] In subsequent elections, the official slate of nominations presented by the executive committee in office was regularly amended by an equal number of nominations made by backbenchers. In 1958, Wehner resigned his parliamentary deputy chairmanship upon his election as a national deputy chairman. In a contest for the position, one of the new

[75] *FAZ*, Oct. 31, 1957; *Vorwärts*, Nov. 1, 1957. The newcomers were Deist, Schellenberg, Heinemann, Mattick, Conrad, Schmidt (Hamburg), and Schanzenbach; the executive nominees defeated were Seuffert, Strobel, and Neumann; the defeated trade unionist was Leber, new in the Bundestag, who did win a seat the following year.

members of the executive first elected the previous year, a noted parliamentary expert on economic questions, Heinrich Deist, won election. Two years later in 1960, two Members who had made outstanding parliamentary reputations in their first term, Gerhard Jahn and Friedrich Schäfer, won seats on the executive committee.[76]

After the Bundestag election of 1961, the parliamentary party again asserted its independence. It rejected the proposal of the national organization that it expand its executive committee to twenty, and include on it all Members, regardless of their parliamentary records, who had campaigned as part of the "government team" which the party had presented to the electorate. Several members of the "team," sensing the way the wind was blowing, finally declined to run. Three nominees of the outgoing executive were defeated, including two members of the "team." Of four newcomers to the executive, three were the nominees of backbenchers. In the same election, two of the newer members of the executive committee, Jahn and Schäfer, were chosen as parliamentary whips along with Mommer, an incumbent; the two other incumbents had resigned.[77]

The parliamentary party elections which occurred after the party's fifth straight electoral defeat in 1965 indicated another effort to bring forth new parliamentary leaders. Although no change was made in the chairmanship or among the whips, two new deputy chairmen were elected in addition to the four incumbents. One of them was Helmut Schmidt, first elected to the Bundestag in 1953, a parliamentary expert on defense policy, and a possible successor to Willy Brandt as the party's candidate for the Chancellorship. The other, Karl Schiller, although just elected to his first term in the Bundestag, had been actively sought by the parliamentary party because it badly needed the expertise in financial policy which he had developed in the Berlin government. In the elections to the executive committee, three incumbents were defeated and replaced by younger Members from those

[76] *FAZ*, June 19, 1958; *Die Welt*, March 16, 1960. In the 1958 contest, Deist defeated Blachstein, 88 to 44.

[77] *Die Welt*, Dec. 8, 1961. The executive nominees who were defeated were Brauer, Steinhoff, and Welke, the first two having been members of the "team." The newcomers were Frehsee, Sänger, Kurlbaum, and Strobel, the first three being nominees "from the floor." Möller, a member of the "team," a prominent *Land* leader and financial expert in the party, but just elected to the House, calculated his chances of winning election to the executive and withdrew. In the elections a year later, he was successful, and before the end of the parliamentary term, he had been elected to a deputy chairmanship.

regions of the country in which the party had done well electorally.[78]

Chairman. For a long time, the chairmanship of the parliamentary party was exempt from the standard that the party in the Bundestag should be led by its ablest parliamentarians. Loyalty to the party's national leader precluded competitive elections to the parliamentary chairmanship under Schumacher and Ollenhauer. Although Ollenhauer was a faithful and respected negotiator for the SPD in the Bundestag, he was neither the party's most effective parliamentary spokesman, nor its most popular figure electorally. Electoral consideration caused the party to nominate the mayor of Berlin, Willy Brandt, as its candidate for the Chancellorship in the election of 1961, but when the party failed to win office, Brandt resigned the Bundestag seat to which he had been elected to return to his position in Berlin, leaving the parliamentary leadership to Ollenhauer.

On Ollenhauer's death in 1963, however, the national and the parliamentary leadership were divided. Still the party's candidate for the Chancellorship, Brandt could not be denied the national chairmanship. But he could not lead the party in the Bundestag while mayor of Berlin. The parliamentary party therefore elected Fritz Erler as its chairman to replace Ollenhauer. A Member of the Bundestag from its beginning in 1949, specialist on foreign and, later, defense policy, he had been elected to the executive committee of the parliamentary party in 1953, and was one of the three new deputy chairmen elected in 1957. His awareness of the need to change the party's position on foreign affairs and defense in the 1950's distinguished him as one of its leading policy innovators, and his skill in debate and committee negotiation added to his effectiveness as a parliamentary leader. Erler's unchallenged elevation to the parliamentary party's chairmanship was a tribute to his outstanding performance in the House. He was re-elected, unopposed, in 1965.

The division between the national and the parliamentary chairmanships has not caused conflict, in part because in the interval since the parliamentary party rebelled against domination by national party officials, it has itself attained a certain domination in the councils of

---

[78] *Die Welt,* November 4, 1965. Because a change in rules (see note 74) had made two incumbent deputy chairmen, Carlo Schmid and Erwin Schoettle, into deputy chairmen ex officio, in their capacity as Vice Presidents of the Bundestag, the way had been cleared for the election of Schmidt and Schiller without a contest.

the national party. At the start of the fourth Bundestag, 26 out of 33 members of the national executive committee were Members of Parliament, although their number decreased after a succession of Members resigned from the House to resume—or assume—positions in *Land* governments. But many of those remaining were parliamentary leaders, whose position in the national executive grew out of their parliamentary prominence. Upon Brandt's election to the party chairmanship, Erler was added to Wehner as national deputy chairman, making seven of the nine leaders in the party's highest council, the presidium, Members of the Bundestag and party leaders there. The only exceptions were Brandt himself, and the party Treasurer, a full-time official. Under these circumstances, the party in the Bundestag was willing to re-elect Wehner to the parliamentary deputy chairmanship he had relinquished six years earlier out of respect for a separation between the parliamentary and the national leaderships.[79]

Sources of Cohesion. The small oligarchy of leaders who occupy the top positions in both the national and the parliamentary organizations contributes decisively to party cohesion. Their authority rests on democratic legitimation, particularly in the case of the parliamentary leaders who have achieved office in the competitive elections of recent years. Their control derives from the multiple positions they occupy (see Table 26). In the decision-making process within the party, the same group of leaders meets repeatedly, in different combinations at the various stages, and surrounded each time by different cadres of secondary leaders. Parliamentary working groups overlap with committees of the national executive; the national executive committee, its presidium, and its chairman and deputy chairmen form an interlocking directorate with the parliamentary executive, "inner executive", and chairmen. The parliamentary caucus includes a majority of the members of the other bodies.[80]

Throughout the policy-making process, the top leaders have the

---

[79] For the election of Brandt as party chairman, see *Die Welt*, Feb. 17, 1964. For the election of Erler to the parliamentary chairmanship, see *Die Welt*, March 4, 1964. In October, 1961, the following members of the national Executive Committee of the party were simultaneously Members of the Bundestag: Ollenhauer, Wehner, Albertz, Arndt, Brandt, Brauer, Deist, Erler, Franke, Heinemann, Herklotz, Keilhack, Menzel, Metzger, Möller, Pohle, Schanzenbach, Schellenberg, Schmid, Schmidt, Schoettle, Steinhoff, Strobel, Welke, Wienand, Zinn.

[80] See the illuminating analysis by Ulrich Dübber, "An den Stellwerken der Macht," *Die Neue Gesellschaft*, X (1963), 101–9.

Table 26. *Interlocking directorate of the SPD: Leadership positions held by Members of the executive committee of the parliamentary party (December, 1964)*

	Parliamentary organization			Party organization		
	Party foreman, Bundestag committee	Chairman, Bundestag committee	Chairman, working group	Party presidium	Party executive	Chairman of a committee of the executive
Chmn, Parliamentary Party						
Erler				—[a]	—	—
Deputy Chmn., Parl. Pty.						
Möller			—	—	—	—
Schmid	—			—	—	—
Schoettle		—		—	—	—
Wehner	—	—		—	—	—
Whips						
Mommer						
Schäfer						
Executive Committee						
Behrendt	—					
Blachstein						
Frehsee						
Heinemann					—	
Junghans	—					
Kurlbaum	—		—			
Leber					—	
Mattick						
Metzger					—	
Sänger						
Schanzenbach	—			—	—	—
Schellenberg		—	—		—	
Schmitt-Vockenhausen		—	—			
Strobel					—	—
Wienand	—		—		—	

[a] Dash indicates other positions held.

advantages of holding the most influential positions, of staying power, and of professional political skill. To achieve support, they can still appeal to traditional feelings of ideological and class solidarity, even though new programs and a slowly changing party composition are weakening these sources of cohesion. The traditional respect for majority rule in the caucus still persuades those who are in the minority on any issue to keep their differences within the family. During the first decade of the Bundestag, these traditions were strongly invoked to preserve party unity in the face of particularly divisive defense and foreign policy issues. Since that time, there has been a noticeable relaxation of discipline. During the first year of the fourth Bundestag, SPD Members in substantial numbers, about thirty in each case, refused to vote with their party in the House on the conspicuous issues of draft extension and the reduction of tariffs on automobile imports.[81] No formal sanctions were applied or threatened, and the leaders even took some pride in this novel demonstration of diversity within the party. Compared with the controversies of the 1950's, many of the differences occurring today are less fundamental, arising from specialization and division of labor among parliamentary Members, and from the differing interests of the various parliamentary constituencies. They do not appear to threaten the essential cohesion of the party but instead promise to increase the party's electoral appeal. However, the traditional feeling for unity places definite limits on how far deviation may go. It is taken for granted that those who disagree with the majority will speak up in the caucus, or inform the whips in advance. More important, it is expected that they will not speak against the party position in the House. Freedom of conscience is permitted, but at a price which robs it of much of its political effect.

Compared to the CDU/CSU, the Social Democratic leadership consists of a smaller, more homogeneous group, which confronts a party whose composition produces unity more readily than factionalism. This explains the SPD leaders' relatively greater influence far more than differences in the sanctions available to them. As the leaders of the Opposition, they control no ministerial positions although, because of the proportional representation of parties in the leadership of the Bundestag, they do have their share of parliamentary offices. Indicative of the relatively stronger position of the leaders in the SPD than in

[81] On the vote on the draft extension, see *Stuttgarter Zeitung*, Feb. 23, 1962; on the automobile tariff, *Dt. Btag.*, 4. W.P., 32. Sitz., May 22, 1962, pp. 1351-2.

the CDU/CSU, the initiative in making committee assignments is taken by the "inner executive" rather than by a special committee. But as in the CDU/CSU, many factors influence committee assignments. They cannot be used for specific disciplinary purposes. As in the other parties, therefore, the leaders cannot easily employ patronage and favors in the Bundestag in order to command support. However, due to the centralization and extent of the party organization nationally, they do have more effective extraparliamentary sanctions. Such extreme weapons as dismissal from party positions, intervention against renomination, and expulsion are employed more frequently in the SPD than they are in the CDU/CSU.

The day-to-day effectiveness of the party in the Bundestag depends on the whips, who do not, however, work as autonomously as their counterparts in the CDU/CSU, serving in a more coordinated fashion as the agents of the executive. Furthermore, the work has been divided among a number of men with separate responsibilities. Foremost among these since 1957 has been Karl Mommer, who has acted as main tactician on the floor, party spokesman in the Council of Elders, negotiator with his opposites in the other parties, and chief of the parliamentary staff. He works together with Friedrich Schäfer, who has at times had special responsibility for coordination between the parliamentary party and its counterparts in the parliaments of the Länder, and with a third whip responsible for legal questions, a role performed with notable skill by Adolf Arndt between 1949 and 1962.

Acutely aware of the disadvantage of the Opposition in not having ready access to the ministerial bureaucracy, the SPD has placed greater emphasis on the development of staff assistance than has any other party. Among the fifty-six employees on its staff, there were eighteen research assistants at the end of the fourth term of the Bundestag, twice as many as in the CDU/CSU, one working group having as many as four assistants. The staff also includes administrative assistants for the chairman and the whips, press secretaries, and office and clerical help. The size and skill of the staff, which primarily serves the leaders, contributes to their technical superiority over the rank-and-file Members of the party.

If the cohesion of the SPD depends on its traditions of solidarity and on a tight-knit leadership, rather than on the balance of power among factions which characterizes the CDU/CSU, the two parties share the problems of a sharp division between the active parliamentary professionals in positions of leadership and the apathy of large numbers of rank-and-file MP's. This is an expression both of the variety of types of Members who are elected to Parliament in both parties and the division of labor within the parliamentary parties produced by the complexity of the issues they confront and the organizational problems of size. In the absence of the interest groups of the CDU/CSU, the SPD contains a large number of backbenchers having no group affiliations within the parliamentary party, whose chief influence comes from their voting power in the caucus. To some extent social contacts enable them to develop common views and to concert their votes, giving the elected executive committee a truly representative character. But their participation in parliamentary politics is otherwise limited, if it exists at all, to narrow specialization in the working groups. The prominence of the parliamentary leadership, and its influence on policy, is all the more striking.

FDP

In form, the Free Democratic party maintains a parliamentary organization comparable to those of the other parties. In effect, however, the organization is quite different, if only because the FDP, with sixty-seven Members at the height of its success in the fourth Bundestag, has been one-fifth to one-third the size of the other parliamentary parties. It also has other distinguishing characteristics. Compared to the CDU/CSU, it has a more homogeneous membership, and a narrower electoral base, drawing its supporters, as well as its Members of Parliament, largely from the Protestant professional classes. Compared to the SPD, it is heir to political divisions rather than to unity and cohesion, and still suffers from controversies that have plagued German liberalism since the middle of the 19th century. Compared to both other parties, it has a far smaller membership, a weaker organization, and more limited financial resources, making it more dependent on individual contributors and more susceptible to their interests.

The party has endured a major split, occurring in 1956 between the Dehler wing in the Bundestag and the party's ministers in the Government, over the question of continued participation in the Adenauer Cabinet.[82] Conflicts among the *Länder* organizations of the party, especially between the conservative northern and the liberal southern

---

[82] *Die Welt*, Feb. 24, 1956.

groups, were frequent during the first decade of the Federal Republic and were reflected in rivalries among leaders and tension between the parliamentary, the national, and the *Land* organizations. The replacement of the irascible Thomas Dehler by Erich Mende as parliamentary party chairman in 1957, the merging of the parliamentary and national leaderships in the hands of Mende between 1960 and 1963, and FDP electoral gains in 1961 and re-entry into the Government diminished these conflicts, more because of the good fortune and skill of individual leaders than because of organizational reforms. In 1965, fourteen out of thirty-four of the members of its national executive committee belonged to the Bundestag.[83]

There has been no clear line of demarcation between the national and the parliamentary organizations. Major policy decisions since 1957 have been taken at joint meetings of the leading organs of both. The rules of procedure of the parliamentary party admit both the national chairman and the honorary chairman of the party, if they are not Members of Parliament, to the councils of the parliamentary party executive, and admit FDP ministers in the *Länder* Governments to the parliamentary caucus and its working groups. Under the rules, the working groups collaborate with their counterparts in the national organization, because the party has felt the need to pool the services of such experts as it has available.[84]

The parliamentary party has established five working groups, dealing with Foreign Policy and Defense, Economic Policy, Social Policy, Internal Policy, and Food and Agriculture. They elect their own chairmen and also select the chairman or party foremen in the relevant Bundestag committee. Policy and proposals are considered in the working groups first, then are submitted to the seven-member executive and then to the caucus. The executive consists of the chairman, two or three deputy chairmen, one or two parliamentary whips, and the Bundestag vice-president belonging to the party.[85]

[83] In June, 1965, the following members of the national executive committee were Members of the Bundestag: Achenbach, Atzenroth, Bucher, Dahlgrün, Dehler, Effertz, Funcke, von Kühlmann-Stumm, Lenz, Mende, Mischnick, Scheel, Starke, Zoglmann.

[84] *Geschäftsordnung der Bundestagsfraktion der FDP*, Nov. 13, 1957 (mimeographed), par. 5, 10. See also Gerard Braunthal, "The Free Democratic Party in West German Politics," *The Western Political Quarterly*, XIII (1960), 335; Rheinhold Maier, "Partei und Bundestagsfraktion," *Südwest Merkur*, Nov. 22, 1957.

[85] *Geschäftsordnung der Bundestagsfraktion der FDP*, par. 5. *Freie Demokratische Korrespondenz*, Nov. 28 and Dec. 10, 1957; *Das Freie Wort*, Oct. 24, 1959.

Because of its relatively small size, the caucus plays a more important deliberative role than in either of the other parties. In a more intimate atmosphere in which microphones are unnecessary, participation is broader and more varied, less under executive control. The sessions are lengthy, lasting four to five hours in every week that the Bundestag is in session. Covering a detailed agenda issued to Members in advance, the arguments, tactics, and speakers to be used in the week's parliamentary debates are determined and motions to be introduced by the party are prepared. Discussion in the caucus is active on controversial points, as there are fewer recognized "experts" to dominate it than in the other parties. It is not unusual for a working group, the whips, or the executive to be overruled. Votes are taken to decide the party position, but willingness to defer to the majority depends on the intensity of the conflict over issues and interests. The voting unity of FDP Members in the House has been consistently lower than that of the other parties.

To maintain its distinctiveness as a party, the FDP has voted with both Government and Opposition, whether it was itself represented in the Cabinet or not, greatly straining normal parliamentary relationships. The attempt to avoid undue friction by the establishment of a "coalition committee" composed of the parliamentary leaders of the CDU/CSU and of the FDP has had only very limited success. The committee, created on the demand of the FDP as part of the "coalition agreement" reached with the CDU/CSU in 1961, started its work in the atmosphere of personal bitterness which the negotiations leading to the formation of the Government had produced at the time. Its regular sessions are often attended by deputies for the leaders, an indication that the negotiations proceed at arm's length. Recurring controversies between the parliamentary group of the FDP and its partner in the coalition have had to be settled *ad hoc,* and have often required the intervention of the Cabinet.[86]

Because of its size, the FDP has a substantially smaller parliamentary staff than the other parties. It consists of seventeen employees, four of whom are research assistants for the working groups. The parliamentary party depends on the national organization and on

[86] For the text of the "coalition agreement," see *Die Welt,* Nov. 6, 1961, p. 6. As an example of controversy between the FDP in the Bundestag and its partner in the Cabinet, see the dispute over children's allowances, recounted in *Die Welt,* March 5, 6, and 7, 1964.

private resources for further staff assistance. Altogether, its size has prevented the FDP from developing the degree of specialization upon which effective committee work depends. But for the same reason, a larger proportion of its Members are active in the Bundestag, especially in debate, than in either of the other parties. The individuality of its Members, and the party's occasionally cavalier disregard of its commitments to the coalition Government, introduce an element of uncertainty into the highly structured framework in which the Bundestag works. More than its larger confreres, the FDP recalls the parliamentary parties of earlier times.

PARLIAMENTARY PARTIES AND PARLIAMENTARY COMMITTEES

The organization of the parliamentary parties affects not only their internal processes of policy formation, but their parliamentary relationships with each other and their performance in the Bundestag and its committees. By their power to appoint their quota of committee chairmen and members, the parliamentary parties collectively compose the committees. In their working groups the parties have organizations parallel to the committees through which they maintain close contact with committee work.

Committee Appointment

The appointment of committee members is one of the most important and challenging tasks of the parliamentary parties. Each must take account of a number of conflicting considerations. Members themselves have strong preferences, on the basis of their competence, interests, and energy, and on the basis also of the interests of their constituency, or, frequently, of the organizations which have advanced their candidacy. Identification with a particular economic or social interest has been, for most Members, a decisive contribution to election. Specialization is, for most, the avenue to recognition in the House. Committee appointment is therefore an important determinant of an individual's parliamentary career. Each parliamentary party systematically solicits the committee preferences of its members at the beginning of each parliamentary term. This is an opportunity not only for new Members, but also for those returning, who may wish to improve their assignments. Since chairmanships are not exclusively awarded according to seniority on a committee, hope for appointment as chairman is no compelling reason to stay put. Close to one-fifth of the Members of the third Bundestag who were re-elected to the fourth changed their primary committee assignment. But the tendency of Members toward specialization is strong, expressing itself in considerable stability in committee membership through successive terms. (See Table 27.) Except in cases of outright insubordination, parties will not change assignments against a Member's will. Characteristically, the SPD merely asks its Members to list their choices.[87] The CDU/CSU issues a full-page questionnaire asking the Member's denomination, marital status, number of children, profession, current occupation, employer, other elective offices, and whether the respondent is a refugee, expellee, or former prisoner of war.[88]

For the party, numerous considerations beyond individual preference are at stake. Considering the importance of the committee stage in legislation, the parties are anxious to have their ablest experts on the relevant committees, and to have their political leaders on Foreign Affairs, and to a lesser extent, on Judiciary and Appropriations, which deal with the broadest political questions. On the other hand, they want a good cross-section of the parliamentary party on each committee, to assure that the committee work of their Members will have caucus support. Furthermore, they must deal with the demands of interest groups anxious to place Members friendly to them, or employed by them, in advantageous positions. In the CDU/CSU and the FDP, there is also pressure from the *Länder* organizations of the party for parity in sectional representation. Finally, the work load must be distributed among the Representatives. Considering that each party must place its share of members as well as alternate members on every one of 23 parliamentary standing committees, in addition to such other parliamentary bodies as special committees, investigating committees, the Mediation Committee with the Bundesrat, various committees partially elected by the Bundestag such as the Committee for the Election of Judges, and the German delegation to the European Parliament and the Consultative Assembly of the Council of Europe, there are approximately three places to be filled for every Member. A few Members, notably those holding Cabinet office, the President of the Bundestag, two or three Members with heavy private, or other

[87] Fraktion der SPD im Bundestag, Rundschreiben Nr. 3, Bonn, Sept. 28, 1961.
[88] CDU/CSU Fraktion, Deutscher Bundestag, "Fragebogen," Bonn, Sept. 18, 1961.

public, obligations, are unable to serve on committees. Furthermore, the work required in different positions varies tremendously.[89] Members assigned to the busiest committees, such as Appropriations and Judiciary, are not generally given a second full assignment, nor are members of the delegations to the European parliaments. This meant that about half the Members of the third Bundestag, for example, had to take two full committee assignments, in addition to assignments as alternate members. To be sure, they had the less onerous assignments; ten committees met less than fifty times during the four years of the third Bundestag. Although the reduction in the number of standing committees in the fifth Bundestag alleviated the burden somewhat, the problem is still one of drafting Members, rather than of rejecting volunteers, for the less glamorous positions.[90]

The initiative in the delicate and important task of appointing committee members is taken by a small group of leaders in each parliamentary party. In the CDU/CSU it is a special "independent" committee composed of one senior Member from each *Land,* in the FDP it is a special committee of three senior Members and the parliamentary whip, and in the SPD it is the "inner executive" in consultation with the chairmen of the relevant Bundestag committees or party working groups in the previous term. These recommendations then go to the respective executive committees where they are further discussed at length. They are finally submitted to the caucus, where some further changes may be made.

The extent of the deliberations should not be exaggerated, however, since the discretion to be exercised is severely limited. The political leaders and the interest representatives, in effect, appoint themselves, and the seniority of the more experienced Members is respected both because it contributes to the competence with which the party is represented, and because it is generally accompanied by influence within the party. The membership of committees shows a high degree of continuity from one Bundestag to another, an index of the extent of Member specialization in committee work. Over five-eighths of the Members serving throughout the first three terms of the Bundestag, and fully half of those holding their seats for the first four terms, never

[89] See pp. 147–8, *supra.*

[90] The general principles governing committee assignments are well described in Dechamps, *op. cit.,* pp. 143–8, although the description given there of the detailed procedure within each party is no longer up-to-date.

Table 27. Continuity and change in committee assignments, 1949–1965
(in per cent of each party group and total membership)

Committee seniority	Seniority in the Bundestag				
	Two terms [a]				
	CDU (n = 80)	CSU (n = 26)	SPD (n = 59)	FDP (n = 10)	Total (n = 175)
One term	19	23	15	40	19
Two terms	81	77	85	60	81
Three terms	—	—	—	—	—
Four terms	—	—	—	—	—

Committee seniority	Seniority in the Bundestag				
	Three terms [b]				
	CDU (n = 55)	CSU (n = 8)	SPD (n = 70)	FDP (n = 8)	Total (n = 141)
One term	9	0	11	0	9
Two terms	24	75	23	50	28
Three terms	67	25	66	50	63
Four terms	—	—	—	—	—

Committee seniority	Seniority in the Bundestag				
	Four terms				
	CDU (n = 35)	CSU (n = 6)	SPD (n = 48)	FDP (n = 6)	Total (n = 95)
One term	20	0	21	17	19
Two terms	8	0	6	0	6
Three terms	26	67	19	33	25
Four terms	46	33	54	50	50

[a] Includes only Members of the third Bundestag who served one term prior to 1957.

[b] Includes only Members of the third Bundestag who served both terms prior to 1957.

changed their primary committee assignment. (See Table 27.) The rate of committee change has averaged below 20 per cent of those Members re-elected from one term to the next. It has been slightly lower in the SPD than in the CDU, probably because movements in and out of Cabinet positions among the members of the largest governing party have produced some additional committee reshuffling.

The effective appointing power of the parties is now limited to about two-fifths of the Members of each new House, counting those 25 per cent or so who are new, and a relatively small proportion of those returning.

The largest number of decisions concern the new Members. If they have achieved prominence in the party organization, or have powerful patrons or needed skills, they may receive important appointments from the start. Erik Blumenfeld, for example, who was chairman of the CDU organization in Hamburg upon his election in 1961, immediately received a place on the coveted Foreign Affairs Committee. Ulrich Lohmar, a noted SPD journalist and intellectual, was given his first choice, a place on the Committee on Cultural Policy and Publishing, upon his election in 1957. Ernst Benda, a young CDU attorney prominent in the CDU party organization in Berlin, and Gerhard Jahn, a young SPD attorney from Marburg, went straight to the prestigious Judiciary Committee upon their election in the same year, because their parties badly needed their skills there; in fact Jahn would have preferred the Appropriations Committee and Benda the Defense Committee. Hans Merten, chairman of an organization of former prisoners of war, started on the important Veterans Committee. Hans Wellmann, moving into Brandt's place on Brandt's resignation from the Bundestag after the 1961 election, immediately received his first choice, a seat on the Appropriations Committee.

The obstacles in the way of altering the committee assignments of powerful Members was revealed in 1961 by the unsuccessful effort of Richard Jaeger, chairman of the Defense Committee, to reduce the size of that committee from twenty-seven to fifteen members in order to contribute to the preservation of military confidences. The Members who wished to stay on this committee could not be budged. Although the parliamentary whips of all parties made pious assertions of support for Jaeger's move, the SPD and FDP even advocating it formally in the Council of Elders, they agreed privately to do nothing. In the showdown, no one was prepared even to move the reduction, and Jaeger limited himself to a formal statement explaining his abstention in the vote by which the original size of the committee was retained.[91]

Only new Members of the House, rising from lowly positions in the party organization, are subject to direction from those making the appointments. They frequently have their hopes and preferences dis-

[91] *Dt. Btag.*, 4, W.P., 3. Sitz., Nov. 8, 1961, p. 12.

appointed, but they are in no position to protest. Actually, since the total number of positions to be filled is so great, it is not difficult to give some satisfaction to nearly everyone, even if, in the last resort, it is only the prospect of reassignment in the next term.

Selection of Chairmen

In the distribution of chairmanships, on the other hand, the number of awards which each party can make is small. About half the positions fall vacant in each new Parliament because of the death, resignation, defeat, or promotion of incumbent chairmen or because of a change in the quota to which each party is entitled. In 1957, the SPD and FDP were each able to make two new appointments, the CDU/CSU nine; in 1961, the CDU/CSU and SPD each made six, the FDP three. Parties rarely remove their chairmen, unless they are causing them major embarrassment. Two such examples occurred successively in the third Bundestag in the Committee on Restitution. Its first chairman resigned under pressure from his party because of conflict of interests; his successor resigned under indictment for treason. But dramatic as these cases were, they are very infrequent. Of the twenty-six committee chairmen appointed at the start of the third Bundestag, seven had had one previous term as chairman and six had had both previous terms. Half of them were reappointed to their positions in the fourth Bundestag. Of the remainder, six did not stand again or were not re-elected, one died before the new House was constituted, one received Cabinet appointment, one became a Bundestag vice-president, and two others became deputy chairman and parliamentary whip of their parties respectively. Only two of the re-elected committee chairmen, both heading minor committees, failed both to retain their positions and to go on to better things, and one of these was a party leader whose failure to be reappointed was not conceivably a case of involuntary dismissal.

Seniority in the House is generally an important consideration in the appointment of new committee chairmen. In the third Bundestag 19 out of 26 committee chairmen had served both previous terms, in the fourth Bundestag 13 out of 28 had served in all three previous terms, and 7 others had served two terms. The chairmen of committees dealing with the broadest political questions are drawn from among the professional politicians of the House; half of the committee chairmen in the third Bundestag fitted this category. But in those committees which directly affect organized interests—the committees on Economic Affairs, Foreign Trade, Small Business, Agriculture, Labor, Housing, Veterans, Family and Youth—the chairmanship has regularly gone to representatives of the interests within the committee's jurisdiction. The Economic Affairs Committee, for example, has consistently had a chairman closely identified with business interests. In 1956, while the committee was considering a major piece of legislation to regulate cartels, the CDU/CSU, which was entitled to name the chairman, nominated Fritz Hellwig, who was then managing director of the Institute of German Industry, the main public relations organization for German industry. The chairmanship in the fifth Bundestag fell to the FDP, which chose Alexander Menne, vice-president of the Federation of German Industry. Since 1953, the Agriculture Committee has been headed by Bernhard Bauknecht of the CDU, a member of the presidium of the largest agricultural interest group, the German Farmers Association. For twelve years before its amalgamation with the Economic Affairs Committee in 1965, the Foreign Trade Committee had in Reinhold Bender and Günther Serres chairmen who have been employees of business interest groups.

Interest Representation

The composition of the committees follows a similar pattern. In the third Bundestag, the parliamentary leadership itself occupied nearly two-thirds of the places on the Committee on Foreign Affairs, and over one-third of the seats on the Judiciary and Appropriations committees, all of which belong to the top policy-making bodies in the House. One-sided interest representation was especially strong on the committees on Economic Affairs, Foreign Trade, Small Business, Agriculture, Labor, Veterans and Housing. Public employees formed a substantial interest group on the Interior Committee, and local government officials, present and past, actually made up a majority on the Committee on Local Government and Public Welfare. A greater variety of affected interests was represented on the committees on Family and Youth, Cultural Policy (Education), Health, and Social Policy. (See Table 28.)

The committee membership of Representatives belonging to the labor group within the CDU/CSU is a striking illustration of the ability of an interest group within a parliamentary party to place its Members on the committees of greatest concern to it. Members of the

Table 28. *Composition of Bundestag committees by types of Members,* [a] *1957–1961 (in per cent of committee membership)* [b]

Name of committee	Professional politicians	Public employees	Interest representatives	Part-time private occupation	Parliamentary Leaders [c]	Parliamentary Backbenchers [c]
Average for all committees	24	10	32	33	28	72
Election Validation, Immunity, and Rules	**35**	12	12	35	35	65
Petitions	28	10	21	41	21	79
Foreign Affairs	**41**	0	24	31	66	34
All-German and Berlin Questions	**31**	7	14	**41**	24	76
Defense	**31**	10	28	31	27	73
Interior	24	**28**	14	34	31	69
Restitution	24	6	18	**41**	35	65
Cultural Policy and Publishing (Education)	**31**	3	10	**51**	27	73
Local Government and Public Welfare	24	**17**	38	21	14	86
Family and Youth	17	**17**	26	39	26	74
Health	17	**17**	13	**52**	30	70
Judiciary	17	**21**	10	**52**	34	66
Appropriations	24	**21**	10	**45**	34	66
Finance	10	10	38	34	24	76
Equalization of Burdens	24	12	**41**	24	35	65
Economic Affairs	24	0	**41**	34	31	69
Foreign Trade	14	0	**45**	34	21	79
Middle Class (Small Business)	3	0	**45**	31	22	78
Food, Agriculture and Forestry	3	7	**59**	21	17	83
Social Policy	14	10	**66**	10	27	73
Labor	14	**14**	**52**	21	21	79
War Victims and Repatriates (Veterans)	26	9	26	39	30	70
Transport, Post Office, and Telecommunication	17	10	28	41	21	79
Housing and Town and Country Planning	14	7	**41**	28	17	83
Refugees	**30**	0	26	26	23	77
Atomic Energy and Water Resources	17	7	31	34	17	83

[a] For explanation of Member types, see pp. 121–8, *supra.*

[b] First four columns across do not quite add up to 100% because Members classified "other" are not included. *Percentages one-fourth or more above average are in boldface.*

[c] For definition of parliamentary leaders and backbenchers see Table 18.

labor group made up 18 per cent of the CDU/CSU delegation in the Bundestag in 1957, and 23 per cent in 1961. In both Parliaments, how- ever, its Members occupied over 55 per cent of CDU/CSU seats on the committees on Social Policy and on Labor, where they could ally with SPD Members having similar views on some issues. In the Economic Affairs Committee, for another example, representatives of business from both CDU/CSU and FDP combine to defend their interests across party lines. In the fourth Bundestag, nine of thirteen CDU/CSU Members on this committee were closely allied with busi- ness, including Gustav Stein, managing director of the Federation of German Industry; all three of the committee's FDP Members were likewise business representatives. A similar alignment existed in the Foreign Trade Committee.[92]

The ability of the party leaders to influence the committees through their appointing power therefore varies with their subject. The direct participation of these leaders in the basic policy-making committees contrasts with the interest-group character of the committees in some areas of domestic policy. The dominance of interest representatives on these bodies is due both to the influence of the interests within the parliamentary parties, especially in the CDU/CSU and FDP, and to the dependence of party leaders on the subject expertise which often only the "interested" Member can supply.

Party Efforts to Control Committees

The power of appointment to the committees is in another sense quite limited as a form of influence over committee deliberation, since the power to appoint falls far short of the power to compel attendance, let alone conscientious work. Counting both primary and alternate assignments, 60 per cent of the Members of the third Bundestag had three places on legislative committees, 20 per cent had four, and eighteen Members actually had five. Due to other committee and party assignments, and the large proportion of Members for whom the mandate is a part-time obligation, committee attendance is very poor.

[92] For the analysis of the committee assignments of members of the CDU/CSU labor group, see Deutsches Industrie Institut, "Der linke Flügel der CDU/CSU," *op. cit.*, p. 28. For the analysis of the composition of the Economic Affairs and the Foreign Trade Committees, see Gerard Braunthal, *The Federation of German Industry in Politics* (Ithaca: Cornell University Press, 1965), pp. 170–71. See also Domes, *op. cit.*, pp. 158–9. The relationship between Members' occupations and their committee work is also discussed on pp. 112–13, *supra*.

Despite the appointment of an alternate for every committee member, the severity of the attendance problem has produced the custom of permitting any Member to substitute for any other. Although no party likes this practice, which in effect robs it of control over committee membership, the difficulty of finding substitutes to maintain a party's strength on a committee is often so great that all parties wink at the practice. The result is a tendency to have committee work performed, and committee decisions made, by those Members most interested in them, not only in the intellectual but in the material sense. Although each parliamentary party obliges its members to perform their committee work, none is able effectively to enforce the obligation.[93]

Limited in the control they exercise over the committees through their appointing power, party leaders have tried to organize other forms of supervision. The rules of the CDU/CSU parliamentary party state that "the members of a committee are requested to remember that they do not belong to the committee only as individuals, but are regarded in the Bundestag and in public as representatives of the parliamentary party." [94]

The principle applies equally in the other parties. Each of them appoints a party foreman to head the party's delegation in each committee. In the CDU/CSU the foreman is, in three-quarters of the committees, either the chairman or the deputy chairman of the committee, depending upon which of these offices belongs to the party. In the other committees, where conflicts of viewpoint or personality exist within the party, as during the fourth Bundestag in the Defense, Family and Youth, Agriculture, and Federal Property committees, the duties of foreman are exercised by another Member, usually the chairman of the relevant party working group. In effect, this division of leadership also existed in the Judiciary, Small Business, and Veterans committees. In the SPD and FDP the foreman is the chairman or deputy chairman if one of these belong to the party, another Member if not, and is often simultaneously the chairman of the party's working group. Elected by the caucus, the foremen are responsible for the organization of the party's work in their committee, are answerable for committee attendance to the parliamentary whip of the party, give

---

[93] See, for example, Carlo Schmid in the *Süddeutsche Zeitung*, Feb. 8, 1958. Cf. *FAZ*, Feb. 26, 1960.

[94] *Arbeitsordnung der CDU/CSU Bundestagsfraktion*, par. 9.

status reports on committee progress to party leaders, and make public statements on the party position in the committee.

Substantive responsibility for each subject before a committee is separately assigned in each case to a particular party member on the committee. In the CDU/CSU and the SPD the party members on each committee distribute these assignments among themselves; in the smaller FDP the executive makes the assignments. It is the subject specialist's responsibility to initiate the formulation of the party's viewpoint on the particular matter in the working group, to defend that formulation in the executive committee and the caucus, and to express the party's position and cast the party's vote in the committee. How frequently and how intensively the subject specialist consults with his delegation on the committee, with the relevant party working group, and with the executive and the caucus, depends upon his authority within the party and on the nature of the question. The limits are set by his ability to obtain the eventual support of his party for the positions he takes in the committee. A party leader may for this reason act with a high degree of independence; an expert on a narrow technical issue is likewise on his own. In either case, the party is likely to follow. But where the issues are broad and party interest great, consultation becomes closer in order to avoid party repudiation of decisions taken in its name within a committee.

The most continuous contact is between the committee delegations and the working groups or their subgroups. Thus the working groups are the chief instruments of communication between party and committee. Since many legislative measures are simultaneously under discussion in several committees, the working groups supply the means of communication among party members on these related committees and permit the coordination of their activities. The executive committee and the caucus, on the other hand, are not closely consulted between the initial decision of the party, taken when a subject is first introduced in the Bundestag, and the final decision before the second reading debate. The exceptions are major pieces of legislation which undergo significant alteration during committee discussion.[95] Despite the complexity of the organization, coordination is not assured. Cau-

[95] Dechamps, *op. cit.*, pp. 148–54, although somewhat dated in the failure to emphasize the role of the working groups, gives a good description of the respective roles of the foreman and the subject specialist.

cuses do, from time to time, repudiate the committee action of their members. Occasionally they are trapped when repudiation is publicly too embarrassing.

The reciprocal relationships which exist between the party caucuses and their members on the Bundestag committees do not give the leaders of the parliamentary parties control over committee work. Whether the leaders control their committee members, or the committee members control the caucus, varies with the issues, the committees, and of course with the men concerned. The organization of foremen, specialists, and working groups has grown in response to the problem of maintaining party unity in the face of the growing size and diversity of the parliamentary parties, and the multiplication of the quantity and complexity of the issues. But the organization cannot be controlled from any single locus of power. This is particularly true in the case of the CDU/CSU, with its substructure of organized interest groups. When Brentano resumed the chairmanship of that parliamentary party in 1961, after an interval of six years, he asserted that it was his aim to have the party's work on the committees done "more strongly according to political than technical-legislative considerations." [96] But the review of party organization which he instituted to that end has not yet led to any reforms, nor have the other parties solved the problem. For the same forces which have made the committees of the Bundestag more powerful than the formal Rules imply, have made the specialized subgroups of the parliamentary parties more powerful than the party leaders like.

COUNCIL OF ELDERS

Although autonomous centers of power exist within the committee structure which escape the control of the party leaders, these leaders do effectively control the public performance of the Bundestag, and the distribution of parliamentary patronage among the parties. Through the Council of Elders, the parties, having parceled out the appointments of presiding officers among themselves, control the exercise of important aspects of presidential power. The Council, originally formed in the nineteenth century as an informal meeting of party

[96] *Die Welt*, Jan. 19, 1963.

Plate VII. A regular luncheon meeting of the Council of Elders. (Courtesy of Georg Munker, Bonn.)

Plate VIII. A meeting of the FDP parliamentary party. (Courtesy of Presse- und Informationsamt der Bundesregierung.)

leaders to enable them to arrange the business of the House and to bargain on appointments,[97] has attained an official status. The Rules provide that

the Council of Elders has the task of supporting the President in his conduct of business, in particular to contribute to agreements among the parliamentary parties on the agenda of the Bundestag, and the appointment of committee chairmen and deputy chairmen. It is not empowered to make decisions. (Par. 14)

The Council consists of the President, who is chairman, the vice-presidents, and twenty additional members including the whips, divided proportionately among the parties and appointed by them. One Cabinet minister as well as the chief of the Bundestag staff also attend. Significant of the formal distance between Government and Parliament, the Cabinet has always been represented on the Council by a minor figure, often, strangely enough, the Minister for Bundesrat Affairs.

Originally, in the first Bundestag, the Council was a gathering of party chairmen, but as specialization developed within the parties, it has become a meeting in which the parliamentary whips play the main part. The Council cannot reach binding decisions. Any of its proposals can be made the subject of contested motions in the House. It can therefore only "decide" when all parties agree. The whips are the agents of their parties in the Council. The agenda of the meetings of the Council is discussed in advance by each party executive committee with its whips. Although the Council cannot bind the House, when it reaches unanimous agreements on behalf of the parties, it effectively binds the President. This is in fact its chief function. For the President cannot ignore what the parties unanimously support, regardless of the Rules of Procedure. "Even the President in the chair is powerless against the arrangements of the parties," Vice-President Schoettle responded, when the CDU whip objected to his recognition of a speaker and asked him instead to take up a different agenda item "as has been agreed among the parties." [98]

In the presence of the President, the Council is the place for negotiation and registration of interparty agreements on the agenda of the

[97] Hatschek, *op. cit.*, pp. 175–85; 192–5.
[98] *Dt. Btag.*, 4. W.P., 164. Sitz., Feb. 17, 1965, p. 8102.

Bundestag, the order and the number of speakers in debate, and the designation of the committees to which bills are to be referred. It also informs the President of any disagreements among the parties on these points, prepares him for the procedural problems to be faced in the coming session, and prepares the parliamentary whips for such procedural rulings as the President may intend to make. The minutes of its meetings, which take place weekly, in advance of the sessions of the Bundestag and the party caucuses, are circulated to half a dozen members of the Bundestag staff and, through the member of the Cabinet present, to the Government. Through the whips, the results of the meetings of the Council are reported to the caucuses and, summarily, to the press. Consequently, the presiding officers, their staff, the parties, and the public, to different extents, know in advance the plan for the coming sittings of the House.

On some subjects, the Council serves as a deliberative body. Since it plans the day-to-day procedure of the Bundestag, it is naturally the place where proposed changes in the Rules or their interpretation are discussed, effectively taking that subject out of the province of the Bundestag Committee on Rules where it is formally assigned. It is also the place where matters partly or wholly within the formal competence of the presiding officers are discussed. These include conduct within the House of individual Members, of the press, and of the public, permission to report parliamentary sessions by radio or television, and the calendar of sittings. Questions of parliamentary staff and budget are reserved for the Bundestag Executive Committee, but by a Rules change in 1961, the parliamentary whips have become members of this body also (par. 6). The Council is occasionally the place of negotiation between Cabinet and Bundestag on the question of scheduling Government business. Agreement exists in general that bills proposed by the Cabinet will be placed on the agenda, but occasionally there have been bills which the governing parties in Parliament have preferred to suppress. These have been long, or even indefinitely, postponed, protests of the Cabinet representative on the Council notwithstanding.[99]

[99] This was notably the case in the third Bundestag with the *Ehrenschutzgesetz* (Drs. 1237), a proposed revision of libel law, and with the proposed reform of the Criminal Code (Drs. 2150). The latter was also kept off the agenda of the 4th Bundestag for 18 months (see *Die Welt*, Jan. 9 and 24, 1963). In both

At the beginning of the parliamentary term, the Council is the scene of interparty bargaining on the number of vice-presidencies, the number and size of committees to be constituted, and the distribution of chairmanships. Well-established customs regulate the distribution of seats and chairmanships among the parties through a precise calculation of proportional representation by the d'Hondt system. The particular chairmanships given each party are generally settled by agreements among the parties, whose aim it has been to preserve the places of incumbent chairmen so far as is possible within the limits of proportionality. An effort by the CDU/CSU in 1961 to give "its" Foreign Affairs Committee chairmanship to the FDP as part of the general agreements on the formation of the coalition Government caused the interparty negotiation on the chairmanships to break down for the first time in the history of the Bundestag. The parties resorted to a custom first employed in 1912 by which each chose chairmanships in turn in the order in which the places fell to them by the d'Hondt calculation. According to its strength, the FDP was not entitled to a chairman until seventh choice, the CDU/CSU being entitled to choices 1, 3, and 5, the SPD to choices 2, 4, and 6. Unwilling to see a question of parliamentary organization made part of a coalition deal, the SPD warned that it would take the Foreign Affairs chairmanship with its sixth choice unless the CDU/CSU had taken it by then, in order to prevent its falling to the FDP. The order in which the parties chose the chairmanships in this instance gives an interesting index of the importance which they attach to the respective committees. Each made an effort to hold those chairmanships which it had had in the previous House, in order to preserve the positions of its incumbent chairmen. The parties had agreed in advance to make this possible within the limits of the shift in party strengths by which the CDU was compelled to give up one chairmanship to each of the two others. But the antagonism between the SPD and FDP had become so great that the SPD, in the seventeenth turn, chose the chairmanship of the Atomic Energy Committee which the FDP had held, after the FDP, in the fifteenth turn, had chosen the chairmanship of the new Committee on

---

cases the proposed bills were potentially embarrassing to the CDU/CSU. It happens more frequently that private members' bills are kept off the agenda, as was the proposed reintroduction of the death penalty (Drs. 133, 389, 390, and 391) during the third Bundestag. See also p. 306, *infra*.

Foreign Aid, which the SPD had sought. The SPD's subsequent offer to trade was turned down angrily.[100]

The Council of Elders is important as a means of communication between the parliamentary parties and the President. It is a place where interparty controversies on procedure and organization can be settled, or at least expressed in the presence of the presiding officers, in a dignified, confidential, collegial atmosphere. It is the arena of the professional politicians. For the party leaders, the Council is above all the instrument through which they can control the course of the public sessions of the Bundestag. If they can agree, they can impose their will on the President. The incentive to do so is high.

MANAGED PROCEDURE

Formal Rules in a Changing Political Context

Out of the agreements among the parties which the members of the Council of Elders have negotiated and registered, a body of informal procedural norms has gradually developed which supplement and, in effect, amend the formal Rules of Procedure of the Bundestag. The chief authors of these new norms are the parliamentary whips. As the main participants in the constant negotiations among the parties which are required to arrange the business of the House, they have been

[100] The order of choice was as follows:

1. CDU—Defense	16. CDU—Foreign Trade
2. SPD—Appropriations	17. SPD—Atomic Energy
3. CDU—Finance	18. CDU—Labor
4. SPD—Interior	19. SPD—Refugees
5. CDU—Foreign Affairs	20. CDU—Local Government
6. SPD—All-German Questions	21. CDU—Equalization of Burdens
7. FDP—Economic Affairs	22. SPD—Rules
8. CDU—Judiciary	23. FDP—Health
9. SPD—Social Policy	24. CDU—Family and Youth
10. CDU—Agriculture	25. SPD—Petitions
11. CDU—Housing	26. CDU—Middle Class (Small Business)
12. SPD—Transport	
13. CDU—Cultural Policy (Education)	27. SPD—Restitution
14. SPD—War Victims (Veterans)	28. CDU—Federal Property
15. FDP—Foreign Aid	

CDU and CSU choose jointly. See *Der Spiegel,* XVI, no. 4 (Jan. 24, 1962), 17–19; cf. *Die Welt,* Dec. 13, 1961, and Jan. 5, 10, 11, 12, 17, 18, and 19, 1962; *FAZ,* Jan. 13 and 17, 1962.

acutely aware of new possibilities for procedural consensus arising from the new party configuration in Parliament.

The formal organization and procedure, and the conventions surrounding them, which the Bundestag inherited, had been developed by a multiparty Parliament in which no one group even approached majority status, a Parliament, furthermore, which was, until 1917, entirely separated from the Government and which thereafter confronted Governments of short duration which were unable to lead a definite majority in the House. The customs governing the appointment of committees, committee chairmen, and the officers of the House reflected the agreement of a multiplicity of parties to share the spoils. The institution of the Council of Elders satisfied the need for a regular meeting among the various party leaders to negotiate all those procedural questions which, under the Rules, are subject to majority decision, but which in the traditional party system required multiparty arrangements. These included setting the agenda of the House, determining the length and order of debate, electing the officers of the House, and interpreting the Rules in case of disputes. The inherited Rules reflect the separation between Government and Parliament by granting special rights to members of the Government, notably to be recognized to speak at any time, ignoring the possibility that the Government might be composed of Members of the House (par. 47). Also, the Rules elaborate a carefully graded set of minority rights, designed to guarantee a balance of power in a fragmented parliamentary party system. Every Member has an unlimited right to move amendments on second reading of bills (par. 81); five Members can block consideration of a subject not on the agenda (par. 26, sec. 3), can insist on observing prescribed intervals between the readings of bills (par. 93, sec. 2) or on postponing debate until motions are available in print (par. 99, sec. 2), or can question the existence of a quorum (par. 50, sec. 1). Under the Rules, as many Members as are needed to constitute a parliamentary party—fifteen since 1952—can move bills and resolutions and third reading amendments (par. 86, 97), put written questions to the Government (par. 110), and demand postponement of a final vote until all amendments adopted are available in print (par. 88). A motion for closure (par. 30, sec. 2), postponement of the session (par. 31), and the interpellation of the Government (pars. 105–108) can be made by any group of thirty Members. Fifty Members can demand a recorded vote (par. 57), one-quarter of the membership can require the establishment of an investigating committee (par. 63) or move the replacement of the Chancellor (par. 98, sec. 2), and one-third of the Members can compel calling a special session of the House (par. 25, sec. 2), while one-third plus one can block consideration of bills which have not been available in print for two full days (par. 77, sec. 2).

The elections of 1953 and 1957 completely altered the political conditions for the employment of these Rules and conventions. For the first time in German parliamentary history, a single party held a majority of seats in the House, and was committed to the support of a Cabinet composed of its leaders. A single Opposition party controlled over one-third of the seats. Under the prevailing Rules, the governing majority could control the agenda and length of debate, while its leaders in the Cabinet could demand unlimited speaking time. The Opposition, on the other hand, in addition to holding a proportionate share of committee chairmanships, could obstruct business by the employment of the entire range of minority rights. Carried to its permissible extremes under the Rules, a ruthless majority tyranny faced by an obstructive minority could have made parliamentary government impossible. These conditions, which were not materially altered by the subsequent general elections, alone provided a strong incentive for the parties to reach tactical and procedural arrangements beyond the formal Rules.

The Development of Informal Norms

Increased specialization within the parliamentary party organizations also encouraged this development. The creation of the position of the whip, charged with the tactical leadership of the party on the floor of the Bundestag, centralized in the hands of one or two Members in each party the function of negotiating the necessary procedural arrangements with the other parties. The reduction of the number of parties to four in the third Bundestag and three in the fourth and fifth, and the pre-eminent importance of two of them, greatly simplified the task of making these arrangements by reducing the number of groups needing to agree.

A number of less tangible considerations also helped the development along. The elimination of the extreme radical parties from the Bundestag allowed those remaining to negotiate with each other on the broad common ground of support of the parliamentary system. All parties were interested in avoiding the use of tactics which appeared destructive of the parliamentary order, and this included both the ruthless use of majority power or minority rights, and engagement in endless procedural wrangles. The reduction of the substantive divisions between the parties, after the SPD's adoption of the Godesberg Program in 1959 and its foreign policy shift in 1960,[101] also broadened the common ground on which procedural and organizational questions could be settled. SPD hopes for eventual inclusion in a governing coalition contributed to the atmosphere of harmony.

The sheer informality and privacy with which agreements among the parties could be made also facilitated them. What could be arranged could be kept out of the limelight; what could not be arranged had to be openly controverted. The majority would then prevail, but at the price of an open dispute. This consideration tended to set the limits of possible agreements. Any procedural position which a party felt it could advantageously publicize was relatively resistant to settlement by agreement.[102]

Under these circumstances, the parliamentary whips of the parties, notably Will Rasner of the CDU and Karl Mommer of the SPD, became the authors of a new body of parliamentary conventions and usages based upon interparty arrangement. These include the customs pertaining to the distribution of committee chairmanships and vice-presidencies, based on the common interest of all parties to preserve the places of their incumbents. They include the agreement reached in 1961, not to create committees of such size that they will give the largest party a majority of seats according to the calculation of proportionality by the d'Hondt system when that party does not possess a majority in the House.[103] They also include norms determining the daily procedure of the Bundestag.

Informal Procedure

Elaborate conventions govern the preparation of the agenda of the House. Their basic premise is that any point desired by any party

---

[101] See *Grundsatzprogramm der SPD*, Beschlossen vom Ausserordentlichen Parteitag der Sozialdemokratischen Partei Deutschlands in Bad Godesberg, Nov. 13–15, 1959, and the speech of Herbert Wehner, *Dt. Btag.*, 3. W.P., 122. Sitz., June 30, 1960, pp. 7052 ff.

[102] For example, the SPD, against the will of the majority, insisted on a motion to place on the agenda the first reading of its bill providing public employees a Christmas bonus (Drs. 54/55), as well as bills raising veterans' pensions (Drs. 82), *Dt. Btag.*, 4. W.P., 8. Sitz., Dec. 13, 1961, pp. 143–6.

[103] See p. 151, *supra*.

should be admitted to the agenda, unless the subject is sufficiently embarrassing to the majority that it is willing openly to vote the matter down. Preparation of the agenda for the Bundestag begins a week in advance of the meetings for which they are intended, when all the agenda items which have been submitted to the clerks' office (*Antrags-annahmestelle*) by individual Members, the Cabinet, parties, or committees, are circulated among the parliamentary whips for their comments. The whips, after consulting with their respective executive committees and, in the SPD, with the research assistants of the working groups, indicate any additions, subtractions, or changes of order which they desire. A correspondingly revised agenda is then submitted by the clerks' office to the whips, enabling them to negotiate any disputed points among themselves, or in the Council of Elders, which meets at noon on Tuesdays, the day before the first sitting of the House in each week. If the whips reach agreement, they can effectively exclude points from the agenda, whether proposed by individual Members, committees, or even the Government, on the assumption that their parties will support them. A small number of bills each term fail to reach the agenda in this way.[104]

The weekly negotiations take place within the framework of a general agreement among the parties concerning the order of consideration of major issues over a period of two to three months. On the agenda of any particular week, it is customary to begin each sitting with a question period, and to follow with interpellations, second reading debates, and first reading debates, in that sequence, an order of priority which gives precedence to the most interesting items from the public's point of view. Time hardly ever runs out before completion of the agenda, since the whips, in consultation with their executives, also agree on the number of speakers each party will send into the debates, on the order in which they are to be recognized, and on whether the speeches should be long (up to an hour) or short (fifteen to thirty minutes). Tacit acceptance of equal time for all parties has replaced the traditional division of debating time among the parties in proportion to their size, as the formal Rules provide.

Even if full agreement is reached on the agenda in the Council of Elders, it is still only provisional. At the party caucus which follows immediately upon the meeting of the Council, a party will occasionally

[104] See n. 99, *supra*.

overrule an agreement entered into by its whips. This happened, for example, near the end of the fourth term of the Bundestag, when the FDP refused to abide by an agreement reached in the Council that bills submitted at the last minute—including some designed for exploitation during the coming election campaign—be kept off the agenda.[105] In these circumstances, or when no agreement is reached in the Council, a motion may be made at the start of the meeting of the House to include the disputed items on the agenda, and the majority decides. This procedure rests on a convention directly contradicting the formal Rules, which provide that at the end of each sitting, the President will proclaim the agenda for the next one, and that "subjects which are not on the agenda can only be discussed if five Members do not object" (par. 24, par. 26, sec. 3). Since in practice the task of establishing the agenda has been undertaken by the Council of Elders, and the necessary negotiations among the parties cannot be completed sufficiently early to permit the President to announce the agenda in advance, the Rules of Procedure were suitably "interpreted" by agreement among the parties. In a footnote to the paragraph which explicitly prohibits consideration of any item not on the agenda if five Members object, an annotation explains that

in accordance with an agreement reached in the Council of Elders on April 26, 1955, if unanimity is not attained in the Council regarding the inclusion of a subject on the agenda of the House, any Member may move the inclusion of this subject on the agenda before the first item on the printed agenda is taken up. In this case paragraph 26 (3) is not applicable, but the decision on the motion is taken by majority vote.[106]

Even after this vote is taken, the agenda is not necessarily followed. If it suits the convenience of the parties, points may be taken up out of their printed order. An indication to the President that a corresponding agreement exists among the whips is all that is needed. Agreements not to call up matters requiring votes during the dinner hour are common, and, at the end of the parliamentary term, a complete disregard of the order of items to facilitate the accomplishment of a large volume of business is standard practice. Members prepared to speak to particular points find themselves completely at the mercy of

[105] Dt. Btag., 4. W.P., 191. Sitz., June 23, 1965, pp. 9569–73; 9610–14. Cf. Die Welt, FAZ, June 23 and 24, 1965.

[106] Geschäftsordnung des Deutschen Bundestages, op. cit., note to par. 26, p. 24; cf. Trossmann, Der Deutsche Bundestag, p. 32.

the whips, and it has happened that a Member of a minor party has been done out of a speech which the major parties expected to be embarrassing, by joint action of the whips to call up the point, out of order, when the Member was not present.[107] The sometimes chaotic result is partially mitigated by regular announcements of the rearrangement from the chair. Vice-President Schmid's announcement during the final sessions of 1960–1961, is typical:

Perhaps I should let you know what the parliamentary whips have in store for us during the next hours [hilarity]. Next, point no. 15, then the points nos. 17, 18, 19, 20, 23, 24, 25, 31, and 44. They hope that that can be finished during the dinner hour.[108]

But even after such announcements, the order may subsequently be rearranged, as it was in this case.

Although agreements on the agenda are among the most important, other aspects of the formal procedure have been altered or supplemented by arrangement. In violation of express provisions of the Rules forbidding it, Members are permitted to give oral explanations of their vote (par. 59).[109] Written questions to the Government and their replies are not printed in the stenographic report, which has only an indication of the number of the document containing the answer despite a contrary provision of the Rules.[110] The provisions requiring an interval of two full days between the printing of bills and their first reading, one full day between first and second readings, between the committee report and the second reading, and between the second and third readings if amendments have been adopted (par. 77, sec. 2; par. 80, sec. 1; pars. 85, 93), are rarely applied by any of the parties against each other. In return, by agreement, each party supplies the others in advance with a text of any bills or motions it intends to submit. As a result, the three-readings' sequence of the legislative process has largely been replaced by a single stage of public deliberation after the committee report. Furthermore, by agreement, the par-

[107] This was done in the closing days of the 1961 session, to avoid a speech by Herbert Schneider (DP), criticizing the exclusion of former SS members from the rights guaranteed under art. 131 of the Basic Law.

[108] *Dt. Btag.*, 3. W.P., 165. Sitz., June 29, 1961, p. 9608. Cf. *ibid.*, pp. 9631, 9655, 9664; *Dt. Btag.*, 3. W.P., 166. Sitz., June 30, 1961, pp. 9723, 9762.

[109] *Geschäftsordnung des Deutschen Bundestages, op. cit.*, note to par. 59, p. 38.

[110] *Ibid.*, note to par. 110, p. 62.

ties are extremely hesitant about demanding recorded votes, although fifty Members can insist on it under the Rules. The object of restraint in the use of this right appears to be the mutual interest party leaders have in anonymous voting, because it helps them to persuade Members that it is safe to follow the party line.[111]

The registration of this new body of procedural conventions and usages is haphazard. Certain detailed agreements, such as those revising the procedure of the question hour, those establishing the hour debates on current subjects, and those governing questions interpolated during debates from the floor, are formulated in writing as agreements of the Council of Elders, and are printed as appendices to the Rules of Procedure, with or without perfunctory ratification by the House.[112] Others are noted in the minutes privately kept by the Council, and are available only to its members and to the staff parliamentarians. A few appear as annotations in the officially published Rules of Procedure. But many others merely take the form of personal agreements among the whips. While the staff parliamentarians maintain a file of precedents, these of course include only those norms of procedure which have been recognized in a public session, not those growing informally out of the agreements among the parties.

The Relation between Formal and Informal Procedure

As the custom of making arrangements among the whips has grown, the intimate collegial spirit in which they are made has further facilitated them. The President has ruefully referred to "the trade union of the parliamentary whips" to allude to what many regard as the tendency of the whips to make agreements of convenience with each other at the expense of the interests of the Members, the parties, and the public. The limits to this development are set by the control which parties exercise over their whips. On matters of major strategy, the whips must consult closely and constantly at least with the executive committees. But one of the consequences of the need for specialization, which prompted creation of the position in the first place, is to allow the whips considerable freedom on tactics, a freedom they

[111] The number of roll calls in a four-year period was 167 in the 2d Bundestag, 46 in the 3d, and 38 in the 4th.

[112] *Geschäftsordnung des Deutschen Bundestages, op. cit.,* app. 1, 2, 6, pp. 73–77.

exercise hour by hour on the floor of the Bundestag, and day by day in their direct contacts. Their skill in distinguishing between what their parties will and will not support is borne out by the infrequency with which their decisions have been overruled. The extent to which each whip must consult his party executive is dictated by the internal structure of his party. Within the complex balance of power which exists in the CDU/CSU, the whip appears to have greater autonomy than in the more strongly led SPD. Half defending his functions to the party rank and file, half pointing with pride to his accomplishments, SPD Whip Mommer declared to an SPD party congress that

I can say, to my great satisfaction, and to the good fortune of German democracy, that the relationship among the parliamentary parties is governed by the unanimous desire to respect the rules of the game. Everyone would regard the charge that he has dealt unfairly [with another party] as a severe criticism and an embarrassment. Since that is the case, the business of the Bundestag fortunately goes smoothly, there are seldom procedural debates and even less often ugly controversies over procedure. That is why there are no scenes, as the Reichstag of the Weimar Republic knew them. . . . This is a great gain for our democracy.[113]

What Mommer failed to add was that the rules of the game which work so nicely are in important respects the creation of those few men who play the game. For the game that works so well depends on the willingness of most Members to regard procedure as a technical matter to be left to the specialists, and to forego the knowledge and the use of such rights as they are granted by the formal Rules.

The transfer of procedural authority in so many important matters from impersonal rules, subject to nonpartisan interpretation and enforcement, to party leaders, especially empowered for the purpose, has reduced the function of the formal Rules of Procedure, and of those whose task it is to apply them, interpret them, preserve precedents, and reform them. In the first Bundestag, the smaller parties still made active use of their rights under the Rules. This was especially true of the Communists, who knew how to use the Rules effectively and kept presiding officers and the parliamentarians on their toes. The decline in the function of the Rules set in during the second Bundestag with the disappearance of the Communists, the decline in the number of parties altogether, and a reduction in the number of meetings of the

---

[113] SPD Parteitag 1962, May 29, 1962, uncorrected transcript, p. 42.

House.[114] As the possibilities of interparty agreements among the parties increased, the incentive to use minority rights under the Rules declined, and the simplest forms of procedure were favored. The relatively primitive condition of the parliamentary precedents—for half a century no later commentary on German parliamentary law existed than the incomplete work of Hatschek published in 1915—played its part, by leaving the parties relatively unaware of the procedural possibilities.

When the Bundestag adopted its "permanent" Rules in December, 1951,[115] basing them largely on the Rules of the Weimar Reichstag, no one could yet be aware that profound changes in the party system and in the relationship between Parliament and Government made them inappropriate in many respects. By 1957 the need for reforms was widely recognized. But efforts by the Committee on Rules to prepare a revision encountered serious obstacles. In the first place, the power to make effective changes was already being exercised by the parliamentary whips and registered in the Council of Elders, thereby bypassing the competent committee. Secondly, the Rules Committee was also charged with dealing with the parliamentary immunity of Members in individual cases and in general, and with scrutinizing the validity of their election. These tasks continually preoccupied it. Third, neither the President nor the Director of the Bundestag staff, who is the chief parliamentarian, were convinced that a wholesale revision was desirable. When there was agreement that particular provisions needed to be changed, as those dealing with the question hour, they were changed informally by agreement among the parties, presented to the House for perfunctory approval, and published as an appendix to the Rules.[116] A ruling by the Federal Constitutional Court, declaring unconstitutional the Bundestag's financial procedure, compelled the House to adopt a new provision in 1955.[117] Two minor changes on the election of the Secretaries and the composition of the Executive Committee of the Bundestag were made in 1961.[118] In 1964, a

[114] The number of plenary sessions was 282 in the first Bundestag, 227 in the second, 168 in the third, and 198 in the fourth.
[115] Dt. Btag., 1. W.P., 179, Sitz., Dec. 6, 1951, pp. 7411–68.
[116] Geschäftsordung des Deutschen Bundestages, op. cit., app. 1, pp. 73–5. Cf. Dt. Btag., 3. W.P., 121. Sitz., June 29, 1961, pp. 6960, 7031–2.
[117] BVerfGE. 1, 144–62. The affected provision was par. 96.
[118] Par. 3, 6. For the adoption of the change, see Dt. Btag., 4. W.P., 8. Sitz., Dec. 13, 1961, p. 171.

novel provision was added enabling the Bundestag to issue regulations to safeguard any secret documents used in parliamentary deliberations.[119] The following year a change was adopted to make it possible for the parliamentary Defense Commissioner to speak before the House.[120] But besides these five specific alterations, there have been no formal amendments to the Rules, which remain substantially intact as adopted in 1951, despite the fundamental changes in their application. Two complete revisions, prepared respectively in the names of Vice-President Carlo Schmid and Rules Committee Chairman Heinrich Ritzel, designed at least to rationalize existing procedure, have been filed and forgotten.[121] A pragmatic approach dominates, favoring experimentation, informality, and caution about freezing existing procedure into formal provisions.

THE INFORMAL PARLIAMENT

The rapid and significant development of the structure of the Bundestag in the last decade has come in response to a fundamental change in the party system in Parliament, to a closer relationship between parliamentary majority and Government than has ever been known before in Germany, and to the great complexity of the issues. The decline in the number of parties, their increase in size, the pressures upon them for internal specialization, and the appearance of a governing and an opposition party, have been the motive forces. The formal structure inherited from another political age, an age with which Members had had very little direct contact, has been informally adapted and bypassed, though not always completely.

---

[119] Par. 21a, 73(6). For the adoption, see *Dt. Btag.*, 4. W.P., 132. Sitz., June 24, 1964, p. 6498. Under these provisions, a set of Regulations (*Geheimschutzordnung des Deutschen Bundestages*) was issued (see *BGBl.* I, pp. 713–14).

[120] Par. 116a-c. For the adoption of the change, see *Dt. Btag.*, 4. W.P., 159. Sitz., Jan. 27, 1965, pp. 7844–6.

[121] They are contained in a synopsis published by the Rules Committee, *Zusammenstellung der gültigen Geschäftsordnung mit den Neuredaktionsentwürfen des Abg. Schmid* (Frankfurt) *und des Abg. Ritzel* (Ausschussdrucksache 5 verändert), Ausschussdrucksache 10, June 25, 1959. Another revision prepared by the assistant of the Rules Committee, Bücker, was published as *Ausschussdrucksache* under the name of chairman Ritzel in July—August, 1961. None have made any headway toward adoption. In a letter to *Der Spiegel*, July 22, 1959, Ritzel wrote that ". . . I have learned that particularly in the law of procedure loopholes can be filled by conventions and only then be adopted as paragraphs in the Rules."

Party organization is the chief determinant of the distribution of power within this structure. Varying considerably from one party to another, it does not permit the exercise of complete authority by a small group of leaders in any of them, least of all in what has continuously been the largest party. A complex sharing of power exists between Government leaders, at the head of the executive bureaucracy; a group of party leaders, at the head of the caucuses; their parliamentary whips, authors of much of the effective procedure; and the subject specialists, who dominate many of the committees and the decisions on substantive issues.

Some of the greatest tensions in the present system seem to be the result of an uneven rate of change in various aspects of the structure. Difficulties in the relationship between the Cabinet and the parliamentary majority, for example, are partly due to the complete separation between the organization of Cabinet and of parliamentary party leadership, despite the development of government by a parliamentary majority. The complexity of the relationship between party leaders and their committee members is due to the almost uncontrolled development of subject specialization without the growth of new sources of leadership influence.

The great reliance on informal arrangements to supplement, and alter the effect of, the overt Rules, and to change the authority of the formal officers of the House, represents adaptation of an inherited organization and procedure to the new political system. But it leaves the effectiveness of the norms of parliamentary behavior extraordinarily dependent on arrangements among a few leaders and on the particular relationships which exist among the political parties at the moment.

The success of the Bundestag in adapting the structure which it has inherited to the requirements of the new party system, the new relationship between Government and Parliament, and new types of political issues, has given Parliament its present vitality. But the failure so far to formalize this new framework with written rules and published precedents, impersonally applied, is a failure to institutionalize the new pattern of power. It leaves the new pattern tenuous, largely hidden from public view by traditional rules and offices which, particularly in a legalistic political culture, are the chief objects of attention and veneration. Under these circumstances, many Members, the parties, and the interested public lack an accurate perception of the norms of behavior which comprise the framework of parliamentary action—a perception on which the long-term survival of Parliament depends.

This conclusion runs parallel to that of the previous chapter, where we indicated that the membership of the Bundestag includes a corps of professional politicians possessing the requisite skills for parliamentary leadership, in spite of public disparagement of this type of Representative. We can now say that despite public appearances to the contrary, the Bundestag has developed the procedural and organizational structure it requires in its present political setting. The analysis so far suggests that these characteristics of personnel and structure are partial responses to the position of the Bundestag in the political system, although, in turn, its composition and structure also help to determine that position. The succeeding chapters, which deal successively with the major functions which the Bundestag performs in the political system, will offer additional evidence of the reciprocal relationship between the shape of the institution and its performance.

V

Forming the Cabinet

THE Basic Law assigns certain important powers to the Bundestag: it must elect the Chancellor; legislation requires its assent. To the extent that it exercises such constitutional powers, the Bundestag performs vital political functions: the selection of the executive head of government; participation in the formulation, and the ratification, of enforceable rules. We will begin our analysis of the performance of Parliament in the German political system by examining how the Bundestag exercises its constitutional powers, and with what consequences for the system. But since political institutions may also perform functions which do not derive from their exercising—or failing to exercise—specific constitutional powers, we will propose hypotheses about the political functions which a representative institution might perform as a result of its composition and its structure, and then consider to what extent the Bundestag carries out such functions. Proceeding from the specific to the more general, we will look first at the role of Parliament in electing the Chancellor and selecting his colleagues in the Cabinet, then take up the role of the Bundestag in the legislative process, and finally deal with the representative function of Parliament.

THE SELECTION OF THE CHANCELLOR

Historical Experience and Constitutional Provisions

When a newly elected Bundestag is constituted, its first major task is to elect a Chancellor to head the Cabinet. From the viewpoint of German parliamentary development, this is the power it has acquired last. Early proposals for the "parliamentarization" of the Government, pressed with growing insistence in the waning years of the Empire, sought to make Cabinets accountable to Parliament and subject to its dismissal, but did not generally contemplate that Cabinets would be elected by Parliament or be composed of its leaders. The Weimar Constitution adopted that pattern, leaving the power to appoint the Chancellor to the President of the Republic, who acted in this respect, as in others, like a republican emperor. That this vestige of the imperial system has not survived is due to the irresponsible use of presidential power in the critical final period of the Weimar Republic. The prerogative of choosing the Chancellor gave President Hindenburg the power to replace parliamentary with presidential Cabinets in 1930. He appointed Chancellors to his own liking, representative at most of the narrow clique around him, regardless of their lack of parliamentary support, and kept them in office at his pleasure, by permitting them to govern by the use of the President's power to issue emergency decrees, and by repeatedly dissolving Parliament.

The dominant interpretation of this experience among the authors of the Basic Law for the Federal Republic was that presidential power is perilous in a multiparty system in which a popularly elected President is not likely to be chosen from among party leaders. They believed, furthermore, that a strong presidency is not in any case consistent with parliamentary government. It appeared to them that giving the President the power to appoint the Chancellor provided parliamentary leaders with a dangerous escape from their responsibility for creating a Government having the confidence of Parliament. Without much controversy, therefore, they assigned the main role in the process of selecting the Chancellor to the Bundestag.[1] According to the Basic Law, a Chancellor can be appointed only after he has been elected by the Bundestag. The President is reduced to making a single nomination. If his nominee fails to be elected by an absolute majority vote, he must formally appoint whomever the Bundestag may choose by such a vote. The President has discretion only if the Bundestag is unable to agree upon a candidate by the required majority after trying for fourteen days. He may then appoint as Chancellor the person who has

---

[1] Klaus-Berto von Doemming, Rudolf Werner Füsslein, and Werner Matz, "Die Entstehungsgeschichte der Artikel des Grundgesetzes," in Gerhard Leibholz and Hermann von Mangoldt, eds., *Jahrbuch des öffentlichen Rechts* (Tübingen: Mohr, 1951), Vol. I n.f., pp. 397–406, 426–33. Cf. J. F. Golay, *The Founding of the Federal Republic of Germany* (Chicago: University of Chicago Press, 1958), Ch. III.

received the greatest number of votes short of an absolute majority, or dismiss the Bundestag and call for new elections.[2]

Ironically, while these provisions in a sense completed the "parliamentarization" of Government, others reversed it. Again under the influence of their interpretation of the Weimar experience, the authors of the Basic Law sought constitutional remedies for that instability of Governments which had been exhibited in the succession of twenty Cabinets in the fourteen Weimar years. Although only two of these Cabinets had resigned because the Reichstag had withdrawn its confidence from them, it nevertheless appeared in retrospect that "negative" majorities of Nazis and Communists, combining in the Reichstag to overthrow Governments without being able to replace them, had been the chief cause of instability, at least in the critical period. Constitutional draftsmen after the war believed that if negative majorities could be disarmed, even governing pluralities could survive. To this end they wrote into the Basic Law a provision, already established in several *Land* constitutions, which restricts the power of the Bundestag to dismiss the Government. By this attenuation of the parliamentary relationship, the Chancellor alone is constitutionally subject to parliamentary removal, and the Bundestag can overthrow him only by electing a successor by an absolute majority vote.[3]

[2] *Basic Law*, art. 63. For an authoritative commentary, see Hermann von Mangoldt and Friedrich Klein, *Das Bonner Grundgesetz*, 2nd ed. (Berlin and Frankfurt: Verlag Franz Vahlen, 1957–1961), II, 1224–40. The most complete analysis of the constitutional position of the Chancellor is Jean Amphoux, *Le Chancellier Fédéral dans le regime constitutionnel de la République Fédérale d'Allemagne* (Paris: Librairie générale de droit et de jurisprudence, 1962).

The Federal President is elected for a five year term—once renewable—by a Federal Assembly composed of the Members of the Bundestag and an equal number of members elected by the Landtage (*Basic Law*, art. 54).

[3] *Jahrbuch des öffentlichen Rechts*, I, (1951), pp. 442–7; von Mangoldt-Klein, *op. cit.*, pp. 1288–1303. The two Weimar Governments dismissed by vote of the Reichstag were those of Chancellors Luther and Marx, both in 1926; the Government of von Papen only barely escaped votes of no confidence in two cases by dissolving the Reichstag. The basic principle underlying the new provision prohibiting any but constructive no-confidence votes had been discussed by German constitutional lawyers as early as 1929, both by those, like Alexander Rüstow, concerned to preserve the parliamentary system by strengthening the Chancellor, and those, like Otto Koellreutter, intent on replacing it with an authoritarian system. Rüstow's lecture of July 5, 1929, is reprinted in *Vierteljahreshefte für Zeitgeschichte*, VII (1959), 87–102, esp. 9–99; Koellreutter's lecture of December 20, 1932, is reprinted in Fritz Berber, ed., *Zum Neubau der Verfassung* (Berlin: Junker and Dünnhaupt, 1933), esp. pp. 33–4.

Influence of the Elections

Increasing the power of Parliament to appoint the Government while decreasing its power to dismiss it, the Basic Law of 1949 was designed with the memory of the party system of 1930 in mind. But for reasons having little to do with the Basic Law, the party system which developed in the postwar period was significantly different from that of Weimar. The new constitutional arrangements have therefore worked in some unintended ways. The electorate has significantly affected the selection of the Chancellor and the composition of the coalition. The prospective Chancellor has shared the power to appoint the Cabinet with the members of the Bundestag belonging to the coalition parties. The intention of the Constitution has been fully realized in only one respect: the President's role in the creation of the Government has been effectively limited.

These results appeared only gradually as the new configuration of party power emerged between 1949 and 1957. The election of the first Bundestag did not yet produce results clearly different from those of the Reichstag elections of the 1920's. There was a close division between the CDU/CSU, with 35 per cent of the seats, and the SPD with 33 per cent, eight parties sharing the remainder.[4] The leading party, the CDU/CSU, did not yet have any national organization, but it did have leaders who had acted on a national stage in the Parliamentary Council, which enacted the Basic Law, and in the Bizonal Economic Council, in which domestic policy for the western occupation zones had been made for two years. Konrad Adenauer's response to the close election result helped the emergence of a new party pattern. Although he was formally only the chairman of a conference of CDU *Land* chairmen, he was the party's most conspicuous national leader since he had been President of the Parliamentary Council. Taking the initiative within his own party, he advocated the formation of a coalition Government headed by the CDU/CSU but excluding the SPD, a Government led by the largest party and leaving the runner-up in the Opposition. His argument was that the chief differences between the parties were over economic policy, that the electo-

[4] CDU/CSU, 139; SPD, 131; FDP, 52; Bavarian Party, 17; German Party, 17; Communist Party, 15; Economic Reconstruction League, 12; Center Party, 10; German Reich Party, 5; Independents and others, 4; not including Berlin Representatives, whose vote does not count in the election of the Chancellor.

rate had supported the "social market economy" advocated by the CDU and rejected socialist economic planning, and that a compromise between the two would obscure the issues. Kurt Schumacher, the SPD leader, independently came to the same conclusion, both men possibly motivated in part by their unwillingness to serve together in the same Cabinet. This line-up between the CDU, governing together with smaller coalition partners, and the SPD, in opposition, had been the pattern in the Bizonal Economic Council, but not in many of the *Länder,* where coalitions including both the CDU and the SPD existed. Out of their own experience, the CDU *Land* chairmen therefore opposed Adenauer. But in the absence of a national party organization, Adenauer was in a dominant position in national politics. His national reputation assured him of election as chairman of the CDU/CSU caucus in the Bundestag, and from this vantage point, with the tactical skill for which he later became notorious, he was able to make his view prevail within his party. As chairman of the largest party in Parliament, he was able to negotiate successfully with the leaders of the other prospective coalition parties.[5] By obtaining leadership of the Government on the basis of a very narrow electoral victory, Adenauer created a presumption that the largest parliamentary party would be the chief governing party, and that its parliamentary leader would be Chancellor. In 1950 the CDU held its first national convention and elected Adenauer as party chairman, thereby clearly establishing his primacy in the party.[6]

Because of the success of the domestic and foreign policies of the Adenauer coalition, the CDU/CSU conducted the parliamentary campaign of 1953 as a plebiscite on Adenauer's Government, and the electorate responded to the suggestion that a vote for the CDU/CSU was a vote for the continuation of that Government. The result was the first parliamentary majority ever attained by a German political party in a constitutional election, and the first time that a parliamentary election conclusively determined the designation of the Chancellor.

[5] Arnold J. Heidenheimer, *Adenauer and the CDU, The Rise of the Leader and the Integration of the Party* (The Hague: Nijhoff, 1960), pp. 178–85. The first post-election meeting between Adenauer and other CDU leaders is described in detail in the authorized biography by Paul Weymar, *Adenauer* (New York: Dutton, 1957), pp. 264–9. For Schumacher's reaction to the election, see Lewis J. Edinger, *Kurt Schumacher, A Study in Personality and Political Behavior* (Stanford: Stanford University Press, 1965), pp. 120, 208–10.

[6] Heidenheimer, *op. cit.,* pp. 196–205.

This success was repeated with an even greater majority in 1957. By 1961 the SPD felt compelled to follow suit by announcing its "Chancellor candidate" in advance of the election, basing its campaign appeal also on its nominee for the highest office.[7] In 1964 it elected him national party chairman and again named him as its candidate for Chancellor.[8] Meanwhile, both before the elections of 1961 and those of 1965, the Free Democrats, the only other surviving parliamentary party, made advance commitments to enter coalitions with the CDU/CSU but not with the SPD, after voters and backers had shown a reluctance to buy a pig in a poke.[9]

Although the CDU/CSU failed to obtain an absolute majority in the Bundestag in the election of 1961, it widely outdistanced its nearest competitor, the SPD, with 242 seats to 190. While this reversal was widely regarded as a personal defeat for Adenauer, especially since the FDP had gained seats after a campaign in which it promised not to enter a coalition under his Chancellorship, he was elected Chancellor for a fourth straight time as leader of the largest party in the Bundestag, with the support of the FDP. In a weakened position, he successfully exploited the unwillingness of his party to repudiate him at a critical moment under pressure from another party. He first secured the support of the federal executive committee of his party, next the unanimous approval for his candidacy from his caucus without a word of opposition spoken, even by those prepared to write critically about him, and only then the reluctant support of the coalition partner.[10] The parliamentary party could have repudiated the claim to leadership of the man who had led it in the election only at the risk of a severe division at the critical moment when a plurality at the polls had to be transformed into a majority in the House. This gave it little real choice, and no alternatives were considered.

The only change in the Chancellorship in the history of the Federal

---

[7] The "Chancellor effect" on the German party system has been explored by Arnold J. Heidenheimer, "Der starke Regierungschef und das Parteien-System: Der Kanzlereffekt in der Bundesrepublik," *Politische Vierteljahresschrift*, II (1961), esp. 254–62.

[8] *Die Welt*, Feb. 17, 1964.

[9] *FAZ*, Sept. 15, 1961, p. 4; *Die Welt*, June 2, 1964.

[10] *Die Welt*, Sept. 20 and 28 and Nov. 3, 4 and 6, 1961; *Welt am Sonntag*, Nov. 5, 1961. Although Bucerius, a leader of the internal opposition against Adenauer, wrote against his continuation as Chancellor and voted against the final coalition agreement, he did not raise his voice in the first CDU/CSU post-election caucus in which approval was given to the party decision to support Adenauer once more (see Bucerius' article in *Die Zeit*, Oct. 6, 1961).

Republic appears to have taken place without any electoral influence, since it came between general elections. The action formally initiating the change was a recommendation from the CDU/CSU parliamentary party to the Federal President saying that it favored the appointment of Ludwig Erhard to succeed Adenauer upon his retirement. But even in this case the parliamentary party acted largely in response to electoral considerations. Erhard's claim to the succession rested largely on his superior electoral appeal over such potential rivals as Gerhard Schröder, Heinrich von Brentano, Heinrich Krone, and, at an earlier time, Franz Etzel and Eugen Gerstenmaier. The timing of the decision, which came in the middle of the parliamentary term, was strongly influenced by a succession of CDU losses in six Landtag elections, a trend which the party's leaders in the *Länder* regarded as an expression of voter dissatisfaction over Adenauer's continuation in office.[11] In early April, 1963, with another Landtag election in prospect, local party chiefs placed the parliamentary leadership under strong pressure to act on the succession. Opinion polls revealed that Erhard was at the peak of his popularity, far outdistancing all other party leaders.[12] The need to establish the new leader well in advance of the next parliamentary elections was urgently felt. While Adenauer's promised retirement was still six months away, the parliamentary party formally voted to advise the Federal President that Erhard was its choice as the next Chancellor. Although Adenauer prompted them, Schröder, Krone, and Brentano refused to be considered as alternatives. In the ballot taken in the caucus, 159 favored the motion for Erhard, 47 were opposed, 19 abstained, and 25 were apparently absent.[13] If this vote indicated some internal opposition to Erhard, from loyal friends of the old Chancellor, and from those members of the farm bloc and others who were distrustful of the new man's economic liberalism, it was also evidence that in the face of electoral considerations, the delaying and dividing tactics Adenauer had employed for four years had failed. By the time he was elected Chancellor half a year later, the internal opposition to Erhard had melted considerably, as the 279 votes which were cast for him in the Bundestag indicate. Even if, at most, 67 of these came from the FDP, at least 212 Members from his own party supported him.[14]

Although the CDU/CSU failed by four seats to gain an absolute

[11] *Die Zeit* (U.S. ed.), April 12, 1963.
[12] *Die Welt*, April 20, 1963; *Die Zeit* (U.S. ed.), May 3, 1963.
[13] *Die Welt*, April 24, 1963.   [14] *Die Welt*, Oct. 12 and 17, 1963.

majority in the Bundestag in the election of 1965, it was once again returned as the largest party in the House. The campaign which had given it a greater victory than four years earlier had been clearly led by Chancellor Erhard. The morning after the election, the party publicly committed itself to the continuation of Erhard's Chancellorship, and on the following day its chairman officially informed the Federal President of its position, eliminating the selection of the Chancellor from further negotiation.[15]

For the fifth straight time, therefore, the outcome of the election effectively determined the choice of the Chancellor. Twice, in 1953 and in 1957, the electorate has determined which party would form the Government and has, in effect, made its leader Chancellor. The President and the Bundestag had no alternative in these instances to the man who was the undisputed leader, both in the country and in the House, of a party commanding an absolute majority of seats. In the other three instances, in 1949, 1961, and 1965, the election result has prompted the formation of a Government headed by the party obtaining the largest number of Bundestag seats. In 1963, Erhard's election as Chancellor was also governed by electoral considerations.

The decisive influence of the election on the appointment of the Chancellor has three sources. First, the reduction in the number of parties has helped to produce relatively clear electoral decisions. Second, the requirements of the campaign have induced the two largest parties to commit themselves to their candidates for the Chancellorship in advance of the election, explicitly in the case of the SPD, implicitly in the CDU/CSU. This has greatly narrowed the possibilities of parliamentary bargaining on the Chancellorship after the election, and correspondingly strengthened the position of the Chancellor "candidate" of the largest party before his actual appointment. The Free Democrats learned this to their dismay in 1961, when they were unable to make good on their campaign promise to enter into a coalition with the CDU/CSU, but without Adenauer. Finally, the third party, the FDP, has lost its field of maneuver between its larger rivals, by committing itself, again for electoral reasons, to coalition with one and against coalition with the other. This greatly restricts the possibility of parliamentary bargaining on the party composition of the Government after elections.

[15] *Ibid.,* Sept. 21 and 22, 1965.

The Role of the President

With the designation of the Chancellor so largely determined by the outcome of the election to the Bundestag, the President's right to make a single nomination for the office has been largely perfunctory. He has in all six instances proposed the leader implicitly or explicitly supported by the largest party in the House, Adenauer in the first four cases, Erhard in the last two. In the absence of an absolute majority for the CDU/CSU in 1961, and in doubt about the extent of Free Democratic support which Adenauer would have in the secret ballot, by which the House elects the Chancellor, President Lübke asked for, and received, from FDP leader Mende, the result of a secret canvass of that party's parliamentary membership on the question of voting for Adenauer. Thereby he assured himself in advance that his nomination would succeed.[16] In 1963, nearly six months before Adenauer's resignation, the CDU/CSU formally advised the President that Erhard was its choice as a successor.[17] In 1965, it gave the same advice immediately after the Bundestag had been elected.

In the face of his heavy dependence on the outcome of the general election, and on the commitments of the parliamentary parties to their leaders and their alignments, the President is relatively weak. A presidential nomination, not assured in advance of parliamentary support, seriously risks presidential prestige, since the Basic Law leaves the President unable to compel the House to vote on a second nomination from him should his first fail.[18] He may, of course, in his consultations with party leaders, attempt to influence their decisions, as Lübke reportedly did in 1961 in an effort to secure support for a CDU successor to Adenauer and for an all-party coalition.[19] But the President's powers of persuasion are only personal. In 1965, Lübke's efforts to exercise influence misfired completely. Persuaded that the election

---

[16] *FAZ*, Oct. 23, 1961, p. 4; *Die Welt*, Nov. 4, 1961, p. 2.

[17] *Die Welt*, April 24, 1963.

[18] von Mangoldt-Klein, *op. cit.*, pp. 1229–30.

[19] *Der Spiegel*, XV, no. 46 (Nov. 8, 1961), 21–3. According to Rudolf Wildenmann, who directed the most thorough study of the 1961 election and its results, the President told the party leaders that if they could not agree on a coalition, he would neither appoint a Cabinet having the support of only a plurality of the House, nor call for new elections. The implication was that he would try to compel the formation of a Cabinet composed of all parties (Rudolf Wildenmann, "Parteipolitische Malaise?" in Egon Klepsch, Günther Müller, and Rudolf Wildenmann, *Die Bundestagswahl 1965* [Munich: Günther Olzog Verlag, 1965], p. 11).

would be close, he wrote to party leaders immediately before voting day asking them not to make public commitments to candidates for the Chancellorship before consulting with him. When the returns indicating a clear CDU/CSU plurality were in, that party's open recommendation to the President that Erhard be nominated as Chancellor came the more quickly and clearly for the President's attempted intervention.[20]

The President's act of nomination does set a timetable in motion which can force the Bundestag to come to a decision, for the House must vote promptly on the presidential nomination, and, if it defeats it, has only fourteen days to agree on an alternative before the decision is taken out of its hands. For at that point presidential discretion comes into play, enabling the President either to appoint the candidate having received a plurality on the final Bundestag ballot, or to dissolve the House. Since the negotiations among the parties following the election have occupied extensive amounts of time, the President's power to force a decision, or to threaten to do so, can be of some importance. In 1949, with all the organs of the Federal Government being constituted for the first time, 32 days passed between the general election and the election of the Chancellor; in 1953 there were 33 days, in 1957 the interval was 37 days, in 1961 it took a record 51 days, and in 1965 it was back to a more normal 32.[21] In 1953, presidential intervention helped to push party deliberations to a conclusion when President Heuss persuaded the Free Democrats to withdraw Thomas Dehler and the CSU not to insist on Hans Schuberth, as ministerial candidates. Both candidacies were obstacles to the formation of the Government.[22] In the record interval of 1961, Lübke twice threatened to make his own nomination if agreement on an Adenauer Government were not reached, possibly adding thereby to the pressure to complete

[20] The text of Lübke's letter to the party leaders was published in *Die Welt*, Sept. 25, 1965. Lübke revealed his preference for a "Great Coalition" in a subsequent interview (see *Die Welt*, Jan. 5, 1966; *Der Spiegel*, XX, no. 3 [Jan. 10, 1966], 15–6).

[21]

Year	*General election date*	*Date of Chancellor's election*
1949	August 14	September 15
1953	September 6	October 9
1957	September 15	October 22
1961	September 17	November 7
1965	September 19	October 20

[22] Jürgen Domes, *Mehrheitsfraktion und Bundesregierung* (Cologne and Opladen: Westdeutscher Verlag, 1964), p. 60.

the negotiations.[23] But although the President has not always waited until all agreements have been made, he has never acted until he has been confident that his nominee would be elected.

Within the important limits set by the outcome of the general election, and the formalities of presidential action, the making of the Cabinet is the work of the parliamentary parties constituting the prospective coalition. Ironically, although the Basic Law grants the power to elect the Chancellor to the Bundestag, the actual choice of the head of Government has largely escaped the House. The parliamentary election of the Chancellor tends merely to confirm what the general election has decided. But although the Basic Law says nothing about the role of the Bundestag in the appointment of the remainder of the Cabinet, it is here that some Members of Parliament exercise great influence. For the leaders of the parliamentary parties which, as a result of the election, constitute the prospective coalition are the chief negotiators on the composition of the Cabinet, as well as the nearly exclusive recipients of the spoils of office.

THE ROLE OF THE PROSPECTIVE CHANCELLOR

Party Leader

In the bargaining over the appointment of the Cabinet, the man who is, as the result of the election, the prospective Chancellor has several important sources of power. He is likely to have strong influence within his national party organization, if indeed he is not his party's chairman. Erich Ollenhauer retained the party chairmanship even after Willy Brandt had become the party's candidate for the Chancellorship in 1959. But upon Ollenhauer's death in 1963, it was inevitable that Brandt, as his party's candidate for the nation's highest office, would also be its national chairman. Adenauer, who had combined the Chancellorship with the party chairmanship for thirteen years, retained the chairmanship even after his resignation as Chancellor. But this was a transitional division of the offices, the result of the particular combination of Adenauer's tenacious hold on party power

[23] *Der Spiegel*, XV, no. 46 (Nov. 8, 1961), 21–3; *FAZ*, Oct. 20, Nov. 4, and Nov. 6, 1961. A number of prestigious newspapers urged the President to take the initiative in making a nomination even if the parliamentary parties had not reached an agreement (see "Stunde des Bundespräsidenten?" *FAZ*, Sept. 23, 1961; "Das Mass ist voll! Die Stunde des Bundespräsidenten ist gekommen," *Die Zeit*, Nov. 3, 1961).

and Erhard's initial reluctance about partisan involvement.[24] Normally, the prospective Chancellor occupies the chairmanship of the party he has led to electoral victory. The value of the influence this gives him was well demonstrated by Adenauer in 1961, when his first step after the election was to secure the support of the party's federal executive committee for both his continuation as Chancellor and his leadership of the negotiations on behalf of his party.[25] In the weeks that followed, Adenauer's strategic position enabled him to play off against each other the contending groups within the party, notably the business and labor wings. The first came to Adenauer's support out of fear that he might otherwise be driven to make arrangements with the Social Democrats, the latter in order to retain an influence over the social policies of the new Government.[26]

Appointing Power

Even if the prospective Chancellor is not also the incumbent, as Adenauer was in 1953, 1957, and 1961, and Erhard was in 1965, he can employ his powers as head of the Government—whether they are actual or potential—during the negotiations on the composition of the Cabinet. As head of Government he will control patronage. Appointment to, and dismissal from, ministerial office is made by the President on the recommendation of the Chancellor. The prospective Chancellor may therefore veto particular candidates for Cabinet posts, as Adenauer did in the cases of Brentano, Schuberth, and Dehler in 1953, and in the case of Fritz Schäffer in 1957.[27] Furthermore, under German

---

[24] *Die Zeit* (U.S. ed.), March 27, 1964, p. 3. Erhard believed that it was preferable for the Chancellor to be free of too close a tie to the party (*Die Welt*, March 17, 1964). It was soon evident that this "freedom" deprived the Chancellor of a source of control over his parliamentary majority (see "Der Volkskanzler," *Die Zeit* [U.S. ed.], Aug. 14, 1964, p. 1). After an unsuccessful attempt to establish one of his supporters in the chairmanship to succeed Adenauer, Erhard finally decided to accept the position himself. He was elected at the 1966 party conference (*Die Welt*, March 24, 1966).

[25] *Die Welt*, Sept. 20, 1961; *Der Spiegel*, XV, no. 40 (Sept. 27, 1961), 25–8.

[26] Peter H. Merkl, "Equilibrium, Structure of Interests and Leadership: Adenauer's Survival as Chancellor," *The American Political Science Review*, LVI (1962), 637–42; *Der Spiegel*, XV, no. 42 (Oct. 11, 1961), 27–8; *Die Welt*, Sept. 25, 26, 28, and 29, 1961; *FAZ*, Sept. 25 and 28, 1961.

[27] Domes, *op. cit.*, pp. 53, 57, 58, 60, 61, 71, 90. Adenauer and Erhard both successfully turned back presidential attempts by Heuss in 1949, and by Lübke in 1961 and 1965, to exercise a similar veto power over appointments recommended by the Chancellor (see *Der Spiegel*, XIX, no. 42 [Oct. 13, 1965], 31–2. *Die Zeit* [U.S. ed.], Oct. 19, 1965, p. 3).

constitutional law, the Chancellor determines the number of ministries which will exist in a Government and their respective jurisdictions, thereby controlling the number of offices to be filled.[28] This power is, of course, potentially subject to parliamentary approval of the necessary appropriations. Since only the top position in each ministry is filled by a political appointee in Germany, and there are no parliamentary secretaries as in Great Britain, the number of jobs available is relatively small. Cabinets have varied in size from fourteen to twenty-two members. The Chancellor's ability to create additional Cabinet positions, including some without administrative responsibilites, can therefore be an important factor in negotiations. In 1953 Adenauer suggested the creation of four new ministries. In the face of criticism from conservative financial circles in the parliamentary party and from others fearful of the exercise of this patronage power, only one new ministry was created, but four ministers for rather ill-defined "special assignments" were appointed and the Cabinet thus had nineteen members instead of the fourteen originally appointed in 1949. In 1957 Adenauer proposed two new ministries; one was finally created and the new Cabinet consisted of 18 members, all of them, however, heading ministries, since two new ministries had been created during the previous administration.[29] Again in 1961, the number of offices was increased to facilitate coalition agreement, two new ministries being established on Adenauer's decision and, with the appointment once again of a minister without a department, the size of the Cabinet reached a high of twenty-one.[30] In the reorganization of the Cabinet in 1962, the Ministry for Atomic Energy was recast and enhanced as a Ministry for Scientific Research. This was done to compensate the FDP, which got the new ministry, for the loss of the Ministry of Federal Property, which it had had to yield.[31]

[28] von Mangoldt-Klein, op. cit., pp. 1214–16; Theodor Eschenburg, Staat und Gesellschaft in Deutschland (Stuttgart: Schwab, 1956), pp. 759–60. See also Eschenburg's articles in Die Zeit (U.S. ed.), Jan. 4 and Feb. 22, 1963, and his exchange with Ulrich Scheuner in the issue of March 8, 1963, on the advisability of transferring this power to the Federal President. The most thorough study of the subject is Ernst Wolfgang Böckenförde, Die Organisationsgewalt im Bereich der Regierung, Eine Untersuchung zum Staatsrecht der Bundesrepublik Deutschland (Berlin: Duncker & Humblot, 1964).

[29] Domes, op. cit., pp. 57–61, 91.

[30] The new positions were the Ministry of Health and the Ministry of Economic Cooperation. The first was created under combined pressure for the appointment of a woman minister and, from physicians' groups, for the creation of such a ministry; the second was created as a fifth post for the FDP.

[31] Die Zeit (U.S. ed.), Jan. 4 and Feb. 22, 1963.

Chief Policy Maker

As head of Government, the Chancellor determines general policy. To the extent that the formation of the Government includes policy agreements, the Chancellor cannot be bound to them. When the Free Democrats attempted to impose extensive agreements on policy in 1961, in the form of a treaty of coalition, Adenauer responded with a tactically inspired assent and a barely concealed cyncism.[32] Adenauer also demonstrated that when the potential Chancellor is in office during the negotiations, if only in a "caretaker" capacity, he can employ inside information on policy problems, and also his international prestige as head of Government, to bolster his bargaining position.[33]

Dismissal Power

Once appointed, ministers serve at the Chancellor's pleasure. He can retain them in office, even against the will of their parliamentary party. Adenauer did this, for example, when he refused to dismiss Waldemar Kraft and Theodor Oberländer on the demand of the All-German Bloc, after the two men had resigned from this party in 1955, and again when he kept in office Franz Blücher, Fritz Neumayer, Viktor-Emmanuel Preusker, and Hermann Schäfer, after their resignation from the Free Democrats in the following year. In both cases, the frustrated parties quit the coalition, but the CDU/CSU, with an absolute majority, was able to carry on undisturbed. The men concerned eventually succumbed to the lack of parliamentary support, even though the first two joined the CDU and the latter group attempted to form their own party.[34] Although none of these men re-

---

[32] A text of the treaty was published in the *FAZ* on November 4, 1961, and in *Die Welt*, November 6, 1961. In an early critique of the treaty, Eschenburg wrote that "there is hardly any prospect that this pact can really be observed" (*Die Zeit*, Nov. 10, 1961). For Adenauer's attitude toward it, see *Der Spiegel*, XV, no. 45 (Nov. 1, 1961), 21–3. A good survey of the sources of the Chancellor's power to determine general policy is given by Wilhelm Hennis, *Richtlinienkompetenz und Regierungstechnik* (Tübingen: Mohr, 1964).

[33] For Adenauer's use of his special relationship with President Kennedy in 1961, see *Welt am Sonntag*, Nov. 5, 1961, p. 1; *Der Spiegel*, XV, no. 44, Oct. 25, 1961, 23–4.

[34] Eschenburg, *Staat und Gesellschaft in Deutschland*, pp. 598–9. Cf. Alfred Grosser, *La démocratie de Bonn, 1949–1957* (Paris: Librairie Armand Colin, 1958), pp. 72–3; German ed., *Die Bonner Demokratie* (Düsseldorf: Karl Rauch

Table 29. Members of the Cabinet, 1949-1965

Ministry	Date of Appointment												
	9/20/49	10/11/50	3/15/51	7/15/52	10/20/53	6/7/55	10/20/55	10/16/56	10/29/57	9/30/59	10/27/60	11/14/61	12/14/62
Chancellor	Adenauer (CDU)												
Foreign Affairs			Adenauer (CDU)			Brentano (CDU)						Schröder (CDU)	
Interior	*Heinemann* ‡ (CDU) ..... /Lehr (CDU)				Schröder (CDU)							Höcherl (CSU)	
Justice	Dehler (FDP)				Neumayer (FDP)			Schäffer (CSU)				Stammberger (FDP)	Bucher (FDP)
Finance	Schäffer (CSU)								Etzel (CDU)			Starke (FDP)	Dahlgrün (FDP)
Economics	Erhard (CDU)												
Food, Agriculture and Forestry	*Niklas* (CSU)				Lübke (CDU)					Schwarz (CDU)			
Labor and Social Policy	Storch (CDU)								Blank (CDU)				
Defense							Blank (CDU)	Strauss (CSU)					von Hassel (CDU)
Transport	Seebohm (DP)												
Post Office and Telecommunications	*Schuberth* (CSU)				*Balke*[1] (CSU)				Stücklen (CSU)				
Housing and City Planning	Wildermuth (FDP)			Neumayer (FDP)	Preusker (FDP)				Lücke (CDU)				
Expellees, Refugees and War Victims	*Lukaschek* (CDU)				Oberländer (GB)						Merkatz (CDU)	Mischnick (FDP)	
All-German Questions	Kaiser (CDU)							*Lemmer*[2] (CDU)			Merkatz (CDU)		Barzel (CDU)
Bundesrat and *Länder* Affairs	Hellwege (DP)					Merkatz (DP)							Niederalt (CSU)
Family and Youth					Wuermeling (CDU)								Heck (CDU)
Scientific Research *							Strauss (CSU)	*Balke* (CSU)					Dollinger (CSU)
Federal Property									Lindrath (CDU)		Wilhelmi[3] (CDU)		Lenz (FDP)
Economic Cooperation †	Blücher (FDP)											Scheel (FDP)	Lenz (FDP)
Health												Schwarzhaupt (CDU)	
"for Special Assignments"					Kraft (GB)								Krone[4] (CDU)
"for Special Assignments"					Schäfer (FDP)								
"for Special Assignments"					Strauss (CSU)								
"for Special Assignments"					Tillmanns (CDU)								

* Before 1962 called Atomic Energy
† Before 1953 called Marshall Plan Affairs
‡ Italics indicate ministers who were not Members of the Bundestag at the time of appointment
| Died in office

/ Resigned from office
.... Continued in office
→ Appointed to another office
⇢ Appointed to another office after an interval without appointment
: A colon indicates end of term of Bundestag

[1] Appointed 12/9/53
[2] Appointed 11/14/56
[3] Appointed 4/12/60
[4] Appointed 6/25/64

mained in the Government by 1960, the Chancellor, with the support of an absolute majority in the Bundestag, had proven stronger than the parliamentary parties in controlling his ministers and had actually induced splits in their parties. The lesson was not lost on the Free Democrats, who successfully demanded the resignation of their ministers from the Cabinet in 1962 over the "*Spiegel* affair." But in this case the party leaders had cautiously remained outside the Cabinet, Adenauer's tenure was clearly coming to an end, and the Chancellor needed the FDP to give him a parliamentary majority.[35]

Constitutionally, the Chancellor may recommend dismissal to the President in the same way as he recommends the appointment. But the power to dismiss ministers has been only sparingly demonstrated. In the two main cases, that of Oberländer in 1960 and Hans Krüger in 1964, in both instances on charges of high level participation in the National Socialist Government, resignations were forthcoming on the Chancellor's prompting.[36] In the first case, the Chancellor acted only after prolonged pressure from the press and from the Bundestag. Ministers have, on the whole, enjoyed a remarkable tenure in office. Fifty-six men held ministerial positions during the first sixteen years of the Federal Republic, for an average term of nearly five years, one year longer than the life of a Parliament. Of thirty-four replacements of men in office, thirteen were due to death or voluntary resignations, four were in effect dismissals or unwillingness on the part of the Chancellor to reappoint, and the other seventeen were due to changes in support within or among the parliamentary parties.[37] (See Table 29.) The tendency has clearly been to retain the services of a minister rather than to replace him, even in the face of public and parliamentary criticism, in part because each dismissal reopens negotiations on appointments and hence challenges the Chancellor's control over

Verlag, 1960), pp. 101–2. U. W. Kitzinger, *German Electoral Politics; A Study of the 1957 Campaign* (Oxford: Clarendon Press, 1960), pp. 12–4. Schäfer, Neumayer, and Kraft resigned later in 1956, Oberländer in 1960; Preusker and Blücher were not reappointed to the Government in 1957.

[35] *Die Welt*, Nov. 20, 1962, p. 1; Nov. 21–22, 1962, p. 3.

[36] *Die Welt*, May 5, 1960, and Feb. 1, 1964, respectively.

[37] Died in office: Lindrath, Tillmanns, Wildermuth.

Voluntary resignations or unwillingness to serve another term: Heinemann, Brentano, Lübke, Niklas, Lehr, Kaiser, Hellwege, Etzel, Schäffer, Bucher.

Dismissal or unwillingness to reappoint: Oberländer, Krüger, Schuberth, Dehler.

The ministerial changes after the "*Spiegel* affair" in 1962, including the failure to reappoint Strauss, were not voluntarily undertaken by the Chancellor.

his Government. Because expertise is valued, it is rare even to reshuffle portfolios among the same group of men.

The Chancellor's Tenure

The Chancellor himself is not readily subject to dismissal, thanks to the constitutional limits on the Bundestag's power to compel his resignation. Since parliamentary coalitions merely for the purpose of overthrowing the Chancellor are constitutionally ineffective, loss of coalition support can force a Chancellor out only if a new governing coalition headed by a new Chancellor can be found. This, however, requires a realignment of parties which is very risky for the Free Democrats, in view of the pre-election coalition commitments they have made in recent years. Their switch from CDU to SPD in the North-Rhine–Westphalian Landtag in 1956 was followed by a loss of votes in the following election. The party regarded this loss as an indication that it could not exercise its freedom of maneuver with impunity, against the expectations of its financial supporters, its members, and its electorate.[38] Negotiations between Adenauer and the SPD in 1962 for a "Great Coalition" indicated substantial obstacles within each of the large parties to such a realignment.[39] Party alignments in the Bundestag are rigid so far as the formation of governing majorities is concerned. Adenauer therefore survived, in 1962, the most severe coalition crisis of his career, although all his ministers resigned and the Cabinet was reconstituted. This illustrates that, even when his Government rests on a coalition, the Chancellor can be forced out only if his own party turns against him. Adenauer's survival, through all the efforts to unseat him in the four years following the withdrawal of his offer to vacate the Chancellorship for the Presidency in 1959, indicates the inhibitions that exist to this type of internal party revolt. As long as his party regards his leadership as an asset, a Chancellor can defiantly challenge it to introduce a no-confidence motion against him if it is dissatisfied with a particular action he has taken, as Adenauer did in

[38] For an analysis of FDP electoral strength, see Gerard Braunthal, "The Free Democratic Party in West German Politics," *The Western Political Quarterly*, XIII (1960), esp. 345–7. An analysis of the restrictions on the FDP's freedom of maneuver is given by Peter Merkl, *op. cit.*, pp. 642–9. For its relationship with its financial supporters after the events of 1956, see Rupert Breitling, "Das Geld in der Deutschen Parteipolitik," *Politische Vierteljahresschrift*, II (1961), esp. 358–61.

[39] *Die Zeit* (U.S. ed.), Dec. 14, 1962; *Die Welt*, Dec. 4, 5, 6, 7, 1962.

response to criticism over his attitude toward the Presidential nomination in 1959, and Erhard did in answer to foreign policy criticism he encountered in 1964.[40] In these cases the Chancellor was secure in the realization that his party could not survive electorally if it disowned him. But in 1963, after his position in the party had been weakened, Adenauer was unable to stop the parliamentary caucus from recommending Erhard's succession and thereby enforcing his promise to resign in the middle of his fourth term. In that event, however, there was no resort to a formal vote of no-confidence, but only a clear assertion of the Chancellor's ultimate dependence on the support of his party in the Bundestag.

THE ROLE OF THE COALITION PARTIES

Dominance of the Parliamentary Leaders

In the creation of a Government, therefore, the prospective Chancellor occupies a position of strength but not of omnipotence. His partners in negotiation are the leaders of those parties which must constitute the coalition as a result of the outcome of the election. Their chief negotiators are their parliamentary leaders. Participation of the party leaders in the *Länder* has been limited, occurring mainly in the first stage when a party decides to open coalition discussions with another party, and in the final stage, when the negotiated agreements require ratification on behalf of the entire party. The issues and personalities considered in the detailed negotiations are largely national, the concern almost exclusively of the national leaders, most of whom occupy prominent positions in the Bundestag.[41] In the CDU, the federal executive committee is, both by party statute, and as a result of its subordination under Adenauer so long as he was Chancellor, a weak institution.[42] Franz-Josef Strauss has likewise been able to dominate the CSU executive committee and to use it to support his parliamentary tactics. Erhard may not dominate his national party organization as Adenauer did, but the group with which he shares power consists almost entirely of parliamentary leaders: ten of the twelve

[40] Domes, *op. cit.*, p. 108; *Die Welt*, July 13, 1964.

[41] Sixty per cent of the members of the federal executive committee of the CDU were Bundestag Members in 1960; for the FDP the figure was 50 per cent (see Domes, *op. cit.*, p. 47; Braunthal, *op. cit.*, p. 335).

[42] Heidenheimer, *Adenauer and the CDU*, pp. 201–4.

members of the party presidium elected at the 1966 conference belonged to the Bundestag. In the FDP, decentralization and disunity
existed at all levels of the party during the 1950's, expressing themselves occasionally as conflicts between the parliamentary and the
extraparliamentary organizations. But this type of division ended
when Erich Mende assumed the federal chairmanship of the party in
1960, combining the parliamentary and extraparliamentary leadership.[43] The main potential challengers to the parliamentary leaders in
both parties are individual *Land* leaders, and their interests are not
usually national.

In 1949 Adenauer knew that the *Land* chairmen of the party, for
their own parochial reasons, opposed a national coalition which did
not include the SPD. To evade their opposition, he initiated the
negotiations for the first Government with a group of CDU leaders
who had been prominent in the Parliamentary Council and the Economic Council of the Bizonal Administration—in other words, with
the party chieftains who had served on national bodies. On the excuse
that "there was no party organ authorized to speak for all three
zones,"[44] Adenauer invited this group of men, *ad hoc,* to discuss the
formation of the Government and conspicuously excluded the *Land*
leaders who had not served nationally or campaigned for seats in the
Bundestag. Although the ministers-president of the *Länder*—five representing the CDU/CSU, five the SPD, and one the FDP—"emphati-
cally expressed themselves in favor of a grand coalition" of all three
parties, Adenauer got the CDU/CSU Members of the Bundestag, at
their first meeting, to agree to a coalition without the SPD, on the
pattern of the Bizonal Council. With this support, he conducted negotiations with the parliamentary leaders of his prospective coalition
partners, Blücher of the FDP and Heinrich Hellwege of the DP.[45]

By 1953, the pattern was established. Adenauer, now formally the
national chairman of his party, and implicitly its nominee for the
Chancellorship, negotiated with the members of the incumbent Cabinet and with the parliamentary leaders of the existing coalition, Brentano and Krone for the CDU, Franz-Josef Strauss for the CSU,
Blücher, Schäfer, Willy Rademacher, and Mende for the FDP, and
Kraft and four colleagues for the newly elected All-German Bloc. The
federal executive committee of the CDU, which includes CDU *Land*

[43] Braunthal, *op. cit.,* pp. 334–5.   [44] Heidenheimer, *op. cit.,* p. 180.
[45] *Ibid.,* pp. 180–5.

Plate IX. A meeting of the SPD parliamentary party. On the rear wall is a picture of former SPD leader Kurt Schumacher. (Courtesy of Georg Munker, Bonn.)

leaders, together with the CSU *Land* executive, met in the first stage of the deliberations, four days after the election, to agree to continue the existing coalition and to consider adding to it—in order to secure a two-thirds majority in the House—members of the All-German Bloc. Once the Bundestag and its caucuses had constituted themselves, one month after the election, the parliamentary parties and their executives became Adenauer's main negotiating partners. Four full meetings of the CDU/CSU caucus took place at critical stages during the final two weeks of negotiations.

In 1957, this caucus exercised an even more extensive influence, after the CDU/CSU victory at the polls had brought the party 270 out of 497 Bundestag seats, and only the 17-Member DP remained as a prospective coalition partner. It had survived electorally only by the grace of alliances in certain constituencies with its larger associate, and it had therefore become a satellite of the CDU. The departure of the FDP from the Government in 1956, and the failure of the All-German Bloc to win any seats in the House in the 1957 election, determined their exclusion from the new coalition. The opportunity which Adenauer had had in 1953 of playing the various coalition parties off against each other did not exist four years later. One measure of the shifting focus of the negotiations is the fact that while 17 out of 28 official discussions over the formation of the Government in 1953 had taken place between Adenauer and the minor parties, 20 out of 26 official meetings in 1957 were with delegations of the CDU/CSU parliamentary party. The federal executive of the CDU again met, together with the CSU *Land* executive, four days after the election; then it retired into the background. Subsequently, the CSU named a separate negotiating committee consisting of its chairman, Hanns Seidel, and three parliamentary leaders, Richard Stücklen, Werner Dollinger, and Hermann Höcherl. It was active throughout the deliberations, and its Bundestag Members remained in close touch with the *Land* leadership.

The CDU/CSU caucus constituted itself this time within three weeks after the election, a week in advance of the first meeting of the Bundestag, but interested groups of its Members, many of them by now organized as factions, had met with Adenauer even earlier. These included delegations of Members from particular *Länder*, including Schleswig-Holstein, North Rhine–Westphalia, and Baden-Württemberg; a deputation from the labor group of the CDU, which had named a special negotiating committee of four Members to present its demands; an "economic committee" of the CDU, composed of Members identified with business; and groups of Members representing agricultural and expellee interests. The full caucus was the scene of heated discussions on the composition of the new Cabinet in four sessions during the two weeks preceding the election of the Chancellor. One meeting was held just two hours before the vote.[46]

After the 1961 election in which the CDU/CSU lost its absolute majority and the FDP had campaigned on a promise not to enter a Government that included Adenauer, the negotiations were particularly difficult. The CDU/CSU held 241 out of 499 seats while the FDP had raised its strength from 41 to 67, seeing in this gain a confirmation of its campaign position. The CDU federal executive committee, which Adenauer had called into session immediately after the election to extract from it a public statement of support for his continuation as Chancellor, saddled him with a twelve-man negotiating committee which included, in addition to parliamentary and Cabinet leaders, four *Land* leaders of the party. The CSU and the FDP each appointed seven-man committees, led and dominated by their parliamentary leaders, but including, for the FDP, three prominent *Land* leaders.[47]

In the course of the wearying six weeks of negotiations, however, the parliamentarians, generally favoring a coalition, dominated the discussions and prevailed over the *Land* leaders, who were, especially in the CSU and the FDP, most hesitant. Eighteen joint meetings of the negotiating committees were held, mostly consisting of the parliamentary leaders who headed them. There were eleven sessions of the FDP caucus, seven of the CDU/CSU caucus and five of its executive, and countless smaller meetings on each side. The parliamentary caucuses entered the negotiations earlier than ever. The Free Democrats called their lame-duck and newly elected Members together with their federal executive committee two days after the election. A comparable CSU meeting and a session of the executive committee of the CDU/CSU caucus followed on successive days, and the CDU/CSU caucus itself met six days thereafter.[48]

[46] Domes, *op. cit.*, pp. 50–74.

[47] *Die Welt*, Sept. 20, 1961. The *Land* leaders on the CDU negotiation committee were Peter Altmeier, Josef Dufhues, Kurt-Georg Kiesinger, and Kai-Uwe von Hassel; in the case of the FDP they were Wolfgang Haussmann, Willi Weyer, and Edgar Engelhard.

[48] *Die Welt*, Sept. 20, 21, 22, and 28, 1961.

The Free Democrats, in some danger of a party split for reneging on their pledge not to serve under Adenauer, called a meeting of the main committee of the party's national conference to ratify the parliamentary party's decision in favor of coalition. Despite a heated and lengthy discussion, the parliamentarians prevailed, and thereafter had full control over the detailed negotiations on personnel for the new Government.[49] In the CSU, the parliamentarians were similarly in control, despite efforts by Strauss to assert independent influence by relying on the hostility to Adenauer on the part of *Land* leaders in Bavaria.[50] For the CDU, the negotiations were primarily conducted by Krone, on behalf of the parliamentary party.

The fourth Adenauer Government, so arduously formed, lasted only a year. The event which upset it was the decision taken at a joint meeting of the federal executive and the parliamentary caucus of the FDP for the collective resignation of the five Free Democratic ministers over the "*Spiegel* affair." The resignation of the CDU/CSU ministers followed a similar meeting of CDU/CSU parliamentary and national leaders. But in negotiating the reconstitution of the Government, the CDU/CSU and the FDP parliamentary groups asserted their primacy by naming a negotiating committee entirely composed of Members of the House.[51] With no new coalition required, and no new election results to be interpreted, the extraparliamentary leaders stayed out. The long-drawn-out and less formal discussions attending the reorganization of the Cabinet upon Erhard's succession the following year were also entirely in the hands of the parliamentary leaders.

In 1965 the party caucuses constituted themselves with even greater speed than before. Their executive committees met the day after the

[49] The 67 FDP parliamentarians, many of whom were on the 96-member main committee, favored entry into the Government by a five-to-one margin. The 26 delegates from the two largest *Länder*, North Rhine–Westphalia and Baden-Württemberg, were likewise in favor, partly because coalitions with the CDU/CSU existed in these states, partly because their leaders had participated in the national coalition negotiations. This made a majority in the Committee in favor of joining the Government. Opposition came mainly from the small, northern *Länder*, Schleswig-Holstein, Bremen, and especially Hamburg, where a *Land* election due within two weeks made the local leaders extremely desirous of keeping campaign pledges. *Die Welt*, Oct. 23, 1961; *FAZ*, Oct. 20, 1961; *Die Zeit*, Oct. 20, 1961. See also Merkl, *op. cit.*, p. 649.

[50] *Der Spiegel*, XV, no. 43 (Oct. 18, 1961), 25–33.

[51] *Die Welt*, Nov. 20, 21–22, and 29, 1962.

elections and the entire parliamentary parties followed one to three days later. The delegations chosen to negotiate with the prospective Chancellor consisted of seventeen members, twelve of them party leaders in the Bundestag. The parliamentarians clearly dominated the critical phases of the bargaining, using the extraparliamentary organs of the party mainly to ratify their decisions. The subordination of the national to the parliamentary officers of the parties was demonstrated with particular sharpness by the conspicuous failure of Adenauer, relying on his powers as CDU chairman, to exert influence on the composition of the Cabinet.[52]

Sources of Parliamentary Influence

Clearly established as the chief negotiating partners of the prospective Chancellor, the parliamentary leaders, for their part, have several sources of influence to offset his. The formation of the Government cannot take place until an absolute majority of the Members of the Bundestag have elected the Chancellor in a secret ballot, in which the Members are free of overt party discipline. Even if their eventual choice is largely a foregone conclusion, the prospective Chancellor must satisfy his constituency in the House before he can take office. The vote in six Chancellorship elections indicates that the candidate has always fallen somewhat short of winning the full support of the coalition parties. Adenauer's 202 votes in 1949—a bare majority—were 3 short of the total number of Members belonging to the coalition parties who were not marked absent from the session at which the balloting took place. His 305 votes in 1953 fell 19 short; in 1957 his 274 votes were 7 short; and in 1961, after six weeks of hard bargaining, his 258 votes, just 8 more than the absolute majority, were 47 short.

[52] The negotiators for the CDU included three representatives of the national party, its chairman, Adenauer, himself of course also a Bundestag Member, its managing chairman, Dufhues, and its North-Württemberg chairman, Scheufelen. The other members of the delegation were the chairman and vice-chairmen of the parliamentary party, Barzel, Brand, and Struve, its whip, Rasner, and the leader of its labor wing, Katzer. The CSU was represented by Strauss, who was both party chairman and chairman of the parliamentary group, as well as by Dollinger, incumbent minister and former leader of the parliamentary group, and Huber, a *Land* leader. The FDP negotiators consisted, in addition to party chairman and Bundestag Member Mende, of parliamentary chairman and vice-chairman, Kühlmann-Stumm and Mischnick, two other parliamentarians, Bucher and Genscher, and one *Land* leader, Weyer. Near the end of the negotiations, the party's main committee met to ratify the course of the negotiations (*Die Welt,* Sept. 24, 25, Oct. 6, 18, 1965).

Erhard's election, in 1963, by 279 votes, was 25 short of the 304 members of the CDU/CSU and FDP in attendance.[53] In 1965, FDP leaders threatened to absent their entire membership in the Bundestag from the meeting to elect the Chancellor, unless their demands were first met. In that way, they sought to prevent any of their Members from secretly voting for Erhard, whose own party was only four votes short of the required absolute majority. The prospective Chancellor thereupon yielded two days before the scheduled election on the crucial question of FDP leader Mende's retention of the Ministry of All-German Questions.[54] The Bundestag then elected Erhard Chancellor, giving him 272 votes, 19 less than the number of coalition members present; 15 of them must have abstained, and 4 voted against him.[55] This fluctuation in the extent of support that the candidate for the Chancellorship has received from the members of the coalition indicates that they are not ciphers whose electoral support can be taken for granted.

A prospective Chancellor must not only satisfy his constituency in the Bundestag *before* he takes office. Once established, his Government continues to require the support of at least some majority in the House for the passage of each item in its legislative program, for every appropriation it requires, and for protection against the various harassments of which the Parliament is capable, such as investigations, interpellations, and the passage of policy resolutions. The power of the parliamentary majority over the composition of the Cabinet was demonstrated, for example, in the case of the dismissal of Minister Oberländer. In this instance, it was the signature of nearly a hundred Members of the CDU/CSU to a motion demanding the creation of an investigating committee to look into the charges of the minister's wartime activities which finally compelled the Chancellor to request his resignation.[56] The continuing dependence of the Cabinet on parlia-

[53] The results of the votes can be compared with the list of excused Members, in *Dt. Btag.*, 1. W.P., 3. Sitz., Sept. 15, 1949, pp. 13–4; 2. W.P., 3. Sitz., Oct. 20, 1953, pp. 7–8; 3. W.P., 2. Sitz., Oct. 22, 1957, pp. 13–4; 4. W.P., 2. Sitz., Nov. 7, 1961, p. 10; 4. W.P., 87. Sitz., Oct. 16, 1963, p. 4171. See also Domes, *op. cit.*, pp. 58, 73, whose figures for 1953 and 1957 are slightly different. For Erhard's 1963 election, also see *Die Welt*, Oct. 17, 1963.

[54] *Der Spiegel*, XIX, no. 43 (Oct. 20, 1965), 38. *Die Welt*, Oct. 20, 1965.

[55] *Dt. Btag.*, 5. W.P., 2. Sitz., Oct. 20, 1965, pp. 8–9. Although six of the 202 SPD Members were absent, 200 votes were cast against Erhard. There were 15 abstentions. Three CDU Members were absent.

[56] *Die Welt*, May 5, 1960.

mentary majorities derives from traditional parliamentary relationships rather than from new constitutional provisions for the election of
the Chancellor. The influence of Parliament on the Cabinet is greater
today than it was under the Weimar Republic because of the effective
concentration of party power in the parliamentary leadership of a
small number of parties, and the elimination of the most tempting
forms of emergency government without Parliament.

The election of the Chancellor has taken place each time before the
negotiations on the composition of the Government are completed,
indicating that parliamentary influence hardly lapses with the election.
The parliamentary leaders would otherwise resist this timing. Nine of
nineteen Cabinet appointments were decided after the election of the
Chancellor in 1953, three of eighteen in 1957 along with designation of
the Vice Chancellor, and four of twenty-one in 1961. The reconstitution of the Government in 1962, involving changes in eight ministerial
positions, of course took place without any new Chancellor election,
since Adenauer remained in office. Nevertheless, it was carried out
under heavy parliamentary influence, originating in the withdrawal of
parliamentary support and governed in the new appointments by
parliamentary considerations. Erhard's first Government was completely formed on the day of his election. Although prior to his
election in 1965, Erhard had given assurances to the FDP regarding
the retention of Mende, and to the CSU that it would have five
ministers in the Cabinet, a number of specific appointments were still
uncertain, including the ministries of the Interior, Justice, Expellees,
Housing, and Scientific Research.[57]

BARGAINING

Objects

The chief prizes for which the parliamentary parties and the prospective Chancellor bargain are the ministerial positions, but these are
not the only stakes. In 1949 the presidency of the Republic and of both
the Bundestag and the Bundesrat were included in the negotiations.

[57] Domes, *op. cit.*, pp. 58–9, 72–3, 78–9. In 1961 the appointments remaining at
the time of the election were those to the Ministries of the Interior and Justice,
and the appointments of a Minister of Health, and a Minister for Special
Assignments, were also still to come (*FAZ*, Nov. 8, 11, 14 and 15, 1961; *Die Welt*,
Oct. 16, 1963; *Die Welt*, Oct. 20 and 21, 1965; *Der Spiegel*, XIX, no. 43 [Oct. 20,
1965], 43).

Also part of the bargain were ambassadorships and appointments to the positions of state secretaries, the seconds in command in each department, who have traditionally been recruited from the civil service but subject to political appointment.[58] State secretaries were once again the objects of avid bargaining in 1961. Bundestag vice-presidencies for the CSU in 1953 and 1961, and for the DP in 1957, have also been included, as well as the chairmanship of the Foreign Affairs Committee in 1961. The presidency of the Bundestag became involved in the negotiations in 1965, when the FDP implied that it might support an SPD candidate for that office if it were not included in the governing coalition.[59] Finally, Government policy and the size of the proposed Cabinet may be objects of bargaining. Indeed, any objects the negotiators feel they can control are negotiable. But this also sets the limits. In fact, in 1949, the Bundesrat rebelled against the agreement of the Cabinet negotiators that the Bavarian, Hans Ehard, should be elected President, and elected Karl Arnold of North-Rhine–Westphalia instead.[60] There was strong opposition in the Bundestag to a vice-presidency for the small DP in 1957, and it took half a year of intraparliamentary bargaining to make good the agreement.[61] In 1961, the SPD successfully blocked the effort of the CDU/CSU to turn the chairmanship of the Foreign Affairs Committee over to FDP leader Mende as part of the coalition agreement, and the efforts that year to tie down Government policy in a lengthy coalition treaty also failed. The Chancellor and the competent ministers also largely blocked the political appointment of the quota of state secretaries promised the Free Democrats.[62]

[58] Heidenheimer, *op. cit.*, pp. 181–5; Eschenburg, *Staat und Gesellschaft in Deutschland,* pp. 758–9; Theodor Eschenburg, *Ämterpatronage* (Stuttgart: Schwab, 1961), pp. 62–6, 71–5. Theodor Eschenburg, "Staatssekretär nach Proporz," *Die Zeit* (U.S. ed.), Sept. 13, 1963.

[59] On the vice-presidencies in 1953 and 1957, see Domes, *op. cit.*, pp. 54, 63; on the vice-presidencies in 1961, see *Dt. Btag.,* 4. W.P., 1. Sitz., Oct. 17, 1961, pp. 6–7; on the unsuccessful attempt to give FDP leader Mende the Foreign Affairs Committee chairmanship in 1961, see *Die Welt,* Dec. 13, 1961, and Jan. 5, 10, 11, 12, 17, and 19, 1962; *FAZ,* Jan. 17, 1962; on the presidency in 1965, see *Der Spiegel,* XIX, no. 44 (Oct. 27, 1965), 31, 34.

[60] Heidenheimer, *op. cit.*, p. 184.

[61] *Dt. Btag.,* 3. W.P., 24. Sitz., April 23, 1958, pp. 1291–3, 1304.

[62] *Die Welt,* Nov. 21, and Dec. 21, 1961, Jan. 4, 12, 16, 17, February 8, and March 1, 1962; *Der Spiegel,* XVI, no. 4 (Jan. 24, 1962), 19–20; XVI, no. 29 (July 18, 1962), 20, 22; *Die Zeit* (U.S. ed.), Nov. 9, 1962.

Recruitment Pattern

A good index of parliamentary influence on the formation of the Government is the strong tendency to recruit the Cabinet from the membership of the Bundestag. Parliamentary government did not traditionally mean government by parliamentarians in Germany. Even in the Weimar Republic, three-eighths of Cabinet members, including four out of twelve Chancellors, were not and had never been Reichstag Members, and in the parliamentary regimes of the *Länder* today, the practice of making ministerial appointments only from the Landtag is not yet fully established.[63] In the first Adenauer Government of 1949, four out of fourteen members were from outside the Parliament, though one of these, Wilhelm Niklas, entered it less than two years later.[64] *Land* leaders, whom Adenauer had deliberately bypassed in the negotiations, were conspicuously absent from the Cabinet. Five Cabinet members, including two of those not in the Bundestag, had been party or administrative leaders in the Economic Council, and four had served in the Parliamentary Council.[65] In the 1953 Government, only one difficult appointment was made outside the Bundestag, and the appointee entered the House at the next election.[66] The practice recurred only once more, with the appointment of the national deputy chairman of the CDU and minister-president of Schleswig-Holstein, von Hassel, as Minister of Defense, in the reorganization of 1962.[67] He had served in the Bundestag for only a year of the term to which he was elected in 1953; then he resigned to head the *Land* government. But he, too, re-entered the House at the next election.

The appointment of Erhard's chief of staff, Ludger Westrick, to ministerial rank in 1964 and his reappointment in 1965 was solely for the purpose of retaining the service of a man who faced compulsory

[63] On recruitment in the Weimar Republic, see Maxwell E. Knight, *The German Executive, 1890–1933* (Stanford: Stanford University Press, 1952), pp. 15, 17. The non-parliamentary Chancellors were Cuno, Luther, von Papen, and von Schleicher. About one-quarter of the ministerial appointments in the *Länder* have been made outside the Landtag in the postwar period, though the proportion appears to be declining and the non-parliamentary appointments tend to be made to the lesser offices.

[64] Heinemann, Lukaschek, Niklas, Schuberth.

[65] From the Economic Council: Blücher, Erhard, Niklas, Schuberth, Storch; from the Parliamentary Council: Adenauer, Dehler, Kaiser, Seebohm.

[66] Minister for the Post Office, Balke.   [67] *Die Welt,* Dec. 12, 1962.

civil service retirement because of age, and is not therefore a genuine case of ministerial appointment outside of Parliament.[68] Even press speculation about ministerial candidacies, which took little account of parliamentary membership in 1949 and 1953, has been largely limited since 1957 to Members of Parliament, indicating a new recognition of the importance of this qualification.[69] Some men have sought Bundestag seats largely to become eligible for ministerial positions. Franz Etzel, for example, left the High Authority of the Coal and Steel Community in 1957 to campaign for a seat, and was appointed Minister of Finance upon his election victory. Only five of the eleven members of the "governing team" which the SPD presented to the electorate in 1961 belonged to the Bundestag at that time, but five others contested and won seats in that election, two of them resigning once the Government had been formed without them. Seven of ten party leaders whom Brandt named at the 1964 party conference as members of a prospective SPD Government were Members of the Bundestag, and nine of them were candidates for the House in 1965.[70]

Not parliamentary membership alone, but additional parliamentary qualifications among ministerial appointees, give further evidence of parliamentary influence on the selection process. Half the members of the first Adenauer Government, including the four who were not parliamentarians, possessed political experience only on the executive-administrative level at the time of their appointment.[71] Among the other half, six had had Landtag experience, and one had sat in the Weimar Reichstag; three among these had served in the Parliamentary Council which drafted the Basic Law.[72] But these proportions changed

[68] *Die Welt,* June 17 and 18, 1964. See the critical commentary of Theodor Eschenburg, *Die Zeit* (U.S. ed.), July 3, 1964, p. 2.

[69] Domes, *op. cit.,* p. 80.

[70] Of the 1961 "team," Deist, Erler, Jaksch, Schmid, and Strobel were Members of the Bundestag; Brandt, Brauer, Möller, Steinhoff, and Zinn won seats that year, but of the latter, Brandt and Zinn resigned their seats after the election. Of the 1965 "team," Erler, Heinemann, Möller, Schellenberg, Carlo Schmid, Strobel, and Wehner were Members of the Bundestag; Helmut Schmidt had resigned the seat to which he had been elected in 1961 to assume a position in the Government of Hamburg, and was elected again in 1965; the other two, Schiller and von Knoeringen, had never been in the Bundestag, but Schiller was elected in 1965.

[71] Erhard, Heinemann, Lukaschek, Niklas, Storch, Schuberth, Wildermuth.

[72] Adenauer, Blücher, Dehler, Hellwege, Schäffer, and Seebohm had had Landtag experience, Kaiser had been a member of the Reichstag, and Adenauer, Dehler, and Kaiser had belonged to the Parliamentary Council.

substantially in subsequent Governments. Not only membership but seniority in the Bundestag has become a conspicuous ministerial qualification. Sixteen of the nineteen members of the second Adenauer Cabinet who were Members of the House had belonged to the Bundestag throughout the previous term; another had served for one year of that term.[73] Among the eighteen members of the third Adenauer Cabinet, fourteen had served two terms in the House, three had had one term, and only one had just entered.[74] The trend continued in the Cabinet appointed in 1961, among whose twenty-one members twelve had been Bundestag Representatives throughout the three previous terms, seven had been Members for two terms, and only two for just one term.[75] Although the reorganizations of the Cabinet in 1962 and 1963 brought in ten fresh faces, the nine Members of the House among them had an average Bundestag seniority in excess of two Bundestag terms at the time of their appointment. Of the four new additions to the Cabinet in 1965, one had served in the Bundestag from the beginning; the others had each had two previous terms.

Furthermore, the tendency has been to recruit ministers from among the leadership of the parliamentary parties, partly from among committee chairmen but to a far greater extent from the executive committees of the parliamentary parties, the same bodies which largely conduct the negotiations. Their ability to get their own members into office is another measure of their influence. Five of the ten newcomers to the second Adenauer Government had served on the executive committee of their parliamentary party in the first Bundestag, constituting all but one of those who had had a previous full term in the House; one had also been a committee chairman.[76] Brentano and Hans Joachim von Merkatz, added to the Cabinet in mid-term, were the chairmen of their respective parliamentary parties. Two of the four new members of the third Cabinet also came from the caucus execu-

[73] The exceptions were Kraft and Oberländer of the All-German Bloc, which had just contested its first national election.

[74] This was Siegfried Balke, who had belonged to the previous Cabinet as the only nonparliamentary minister.

[75] Balke, and Mischnick of the FDP.

[76] Schröder, who had been deputy chairman of the caucus, Strauss, who had been chairman of the CSU group and of the Bundestag Committee on Youth, Tillmanns and Wuermeling, who had served on the CDU/CSU executive, and Schäfer, who had been chairman of the FDP caucus.

tive, three of them also having held committee chairmanships.[77] In the fourth Cabinet formed by Adenauer, all three new CDU/CSU members had belonged to their parliamentary executives; one of them, Krone, had been its chairman, the other two, Höcherl and Elisabeth Schwarzhaupt, deputy chairmen. The FDP leadership, because it had made the compromise of accepting Adenauer's continuation as Chancellor, felt unable to join the Government. Nevertheless, the new FDP members of the Cabinet included the deputy chairman of the caucus, one of its parliamentary whips, and a Bundestag committee chairman; of the other two, one had served on the federal executive committee of the FDP.[78] In the course of the cabinet reshuffles in the following two years, the FDP's new appointees included Mende, its chairman; Ewald Bucher, its parliamentary whip; and Rolf Dahlgrün, a Bundestag committee chairman; and six of the seven new CDU/CSU Cabinet members who were in the Bundestag were drawn from the executive of the parliamentary party, including two of its deputy chairmen and one of its parliamentary whips.[79] Three of the four newcomers to the Cabinet in 1965 were members of the CDU/CSU executive committee; one was a Bundestag vice-president, and chairman of the Defense Committee.[80]

There has also been some interchange between Cabinet and parliamentary executive positions. Dehler became FDP caucus chairman in 1953 after he had left the Government, and Brentano did the same when his party elected him chairman in 1961. He had been caucus chairman when he was appointed Foreign Minister in 1955. Strauss became chairman of the CSU parliamentary group on his dismissal from the Government in 1962; Barzel became first acting chairman, then chairman, of the CDU/CSU caucus, when he failed to be reappointed as minister in the reshuffle of 1963. Lemmer was elected

[77] Etzel had been chairman of the Economics Committee during the first Bundestag; Lücke, chairman of the Housing Committee during the first and second Bundestag, and on the caucus executive during the second; and Stücklen, chairman of the Committee on Middle Class (Small Business) Affairs during the second Bundestag, as well as chairman of the CSU group and deputy chairman of the CDU/CSU caucus.

[78] Lenz, Mischnick, Stammberger, and Scheel, respectively.

[79] Dollinger, deputy chairman and chairman of the CSU group, Schmücker, deputy chairman, Heck, parliamentary whip, and Barzel, Niederalt, and Krüger, members of the executive committee.

[80] Gradl, Katzer, Stoltenberg, and Jaeger, respectively.

deputy chairman when he was not reappointed in the reorganization a year earlier, and Blank secured the same position on leaving the Cabinet in 1965. Men may therefore move back and forth between the two bodies over a period of time. At any given moment, furthermore, there is close contact between the Cabinet leaders and the leaders of the parliamentary majority. Ministers, and even senior civil servants, regularly attend meetings of the executive committee of the parliamentary party, while a parliamentary leader may, on a special occa-

Table 30. Types of Members on the front benches, 1957–1961[a] *(in per cent of categories at top of each column)*

Types	All Members of Bundestag (not incl. Cabinet) (n = 501)	Members of the executive committees of parliamentary parties (n = 73)
Part-time private occupations	33	29
Interest representatives	31	23
Public employees	10	11
Professional politicians	24	37
Others	2	0

[a] For explanation of types, see pp. 121–8, *supra.*

sion, attend a Cabinet meeting. But the traditional organizational distinction between Government and parliamentary leadership has been preserved. The separation has been maintained not only because ministers identify themselves with the executive bureaucracy, but because the parliamentary leaders value their independence, knowing it is the source of their influence over the Government. The potentialities of independent parliamentary leadership, long obscured by Adenauer's personal dominance, became more apparent when ambitious politicians like Barzel and Strauss took over the chairmanship of CDU and CSU in the Bundestag, while Erhard succeeded to the Chancellorship. Thus the separation of leadership organizations has persisted despite recruitment of the Cabinet from the parliamentary front benches.

The recruitment pattern favors the full-time Member of Parliament, and especially the professional politicians in the House, for they constitute the largest group among the members of the executive committees of the parliamentary parties. (See Table 30.) Furthermore, they tend to occupy the leading positions on these committees. However, especially in the CDU/CSU, which has supplied by far the largest proportion of ministerial personnel in the first decade and a half of the Federal Republic, interest groups within the parliamentary party exert strong pressure for the proportionate inclusion of their leaders in the Cabinet. Close inspection reveals that the members of the Government, though primarily drawn from the parliamentary leadership of the coalition parties, painstakingly represent the various factions in these parliamentary parties.

SEVEN CABINETS

An examination of the composition of the seven Cabinets appointed between 1949 and 1965 reveals the pattern of representation of regional, religious, and economic interests which results from the control which the parliamentary parties exercise over the formation of the Government.

1949

Even in the appointment of the first Government, where parliamentary influence was still relatively weak, the alliances within and between parties, which Adenauer had made, were apparent. The small parties received heavy representation, with five of thirteen portfolios, as did the CSU wing, with three. The appointment of Gustav Heinemann, more prominent as a Protestant than as a political leader, as Minister of the Interior, illustrated a concern for religious proportionality in the CDU/CSU, since it was motivated by the desire to have a second Protestant, in addition to Erhard, among that party's eight ministers. Five members of the Cabinet came from Bavaria, three each from North Rhine–Westphalia and Lower Saxony, two from the states of the Southwest, and one from the East, showing a definite concern for representation of those regions in which the coalition parties were strongest. State secretaries under these ministers were appointed in such a way that they would, insofar as possible, come from a region, a denomination, and a party other than that of the minister under whom they served.[81] The party leaders from the Economic Council were clearly in evidence in the Cabinet; the *Land* leaders were not.

[81] Eschenburg, "Staatssekretär nach Proporz," *Die Zeit* (U.S. Ed.), Sept. 13, 1963.

1953

By 1953, representation in the Cabinet of the coalition parties and their factions had become more complex, and by 1957, intraparty group interests were so well organized, especially in the CDU/CSU, that an intricate and arduous bargaining process had developed to enable them to make their claims on Cabinet positions.[82]

Although the CSU and the CDU have combined as one parliamentary group in the Bundestag, the CSU has always had a separate party organization and has always insisted on distinct consideration for itself in the assignment of Government positions. To that end it has bargained through its own spokesmen. In 1953, five days after the election, Strauss, as leader of the CSU group in the Bundestag, conferred with Adenauer to advance his claims for three ministries, the first deputy chairmanship of the parliamentary caucus, and a Bundestag vice-presidency. With fifty-two seats, the CSU regarded itself as the second strongest party in the coalition, ahead of the FDP, which has won only forty-eight. Its group in the Bundestag constituted itself eight days after the election, over three weeks before the first meeting of the new House. In the end, the CSU received its three ministries, including a position for its parliamentary leader, Strauss, and the continuation of its Finance Minister Schäffer, although the latter was not designated vice-chancellor, as the party had demanded. Schuberth, its incumbent Minister of the Post Office, however, had to yield to Adenauer's insistence that there be a Protestant among the CSU ministers, to maintain religious parity in the CDU/CSU group in the Cabinet. The CSU finally nominated an outsider, Siegfried Balke, for that position, after the personal intervention of the President, who asked that the appointment of the Cabinet not be delayed by this problem. However, Balke's appointment did not come until six weeks after the remainder of the Cabinet had been sworn in, and after the CSU leader in Munich had expressed public outrage. The appointment of Robert Tillmanns as minister "for special assignments" added a fourth Protestant to the group of eleven CDU/CSU ministers, incumbents Erhard and Schröder being the other two. The proportion closely reflected the two-to-one Catholic-Protestant ratio in the parliamentary party. The CSU did get its Bundestag vice-presidency, to

[82] The following account of the creation of the Government in 1953 and 1957 is largely based on the excellent treatment by Jürgen Domes, *op. cit.*, pp. 50–74.

which Richard Jaeger was elected, and a deputy chairmanship of the parliamentary caucus, which was given to Stücklen and has been held ever since by the chairman of the CSU group.

Adenauer faced the demands of three other parliamentary parties in 1953. The FDP asked for four ministries, including the continuation of Blücher as vice-chancellor and Dehler as Minister of Justice. The All-German Bloc requested two positions including that of Minister for Expellees, since its electoral appeal was mainly to expellee groups. The DP wanted to maintain its two incumbents. To meet these demands, and yet reserve a proportionate share for his own party, which had increased its parliamentary strength by seventy-seven seats, Adenauer considered a substantial enlargement of the Cabinet over its previous size of fourteen members. There was strong opposition to this move within the CDU parliamentary party, however, which demanded instead a reduction of the small parties' representation.

At its first meeting, a day after the newly elected Bundestag had constituted itself, the CDU/CSU caucus declared it would insist on six Cabinet positions, in addition to the Chancellorship, notably European Affairs for its chairman, Brentano; Economics and Labor, for their respective incumbents, Erhard and Storch; Schröder, to replace the resigning Minister of the Interior; and Lübke as Minister of Agriculture. The best organized economic faction within the caucus, the labor group, also urged ministerial status for Theodor Blank, who was serving as special appointee of the Chancellor for Security Questions; in Anton Storch and Jakob Kaiser it already had two of its members in the Cabinet. After protracted negotiations, in which he had to argue actively in two caucus meetings and various sessions of the executive, Adenauer persuaded his party to accept an enlargement of the cabinet, but with only one new ministry and four ministers "for special assignments."

With the exception of Brentano, who eventually received the Foreign Ministry two years later when Adenauer yielded that post, the men named by the CDU/CSU caucus were appointed. Blank's appointment as Minister of Defense also waited two years, until the London and Paris Treaties formally gave Germany sovereignty in these areas. The implicit recognition that the labor group was thereafter entitled to three positions was demonstrated in 1956 when the CSU's Strauss replaced Blank as Minister of Defense whereupon Ernst Lemmer, another member of the labor group, replaced Balke of the

CSU as Minister of the Post Office. In the expanded Cabinet of 1953 the CDU received two other positions, that of the newly established Ministry of Family Affairs and the appointment of Tillmanns, who, in addition to being a Protestant, had the advantage of being a Berliner. He was nominally placed in charge of "Berlin questions" in the Cabinet.

The smaller parties received the quotas they had demanded, the DP retaining its two incumbents, the Bloc getting the Expellee Ministry as well as a minister "for special assignments," and the Free Democrats obtaining their four places, including all three ministries they had headed before. The resulting Cabinet also had wide regional representation, with ministers from nine of the ten *Länder,* in close proportion to their representation in the parliamentary parties of the coalition, five from North Rhine–Westphalia, four from Bavaria, three from Lower Saxony, two from Rhineland-Palatinate, and one from each of the others except Bremen.

1957

After the smashing victory of the CDU/CSU in 1957, which gave it 270 out of 497 Bundestag seats, its caucus was in a more dominant position in the negotiations on the Government than it had been four years earlier; the factions within it were also more highly organized. The small DP was the only coalition partner; it was put off with the continuation of its two incumbents in office. The two ex-FDP ministers, who had joined the CDU and remained in the Cabinet after the FDP had withdrawn from the coalition, were refused reappointment. One of them, however—Preusker—was promised a Bundestag vice-presidency.

Within the CDU/CSU the bargaining was hard. The CSU, having triumphantly won fifty-five seats, including all the single-member constituencies in Bavaria, authorized its *Land* chairman and its parliamentary leadership to insist on additional Cabinet representation. It demanded a fourth post in addition to the continuation of its three incumbents—Strauss, Balke, and Schäffer—and suggested the chairman of its parliamentary group, Stücklen, for the position.

With additional places available for the CDU/CSU in the next Cabinet, the problem was not with the quota but with the person of Schäffer, who had drawn the criticism of various economic groups for his rigid high-tax policies and his opposition to agricultural subsidies and to the sale of public enterprises into private ownership. Newspapers associated with business interests conducted a campaign of criticism against him, the Federation of German Industry exerted its influence, and a group of CDU Members, calling themselves the "economic committee," organized to oppose his reappointment. The CSU meanwhile repeatedly asserted its support of Schäffer in public statements and in meetings with Adenauer, including a hastily convened session of CSU Members on the eve of decision on the Finance Ministry, a month after the election. As a compromise, Adenauer offered to appoint Schäffer to a newly created Ministry of Federal Property and to name him vice-chancellor. The matter was not yet settled when the re-election of Adenauer as Chancellor took place. In the end, Schäffer and the CSU accepted the counteroffer of the Ministry of Justice, and Etzel of the CDU was appointed Finance Minister. Retaining the Defense Ministry, the Ministry on Atomic Energy, and the Postal Ministry, which it had held for all but the last of the previous eight years, the CSU had obtained most, but not all of its demands.

This time, regional demands other than those of the Bavarian CSU were presented to Adenauer by delegations of Members organized for this purpose. The North Rhine–Westphalian Representatives caucused and presented their case for proportional consideration, as did the Northerners and the group of Members from Baden-Württemberg. With the eventual appointment of Hermann Lindrath, two ministers came from the Southwest, six from North Rhine–Westphalia, and four from Bavaria. With three from Lower Saxony, and one from each of the other *Länder* except Hamburg, Bremen, and the recently acceded Saar, regional representation was again very broad, although Schleswig-Holstein did not receive recognition until Werner Schwarz was appointed to replace Heinrich Lübke as Minister of Agriculture, after Lübke's mid-term election as Federal President.

Lübke's reappointment as Minister of Agriculture in 1957, in the face of strong opposition from agricultural interest groups, had demonstrated that interest groups could not necessarily control "their" ministry if an incumbent minister had organized backing within the parliamentary party. Lübke had had strong and active support among CDU/CSU Members. The appointment of Schwarz two years later was, however, satisfactory to the agricultural organizations.

In 1957 the labor group within the CDU/CSU named a formal

negotiating committee to present its continuing claim to three Cabinet positions, including the Ministry of Labor. Given the opportunity to name their candidate for the latter post, the group found it difficult to decide between the incumbent Storch and former Defense Minister Blank. Its negotiators finally designated Blank, and Adenauer accepted him. The continuation of Lemmer in the Cabinet, and the appointment of Paul Lücke as Minister of Housing, gave this faction its representation of three. The group of Members organized to represent small business interests placed one of their members, Stücklen of the CSU, in the Cabinet for the first time. Furthermore, a careful balancing of denominations, due in part to the intervention of leading Protestant Members, produced a Cabinet in which there were nine Catholic CDU/CSU ministers to seven of Protestant persuasion, and over-all an equal number of members of the two faiths, in spite of the increase in CDU/CSU representation in the Government.

The CDU/CSU caucus as a whole took several stands and prevailed in each. It successfully supported reappointment of the incumbent Minister of Family Affairs, opposed the appointment of a Minister of European Affairs, and pressed for the designation of Erhard as vice-chancellor, a title having chiefly symbolic significance.

1961

Because Adenauer was greatly weakened by the outcome of the 1961 election, the formation of the Government stood more than ever under the influence of the parliamentary parties. Adenauer depended for his continuation in office on specific endorsement from the CDU/CSU caucus, and he was forced to accept the condition that he would resign at mid-term, a commitment he made in writing to the chairman of the parliamentary party.[83] After their substantial gain in Bundestag seats, and their control of the balance of power in the House, the Free Democrats insisted on five ministries, including the key positions of Justice and Finance, and five state secretaries in the ministries they would not head. Having gained acceptance of these demands, the FDP found it relatively difficult to find suitable candidates to fill them, since their leaders were unwilling to serve under

[83] *Die Welt*, Oct. 18 and Nov. 9, 1961; *FAZ*, Oct. 20 and Nov. 9, 1961. On the formation of the 4th Adenauer Government, see Jean Amphoux, "Le quatrième Gouvernement de la République Fédérale d'Allemagne," *Revue du droit public et de la science politique*, LXXVIII (1962), 664–98.

Adenauer in view of their campaign promises. The party also lacked high-level administrators for the state secretarial positions. The FDP caucus took votes to choose ministerial candidates; the filling of the other positions became the subject of long-drawn-out and ultimately unsuccessful negotiations, because the Free Democrats were unable to find candidates whom Adenauer and the respective minister, who held the appointment power, would accept as competent.[84]

The elaborate efforts of the FDP to tie the Government down to particular policies by means of an agreement that the coalition would always vote together in the Bundestag, and by forming a coalition committee to iron out differences, were likewise unsuccessful. They offended not only against constitutional provisions concerning the independence of Members and the policy-making prerogatives of the Chancellor, but also against political realities which soon led the Free Democrats themselves to vote against the CDU/CSU on some conspicuous issues.[85] Unsuccessful also in their effort to obtain the chairmanship of the Foreign Affairs Committee for Mende in violation of the parliamentary mores governing chairmanship appointments, the Free Democrats entered the Government essentially frustrated in their objective of controlling the CDU/CSU majority by opposition from within the coalition.[86]

Since the CSU insisted on retaining its quota of four ministries and the FDP would have five, the new Cabinet was the largest yet created. A new Ministry of Health was set up, and the first woman ever appointed as minister in Germany, Elisabeth Schwarzhaupt, was named to it, in response to strong pressure from women Members in the CDU/CSU.[87] In addition, a new Ministry for Economic Cooperation was established and given to the FDP to fill.[88]

The heaviest controversy surrounded the appointment of the Foreign Minister. Anxious for some evidence of success in altering the Government's course, the Free Democrats urged the replacement of

[84] *Die Zeit,* Nov. 24, 1961, p. 2. *Cf. Die Welt,* Oct. 26 and 27, 1961; *FAZ,* Oct. 26 and 27, 1961. See also n. 62, *supra.*

[85] See, for example, *Die Zeit,* Feb. 9 and July 6, 1962. For a summary of the difficulties within the coalition, see *Der Spiegel,* XVI, no. 29 (July 18, 1962), 17–25.

[86] *Die Zeit,* Oct. 27, 1961.

[87] *Die Welt,* Nov. 13 and 14, 1961.

[88] The intrigues surrounding the creation of this ministry are detailed in *Der Spiegel,* XV, no. 47 (Nov. 15, 1961), 23–6.

Brentano, who had been identified with Adenauer's foreign policy for six years. In his weakened position, Adenauer was unwilling to insist on Brentano's continuation, and this was enough to prompt all sides to seize this position as the one for a conspicuous compromise.[89] Schröder was chosen as the new Foreign Minister, against the opposition particularly of Berlin Representatives who recalled his legal arguments against allowing Berlin delegates to vote in the 1959 presidential election and his draft law restricting travel between East and West Berlin.[90] To placate them, as well as to promote relations between Government and Bundestag, Krone, a Representative from Berlin and the chairman of the CDU/CSU in the Bundestag, was appointed as minister "for special assignments," charged especially with supervising the relationship between Cabinet and Bundestag, and specifically entitled to consultation on all Berlin questions.[91]

Among the sixteen CDU/CSU Cabinet members, Höcherl, who had been chairman of the CSU group in the Bundestag, was the third and last newcomer, taking over Schröder's post as Minister of the Interior.

With such a limited turnover, proportions in group representation did not change markedly. The religious division among the sixteen CDU/CSU ministers was even, but with the addition of the five FDP members, who were all Protestant, the Catholic proportion in the Cabinet as a whole was the lowest of the postwar period. There continued to be three members from the labor group and one from the small business group of the CDU/CSU, and there were ministers from every *Land* except Hamburg, Bremen, and the Saar. Two major efforts on the part of interest groups within the CDU failed. Members representing expellee groups were unable to secure the Ministry of Expellees for the leader of the national expellee organization, Hans Krüger, since that post was given to the FDP; and business groups in the CDU/CSU could not bring about the appointment of business leader Rolf Dahlgrün over his FDP colleague, Heinz Starke, as Finance Minister.[92] In the formation of his final administration, Adenauer pur-

[89] *FAZ*, Oct. 28 and 31, 1961. *Die Welt*, Oct. 31, 1961.

[90] This bill is the subject of a case study (see pp. 294–5, *infra*).

[91] *Die Welt*, Nov. 3, 6, and 15, 1961, and Feb. 6, 1962. Under Erhard, Krone subsequently also became chairman of the Cabinet's defense committee.

[92] *FAZ*, Oct. 24 and Nov. 6, 1961. Gerard Braunthal, *The Federation of German Industry in Politics* (Ithaca: Cornell University Press, 1965), pp. 210–11.

chased a reprieve for his leadership at the expense of yielding full control over five ministerial positions to the FDP and four to the CSU, and of accepting the replacement of his faithful Foreign Minister. In the final caucus meeting which ended with approval of the negotiations, he felt compelled to intervene in the discussions sixteen times. When the vote was taken, only two-thirds of the membership was present, with Gerstenmaier, Brentano, and Erhard among the conspicuous absentees.[93]

The Reorganization of 1962

Within a year, the extent of FDP influence became dramatically clear when the party withdrew its five ministers from the Government to protest Strauss's continuance in office after the exposure of his complicity in the most questionable aspects of the Government action against the influential magazine, *Der Spiegel.* At least one FDP minister, Starke, was reluctant to resign. He rightly suspected that his chances of returning to office were small in the face of opposition from CDU business groups, who disliked his affiliations with small business interests rather than with large industry. Nevertheless the Free Democrats moved as a group after joint deliberation between the parliamentary caucus and the party's federal executive.

Faced with the prospects of a minority Government which would be unable to get its legislative program or its appropriations approved, the CDU/CSU caucus decided upon the resignation of its ministers as well, and the reorganization of the Government.[94] The incident was a clear indication of the influence of the coalition parties in the Bundestag over the tenure of Cabinet ministers. Adenauer's assertion that there had not been a vote of no-confidence in him, and that he could continue in office, appointing whomever he chose, had a hollow ring. His moves toward a "Great Coalition" with the SPD seemed inspired by tactics vis-à-vis the Free Democrats, rather than by the search for an alternative majority.[95] Shortly after his encounter with the prospects of minority government, Adenauer, in spontaneous remarks to the Bundestag, exhibited uncommon regard for the Government's dependence on a parliamentary majority:

[93] *Welt am Sonntag,* Nov. 5, 1961; *Die Welt* and *FAZ,* Nov. 6, 1961.
[94] *Die Welt,* Nov. 20 and 21–2, 1962; *Die Zeit* (U.S. ed.), Dec. 7, 1962.
[95] *Die Welt,* Dec. 6, 7, and 11, 1962.

The work of the Parliament is an absolute necessity for the work of the Government. The work of Parliament . . . is, as a matter of fact, the decisive thing for the German people. . . .

At the moment 53 bills are before you, which have not yet been passed. I may say once again with emphasis, no Government can accomplish anything unless the Parliament places its seal of approval on the work of the Government. The Government is dependent on the Parliament. Its successes depend on the Parliament.[96]

It was significant that without the election of the Chancellor, the formation of a new Government nevertheless occurred under the clear influence of the parliamentary parties and their factions. The FDP replaced Starke with Dahlgrün, who had had high-level industrial experience in a large business enterprise and in leading business groups, including the Federation of German Industry. This met the demands which business interests in the CDU/CSU had advanced the previous year. The Free Democrats also yielded to the pressure of their coalition partners to replace their Minister of Justice, Wolfgang Stammberger, who had been outspoken in the *Spiegel* crisis and had drawn heavy fire from the CSU. They proposed their parliamentary whip, Bucher, in his place. The FDP therefore did not go unscathed in the reshuffle.

On the CDU side, the opportunity was used to replace some of the older ministers, notably von Merkatz, who had only recently joined the CDU after the disintegration of the German party; Josef Wuermeling, who had served for nine years as Minister of Family Affairs; Lemmer, a Cabinet member for six years; and Balke, who had been ready to retire from the Government the previous year after nine years of service.

The replacement of Strauss and Balke left the CSU two positions to fill, for which they named their parliamentary leader, Dollinger, and their prominent executive committee member, Alois Niederalt, incidentally preserving the denominational proportion of three Catholics and one Protestant among the CSU ministers. In addition to von Hassel, who became Minister of Defense in Strauss's place, two leaders of the CDU were appointed to the Cabinet: Bruno Heck, an assistant whip and former national managing director of the party, and Rainer Barzel, then a new member of the executive committee of the parliamentary party, whose popularity in the parliamentary group was

[96] *Dt. Btag.*, 4. W.P., 53. Sitz., Dec. 14, 1962, p. 2333.

demonstrated a year later when it elected him deputy chairman, and later chairman, of the caucus. The reshuffle of 1962 brought about some of the personnel changes which had been evaded in the difficult coalition negotiations the previous year.[97]

Erhard's Accession, 1963

Erhard's accession to the Chancellorship one year later did not therefore bring a large number of additional alterations. Mende, free to enter the Government now that Adenauer had retired, and anxious for a conspicuous ministry as FDP leader, was appointed Minister of All-German Questions replacing Barzel, and vice-chancellor. The CDU received compensation for its loss with the Ministry of Expellees. When Barzel could not be persuaded to move over into that post, the candidate of the expellee groups, Krüger, finally prevailed. It was a short-lived triumph for the interest group, however, since evidence of Krüger's Nazi affiliations led to his dismissal within four months. Erhard's hope of having his state secretary, Westrick, replace him as Minister of Economics, was blocked by the parliamentary party, which insisted on the appointment of the leading member of its small-business group, Kurt Schmücker, who was not only a deputy chairman of the parliamentary party, but had served as chairman of the working group on economic affairs, and of the Bundestag committee on that subject.[98]

1965

The election of 1965 was the first test of Erhard's electoral leadership. That his party bettered its 1961 showing and came within four seats of an absolute majority in the Bundestag greatly strengthened his influence within the party, which committed itself to Erhard's continuation as Chancellor the morning after the election. Furthermore, the party's special success in the northern *Länder* and in Protestant regions strengthened the representatives of these sections within the party.

Erhard was therefore able to insist upon the reappointment of Foreign Minister Schröder, a North-Rhine–Westphalian Protestant, in spite of the opposition of both CDU national chairman Adenauer and

[97] *Die Welt*, Dec. 1, 11, and 12, 1962.
[98] *Die Welt*, Oct. 15 and 16, 1963; October 17, 1963, p. 3. *Die Zeit* (U.S. ed.), Oct. 25, 1963, p. 2.

CSU *Land* chairman Strauss. The northern wing of the party gained additional recognition by the advancement of former Housing Minister Lücke to the Ministry of the Interior, and the appointment of Gerhard Stoltenberg of Schleswig-Holstein as Minister for Scientific Research.

Stoltenberg's appointment also satisfied the party's youth group, which he had once headed. The appointment of Hans Katzer, chairman of the Social Committees of the Christian Democratic Labor Movement, as Minister of Labor, was a special triumph for the labor wing of the party.

The FDP, again holding the balance of power between the CDU/CSU and the SPD, and the CSU, more self-conscious than ever under Strauss's aggressive leadership, were both in a strong position in the bargaining. The Free Democrats were able to compel Erhard to keep their chairman, Mende, in the Ministry of All-German Questions, against the will of the CDU parliamentary leaders, who resented what they regarded as Mende's use of that ministry for partisan purposes. The CSU received an additional portfolio, its fifth, to compensate it for the retention in the Cabinet of Mende, toward whom Strauss felt a personal animosity. Between them, FDP and CSU received 9 out of 22 Cabinet positions—over 40 per cent—although they held only 98 out of the coalition's 295 seats in the Bundestag, barely one-third of the total.

The new Cabinet showed a strong continuity with the old. It had only four new members, two of them identified with the same factions as those whom they replaced. Katzer took Blank's place as a representative of the labor wing; Gradl, a Berliner, supplanted another Berliner, Lemmer, in the Ministry for Expellees. The retention of so many other Ministers was partly due to the staunch backing of their respective supporting groups within the parliamentary party. The rumor that Elisabeth Schwarzhaupt might be replaced as Minister of Health immediately mobilized women's associations within the party in her defense. Schröder's survival was due to the support of the northern wings of the party and the Protestant group.

The failure of some "ministrables" was due to their lack of support where it counted. Minister of Justice Weber was not reappointed, to his great dismay, because he had not been re-elected to the Bundestag. Potential rivals of Schröder, such as Minister-President Kurt-Georg Kiesinger of Baden-Württemberg, and Walter Hallstein, president of the Commission of the European Economic Community, also lacked the necessary support within the parliamentary party because they were not Bundestag members. Erhard offered the Ministry of the Interior to a prominent CDU *Land* leader, Paul Mikat, who, anticipating the trials to which a nonparliamentary minister would be exposed, refused the offer.[99]

Thus Cabinet making after the first election since Adenauer's retirement showed a strong tendency to continue in the pattern of influence which had developed during his long and formative Chancellorship.

PARLIAMENTARY INFLUENCE ON CABINET COMPOSITION

The composition of the seven Cabinets which were appointed through the beginning of the fifth term of the Bundestag reflects the changing party strengths in Parliament, as well as the fluctuation in the bargaining power of the interests organized within the parties of the coalition, and the authority of the prospective Chancellor. As economic and social interests have organized themselves into groups, particularly within the parliamentary party of the CDU/CSU, their claims have become more important than the denominational considerations which originally weighed most heavily in ministerial appointments. The success of the various political parties in pressing their personnel demands has depended not only on the absolute number of seats they hold in the Bundestag, but on the importance of these seats for the formation of a governing majority. The CSU, acting as an independent party in matters of appointments, has been continuously indispensable for the attainment of that majority, and has been correspondingly successful with its demands for Cabinet representation. The success of the smaller parties has varied, reaching a nadir between 1955 and 1961 when their members served in the Government only at the pleasure of the CDU/CSU, which alone commanded the necessary parliamentary majority. The influence of the prospective Chancellor has varied with his electoral success and his standing within his own party. As leader of the largest party, the Chancellorship falls to him as if by popular mandate. Yet he requires parliamentary election to take office, and parliamentary support to govern. He must therefore negotiate the composition of his Cabinet with the parliamentary leaders of

[99] *Die Welt,* Oct. 20, 21, 22, 23, and 25, 1965. *Der Spiegel,* XIX, nos. 41–4 (Oct. 6, 13, 20, and 27, 1965).

the coalition parties who command these majorities. Even near the height of his influence, fresh from his electoral triumph of 1953, Adenauer asserted he would rather fight three election campaigns than appoint a single Cabinet.[100]

The influence of the parliamentary leaders, exemplified by their prominent role in the negotiations, and by the recruitment of nearly all Cabinet members from their midst, is the consequence not only of the constitutional relationship between Bundestag and Cabinet. It is the result also of the new parliamentary party system. Because there are only three parties, the prospective Chancellor cannot readily play them off against one another. He has few, if any, alternatives in building his coalition. He is very dependent on his own party, particularly if it alone holds a majority. The highly developed internal organization of the parliamentary parties puts the parliamentary leaders in positions of great influence over the distribution of political spoils, but, especially in the CDU/CSU, compels them to have due regard for the interest groups in the party. The parliamentary party leaders preside over large coalitions of interests, whose claims they must defend tenaciously in order to preserve party cohesion.

The pattern of negotiations over the composition of the Cabinet is complex. It consists of improvised and time-consuming procedures. Parliamentary power and experience, as measured by election to parliamentary leadership, has become an almost indispensable qualification for appointment to Cabinet office. Unlike its predecessors, the Bundestag has become the nearly exclusive training ground for ministerial personnel. But the inherited political structure in which parliamentary and Cabinet leadership is organizationally distinct, and traditional conceptions which regard parliamentary and ministerial positions as separate, if not mutually exclusive, obscure the functions which the Bundestag performs in the recruitment, appointment, and dismissal of cabinet members. The plebiscitary aspect of the parliamentary election, which appears to give the electorate a decisive influence in the appointment of the Chancellor, and the Chancellor's tenure in office throughout the parliamentary term, likewise hide the influence of Parliament on the Cabinet.

The public does not therefore perceive the extent to which the leading members the Government are recruited from the leadership of

[100] Quoted in an editorial of the *FAZ*, Sept. 21, 1957.

the Bundestag, and the extent to which they depend on the support of a majority of the House for their tenure in office. The result is a failure to comprehend the most recent addition to the major functions which Parliament performs in the political system. With the electorate's influence on the composition of the Cabinet obvious, and easily justified, and presidential appointment of the Cabinet based on traditional concepts of the sovereign's prerogative, only Parliament's role in Cabinet making lacks public understanding. At best, parliamentary influence on Cabinet appointments produces public impatience and cynicism toward the long-drawn-out process of bargaining. At worst, it evokes memories of the Cabinet crises of the Weimar Republic. In the background, it leaves the possibility of public frustration over conceivable differences between what is felt to be the mandate of the general election, and the composition of the Cabinet which follows from it.

VI

Lawmaking

WHILE the functions which the Bundestag performs in the selection of the Chancellor and his Cabinet are the consequence of constitutional and political developments in this century, Parliament's legislative functions have a longer history and are sanctioned by far older constitutional theory. The role which the Bundestag plays in the legislative process still bears some of the marks of the system of constitutional monarchy in which it originated.

THE POSITION OF THE BUNDESTAG IN THE LEGISLATIVE PROCESS

The Traditional Role of German Parliaments in Lawmaking

According to the constitutional theory prevailing in the mid-nineteenth century, when the structure of the modern German Parliament took shape, the function of the representative assembly was to defend the traditional rights of the leading groups and classes of society. In the monarchical political system, the task of Parliament was to deliberate on the Government's executive acts and legislative proposals, judging their compatibility with the moral sense of the community. The practical implication was that Parliament would serve as an instrument of communication between the Government and its subjects, and that it would possess a veto on new legislation.[1] A parliamentary role in the legislative process—albeit a passive one—was therefore accepted long before a parliamentary system of government existed.

The constitution under which Prussia was ruled from 1850 to 1918 contained a provision that "the lawmaking power shall be exercised jointly by the King and by the two Chambers." Both chambers, as well as the King, were given the right to initiate legislation. No bill could

[1] Dieter Grosser, *Grundlagen und Struktur der Staatslehre Friedrich Julius Stahls* (Cologne and Opladen: Westdeutscher Verlag, 1963), pp. 93-4.

become law without the approval of all three, and the budget was specifically subject to annual determination by law.[2] These provisions followed those contained in the constitutions adopted in the southern and southwestern German *Länder* during the previous generation. They were copied subsequently in the Imperial Constitution of 1871[3] and, with appropriate adaptation to the demise of the monarchy and the decline in the power of the *Länder,* in the Weimar Constitution of 1919.[4] When the Basic Law for the Federal Republic of Germany states that "federal laws are adopted by the Bundestag,"[5] it echoes a century-old provision.

The practices which govern the exercise of the Bundestag's constitutional legislative powers are likewise the product of a development of more than one hundred years. In the monarchical political systems of the early nineteenth century, Parliament had been admitted to the legislative process as a consultant with veto power. It was expected to play a passive role in the exercise of powers which had, until then, been exclusively within the royal prerogative. The King's Government continued to take the legislative initiative, and a Parliament composed of spokesmen of the leading classes was expected, for the most part, to support that Government. Large areas of decision continued to remain entirely within the jurisdiction of the executive. Foreign and military affairs, the organization of the departments of Government, the appointment of Government officials, and the administration of policy remained solely within the royal prerogative, subject to executive orders and administrative decrees. The legislative process came into play only where general norms of conduct were involved, especially on subject affecting traditional privileges—"liberty and property"—of the people. That the countless detailed administrative decisions which made up the Government's annual budget should be incorporated in an annual law was an exception to the accepted concept that law consisted only of general norms, and caused the legal theorists no end of trouble. The presumption in favor of executive decision was expressed in a provision of the Prussian Constitution giving the Government the power to issue decrees with the force of law in an emergency,

---

[2] Constitutional Charter for the State of Prussia of January 31, 1850, Arts. 62, 64, 99.

[3] Constitution of the German Empire of April 16, 1871, Arts. 5, 69.

[4] Constitution of the German Republic of August 11, 1919, Arts. 68, 85.

[5] Art. 77(1).

should Parliament not be in session; the Government could also exceed the budget, but this required subsequent parliamentary approval.[6]

The subordination of Parliament in the Prussian system became dramatically apparent in Bismarck's successful defiance of the House of Representatives in 1862, on the question of military appropriations. Unable to obtain approval for the appropriations he had requested, the Chancellor proceeded to tax and spend without parliamentary approval, explaining that in the absence of explicit constitutional provisions for such cases of conflict between Government and Parliament, the King's Government had to be carried on. The episode, settled four years later by retroactive parliamentary approval of the Government's actions, was a traumatic experience in the development of Parliament's role in the legislative process.

The Constitutional Distribution of Lawmaking Powers

The origin of parliamentary participation in lawmaking, and early experience with it, still affect the performance of legislative functions by the Bundestag. Constitutionally, the Bundestag shares the lawmaking power with the Federal Government, and with the Bundesrat, an assembly of members of the *Land* Governments. In the German federal system, these local governments administer most national laws. The Bundesrat, Members of the Bundestag, and the Federal Government may each introduce legislation, according to the Basic Law.[7] In practice, the Bundesrat introduces very few bills. The legislative interests of the *Länder* are usually served more effectively by Bundesrat amendment of Government bills, than by Bundesrat initiatives. The second chamber exercises its right to introduce legislation mainly on local or regional questions, such as the regulation of wine making, for example. It acts on national issues only if the parties controlling the state governments have views substantially different from those of the Federal Government. Rarely does the Bundesrat introduce a measure as a counterproposal to a bill of the Federal Government which it finds objectionable. Ordinarily, the Federal Government has been highly sensitive to the opinions of the *Länder* on its legislative proposals, since the Basic Law requires that Government bills be presented to the Bundesrat for its opinion even before they can be submitted to the

[6] Constitutional Charter for the State of Prussia of January 31, 1850, Arts. 63, 104.

[7] Art. 76(1).

Bundestag. Furthermore, the Bundesrat considers Government bills a second time, after their passage by the Bundestag, and can exercise a suspensive or an absolute veto over them, depending on the subject.[8]

The Legislative Initiative of Bundestag Members

Members of the Bundestag exercise a legislative initiative with far greater frequency. The Rules of the House require that bills must bear the signature of as many Members as are necessary to constitute a parliamentary party—since 1952, fifteen.[9] This precludes the introduction of bills purely to please one Member's constituency. Actually, less than one-fourth of the bills introduced by Members of the House are sponsored by individuals.[10] These are usually the product of interest groups for which Members in the governing parties act as spokesmen. They are used for tactical purposes to influence the details of Government bills, or to press the Cabinet for action. Rarely do their proponents expect them to pass, at least without substantial alteration.[11] Most bills initiated by Members of the Bundestag are officially supported by one or more of the parliamentary parties, and are introduced in the names of the party chairmen. Some of them are nonpartisan measures, supported by all the major parties; a few are coalition measures.[12] The largest number has been made up of the proposals of

[8] Karlheinz Neunreither, *Der Bundesrat zwischen Politik und Verwaltung*, (Heidelberg: Quelle und Meyer, 1959), pp. 86–8.

[9] *Geschäftsordnung des Deutschen Bundestages* (Bonn: Herausgegeben von der Verwaltung des Deutschen Bundestages, July, 1962), par. 97.

[10] In the first Bundestag, 68 out of 292 bills studied bore the signatures of individual Members (Wolfgang Kralewski and Karlheinz Neunreither, *Oppositionelles Verhalten im ersten Deutschen Bundestag 1949–1953* [Cologne and Opladen: Westdeutscher Verlag, 1963], p. 57). In the third Bundestag, this was true of 47 out of 207 bills, according to figures supplied by the Bundestag secretariat.

[11] For a case study of how bills introduced by various factions within the CDU/CSU were employed as a means by which to bargain with the Government on its own draft of a law on cartels, see Viola Gräfin von Bethusy-Huc, *Demokratie und Interessenpolitik* (Wiesbaden: Franz Steiner Verlag, 1962), pp. 26–81. This was also the tactic employed by the veterans interest group within the CDU/CSU which, under the leadership of Maria Probst, introduced a pensions bill which it refused to withdraw until the Government had accepted a far greater increase in pensions than it had originally intended (cf. *Dt. Btag*, 3. W.P., Drs. 957 [the original Probst bill], Drs. 1239 [the Government's bill], and Drs. 957 neu, [the compromise bill]).

[12] In the first Bundestag, out of 80 bills introduced by several parties, 38 were sponsored by parties including the SPD, 31 were the products of the governing coalition, and 11 were initiated by parties including the CDU but not the SPD (Kralewski and Neunreither, *op. cit.*, p. 57). In the third Bundestag, out of 26

the major opposition party, the SPD, which attempts in this way to demonstrate that it offers constructive alternatives, or to counter a Government proposal and obtain leverage in committee deliberations, or to force an issue to a vote. In the first Bundestag, the SPD took initiatives in major legislative areas, even presenting its own bill for the creation of the Federal Constitutional Court.[13] Relying on the drafting skills of its Members of Parliament, of *Land* ministries under its control, of its party staff, or on the legal counsel of trade unions or other closely associated interest groups, the party at first expended great energies on bill drafting. But its activity in this direction declined, both in the number of bills introduced and in their significance. It became apparent that, politically, the most important subjects presented overwhelming drafting problems for the party, and that its influence on legislation depended less on its ability to present its own bills than on its ability to influence the viewpoint of the majority in the committees of the House. The smaller parties found bill drafting in opposition even more difficult.[14]

The CDU/CSU is, however, in a different position. With good access to the ministerial bureaucracy, it is far better equipped to draft legislation than any of the other parliamentary parties. Furthermore, its ministers in Government may use the parliamentary party as their agent in the Bundestag. This has three advantages. First, while bills proposed by the Government must first be considered by the Bundesrat and can be submitted to the Bundestag only after the house of the *Länder* has had three weeks to give its initial opinion, bills initiated in the Bundestag skip that stage. This, at the very least, saves time, although at the cost of arousing the hostility of the *Länder*. Those bills

bills introduced by several parties, 17 were sponsored by all of them, 5 more included SPD sponsorship, and 4 were the products of the governing coalition, according to figures supplied by the Bundestag secretariat.

[13] For a case study, see Kralewski and Neunreither, *op. cit.*, pp. 168–204.

[14] In the first Bundestag the SPD was involved in the sponsorship of 109 bills, 51 of them without the participation of other parties; in the second Bundestag it sponsored or participated in sponsoring 72; in the third Bundestag, it introduced 48 bills, and participated in sponsoring 22 others (Kralewski and Neunreither, *op. cit.*, p. 57; *Jahrbuch der Sozialdemokratischen Partei Deutschlands, 1956–1957* [Bonn: Neuer Vorwärts Verlag, n.d.], p. 12). Figures for the third Bundestag were supplied by the Bundestag secretariat. In the first Bundestag, among other parties introducing at least ten bills, the FDP led with 25, the DP 11, and the Center party 13 (Kralewski and Neunreither, *op. cit.*, p. 57). In the third Bundestag, the FDP inroduced 60 bills, the DP 8.

jointly introduced by the coalition parties in the Bundestag usually
have the purpose of initially bypassing the Bundesrat.[15] Second, bills
drafted in a ministry but introduced by the party in Parliament need
not be cleared with the ministers of the other parties in the coalition,
or with other CDU ministers who may be opposed to it. Third, by
introducing a measure in the Bundestag, the Government can escape
responsibility for a measure it finds politically embarrassing, or, as the
case may be, direct all the credit for the measure to the CDU/CSU. It
is nevertheless occasionally true that a bill introduced by the
CDU/CSU in the Bundestag is not a Government measure in disguise,
but an attempt on the part of the parliamentary majority to press the
Government. The total number of measures introduced by the
CDU/CSU is quite small, however, and most of them are not independent of the Government.[16]

The Legislative Initiative of the Government

The Government introduces a majority of all bills, and three-fourths
of those which are ultimately enacted. (See Table 31.) Its command of
the executive bureaucracy gives it a decisive advantage in bill drafting, which it does not readily share with Members of Parliament. Its
own Rules of Procedure provide that "officials of the Ministries may
not participate in the formulation (of a bill of a Member of the
Bundestag) without the approval of the appropriate Minister." [17] Although ministries generally give drafting assistance to Members in the
formulation of amendments during the committee stage, the power to
assist or to withhold assistance is frequently employed for the tactical
advantage of the Government, especially when entire bills are at stake.
Occasionally this has led to bitter recriminations in private between

[15] There were 31 in the first Bundestag, 4 in the third.
[16] The CDU introduced 17 bills in the first Bundestag, 18 in the third. For an
example of a CDU/CSU initiative in an area on which the Government was reluctant to act, see the case of the Agriculture Act described in Bethusy-Huc,
op. cit., pp. 1–35. The bill denationalizing the Volkswagen company was a
Government measure, introduced by the CDU/CSU in the Bundestag as a bill of
"the representatives Adenauer, Erhard, Blank, Häussler, Arndgen, Hahn, Stücklen,
Cillien, Dr. Elbrächter, Dr. Krone, and the CDU/CSU parliamentary party"; it
was an example of an attempt to bypass the first Bundesrat stage, and to give the
party credit for a popular measure (*Dt. Btag.*, 3. W.P., Drs. 102).
[17] *Gemeinsame Geschäftsordnung der Bundesministerien*, Besonderer Teil
(GGO II), as adopted by the Cabinet August 1, 1958, with the revisions of March
10, 1960 (Hrsg. vom Bundesministerium des Innern, 1960), par. 49.

Table 31. Proposal and disposal of legislation in the Bundestag

| | Sources of bills | | | | | | | |
| | Cabinet | | Bundestag Members | | Bundesrat | | Total | |
Action on bills	No.	Per cent of total introduced	No.	Per cent of total introduced	No.	Per cent of total introduced	No.	Per cent of total introduced
Introduced in Bundestag [a]								
1949–1953	470		301		20		791	
1953–1957	431		414		11		856	
1957–1961	387		207		5		599	
1961–1965	367		245		8		620	
Total	1655		1167		44		2866	
Failed to pass Bundestag								
1949–1953	72	15%	152	51%	8	40%	232	29%
1953–1957	55	13%	280	68%	3	37%	338	39%
1957–1961	35	9%	133	64%	3	60%	171	29%
1961–1965	39	11%	147	60%	5	63%	191	31%
Total	201	12%	716	61%	19	43%	936	33%
Passed by Bundestag								
1949–1953	398	85%	149	49%	12	60%	559	71%
1953–1957	376	87%	134	32%	8	73%	518	61%
1957–1961	352	91%	74	36%	2	40%	428	69%
1961–1965	328	89%	98	40%	3	37%	429	69%
Total	1454	88%	455	39%	25	57%	1934	67%
Subsequent action (for details, see Table 36)								
Failure to pass both Houses and reach promulgation	13		17		0		30 [b]	
Enacted	1441		438		25		1904	

[a] Between 1949 and 1965, 37 additional Cabinet bills and 14 additional Bundesrat bills were formally introduced in the Bundesrat, but not subsequently submitted to the Bundestag by the Cabinet.

[b] Includes four bills passed by both Houses but not promulgated by the Government.

Source: Sekretariat des Bundesrates, *16 Jahre Bundesgesetzgebung* (Bonn: Bonner Universitätsbuchdruckerei, 1965).

ministers and Representatives. To a complaint of a Member of the FDP that the Ministry of the Interior had refused to help the party to formulate an amendment to a Government bill, Minister Höcherl, during a Bundestag debate several years ago, gave a sardonic reply which explicitly revealed what has always been the Government's implicit attitude:

A terrible story has been uncovered by my colleague: that our ministry refused to offer help in formulation against a Government bill. I do not know whether this is an extraordinary occurrence. . . .

There is no law on it, and this whole area is *terra incognita*. . . . But I know that there is a certain conventional rule, that the Government in its noblesse will go so far as to give all sides of the House assistance in formulation, even against a Government bill, *if a majority of the House requests it*. . . .

In other parliaments, Members have staffs which enable them to get along without assistance in formulation from the Government, which might otherwise have to act against its own bills. That is a question which you can decide within your own jurisdiction. . . . But one should not fundamentally assert that it is extraordinary that we will not contribute to destroying, so to speak, our own bill. I do not find that extraordinary at all, but human and understandable.[18]

In addition to its great technical advantages in legislative drafting, the Government has sources of information which are vastly superior to those available to Members of Parliament. Furthermore, its constitutional responsibilities in foreign and military affairs, in policy formulation generally, and in administration, oblige it to take the initiative in the legislative process. Tradition supports its exercise of a role of legislative leadership. Control of a parliamentary majority gives it the means to advance its measures through their parliamentary stages. As a result, the initiative in the legislative process is largely in the hands of the Government. In its regular recourse to resolutions which request the Government to present a bill on a particular subject, the Bundestag testifies to its own shortcomings in the proposal of legislation.

[18] *Dt. Btag.*, 4. W.P., 83. Sitz., June 28, 1963, p. 4061. Emphasis supplied. For the response of another Minister to the question of the relative access of Members of different parties to ministerial assistance, see *Dt. Btag.*, 4. W.P., 189. Sitz., June 15, 1965, pp. 9501–2. The Council of Elders of the Bundestag has adopted the position that Government officials must assist all parties in legislative drafting at the committee stage, but not otherwise, as in the preparation of entire bills.

The Constitutional Position of the Bundestag in Lawmaking

While the Government largely proposes, Parliament disposes. But the Bundestag shares control over the passage of legislation with the Bundesrat. Although the approval of the house representing the *Länder* is not required for all legislation, the constitutional power of the Bundesrat is greater than that possessed by its predecessor in the Weimar Republic, an expression of the large role played by the *Länder* in the creation of the postwar federal system. All Government bills are submitted to the Bundesrat first, for its initial opinion, before they come to the Bundestag. Furthermore, all bills go to the Bundesrat after passage in the Bundestag. Depending on their subject matter, the house of the *Länder* can impose a suspensive or an absolute veto; in either case, it can attempt to influence the text by calling for a meeting of a joint Mediation Committee composed of an equal number of members of both Houses, which has the task of negotiating a mutually acceptable version of a bill in contention.[19] In practice, outright opposition between the two Houses has been rare because of the success of the Mediation Committee in achieving compromises.

Although it thus shares power with the Bundesrat in the passage of legislation, the Bundestag nevertheless occupies a crucial position in the legislative process: no amendment of the Basic Law is possible without the concurrence of two-thirds of its Members, no bill can ordinarily become law without the approval of a majority of those of its Members voting, and no money can be raised or spent outside of the budget and supplementary appropriations which it must pass just like ordinary legislation. Yet this commanding constitutional position which the Bundestag occupies in the legislative process is not entirely unassailable.

The Basic Law permits the Chancellor to request the Federal President to dissolve the Bundestag, should an absolute majority of its Members fail to give the Chancellor a vote of confidence which he has requested.[20] However, this qualified version of the nearly unrestricted dissolution power which the Weimar President enjoyed cannot readily be used to bypass the Bundestag in the legislative process. For one thing, the conditions for dissolution are clearly set out: it can occur only within twenty-one days after the failure of a vote of confidence, and only so long as the Bundestag fails to elect a new Chancellor to

[19] *Basic Law*, art. 77. See also pp. 365–8, *infra*.   [20] Art. 68.

replace the one to whom it has denied confidence. Furthermore, the solid majorities which postwar Governments have enjoyed have precluded votes of no-confidence, although they have by no means assured obedient passage of all Government legislation. Finally, even if the Bundestag were sent packing for a maximum of ninety days until a new House convened, the Government would have no emergency legislative powers to employ in the interval, as it did under the Weimar Constitution.

However, a faint echo of the old presumption in favor of a Government blocked by Parliament can still be heard, not so much in the weak emergency legislative procedure provided in the Basic Law, as in the current effort to strengthen that procedure by a constitutional revision, and in the existing appropriations procedure. The Basic Law contains no counterpart for the notorious Article 48 of the Weimar Constitution, which granted broad lawmaking powers, with few safeguards, to the President, for use in emergencies he himself could declare. There was, however—and still is—concern about the exercise of lawmaking and appropriations power in case the Bundestag cannot, or does not, act. Seared by the experience of the Weimar Republic, and reassured at first by the retention of certain emergency powers by the Allies, the authors of the Basic Law contented themselves, after considerable discussion, with a limited provision for an emergency lawmaking process that short-circuited the Bundestag. According to this provision, the Bundesrat has the power, for a six months' period, to pass urgent Government measures into law, if the Bundestag refuses to pass them after having denied the Government a vote of confidence.[21] The provision has never been used. But the concern for a more extensive emergency lawmaking process has grown as the retention of reserve powers by the Allies for use in emergencies has become increasingly incongruous with the otherwise sovereign status of the Federal Republic in international law. The Government made proposals for relevant constitutional changes in 1960, but was unable to persuade the SPD, whose control of more than one-third of the seats of the Bundestag enabled it to block amendments to the Basic Law. A repeated effort during the fourth Bundestag again failed to produce agreement, indicating the tenacity with which the parliamentary Opposition in particular resists any diminution of the position of the

[21] Art. 81.

Bundestag in the legislative process. In the fifth Bundestag, after six years of failure, the effort to provide for a legislative emergency procedure continued, but with greatly diminished objectives, and a strong appreciation of the need to safeguard the legislative powers of the Bundestag.

Less sensitive, and far more generally accepted in practice, are the provisions of the Basic Law which permit the Government to spend money without prior parliamentary approval.[22] First, these provisions permit the Government to meet its legally established financial obligations in case Parliament has not passed the budget by the beginning of the fiscal year. Action under this clause has been the rule rather than the exception, since the Government has frequently introduced its budget proposals too late for punctual Bundestag deliberations, and the Parliament has never yet enacted the budget in time. Second, the Basic Law allows the Government, with the approval of the Minister of Finance, to exceed the budget, requiring only eventual ratification by means of a deficiency appropriation. The Bundestag has even cooperated with this practice, by authorizing its Appropriations Committee to approve expenditures outside the budget. While the Government may therefore spend without advance parliamentary approval, it also has constitutional power to veto parliamentary appropriations which it has not requested. This provision has proved cumbersome, and too awkward politically to employ against the kind of pork-barrel legislation it was designed to stop. But its existence expresses the constitutional principle of a separation of powers between executive and legislature, and a conviction that the power of Parliament to appropriate requires more qualification than does the Government's power to spend without advance parliamentary approval. That conviction is still widely shared.[23]

The Promulgation of Law

The part which the Government plays in the promulgation of legislation is another reminder of its monarchical antecedents. The Basic Law requires that all bills properly passed by Parliament receive the signature of the Federal President and the countersignature of the

[22] Arts. 111, 112.

[23] Art. 113. For a recent, unsuccessful attempt to invoke this provision, see *Die Welt*, Aug. 13, 1965. For the widespread support for this provision, see *ibid.*, July 10, 1965. See also the proposal of Bundestag President Gerstenmaier that the House restrict its own appropriations power (*ibid.*, July 12, 1965).

Chancellor or the relevant minister.[24] In practice both minister and Chancellor, in that order, have signed all bills before presenting them to the President. But whether the signature requirements permit the exercise of discretion on the substance of the bill in the—unlikely—event that Parliament passes a bill which the Government or the President disapproves is an open controversy. In four minor instances, bills passed by Parliament have not been promulgated, in one case because the Federal President regarded the measure as unconstitutional.[25] Although ministerial and presidential signature of legislation is generally regarded as confirmation of the accuracy of the text and of the procedure of its enactment, the assertion that it is also a judgment of the constitutionality of its content is disputed. This claim, derived from monarchical prerogative, was more readily justifiable in the Weimar political system, in which the President had broad executive powers and most courts did not exercise judicial review, than in the present system, in which the President's position is generally much weaker and a Federal Constitutional Court is charged with the judgment of the constitutionality of legislation.[26] The resignation of the

[24] Arts. 58 and 82.

[25] Gesetz gegen den Betriebs—und Belegschaftshandel, *Dt. Btag.*, 3. W.P., Drs. 747. The bill, introduced in the Bundestag, had been passed on November 9, 1960 (*Dt. Btag.*, 3. W.P., 131. Sitz., p. 7530). After holding it for nine months, the Government finally submitted it to the Federal President on August 15, 1961. He, in turn, was reluctant to sign it, on grounds of its possible violation of Art. 12 of the Basic Law. On September 1, he wrote to the President of the Bundestag explaining his hesitation (Umdr. 995). Although the sponsors of the bill had by then lost interest in it, the principle of presidential veto aroused parliamentary opposition. At the end of the term of the third Bundestag, the Federal President requested the Chancellor to ask the Bundestag to reconsider the measure. But a procedure for such reconsideration does not exist. The controversy over the principle of presidential discretion continued into the next parliamentary term, with a letter from the Federal President to the President of the Bundestag on May 28, 1962, insisting on his right to judge the constitutionality of legislation before promulgating it, and a rejoinder drafted by the Bundestag President, on behalf of the parliamentary leaders, rejecting this claim. In another case, several *Land* Governments brought a case against the Federal President to the Constitutional Court because he had promulgated a law they regarded as unconstitutional. The Court, however, upheld the law (*BVerfGE* 10, 21).

[26] For the justification given at that time, see Gerhard Anschütz, *Die Verfassung des Deutschen Reichs vom 11. August 1919* (Bad Homburg: Hermann Gentner Verlag, 1960; photo-offset reproduction of the 14th ed., 1933), pp. 367-9. For discussions of the present status of the power of promulgation, see articles by Claus Arndt and Georg Anders in *Die Öffentliche Verwaltung*, XII (1959), 604 ff., and XVI (1963), 653 ff., respectively.

Minister of Justice in 1965,[27] because he felt unable to sign the extension of the statute of limitations for war crimes, which he regarded as unconstitutional, resolved the dilemma which the countersignature requirement may present to a parliamentary minister in a manner more consistent with the existing political system.

Judicial Review

Because the problem of promulgation has come up in only a few minor instances, and is unlikely to arise in an important case so long as the Government consists of leaders of the parliamentary majority, the exercise of executive discretion has not substantially challenged the position of Parliament in the legislative process. Judicial review by the Federal Constitutional Court imposes a far more important restriction on the role of Parliament in lawmaking. The Court's broad jurisdiction and the multiple channels of access to it, which enable not only aggrieved individuals or groups, but the Federal and *Land* Governments, as well as a minority of one-third of the Members of the Bundestag—in effect, the Opposition—to bring cases before the court, have enabled it to rule on the constitutionality of a large number of laws, among them measures of major importance. The Court has, for example, invalidated the provision of a federal revenue law taxing the incomes of husbands and wives at the rate applicable to the sum of their earnings, the provision permitting tax deduction for contributions to political parties, and a law for redrawing *Länder* boundaries in the Southwest.[28]

Executive Orders

Not only does the position of the Bundestag in the legislative process bear the marks of more than a century of evolution, but the distribution of the rule-making power in the political system is also the product of this development. Some types of regulations which the King's Government promulgated on its own authority, notably those providing for the establishment, organization, and procedure of the ministries, are still today issued as administrative decrees without

[27] *Die Welt*, March 26, 1965, p. 1; March 27, 1965, p. 1.

[28] Thomas Ellwein, *Das Regierungssystem der Bundesrepublik Deutschland* (Cologne and Opladen: Westdeutscher Verlag, 1963), I, 267–77. Through June, 1965, the Federal Constitutional Court invalidated 10 federal laws entirely, and 40 in part, according to the record kept by the Bundestag Legal Research Department.

parliamentary participation. Originally a part of royal prerogative and implicitly taken over by the President of the Republic under the Weimar Constitution, it is today regarded as within the sole discretion of the Federal Chancellor to determine the number and the jurisdiction of the departments of Government, and within the discretion of the Cabinet to regulate their procedure.[29] Other types of rules originally within the Monarch's authority now take the form of executive orders, which may be issued by the Government, according to the Basic Law, on the authority of any existing legislation. Although the Constitutional Court has not been strict in specifying the terms in which legislative power may thus be delegated, any court may challenge the legal validity of an executive order.[30] The Basic Law requires Bundesrat—but not Bundestag—approval for that large majority of orders which in some way affect the *Länder*.[31] The Bundestag has tried to narrow the field of administrative discretion in the issuance of executive orders by pressing for ever-greater detail in the terms of the authorizing legislation.[32] In a number of areas, mainly in the field of tariff legislation, including regulations issued under the treaty establishing the European Economic Community, the House has reserved the right to approve some orders in advance and to revoke others after their issuance. It has thereby taken on a tremendous and rapidly growing burden of detail, particularly in the field of foreign trade. While it dealt with 43 tariff orders during its third term, when this development was in an early stage, the Bundestag handled 244 such orders during its fourth term, as well as 225 Common Market regulations.[33] Parliamentary supervision over executive orders has narrowed

[29] von Mangoldt-Klein, *Das Bonner Grundgesetz*, 2nd. ed. (Berlin and Frankfurt a. M.: Verlag Franz Vahlen, 1957–1961), pp. 1214–15. See also pp. 230–31, *supra*.

[30] *Basic Law*, art. 80(1). For the lenient interpretation of the Constitutional Court, see *BVerfGE* 8, 274. Cf. Ernst Friesenhahn, *Verfassungsgerichtsbarkeit in der Bundesrepublik Deutschland* (Cologne: Carl Heymanns Verlag, 1963), pp. 53, 60–61.　　　[31] Art. 80(2).

[32] For a criticism of the extent to which this tendency has gone, see Ulrich Scheuner, "Die Aufgabe der Gesetzgebung in unserer Zeit," *Mitteilungen der kommunalen Gemeinschaftsstelle für Verwaltungsvereinfachung* (KGSt), June, 1960, pp. 1–11.

[33] *Dt. Btag.*, 4. W.P., 196. Sitz., July 2, 1965, p. 10031. Figures cited there updated by Bundestag secretariat. For the procedure governing Bundestag consideration of these executive orders, see *Geschäftsordnung des Deutschen Bundestages, op. cit.*, appendix 4. For an enumeration of laws under which the Bundestag reserves the right to review executive orders, see Hans Trossmann, *Der*

Table 32. Executive orders

Issuing Ministry	Number issued		
	First Bundestag 1949–53	Second Bundestag 1953–57	Third Bundestag 1957–61
Agriculture	107	145	131
Atomic Energy	0	0	2
Bundesrat Affairs	7	0	0
Defense	0	7	26
Economics and Economic Cooperation	351	98	121
Family and Youth	0	0	1
Finance and Federal Property	190	320	293
Foreign Affairs	3	1	4
Housing	5	7	9
Interior	55	82	119
Justice	39	10	25
Labor	23	54	81
Post Office	22	18	11
Refugees	11	18	1
Transport	64	238	269
Total	877	998	1,093
Laws enacted during the same period	545	510	424

Source: Federal Ministry of Justice, as given in *Statistisches Jahrbuch für die Bundesrepublik Deutschland*, 1964, p. 145.

their scope, but not their volume. The number of executive orders was more than twice the number of laws passed during the first three terms of the Bundestag. (See Table 32.)

The Changing Role of Legislation

Despite the large output of these types of rules, ordinary legislation has also expanded tremendously in quantity and in political impor-

Deutsche Bundestag, Organisation und Arbeitsweise (Darmstadt: Neue Darmstädter Verlagsanstalt, 1963), pp. 61–5. The procedure for receiving the Common Market regulations, referring them to the appropriate committees, and bringing them to the attention of the House within the legally established time limits, has become so complicated that the fourth Bundestag experimented with the creation of a special Council of Elders (*Integrationsältestenrat*), to supervise the work. It consisted of the party whips, and Bundestag Members belonging to the Consultative Assembly of the Council of Europe. For an example of the usually perfunctory acceptance of such regulations by the House, upon the recommendation of the appropriate committees, see *Dt. Btag.*, 4. W.P., 191. Sitz., June 23, 1965, pp. 9602–4.

tance since Parliament was first admitted to the process of its formulation. Lawmaking first attained modern dimensions in the Imperial
Reichstag. As the industrialization and the urbanization of the country
created new, national political issues requiring legislative settlement,
Parliament's part in the legislative process gained central political
significance. By the first decade of this century, the Reichstag was
enacting an average of 27 statutes a year. Lawmaking activity continued to grow in scope in response to the issues of the interwar years. In
the mid-twenties, 118 statutes were being adopted in an average year.
The even greater demands made on the political system by the problems of reconstruction after the Second World War, and the high
propensity to seek legislative settlements, produced an output of legislation which reached an all-time high of over 135 statutes annually
during the first term of the Bundestag. As a measure of the growing
complexity of the legal norms being adopted, the statute book, which
includes important executive orders, and which contains 141 pages for
the year 1882, for example, was growing at the rate of 630 pages per
year during the Reichstag which sat from 1903 to 1906, while the rate
of growth was 1,749 pages annually during the Reichstag term of 1924
to 1928, and 2,879 pages per year during the third Bundestag.[34]

These necessarily crude, quantitative measures nevertheless provide
an index of the changing role of legislation in the political system.
From setting general norms on matters affecting the traditional liberty
and property of the citizen, law has become an instrument of policy
affecting most of the subjects regulated by modern government. The
political significance of Parliament's role in lawmaking has correspondingly grown with the expanding importance of law in the political system. This becomes even clearer when the subjects of legislation
are considered. In the postwar period, the chief legislative issues
included determination of how the costs of war would be shared, what
forms government welfare services would take, how industry would be
organized and regulated, and how far agriculture would be supported.
To the extent that major foreign policy decisions required the ratifica-

[34] The Reichstag which sat from December 3, 1903, to December 13, 1906,
witnessed the enactment of 81 statutes and the addition of 2,520 pages (in 4
years) to the *Reichsgesetzblatt*. During the Reichstag which sat from December 7,
1924, to March 31, 1928, 240 statutes were promulgated in part 1 of the
Reichsgesetzblatt, and 1,964 pages were added to it; part 2 included 150 statutes
and 3,808 pages. For the enactment of legislation in the postwar period, see Table
31. The *Bundesgesetzblatt* for the years 1958 to 1961 includes 5,072 pages in part
1, and 6,444 pages in part 2.

tion of treaties, the appropriation of money, or the raising of armed forces, they presented issues for legislative determination as well. As soon as these immediate postwar questions had been dealt with, a review of fundamental aspects of criminal law and procedure, and of commercial law, seemed urgent. Parts of the law had been unchanged since the original enactment of the relevant codes at the national level three-quarters of a century earlier, in the first decades of the Empire. The complexity of the issues, and the distrust of administrative discretion, added to the level of detail in a volume of legislation and appropriations far exceeding the output half a century earlier.

Federal-State Relations

The sweep of legislative activity at the national level was hardly restricted by the federal division of powers established by the Basic Law. Among the major subjects of legislation, only the field of education was constitutionally excluded from the national jurisdiction. The constitutional demands of the *Länder* were strongest, and prevailed most successfully, in the division of administrative functions, in the participation of *Land* Governments in national decisions through the Bundesrat, and in the division of tax resources. Conflict between national and *Land* jurisdiction has chiefly arisen not in the field of lawmaking, but in the field of government finance. Originally, the Basic Law left the revenue from the two most important sources of taxation, income and corporation taxes, entirely to the *Länder*, subject only to a claim which the Federal Government might make to a portion of these taxes, by means of a law requiring Bundesrat approval. After two constitutional amendments and numerous legislative changes entailing difficult compromises, the Federal Government now has a constitutional right to 35 per cent of income from these tax sources. But since its financial obligations expand far more rapidly than those of the *Länder*, especially in view of rapidly rising defense expenditures, the Federal Government continues to be financially dependent on the *Länder*, since further revisions of the proportions require Bundesrat approval.[35] In the field of legislation, on the other

---

[35] For a discussion of the original federal settlement, see John Ford Golay, *The Founding of the Federal Republic of Germany* (Chicago: University of Chicago Press, 1958), Ch. II, esp. pp. 87–9, and *Basic Law*, art. 106. The present text of this article was adopted by the law of December 24, 1956, *BGBl.* I, p. 1077. In pursuance of art. 106, a further revision of the distribution of these tax resources

hand, the constitutional competence of the Federal Government, and therefore of the Federal Parliament, is broad.

If the legislative role of the Bundestag today still reflects the confinement of that role under the monarchical system in which it developed, its importance must also be measured by the steadily expanding significance of legislative decisions for the political system. Although other political institutions participate in the legislative process, passage through the Bundestag is an indispensable step in the normal enactment of all legislation. The decision in the Bundestag—and all the forces which act on it—therefore influences every step of the legislative way, both those steps which are taken before a bill reaches the House, which must anticipate Bundestag reaction, and those steps which follow.

STAGES OF THE LEGISLATIVE PROCESS

Seven Steps

From its introduction to its promulgation, a bill usually passes through seven major stages of consideration. In the case of Government bills, which constitute three-fourths of all legislation enacted, one can distinguish (1) the stage of ministerial drafting, (2) the first passage through the Bundesrat, (3) the first reading in the Bundestag, (4) the committee stage in the Bundestag, (5) the second and third readings in the Bundestag, (6) the second passage through the Bundesrat, and (7) promulgation. The influence of the Bundestag on legislation is not limited to those stages at which bills pass through the House. An assessment of the legislative functions performed by Parliament therefore requires us to consider each stage of the legislative process in turn.

The influence of the Bundestag on legislation, furthermore, varies considerably with the origin of the bill, its timing, its subject, and the pattern of political support and opposition which it arouses. In order to illustrate this variety, five different types of bill will be traced, stage by stage, from their proposal to their disposal. Our general analysis of each stage of the legislative process will be followed by an account of the specific treatment which these bills received at that stage.

---

was finally agreed on, after a tenacious struggle between the *Land* Governments and the Federation, with the adoption of the law of March 11, 1964, *BGBl.* I, p. 137, which provides that the Federal Government receives 39 per cent of the income from these taxes for the years 1964 through 1966.

Five Illustrations

Five pieces of legislation cannot, of course, adequately represent the nearly three thousand measures which the Bundestag considered during its first four terms. The examples chosen have been selected, not so much as representative, but as limiting cases of the kinds of treatment which legislation receives in the Bundestag. They indicate the perimeter within which most cases occur.

The first, the Volunteers Bill of 1955,[36] the initial legislative step toward German rearmament, is an unusual example of the ability of the Bundestag to rewrite a Government bill completely when the supporters of a measure are limited to the ministerial bureaucracy, and its critics are found among all parties in the House. The second, the Federal Requisitions Bill enacted in 1956,[37] a measure empowering the Government to requisition private property in an emergency, illustrates the extent to which the Bundestag may serve as an avenue for interest-group influence on legislation. The third, the Federal Schedule of Fees for Lawyers,[38] passed in 1961, is an example of the influence on legislation of a single interest group existing within the House itself. The fourth, a bill intended to regulate travel between the Federal Republic and the Soviet Zone of Germany,[39] introduced in 1960 but pigeonholed in committee, illustrates the ability of the Bundestag to block Government legislation when there are opponents of a bill within the majority party in Parliament. Finally, the Child Benefits Bill of 1961,[40] a measure to increase government payments to families, exemplifies partisan legislation, shaped by the parliamentary majority in the drafting stage, which passes through the Bundestag, unchanged, under the control of the governing party.

MINISTERIAL DRAFTING

The Chief Actors

Before a Government bill is formally submitted to the Bundestag, it passes through numerous phases of drafting and revision, of consulta-

[36] Gesetz über die vorläufige Rechtsstellung der Freiwilligen in den Streitkräften vom 23. Juli 1955, *BGBl.* I, p. 449.

[37] Bundesleistungsgesetz vom 19. Oktober 1956, *BGBl.* I, p. 815.

[38] Gesetz zur änderung der Bundesgebührenordnung für Rechtsanwälte und des Gerichtskostengesetzes vom 19. Juni 1961, *BGBl.* I, p. 769.

[39] Entwurf eines Gesetzes über Einreise und Ausreise, *Dt. Btag.*, 3. W.P., Drs. 2372.

[40] Kindergeldkassengesetz vom 18. Juli 1961, *BGBl.* I, p. 1001.

tion and deliberation. Five major groups participate in the legislative process at this stage, not necessarily including any Members of Parliament except those who belong to the Cabinet. First, the ministry into whose jurisdiction the bill falls has charge of the measure, determines its original conception, and prepares the draft (*Referentenentwurf*). Second, other ministries whose work and interests may be affected by the bill are entitled to consultation, and an interministerial committee headed by the sponsoring ministry may have an important part in negotiating disputed points of the draft. Third, officials of the ministries of the *Land* Governments, which in most cases administer federal laws, are consulted on the problems of implementation. Fourth, representatives of nationally organized interest groups are heard. They are frequently given copies of a draft bill in order to test the reaction of their leaders to its provisions. Fifth, the Chancellor, empowered under the Basic Law to "determine the general policy" of the Government,[41] supervises, through the agency of the Chancellor's Office, the development of the bill from its earliest beginnings.

These actors in the early stages of the evolution of a bill have a formal place in the process. The "Rules of Procedure of the Federal Ministries" prescribe that the initiating ministry must inform the Chancellor's Office "if a politically important bill is being worked on,"[42] and must consult the Ministry of Finance on all questions of revenues and expenditures, the ministries of the Interior and of Justice on questions of constitutionality and legal form, and all other ministries which may be concerned.[43] Furthermore, "preparatory drafts of bills, which touch on the interests of the *Länder*, are to be submitted . . . to the *Länder* ministries whose jurisdiction is involved as early as possible."[44] The Rules also provide that "in order to obtain material for the preparation of laws," "the representatives of the special groups (*Fachkreise*) may be consulted."[45]

Federal Ministries

In a society which regards legal norms with great respect and has a high propensity toward the legal formalization of relationships, even among Government ministers, the specific enumeration of the participants in the early stages of bill drafting is itself significant. But the

---

[41] Art. 65.

[42] *Gemeinsame Geschäftsordnung der Bundesministerien,* Besonderer Teil (GGO II), par. 21.

[43] *Ibid.,* par. 22.   [44] *Ibid.,* par. 24.   [45] *Ibid.,* par. 23.

influence of these participants on the formulation of bills depends not only on procedural norms. Since bills cannot be presented to Parliament until they have been approved by the Cabinet, skillful and thorough interministerial consultation assures the initiating ministry that the bill will obtain the necessary support within the Government. If points of dispute among Government departments are not satisfactorily settled, they will come out at the Cabinet stage, and at the very least delay the bill's progress. Under the Cabinet's own rules of procedure, the ministers of Finance, of the Interior, and of Justice have a suspensive veto on financial matters and on questions of legality, respectively, which can only be overridden by an absolute majority of the members of the Cabinet and the affirmative vote of the Chancellor.[46] It is therefore particularly important to secure the approval of these key members of the Government. If a bill is successfully cleared with all ministries, Cabinet approval is a mere formality. If substantial opposition to it remains within the Government, not only is Cabinet delay likely, but disunity within the Government may handicap the measure in the Bundestag, where Members primed by the aggrieved ministry may revive the dispute, even if a Cabinet majority supports the measure. Exploitation of differences among Government departments gives the Bundestag some of its most effective weapons in the legislative process.

Land Ministries

The source of the influence of *Land* ministries on legislative drafts is likewise found in the role which the *Länder* play in later stages of the legislative process. Most Federal ministries lack the substructure through which legislation is implemented and, in their dependence on the Governments of the *Länder* for the implementation of their policies, they must take account of the administrative expertise and the policy predilections of their counterparts on the *Land* levels. Furthermore, Government bills are twice subject to Bundesrat action, once after they first pass the Cabinet and again after their passage through the Bundestag. Objections of *Land* officials which are not met in the original bill may therefore harden into official opposition of *Land* Governments in the Bundesrat. Furthermore, the views of the *Länder* may be subsequently revived in the Bundestag, which finds in the

---

[46] *Geschäftsordnung der Bundesregierung* vom 11. Mai 1951, *GMBl.* p. 137, par. 26.

Land ministries a counter-bureaucracy offering administrative expertise which can be employed to meet the arguments of federal officials.

Interest Groups

Most remarkable is the position which interest groups occupy at this
stage in the drafting of legislation. The ministerial practice of consulting major private organizations in the preparation of laws affecting
them goes back at least as far as the beginning of the Weimar Republic, had precedents during the Empire, and in some forms even antedates the origin of political parties.[47] The expertise of these groups,
their representation in Parliament, and the need for their cooperation
in the eventual implementation of the legislation make it impossible
for the ministries to ignore them. In the later years of the Weimar
Republic, in an effort to protect ministries against the demand for
consultation of countless small groups and to limit access to those
which were nationally organized, a provision was adopted in the Rules
of Procedure giving interest groups a recognized place in the drafting
of legislation.

In the preparation of laws and important decrees [the provision read] the
representatives of the relevant special groups (*Fachkreise*) should be
consulted promptly. . . . *The groups should have adequate time to consult their subordinate bodies and to take aacount of their opinions.*[48]

The present-day version, cited earlier, which is somewhat less open in
admitting the role of interest groups, is even more specific in singling

[47] The habit of consultation between ministry and interest groups can be traced
back to the relationship which existed between the Government and the quasi-
public Chambers of Industry and Commerce which replaced the medieval guilds
and corporations at the beginning of the nineteenth century. The laws creating
them frequently obliged the Chambers to offer advice and counsel to the Government, as well as to perform administrative functions (see Wolfram Fischer,
Unternehmerschaft, Selbstverwaltung, und Staat [Berlin: Duncker & Humblot,
1964], pp. 1, 29, 35). I am indebted to Volker Knörich for research on this point.
For the origin of modern interest groups, relating them also to medieval organizations, see Gerhard Schulz, "Über Entstehung und Formen von Interessengruppen
in Deutschland seit Beginn der Industrialisierung," *Politische Vierteljahresschrift*,
II (1961), 124–54. For their political activity during the Empire, see Thomas
Nipperdey, "Interessenverbände und Parteien in Deutschland vor dem ersten
Weltkrieg," *Politische Vierteljahresschrift*, II (1961), esp. 268–9. For the present
period, see Wilhelm Hennis, "Verfassungsordnung und Verbandseinfluss," *Politische Vierteljahresschrift*, II (1961), 23–35. The important case study by
Otto Stammer, *et al., Verbände und Gesetzgebung* (Cologne and Opladen: Westdeutscher Verlag, 1965), appeared after this chapter was written.
[48] Quoted in Hennis, *op. cit.,* p. 29. Emphasis supplied.

out those with a preferred status, by providing that "groups which are not nationally organized are not, in general, to be consulted." [49] The Rules reflect the strategic position which interest groups have, as intermediaries between the Government and society, in the contrast between the provisions for them and the provisions for the consultation of professional experts. The latter

may be consulted only when, judging by strict standards, the work cannot be done by staff members. . . . [They] are to be carefully selected. Outstanding and recognized expertise, and complete independence of groups affected by the measure, are decisive [criteria for selection].[50]

The choice of interest groups for consultation is up to the department head. It is of course a possible tactic to keep a draft secret, to refuse to consult. But some ministries are in such continuous contact with the leading interest groups in their area of jurisdiction that consultation is constant as a matter of course. This is true for example, of the Federation of German Industry and the Ministry of Economics —some of the officials on both sides being in almost daily contact.[51] If a bill affecting business interests is considered in the Ministry of Economics, the Federation knows of it at once and keeps tab on it. Over a ten-year period, 83 per cent of the Federation's formal statements of opinion were submitted to executive departments of the Government, while only 7 per cent were addressed to the Bundestag or the Bundesrat, or to their committees.[52] These proportions are a measure of the effectiveness of the access which major interest groups have to the legislative process at its ministerial stage. It is duplicated in the case of other major groups and "their" ministries. The influence of the large, centralized interest groups on the early formulation of legislation reflects not only the expertise which they command in any industrialized society, but also the unusual extent to which they per-

[49] *Gemeinsame Geschäftsordnung der Bundesministerien,* Besonderer Teil (GGO II), par. 23(3).

[50] *Gemeinsame Geschäftsordnung der Bundesministerien,* Allgemeiner Teil (GGO I), as adopted by the Cabinet August 1, 1958, reprinted in Hans Lechner and Klaus Hülshoff, *Parlament und Regierung,* 2nd ed., (Munich and Berlin: C. H. Beck'sche Verlagsbuchhandlung, 1958), par. 61.

[51] Gerard Braunthal, *The Federation of German Industry in Politics* (Ithaca: Cornell University Press, 1965), Ch. X, esp. pp. 218–21, 229–31.

[52] Hennis, *op. cit.,* p. 25. For a list of statements in a typical year, see *Jahresbericht des Bundesverbandes der Deutschen Industrie,* Drs. no. 60 (Bergisch-Gladbach: Joh. Heider Druckerei, 1962), pp. 170–74.

form an interest-aggregating function in Germany, and the relationship between their great financial and organizational power, and the relative organizational weakness of the political parties.

The Chancellor

A decisive part in the formulation of legislation within the Government is played by the Chancellor's Office. Seventy-four high-level officials, organized to parallel the ministries of the Federal Government, supervise the legislative process on behalf of the Chancellor and of his responsibility for setting general policy. The relevant specialists in the Office follow a bill from its inception through the process of negotiation among the leading participants, insuring that it is consistent with the Chancellor's policy and sometimes helping to settle disputed points. The influence of the Chancellor's Office is due to the broad power of the Chancellor to issue general policy directives. The possible use of this power to affect the terms of a legislative draft, or to block it altogether, has occasionally led interest groups to appeal to the Chancellor directly if the drafting ministry has not responded satisfactorily to their demands. Adenauer, who was willing to employ the power of his position fully, acted as the final arbiter on disputed legislative projects in many instances.[53]

The Chancellor's Office also influences the course of legislation by the technical services it performs. It is responsible for the development of a legislative program for the Government, by soliciting the ministries concerning their legislative projects and their recommended order of importance, and by supplying the results to a Legislation Committee of the Cabinet. The proposal of this Committee, when approved by the Cabinet, comprises a legislative program for an entire parliamentary term, complete with an order of priorities. The Chancel-

[53] Hennis, *op. cit.*, p. 35. For an example, see Braunthal, *op. cit.*, pp. 198–200. The contrast between Adenauer's use of the power to determine general policy and Erhard's use of it indicates how vague it is, and how dependent on the style of the particular Chancellor. While Adenauer was generally criticized for overusing the power, to dominate the Cabinet, Erhard was criticized for using it insufficiently. For a general discussion, see Wilhelm Hennis, *Richtlinienkompetenz und Regierungstechnik* (Tübingen: Mohr, 1964), esp. pp. 27–39. But Erhard developed the Chancellor's Office even further than Adenauer had, including in it a policy planning bureau, and a department for maintaining direct contact with interest groups. The total staff of the Chancellor's Office included 192 employees in 1966. For a discussion of its organization, see *Der Spiegel*, XX, no. 24 (June 6, 1966), 32–40.

lor's Office prepares the agenda of Cabinet meetings, receives bills for inclusion on the agenda, assures that they have obtained the necessary clearance from all Government departments and that they constitute an approved part of the legislative program, provides a summary of the issues they raise for the Chancellor and an indication of whether they require Cabinet discussion. Under the Chancellor's direction, the Office keeps a transcript of Cabinet meetings. The Chancellor's Office is also the channel of communication between Government and Parliament in the legislative process, transmitting bills approved by the Cabinet to the Bundesrat, receiving the Bundesrat's opinion and presenting it to the Cabinet for the Government's rejoinder, then submitting bills to the Bundestag, and receiving those passed by both Houses for promulgation. The Office also receives all parliamentary inquiries for transmission to the relevant ministries.

Members of Parliament

Among the five major groups which participate in the legislative process at the ministerial stage, Members of the Bundestag are conspicuously absent. They have no formal position here, as the Rules of Procedure suggest in the offhand inclusion of Members of Parliament among a miscellany of outsiders who may be consulted:

If it seems advisable that ministerial bills or their contents be made available to Members of the Bundestag, the press, or other parties or persons not officially concerned, before the Federal Cabinet has approved them, the relevant Ministers . . . or in cases of fundamental political importance, the Chancellor, shall decide in what form this shall occur.[54]

Members of Parliament have continuously complained that texts of legislative projects reach them, to their embarrassment, through interest groups to which they belong. SPD Members, particularly, may also obtain them through *Land* ministries which their party heads. Through these contacts, many Members are in fact well—but by no means fully—informed of the Government's legislative plans, and even

---

[54] *Gemeinsame Geschäftsordnung der Bundesministerien*, Besonderer Teil (GGO II), par. 25. For examples of the dissatisfaction of Members of the Bundestag with the failure of ministries to consult them early in the legislative process, see the symposium published in *Christ und Welt*, Nov. 27, 1964, in which the chief whips of all parties joined in the complaint (cf. Braunthal, *op. cit.*, p. 219). The matter was also raised by an FDP leader in a general discussion of the status of Parliament (see *Dt. Btag.*, 4. W.P., 164. Sitz., Feb. 17, 1965, p. 8133).

CDU/CSU leaders in the Bundestag are dissatisfied with the level of their information.

Ministerial practice in the consultation of parliamentarians varies widely, with the style of the minister, the subject of legislation, and the possible advantages to a ministry of early clearance with influential Members.

Leaders of the governing parties in the Bundestag have been consulted on legislation controversial within their ranks, especially in the fields of social and economic policy where it is necessary to negotiate with interest groups within these parties. In some instances, these leaders have even participated in Cabinet sessions, although sensitivity to the distinction between Government and Parliament is a strong obstacle to this practice. In a notable case, Maria Probst, a CSU spokesman for veterans groups, who had mobilized enough opposition to a Government pension bill within the parliamentary majority to block it, was invited to a Cabinet session to discuss her counterproposal.[55] The practice occurs also when Members are asked to introduce a measure drafted by the Government as a bill initiated in the Bundestag. Constitutional amendments (such as those pending on government emergency powers) and laws for which all-party agreement is desired (such as the proposed law on political parties) have been the subject of consultation with Members from all parties.[56]

Consultation between committee chairman, committee leaders of both parties, and high officials in the department has regularly occurred between the Bundestag Committee on Social Policy and the Ministry of Labor. But between the Interior Department and the Bundestag Interior Committee, relations were strained, especially in the final years of Schröder's leadership of that ministry. An admirer of the British system, Schröder disliked informal negotiations with Members on bills before their approval by the Cabinet. He also found the gruff, blustery SPD Representative who became chairman of the Committee in 1960 difficult to get along with. But after Schröder had

[55] The revision of the pension law in 1963 provided another instance, when Rasner, Strauss, and Zoglmann as parliamentary leaders of CDU, CSU, and FDP respectively, were invited to the Cabinet meeting to negotiate the necessary compromise between the Government and its followers in the Bundestag (*Die Welt*, Dec. 2, 1963).

[56] See for example *Die Welt*, Jan. 29, 1964: "Were the law (on party finance) to be passed in the form in which it has now been communicated for their information to all party executives. . . ."

failed to win enactment of important legislation, especially the constitutional amendments on emergency powers, his successors, Höcherl
and Lücke, became convinced that only by such negotiations could
their programs pass the Bundestag. Höcherl went so far as to create a
joint negotiating commission between the ministry and parliamentary
leaders of all parties to work out an acceptable emergency powers law.
The variety in the relationship between Members and ministries in the
early stages of the legislative process indicates the dominance of
tactical considerations which have not so far found any stable institutional form.

The general reasons for the arm's-length relationship between Government and Parliament at this stage of the legislative process are not
difficult to discover. In the consultations it conducts during the preparation of its bills, the Government is motivated by the desire to obtain
the support of influential groups before the public and partisan deliberations begin. In return for the right to be consulted, the groups
which participate may implicitly agree to abide by the bargains which
are negotiated. By maintaining the secrecy of these consultations with
the interest groups and with the major Federal and *Land* ministries
concerned, the Government is able to withhold the identity of the
groups consulted, and the nature of the concessions made, from the
opposition parties and from unorganized interests among the public.
This deprives Members of the Bundestag of the power to negotiate the
bargains among these groups themselves, and denies them information
and support for opposing views. The objection of Members to the
Government's procedure is directed at just those features of it which
make it advantageous to the Government. But to the extent that
Members of the Bundestag themselves agree to participate in private
ad hoc consultations with the ministries, they imperil the distinctive
contributions which public parliamentary debate and partisan committee deliberation can make to the legislative process.

The five case studies reveal the various types of consultation which
may take place on a bill at the drafting stage, and the various consequences of these different types of consultation for the treatment the
bill receives in Parliament.

The Volunteers Bill

The Volunteers Bill was drafted in reckless haste. A special Office
for Defense Questions under Theodor Blank—no formal Defense

Ministry was yet in existence—had conducted leisurely deliberations on rearmament legislation, in consultation with a committee of the Bundestag on European Security Questions, over a three-year period between the time the Western Allies had decided, in general, to permit Germany's rearmament, and the ratification of the London and Paris Agreements on May 5, 1955.[57] The Chancellor's first inclination was to present the prepared legislation to Parliament within the following months.[58] A week later he reversed himself, deciding on a quick start to rearmament, in preparation for a round of international negotiations which were due later in the summer and which culminated in the Eisenhower-Khrushchev confrontation in Geneva, and in Adenauer's trip to Moscow.

Within the week, a three-paragraph stopgap measure, which became the Volunteers Bill, was drafted.[59] It provided for the enlistment of volunteers to form a military cadre, pending passage of more extensive legislation to establish an army. Weekend consultations, involving the Chancellor, the chairman of the CDU/CSU parliamentary party, CSU leaders, and military staff members, followed.[60] A Cabinet session the following Thursday gave the bill provisional approval, pending assurance that the parliamentary leaders of the governing parties supported it. To obtain this assurance, the Chancellor accepted a CSU demand placing a March 31, 1956, time limit on the validity of the bill. Thereupon, he obtained the final approval of the Cabinet by circulating its members in writing the next day.[61] The bill was immediately presented to the Bundesrat, although it was the Saturday of the Whitsun holiday weekend. This schedule violated the custom of submitting bills to the Bundesrat exactly three weeks prior to its next scheduled session, to allow the *Länder* Governments the maximum time permitted by the Constitution for their deliberation.[62]

The absence of careful consultation on the bill at the ministerial stage contributed decisively to its difficulties in Parliament, where it became apparent that the measure raised all the major issues con-

[57] *FAZ*, Oct. 15, 1952; SZ, Sept. 26, 1953; *Bulletin des Presse–und Informationsamtes der Bundesregierung* (hereafter cited as *Bulletin*), April 23, 1953.
[58] *General Anzeiger* (Bonn), May 11, 1955.
[59] *Ibid.*, May 21, 1955.
[60] *Kölner Stadt-Anzeiger*, May 23, 1955.
[61] *FAZ*, May 31, 1955; *General Anzeiger* (Bonn), May 31, 1955; *Der Spiegel*, IX, no. 24 (June 8, 1955), 7–8.
[62] Neunreither, *op. cit.*, p. 59.

nected with rearmament which the Chancellor had hoped, for the moment, to avoid. As drafted, the bill failed to meet the demands of powerful interests well represented in Parliament. These included the *Land* Governments, which, concerned over their administrative prerogatives, were able to threaten a veto of the bill in the Bundesrat and, armed with this threat, to influence its provisions through *Land* representatives in the committees of the Bundestag. The major opposition party in Parliament, the SPD, was of course also critical of the bill. While SPD leaders had been consulted by the Government on the terms of basic defense legislation, in part because constitutional amendments requiring SPD support were eventually necessary, the Opposition was not consulted in the hasty process of drafting the Volunteers Bill. It was therefore particularly suspicious.

But even among the Members of the largest party, the bill aroused opposition. The CSU, supporting the ambition of its most powerful leader, Franz-Josef Strauss, to become Defense Minister, was unwilling to delegate any substantial authority to a temporary defense administration. In the CDU, there were young Members idealistically concerned about the proper form of rearmament; business interests, concerned over the effect of military recruitment on the labor market; and ex-army officers, worried about the political criteria to be employed in making high level appointments. The Bundestag Committee on European Security included Members of all parties who were unsure how the stopgap measure would fit into the larger legislative program which the Committee had discussed with Blank over such a long time. All critics could appeal to a sensitive public opinion, hesitant about rearmament generally and entirely unprepared for the suddenness of the first step. Supporters of the measure were limited to the sponsoring ministry. As a result, the bill was completely rewritten in the Bundestag before its final passage.

The Federal Requisitions Bill

By comparison, the Federal Requisitions Bill, which had also been drafted during the long interval between the decision to rearm and the ratification of the necessary international agreements, received more thorough, and more normal, deliberation at the ministerial level. A resolution of the Bundestag in 1951 requested the Government to draft a replacement for the Requisitions Law which had been promulgated by the Nazi regime on the first day of the Second World War and was still largely in effect.[63] Work on such a bill had meanwhile been underway in the Ministry of the Interior for about a year, using the old law as a point of departure. Its main purpose was to empower the Government to requisition private property in emergencies.

The history of the Federal Requisitions Law reveals successive efforts, first at the ministerial, later at the parliamentary level, to protect a variety of private interests against the effects of the law. Before the first complete ministerial draft was ready, in the summer of 1952, municipal government and church groups had been consulted, as well as officials of the *Länder*. As a result of these consultations, churches and religious societies, and public bodies at all levels of government, were excluded from its effects.[64]

But the provisions of the bill were otherwise broadly permissive. Business interests, which had not at that stage been consulted by the Ministry of the Interior, were concerned not only about threats to private property contained in the law, but about having to rely for its administration on a department of Government with which their contacts were not as good as they were with the Ministry of Economics.[65] Within the Government, the Ministry of Economics championed the demands of these interests.[66] On this ministry's insistence, the scope of the bill was considerably narrowed in successive drafts over the following two years, until finally all manufacturing and commercial enterprises had been excluded from its application. A new bill, to be administered by the Ministry of Economics, was drafted covering these enterprises.[67] Neither bill was presented to the Cabinet for approval until the ratification of the London and Paris agreements gave the Federal Government responsibility for defense. Only then did there seem to be justification for the introduction of this type of emergency legislation which was bound to be, in view of its predecessor, widely unpopular. The Bundestag Committee on Interior Affairs, headed by a Member of the Opposition, was not consulted on the terms of the bill before its submission to Parliament in October, 1955.

Parliamentary consideration of the bill indicated that while the

---

[63] *Dt. Btag.*, 1. W.P., Oct. 11, 1951, p. 6865.

[64] Referentenentwurf, Der Bundesminister des Innern, Bundesleistungsgesetz, Az: ZB 2–10–239/52, June 21, 1952, par. 25.

[65] *FAZ*, Aug. 26, 1952; *SZ*, Sept. 1, 1952.

[66] *Frankfurter Rundschau*, Jan. 3, 1953.

[67] *FAZ*, Jan. 7, 1953; *Industrie Kurier*, April 28, 1955; *Handelsblatt*, June 6, 1955; *Die Welt*, June 4, 1956.

major interest groups concerned were generally prepared to accept the measure, numerous demands of smaller groups, championed by the Opposition, and of the *Länder* Governments, acting through the Bundesrat, had not yet been met. Enactment did not occur for over sixteen months after the Cabinet had approved the bill, and during this time it was substantially revised.

The Bill on Lawyers' Fees

The bill revising the schedule of fees for court-appointed lawyers was simply the product of a conference of the ministers of Justice of the *Land* Governments. Since the fees are mainly paid by the *Länder*, the Federal Government was prepared to propose any measure on which the *Länder* could agree. The scale on which they settled, and which the Government draft proposed, had not been negotiated with the German Bar Association. Professional demands were therefore pressed by leaders of the Association, who were strategically situated among the Members of the Bundestag Judiciary Committee. A compromise between the *Länder* and the lawyers' group was worked out in the Committee and accepted by the House without any public discussion.

The Travel Bill

The bill designed to police travel between the Federal Republic and the Soviet Zone of Germany was the product of the Berlin crisis, which followed the Soviet Government's proposals late in 1958 to change the status of the city. In restricting the freedom of travel between the two parts of Germany, the bill obviously departed from the premise of German unity, and was bound to raise many questions and sensitivities. The bill was drafted during 1959 and 1960, without consultation with the *Länder* Governments or with any group outside the Interior Ministry. Minister Schröder presented it to the Cabinet for approval on November 2, 1960, five days after the arrest of a Member of the Bundestag on charges of treason appeared to have created a receptive climate for such a measure. The Minister of All-German Questions, Lemmer, a Member from Berlin, raised only mild objections. The ministers of the Interior of the *Länder* were not consulted until nine days after the Cabinet had approved the bill, and then had the bill communicated to them orally. Parliamentary leaders received its text six days after that, simultaneously with its publication.[68] Opposition was immediate. The SPD condemned the bill at its national conference the following week,[69] press criticism was widespread, and a group of CDU Members from Berlin expressed opposition.[70] Within a week of the bill's publication, Schröder wrote a letter to all CDU Members of the Bundestag refuting, point by point, public criticism of the bill,[71] and three weeks later the Ministry of the Interior published a pamphlet defending the bill, entitled "Against the Red Agent." [72] But Schröder brushed aside early efforts of CDU Members to discuss the measure, expecting that he would be able to obtain the support of his party in the Bundestag in the normal course of events. This was a major miscalculation, leading to the organization of a dissident group within the CDU parliamentary party which it was impossible subsequently to reconcile.

The Child Benefits Bill

The bill on child benefits was the result of promises made by all parties and reiterated by their parliamentary leaders throughout the term of the third Bundestag. The payment of family benefits had begun in the Federal Republic in 1954, after five years of controversy regarding the manner of raising revenues for this purpose. The CDU/CSU viewpoint, influenced by Catholic corporative concepts, had prevailed. The law of 1954 provided that employers would make contributions based on wages to "Family Equalization Payment Agencies," organized on an industry-wide basis, which would disburse payments to families for each of their children exceeding two. The cost of this plan affected businesses unequally, since contributions depended on wage payments. Its unpopularity with business groups assured that the increases, which all parties had promised, would have

[68] *Der Spiegel*, XIV, no. 50 (Nov. 23, 1960), 30. See also Schröder's justification of the procedure, in the debate in the Bundesrat, *Sitzungsbericht*, 227. Sitz., Dec. 22, 1960, p. 569.

[69] *Die Welt*, Nov. 23, 1960, p. 2; Nov. 25, 1960, p. 2; Dec. 12, 1960, p. 2.

[70] *Die Welt*, Nov. 16–17, 1960, p. 1; Nov. 18, 1960, p. 1. *Der Spiegel*, XIV, no. 50, (Nov. 23, 1960), 31. See also *Spandauer Volksblatt*, Dec. 9, 1960, p. 3; *Tagesspiegel*, Dec. 23, 1960. For reports of criticism among refugee groups, see *Die Welt*, Nov. 29, 1960, p. 2; Dec. 5, 1960, p. 3; Dec. 10, 1960, p. 2.

[71] Letter, on the stationery of the Minister of the Interior, with a three page appendix, dated November 25, 1960 (cf. *Die Welt*, Nov. 26, 1960, p. 2).

[72] *Die Welt*, Dec. 14, 1960, p. 2.

to be financed from tax revenues. The opposition parties—the FDP in defense of the interests of businesses with high labor costs, the SPD advocating expanded coverage to include families with two children and higher benefits—both pressed for revision of the 1954 law in the direction of tax financing.[73] The CDU/CSU, committed to an expansion of the existing program, contained groups of Members strongly attached to the existing system. The Finance Ministers of the *Länder* had expressed themselves in opposition to a proposal to disburse benefits through their own departments, which lacked the necessary administrative experience and were, in any case, overburdened. Within the Federal Government, the Ministry for Questions of Family and Youth, which had drafted the 1954 act, was under pressure from Catholic family groups to maintain the principles of the existing system. The Ministry of Labor, sensitive to the pressure of groups interested in the reform of the existing system, notably employers favoring finance by taxation, and trade unions advocating increased benefits disbursed by a new, national administration,[74] favored a new approach. The Chancellor was committed primarily to the fulfillment of the attractive promise which his party had made to increase benefits, regarding the matter with increasing urgency as the parliamentary election of September, 1961, approached.

The formulation of the bill therefore had to be undertaken in the face of highly diverse positions publicly taken by the major participants in the legislative process. The appointment of a professional advisory committee within the Government, with an interministerial committee to evaluate its recommendation,[75] had produced no agreed solution. Neither had a special committee of interested Bundestag Members within the CDU/CSU parliamentary party, in which all the major divisions of opinion were represented. The temptation of all sides to mobilize public support produced prominent press coverage of the controversy during the preparation of the bill, and a succession of questions and interpellations from the Opposition in the Bundestag.[76]

Under the pressure of the approaching election, a Government bill

[73] See *Dt. Btag.*, 3. W.P., 61. Sitz., Feb. 18, 1959, p. 3301; 65. Sitz., Feb. 26, 1959, p. 3057; 130. Sitz., Oct. 28, 1960, pp. 7488 ff. Also, *Dt. Btag.*, 3. W.P., Drs. 799, 803, 1553, 2100.

[74] *DGB Nachrichtendienst,* Bundespressestelle des DGB, Jan. 5, 1961; *DZ,* Jan. 6, 1961.

[75] *Dt. Btag.*, 3. W.P., Drs. 1590.   [76] See n. 73.

was prepared in the Ministry of Labor late in 1960, in consultation with the Ministry for Questions of Family and Youth but generally rejecting its views.[77] The terms of the bill were revealed and publicly defended by the Minister of Labor before the Cabinet had given its approval. This enabled members of the parliamentary majority to press their views on its provisions, both openly and in consultation with the Ministry.[78] Early in 1961, the Chancellor moved to obtain the approval of his parliamentary party for the draft bill, in a series of conferences with parliamentary leaders and interest-group representatives which he himself conducted.[79] On February 7, in the presence of the Chancellor, the Minister of Labor, and the Minister for Questions of Family and Youth, the CDU/CSU caucus accepted the compromise, a stopgap solution, on the understanding that the whole question would be reconsidered after the election. There were no opposing votes, but seven Members abstained.[80] Only after the compromise had received this parliamentary support, did the bill incorporating it receive Cabinet approval.[81]

The terms of the compromise were set by a number of fixed positions. Politically, the inclusion of two-child families among the beneficiaries was irresistible. Financially, such a tremendous increase in the number of recipients could not be supported by raising employers' contributions, but would have to involve tax revenues. Administratively, the "Family Equalization Payment Agencies" could not, and would not, handle the new burden. Ideologically, the existing program continued to have adamant supporters especially among some of the CDU's strongest constituent groups, notably Catholic organizations.

The bill which was sent to the Bundesrat provided for payments of DM 25 monthly ($6.25) to families with only two children, if their annual income did not exceed DM 6600 ($1,650). Tax revenues were to finance these payments, which were to be disbursed by the Federal

[77] *Bonner Rundschau,* Nov. 15, 1960; *FAZ,* Nov. 18, 1960; *Die Welt,* Nov. 18 and 19, 1960; *Industrie Kurier,* Nov. 18, 1960; *Die Welt,* Nov. 25, 1960; *Handelsblatt,* Nov. 30, 1960; *DZ, Frankfurter Rundschau, Handelsblatt,* all of Dec. 7, 1960; *Industrie Kurier,* Dec. 8, 1960; *Bonner Rundschau* and *Handelsblatt,* both of Dec. 9, 1960; *Die Welt,* Dec. 10 and 20, 1960. See also *Dt. Btag.,* 3. W.P., 134. Sitz., Dec. 7, 1960.

[78] *FAZ,* Dec. 19 and 20, 1960.

[79] *Die Welt,* Jan. 27, 1961; *Industrie Kurier, Handelsblatt,* and *General Anzeiger* (Bonn), all of Feb. 2, 1961; *Industrie Kurier,* Feb. 7, 1961.

[80] *FAZ,* Feb. 8, 1961; *DZ,* Feb. 8, 1961.

[81] *Die Welt, FAZ, SZ,* and *DZ,* all of Feb. 25, 1961.

Employment Agency. Benefits were to be paid retroactively to April 1, assuring a substantial first check to millions of families shortly before the election. Meanwhile, the program of child benefits for larger families financed by employers' contributions was to remain unchanged. Defending the bill, the Minister for Questions of Family and Youth called it a temporary compromise, dictated by the irreconcilable positions of interested groups.[82]

Because the bill had originated in parliamentary politics, the Government was unable to draft it in privacy and thus assure itself of the support of all ministries, of the *Länder,* and of the major interests, prior to submitting it to Parliament. Its negotiations were therefore conducted with considerable publicity, and with the full participation of the parliamentary party. The positions which the various interested parties had publicly taken were restated during the parliamentary passage of the bill, since no one was under any compulsion to remain silent in support of a privately negotiated compromise. But since the majority party had been committed in advance to the Government bill, it held its ground during the remainder of the legislative process and the bill was passed essentially intact.

FIRST PASSAGE THROUGH THE BUNDESRAT

Government bills are submitted to the Bundesrat as they clear the Cabinet, with little general regard for the parliamentary timetable.[83] However, in order to give the representatives of the *Länder* the full, constitutionally allotted three-week period to take their initial position, bills are ordinarily sent to the Bundesrat just three weeks before its next regularly scheduled meeting. Within this interval, the relevant

---

[82] *Rheinischer Merkur,* April 14, 1961.

[83] The rate of introduction of bills varies from a low point in the first year of the Government's existence, to a higher level steadily maintained in subsequent years of the parliamentary term, with little regard for the declining ability of Parliament to consider bills as the end of its term approaches. Figures indicating the number of bills submitted to the start of the summer recess of each year, during the 2nd and 3rd Bundestage, are as follows:

2nd Bundestag		3rd Bundestag	
1953–54	29	1957–58	79
1954–55	143	1958–59	99
1955–56	129	1959–60	101
1956–57	125	1960–61	111

Figures supplied by the Bundestag secretariat.

Land ministries must formulate their positions, their delegates in the committees of the Bundesrat must deliberate, the *Land* Governments must decide how they will cast their Bundesrat vote, and the session of the second chamber must take place. Time is short. If the Government presents its legislation less than three weeks before the next regularly scheduled meeting of the Bundesrat, the normal routine is upset. On the other hand, when the Government informally submits its legislation to the *Länder* Governments several days in advance of formal presentation, the time pressure can be somewhat reduced.[84] Furthermore, if the bill has been cleared with the *Land* Governments through effective consultation with officials of the *Länder* ministries at the drafting stage, its passage through the Bundesrat is facilitated. Its reception in the second chamber therefore depends greatly on the Government's preliminary consultations.

But even with the greatest tact and consideration, the Government cannot reduce the Bundesrat stage to a formality. In the Bundesrat the committees are very influential, and in these bodies the main actors are *Land* officials. Although the Basic Law prescribes that the "Bundesrat consists of members of the Governments of the *Länder*,"[85] its committees need not be composed of ministers, who are generally too busy to spend time in Bonn. In their place, their officials, under some degree of instruction from their *Land* ministry, conduct the discussion, motivated largely by the concerns of those who will have to administer the proposed law.[86] While they may have been consulted by the relevant federal ministry at the drafting stage, these officials can now act with the authority of instructed delegates of autonomous governments, and can press their views in the event that they have not been fully accommodated in the bill.

Once the Bundesrat committees have deliberated, the *Länder* cabinets decide how to cast their vote. In the short space of time available, the committee recommendation is bound to carry great weight. Only on highly partisan legislation does the party composition of the *Land* Government outweigh considerations of administrative interests. So far in the history of the Federal Republic, the majority of votes in the

---

[84] Neunreither, *op. cit.*, pp. 57–9.

[85] Art. 51.

[86] E. L. Pinney, *Federalism, Bureaucracy and Party Politics in Western Germany: The Role of the Bundesrat* (Chapel Hill: University of North Carolina Press, 1963), Ch. VI.

Bundesrat has never been in the control of parties which are nationally in opposition. Partisan objections to Government legislation have not therefore prevailed in the Bundesrat, though they have sometimes had influence, and the possibility of Opposition control of the Bundesrat has drawn the national party leaders heavily into *Land* politics.[87] On legislation with direct regional effect, the votes of a *Land* in the Bundesrat may be cast according to local considerations.[88] But although regional and partisan voting exists, the position which the Bundesrat takes on Government legislation is most likely to prevail if it is motivated, or justified, by administrative considerations. The importance of the Bundesrat's decision on bills in their first passage through that House is the influence which the decision will have on the legislative process in the Bundestag. In part, this influence is due to the veto power which the second chamber may exercise over bills after their passage through the Bundestag. Furthermore, the committees of the Bundestag respect the administrative expertise of their Bundesrat colleagues, and are therefore receptive to detailed proposals for the revision of a bill on administrative grounds. But politically or regionally motivated proposals are not similarly persuasive. The Bundesrat can supply the Bundestag with effective ammunition against the bureaucratic expertise which the Federal Government commands. In effect it offers the Bundestag the view of a counter-bureaucracy, which is subject to political and interest group influences at least somewhat different from those prevailing at the federal level. One observer concludes that "the friendly reception which individual [Bundesrat] proposals received [in the Bundestag] when they were objectively justified, has prompted the Bundesrat to present even its political wishes in the form of legal-technical improvements."[89]

As a result, the action of the Bundesrat at this stage of the legislative process tends to consist of detailed proposals for amendments. The Government transmits these, and its responses to them, to the Bundestag, together with the text of its bill. By the time the bill arrives at the clerks' office (*Antragsannahmestelle*), the Members of the Bundestag have had at least three weeks to study it and to follow its reception by the representatives of the *Länder*. The presentation of a Government bill—or of the budget—to the Bundestag therefore lacks all drama. But in compensation, the bill arrives equipped with a critical evalua-

[87] *Ibid.*, Ch. IV.   [88] *Ibid.*, Ch. V.   [89] Neunreither, *op. cit.*, p. 60.

tion. The five case studies illuminate some of the factors determining the Bundesrat's response to Government legislation, and the consequences of that response for the legislative process in the Bundestag.

The Volunteers Bill

The Volunteers Bill came to the Bundesrat two weeks in advance of the next meeting of the chamber, instead of the normal three weeks. As a result, the deliberations were hectic not only on the side of the Federal Government, but on the side of the *Länder*. Although constitutional and policy questions were raised in the Security Committee of the Bundesrat, the controversy there concentrated on the bill's vagueness regarding defense administration. The members of the committee were anxious to have assurance that the Federal Government would not pre-empt the field of defense administration entirely, that civilian supremacy and some *Land* influence would be maintained, and that the legal status of recruits would be clearly defined. They were disturbed by the vagueness of the bill on all of these questions. The provision of the bill that the recruits would have the status of civil servants on probation, and that civil service regulations would be applied to them "where relevant," seemed to *Land* officials to be a misuse of civil service standards.[90]

Assertions by the Chancellor, the Defense Minister-designate, and high-ranking officials that the bill was strictly provisional and did not presume to regulate any of these questions definitively were only partly reassuring. Confusion on the Government side was displayed when, in the midst of the Government's efforts to emphasize the provisional nature of the bill, the Finance Ministry put in a request for an appropriation of DM 83 million (nearly $20 million at that time) to pay for the establishment of a defense administration.[91] The request renewed distrust in the Bundesrat toward the Government's intentions. The report of the Bundesrat committee was strongly critical, complaining of the "almost undignified pressure of time" and referring to the bill as a three-paragraph "secrecy-shrouded 'Blitz' law." Accepting the general purpose of the bill, the committee brought forth a resolution indicating four major reservations regarding its terms and

---

[90] *Dt. Btag.*, 2. W.P., Drs. 1467, par. 1(2).
[91] Vorlage des Bundesministers der Finanzen no. 40/55, zum Vorsitzenden des Haushaltsausschusses des Bundestages vom 6. Juni 1955; cf. Bundesrat, *Sitzungsbericht*, 142. Sitz., June 10, 1955, p. 138.

indicating that it expected the Government to submit a revised version.

The Bundesrat expects [the resolution read] that the Federal Government will complete the bill, will create the legal pre-requisites for its implementation, and will reveal the basic principles of its defense policy.

The resolution emphasized the need to assure parliamentary control over the armed forces and the importance of placing them under a civilian administration, and insisted that any necessary Government decrees be subject to the approval of the Bundesrat.[92]

The sharp reaction of the second chamber, reflecting not only its annoyance over not having been consulted beforehand but also its sensitivity on administrative questions, marked the beginnings of partisan opposition to the bill. The Social Democratic state of Hesse voted against that part of the resolution expressing approval of the bill's general objectives; Berlin abstained. The remarkably sharp language used by the committee reporter, Artur Sträter, a member of the Government of North-Rhine–Westphalia, reflected the dissatisfaction of the left-of-center wing of the CDU—led by the minister-president of that *Land*, Arnold—over the Federal Government's approach to defense policy. But despite the hostile reception which the bill received in the Bundesrat, the Government was so confident of its ability to win passage in the Bundestag, and so much in haste, that it passed the bill along to the other chamber, unchanged, with the laconic statement that it would express its view on the criticism of the Bundesrat later.[93] Bundesrat representatives thereupon pressed their views in the committees of the Bundestag, with considerable success.

The Federal Requisitions Bill

The Federal Requisitions Bill was sent to the Bundesrat on the normal Friday exactly three weeks preceding the next scheduled session of the House. The date was June 3, 1955, just six days after the presentation of the Volunteers Bill; both were part of the legislative activity inspired by the ratification of the London and Paris Agreements the previous month. The bill received the searching scrutiny of no less than nine Bundesrat committees. In passing it on June 24, the

---

[92] Bundesrat, *Sitzungsbericht*, 142. Sitz., June 10, 1955, pp. 134–41. Cf. Neunreither, *op. cit.*, pp. 171–8; Pinney, *op. cit.*, pp. 184–92.
[93] *Dt. Btag.*, 2. W.P., Drs. 1467, p. 1.

second chamber recommended eighty-six individual changes in the sixteen-page, eighty-eight-paragraph bill. The recommendations, each with justification, occupied thirteen pages. Many of them were technical improvements. When the Federal Government submitted the bill to the Bundestag, on October 21, after the Parliament's summer recess, it indicated that it would accept thirty-six of the proposed changes entirely, and three of them partially. These were mainly technical and terminological improvements. But it took exception to others.[94] The more contentious revisions proposed by the Bundesrat were designed to restrict the Government's powers under the law, to protect the property rights of the individual and of local communities, to improve the procedures for seeking redress of grievances, and to preserve the administrative autonomy of the *Länder* in the implementation of the law.[95] Representatives of the Bundesrat championed these proposed changes in the committees of the Bundestag, whose sessions they are entitled to attend. Except on questions directly pertaining to the administrative autonomy of the *Länder*, the revisions proposed by the Bundesrat received a positive reception in the Bundestag and formed a substantial part of the amendments proposed there to the Government bill. The question of *Land* administration was not settled until the final stages of the legislative process, when the Bundesrat called the Mediation Committee to negotiate its differences on this subject with the Bundestag.

The Bill on Lawyers' Fees

The bill altering the Federal Schedule of Fees for Lawyers had been proposed by the Government after a conference of the Ministers of Justice of the *Länder* had worked out its terms. The Bundesrat therefore had no substantive changes to propose. It did, however, express the view that the bill required its assent, and that the introductory clause should therefore read that the bill had been passed by the Bundestag "with the assent of the Bundesrat." The second chamber regarded this formal change as important in principle. Anxious for the maximum expansion of the subjects of legislation over which it could exercise an absolute veto, the Bundesrat argued that although the subject of the bill did not fall within the jurisdiction of the *Länder* or

[94] *Dt. Btag.*, 2. W.P., Drs. 1804.
[95] See the recommendations of the Bundesrat to pars. 1, 3, 5, 6, 20, 23, 47, 59, 66, 76, 82, and 84, given in *ibid.*, pp. 43–55.

require *Land* administration, it was a revision of an earlier law which did contain provisions which made it subject to Bundesrat approval. The Government rejected the claim that any bill amending a statute which had originally required the assent of the second chamber would likewise require its approval.[96] In the Bundestag the claim also fell on deaf ears.

The Travel Bill

When the Bundesrat considered the bill regulating travel into and out of the Federal Republic, party lines on the measure were already drawn.[97] The Interior Committee, which had charge of the bill, recommended its rejection, by a vote of six *Länder* to five. But included in this committee majority was Berlin, which had no vote in the plenary session, and Bavaria, in whose CSU-FDP coalition the Interior Ministry happened to be in the hands of the FDP, which opposed the bill.

Furthermore, in committee each *Land* casts one vote, regardless of size. When the *Länder* governments cast their votes in the formal session of the second chamber, weighted according to their population and excluding Berlin, all twenty-six votes belonging to CDU-led *Land* Governments were cast in favor of the bill. Detailed recommendations for its revision had been drawn up, not only by the Interior Committee as an alternative to the bill's rejection, but also by the Judiciary Committee which favored the bill. But in this instance, the Bundesrat, acting as a partisan body rather than as an expert revising chamber, brushed most of these proposed amendments aside.[98] Instead, it declared that it accepted the necessity of legal regulation of travel into and out of the Federal Republic. In very general terms, it called for further study of two of the bill's most restrictive provisions, those calling for the registration of travelers and requiring exit permits. Finally, it demanded that residents of Berlin be treated equally with residents of the Federal Republic, rather than as outsiders subject to control.[99] In transmitting the bill to the Bundestag, the Federal Government expressed its satisfaction that the Bundesrat had generally accepted the measure, and promised to study the provisions which had been questioned.[100]

[96] *Dt. Btag.*, 3. W.P., Drs. 1892, pp. 1, 5.
[97] *Die Welt*, Dec. 22, 1960, p. 2.   [98] *Die Welt*, Dec. 23, 1960, p. 2.
[99] Bundesrat, *Sitzungsbericht*, 227. Sitz., pp. 560–73.
[100] *Dt. Btag.*, 3. W.P., Drs. 2372, p. 8.

The Child Benefits Bill

On the bill increasing payments for children, the Bundesrat suggested seventeen changes, of which the Federal Government accepted eleven technical improvements. The Government rejected six others, by which the Bundesrat sought to reserve to itself a veto power over subsequent administrative decisions under the act, and to include employees of local governments among the bill's beneficiaries. None of these proposals were readopted in subsequent stages of the bill's passage.[101]

FIRST READING IN THE BUNDESTAG

The legislative process in the Bundestag consists of a number of formal stages, running chronologically from the first reading debate, to committee deliberation and report, and culminating in the second and third readings and final vote. Simultaneously, the bill passes through the various informal stages of the decision-making process of the parliamentary parties. How a legislative proposal survives this course, and in what form, is significantly determined by the stages of drafting and negotiation which it has passed through in the Government and the Bundesrat before it ever reaches the Bundestag. The influence of the Bundestag on legislation depends on the extent to which the demands of interested ministries at the Federal and *Land* levels, of interest groups, and, sometimes, of groups of Members of the Bundestag have been met in prior stages of the legislative process. However, the influence which these groups have on a bill before it reaches the Bundestag depends, in turn, on the effectiveness with which they could press their demands in Parliament if they were not satisfied earlier.

Deliberation in the Party Groups

By the time a bill arrives at the clerks' office in the Bundestag, it has been public knowledge for at least the three weeks of its consideration in the Bundesrat. If it is of sufficiently wide public interest, it has become the subject of a public opinion. For at least this period of time, it has received the attention of the parliamentary parties in the Bundestag, whose procedures vary with their size and with their relationship to the Government.

[101] Dt. Btag., 3. W.P., Drs. 2648, pp. 23–8.

If a Government bill comes with little prior negotiation between the Government and its parliamentary supporters, the executive committee in the CDU/CSU assigns it to a working group and gives it its terms of reference; within the working group, it is assigned to a special subcommittee. If the bill is introduced by CDU/CSU Members, or if it has long been under discussion between interested Members and the relevant ministry, it is likely to have evolved out of the deliberations of a working group and to have been under consideration there for months or even years, in continuous consultation with the executive committee and the Government. In the opposition parties, free of ministerial influence, the working groups exercise the initiative in formulating the party's position both toward Government bills and those proposed by groups of Members. In the SPD, members of working groups each have particular subject specialties; the FDP is not large enough for such a division of labor.

The first deadline under which the working groups of the parties operate is the date of the first reading in the House. That date is set by a consensus among the parties, negotiated by their parliamentary whips and ratified by the Council of Elders. A period ranging from the minimum of three days required by the Rules to several months may be available for this initial stage of deliberation within the parties.

Only very rarely have the parties, by common consent, kept a bill off the agenda altogether. During the third Bundestag, three Government bills and seven bills initiated by groups of Members were suppressed in this manner. In the first group, a bill to tighten the law of libel and one to alter the petroleum tax, both earnestly pressed by the Government, were blocked by the mutual preference of the parties to evade the issues they raised. The second group of bills was composed of isolated efforts of backbenchers to legislate on subjects of special interest to them, including a proposal of Members belonging to the DP to amend the Basic Law to reinstate the death penalty. The party leaders found these bills embarrassing and refused to give them a chance. But this type of pigeonholing is not openly condoned, and only a rare consensus among the parliamentary leaders of all the parties makes it quietly possible. Any Member can move the inclusion of an item on the agenda, but a majority is required to adopt the motion.[102] By the time the first reading of a bill appears on the agenda

[102] *Geschäftsordnung des Deutschen Bundestages,* par. 26 as interpreted, p. 24. The bills not given a first reading were: *Dt. Btag.,* 3. W.P., Drs. 133, 389, 390,

of the Bundestag, each party must have determined whether it wishes
a debate at this stage, and, if so, what general view it will express, who
will speak for it, and, in any case, to what committee or committees
the bill should be referred. On each of these questions the chairmen or
reporters of the working groups make recommendations to their respective parliamentary executive committees, which in turn make proposals to the party caucuses held each week in advance of the sessions
of the House.

Planning the Debate

The parliamentary whips attempt to negotiate a consensus among
the parties on whether a first reading debate is to take place and, if so,
at what length and under what ground rules. This includes a determination of the order of speakers, the number of "rounds" of speeches in
which each party has one turn, and whether speeches shall be "long"
or "short." The prevailing conventions facilitate agreement. On a Government bill, the opening speech in a first reading debate is always
made by the minister in charge, or by a senior official in his department. On legislation initiated by Members of the Bundestag or by the
Bundesrat, one of the movers speaks first. The subsequent order of
speeches varies. The SPD has frequently claimed the right to speak
next, as the chief opposition party, but the CDU/CSU has sometimes
insisted on its right, under the Rules, as the largest party, to be the first
among the parliamentary groups to speak. In maintaining this right,
the party rejects its identity as the party of the Government, falling
back on the conception, derived from the monarchical political system
but still very much alive, that Government and Parliament are entirely
separate entities. This was also the rationale for the insistence of the
CDU/CSU, in an unusual dispute over the distribution of time among
the parties during a foreign policy debate in 1958, that the time taken
by Government speakers should not be charged against its quota. That
case went to the Constitutional Court, which gave judicial sanction to
the applicability of the doctrine of the separation of powers to such a
matter.[103]

Since the elimination of the extremist parties from the House after
the election of 1953, there has been no other recourse to the Rules to

---

391, 1237, 2150, 2403, 2843, 2845, 2964. Nineteen bills, most of them submitted
late in the term, failed to reach a first reading during the fourth Bundestag.
[103] *BVerfGE* 10, 4, at p. 19. See also pp. 397–8, *infra.*

determine the distribution of time in debate. The product of a political system in which a multiparty Parliament confronted a separate Government, these Rules would, under present circumstances and if interpreted literally, permit the Government to dominate the debate. They provide for closure by majority vote, the right of members of the Government to gain recognition "at any time," and the distribution of time among the parliamentary parties by the Council of Elders, whose practice it was in the past to allot time to each party according to its strength in the House.[104] Furthermore, according to the Rules, the President has the power "to determine the order of speakers. He shall have regard for the appropriate dispatch and suitable organization of the deliberation, and for the various party viewpoints and the strengths of the parties." [105]

In practice, the President relies on the arangements made by the parliamentary whips, who experience little difficulty in setting time limits, being quite content to preserve a rough equality among the three parliamentary parties in the number of speakers each one sends to the rostrum, and being willing to reach a rough understanding on the length of speeches. When the CDU/CSU insists on leading off, the others defer to it.

The planning of debate, "behind the Speaker's chair" so to speak, is frequently unnecessary at the first reading. For all parties, there is considerable temptation to forego a debate at this stage altogether. If debate can be avoided, the parties preserve a greater maneuverability at the committee stage than they have if they must take a public position beforehand. As a result, there has been a steady decline in the proportion of bills which are debated at first reading. A large number of technical bills, furthermore, receive no discussion in party caucuses at this stage either, if the working groups in each party are satisfied that they raise no partisan issues. Occasionally, especially among the opposition parties, important issues are overlooked in this way. But in the case of major legislation obviously disputed among the parties, or bills which have raised public controversy, the parties feel obliged to take an initial stand in debate, to indicate the lines along which they are prepared to negotiate in committee, and to commit themselves publicly to positions from which they will not retreat. In these cases

[104] Pars. 30, 47, and 39, respectively.   [105] Par. 33.

the first reading debate can be important, and the parties approach it with care, leaving the speaking to their leaders or experts.

Committee Referral

The question of committee referral can also be significant. The jurisdictions of the various committees frequently overlap, and the necessary choice among them is a choice between committees dominated by different interests and chaired by different Members with different party affiliations. The question of the committee assignment of a bill is first considered in the weekly conference of the committee staff assistants, who act in this matter as representatives of the committee chairmen. The Council of Elders then considers the recommendations of this group. Controversy is frequently evaded by placing one committee in charge of reporting on a bill, but allowing other committees to consider it also. Unchecked, this procedure has at times produced a caricature of the principle of committee referral, as when the so-called "Final Bill on the Consequences of the War" went to ten committees in 1955.[106] Since then, energetic efforts have been made to limit referrals to two committees, in part by the consolidation of committees. On important bills, however, controversy can be great among committee chairmen jealously guarding their jurisdictions and interest groups pressing to get a bill to the committee in which they are best represented. In addition, the Appropriations Committee must consider any bill involving expenditure, and the Judiciary Committee may consider any bill which raises important legal or constitutional questions. Multiple referrals to three or four committees therefore persist, and, occasionally, the question cannot be settled by negotiation among the parties at all and a vote in the House becomes necessary.[107]

When the bill comes up for first reading in the House, the treatment it receives follows a rehearsed script. The parties have prepared their positions, the parliamentary whips know the tactics which they and their opposites will employ, and the presiding officer has been informed of these tactics by the discussion which has taken place in the Council of Elders. In the parlance of the Bundestag, "the bill moves across the stage." To the public observer, it is apparent that the script

[106] *Dt. Btag.*, 2. W.P., 103. Sitz., Sept. 29, 1955, p. 5700.
[107] For an example, see *Dt. Btag.*, 4. W.P., 174. Sitz., March 19, 1965, p. 8739.

leaves little room for ad-libbing. The real drama has taken place behind the scenes. Spontaneity occurs only if the bill has attracted wide public interest, and the time has been too short to secure a unified position within each party and a procedural consensus among them. The case studies illustrate the varieties of treatment which bills receive in the first reading phase.

The Volunteers Bill

Deliberation on the Volunteers Bill began in the parliamentary parties the moment the text became available, upon its submission to the Bundesrat. In each party, the initiative was taken by the Representatives who were members of the Bundestag Committee on European Security, which had been considering defense legislation for three years in considerable secrecy.

The SPD's opposition to rearmament precluded, in principle, its support of the bill. But its foreman on the committee, Fritz Erler, supported by a group of moderate party leaders, was anxious to participate in the formulation of defense legislation in order to be able to influence the shape which the new defense establishment would take. Although SPD votes were not available—or needed—for the bill, eventual SPD support for the constitutional amendment which would be required to authorize the Federal Government to exercise defense powers was likely to be crucial for attaining the necessary two-thirds majority. The Government was generally anxious for the broadest support for its momentous decision to rearm. The Opposition could not, therefore, be ignored, and Erler hoped to be able to exert its influence. His task was delicate, however, because members of his own party, who had been unaware of the party's role in the Security Committee of the Bundestag, had no sympathy for SPD participation in the formulation of any legislation which would implement the rearmament policies which the party rejected. While party leaders, including Erler, therefore spoke out strongly against the Volunteers Bill, both publicly and in the first party caucus after its publication,[108] Erler and his SPD colleagues on the Security Committee quietly explored the prospects for revising it. They met with the newly named Minister of Defense, Theodor Blank, who, for four years as Special

---

[108] Fritz Erler, "Gefährliche Hast," *SPD Pressedienst*, P/X/129, June 7, 1955. Cf. *Neue Rhein Zeitung* (Cologne), June 7, 1955; *Vorwärts*, June 10 and 17, 1955; *FAZ* and *Die Welt*, both of June 8, 1955; *Die Welt*, June 14, 1955.

Assistant to the Chancellor on Defense Questions, had become a familiar figure in the committee. Erler, as committee deputy-chairman, also began a series of informal negotiations with the chairman of the committee, Richard Jaeger.

Although he was a prominent leader of the CSU, the Bavarian wing of the governing party, Jaeger approached the Volunteers Bill skeptically. It had never been discussed in his committee. Furthermore, Jaeger acted on behalf of the CSU's strongest leader, Franz-Josef Strauss, whose ambition it had long been to become Defense Minister. Now a member of the Cabinet "with special assignments," Strauss had preceded Jaeger as committee chairman. He had also been chairman of the CSU group in the Bundestag and was still the effective leader of its fifty-two members. The objective of the two men was to restrict the Volunteers Bill so that the incumbent minister could not, under its terms, make the fundamental rearmament decisions. Meanwhile, they sought to shape subsequent defense legislation and to obtain commitments on personnel questions.[109]

There were also other factions in the CDU/CSU which approached the Government bill critically. Left-wing party leaders in North Rhine–Westphalia, notably Minister-President Arnold, were anxious to add safeguards to the measure. Their spokesman led the hostile reaction to the bill in the Bundesrat, and their view was expressed in a leading CDU paper in Cologne, the *Rheinischer Merkur,* which rarely criticized the Government.[110] In both the CDU/CSU and its coalition partner, the FDP, individual Members with professional military backgrounds advanced criticism of the bill with special authority. Two of the three FDP Members of the Bundestag Security Committee, Erich Mende and Hasso von Manteuffel, had been career soldiers, the latter a prominent general in the Second World War.[111] They advocated a revision of the vague measure, in order to spell out its provisions on the status of recruits, the hierarchy of command, and the organization of a defense establishment.

A desire for substantial amendment of the bill therefore cut across party lines. It was widely echoed in the press. The Government's

[109] *Münchener Merkur,* June 14, 1955; *Neue Rhein Zeitung* (Cologne), June 15, 1955; SZ, June 24, 1955.

[110] "Die Bundeswehr," *Rheinischer Merkur,* June 3, 1955.

[111] *Bremer Nachrichten,* June 10, 1955; *Der Spiegel,* IX, no. 26 (June 22, 1955), 9, and IX, no. 30 (July 20, 1955), 8.

commitment to quick passage weakened its position. Despite the criticism of the bill in the Bundesrat, it had been submitted to the Bundestag five days later without the usual Government reply to the Bundesrat's proposals.

Erler took advantage of the Government's unpreparedness and haste by launching into a criticism of the bill during an appropriations debate taking place in the Bundestag the same day as the measure was being officially submitted to the House. In his first appearance as Defense Minister, Blank was disorganized and ill at ease in justifying the bill, but promised that the Government would clarify its entire defense policy before the first reading.[112] The debate did not end until the FDP had also indicated its demands for revision of the measure and Jaeger, after a backhanded compliment for Blank's past accomplishments, announced that "in this form [the bill] will not receive the approval of my political friends." [113] When both Blank and Jaeger, somewhat undiplomatically, expressed the hope that the SPD would join in the passage of a modified bill, Erler felt compelled to make an immediate rejoinder that the Opposition would not vote for the bill under any circumstances, though it might participate in its revision.[114] The debate was lively precisely because of the absence of prepared positions on all sides. It revealed the existence of a large negotiable area.

In the relative privacy of the CDU/CSU caucus the following week, a large number of Members joined in criticism of the Volunteers Bill in Blank's presence. The minister promised that the Government would accept all reasonable amendments. An official press communiqué on the session said vaguely that "insofar as doubts were expressed [about the bill] within the CDU/CSU, they did not pertain to the need to implement the [London and Paris] treaties without delay." [115] The FDP caucus was divided on the bill,[116] the SPD united, at least in the sense of opposing the measure in principle.[117]

Despite these signs of lack of parliamentary support, the Govern-

[112] *Dt. Btag.*, 2. W.P., 87. Sitz., June 15, 1955, pp. 4856–74. Cf. SZ, June 16, 1955; *Die Tat*, June 17, 1955.

[113] *Dt. Btag.*, 2. W.P., 87. Sitz., June 15, 1955, p. 4871.

[114] *Ibid.*, p. 4873.

[115] *Deutschland Union Dienst*, IX, no. 116, June 21, 1955, pp. 3–4. Cf. *Neue Rhein Zeitung* (Cologne), June 21, 1955; *Kölner Stadt Anzeiger* and *FAZ*, both of June 25, 1955.

[116] *Die Welt*, June 13, 1955.   [117] *FAZ*, June 25, 1955.

ment pressed for speed. Adenauer insisted, in a meeting of the parliamentary executive committee of the CDU/CSU, that the first reading take place the following week, although no sessions of the House had been planned for that time. Under these circumstances, the normal agreement on the parliamentary schedule among the parliamentary parties became impossible. A CDU/CSU motion for a special session to give the bill its first reading passed against SPD opposition.[118] The debate therefore took place under circumstances of uncommon division both within and between the parties.

On the surface, the conflict between Government and Opposition was sharp. Underneath, however, there was a strong common desire on both sides to revise the bill. Members of the governing parties belonging to the Bundestag Committee on European Security were drawing up alterations in the bill in consultation with the Defense Minister. Jaeger, leading these Representatives, was informally conferring with Erler and the SPD members of the committee, who were likewise drawing up proposed changes.

The first reading debate therefore gave signs of improvisation. It began with the promised declaration of the Government's defense policy. Blank, in a concise one-hour speech, outlined the legislative program which the Government expected to introduce, and justified the Volunteers Bill as an introductory measure designed merely to cover the interval while the basic legislation was being considered.[119] The debate continued the following morning and went on for a wearisome ten and one-half hours. Fourteen Members, including the Chancellor, the Defense Minister, the leader of the Opposition, and the defense experts of the various parties, spoke for an average of forty minutes each.

Opening the discussion, Jaeger expressed his regret that the Government had not seen fit to revise the bill after the criticism it had encountered in the Bundesrat. "Perhaps it is an honor for the lawyers in this House," he said, "that one trusts them to undertake those changes, which the Government's lawyers were apparently in no position to make." [120] He went on to state his satisfaction with the Government's declaration of defense policy, expressed the hope that all parties would cooperate in the passage of the necessary constitutional

[118] *Dt. Btag.*, 2. W.P., 91. Sitz., June 23, 1955, p. 5201.
[119] *Dt. Btag.*, 2. W.P., 92. Sitz., June 27, 1955, pp. 5213–20.
[120] *Dt. Btag.*, 2. W.P., 93. Sitz., June 28, 1955, p. 5224.

amendments, but hinted only vaguely at the amendments he might propose for the bill in question. Other CDU/CSU speakers followed suit, varying in their degree of criticism of the measure. FDP and SPD speakers expressed their hesitation about any military legislation until constitutional changes had established the legal basis for a defense establishment. Their emphasis was dictated in part by their greater bargaining power on constitutional questions, which require a two-thirds vote, than on ordinary legislation, which the CDU/CSU, with its majority of one over all other parties, could pass by itself. Erler, for the SPD, enumerated the important questions which he felt would have to be settled "before the first man puts on a uniform." They included the matter of civilian control over the military, the administrative organization of the defense department, parliamentary supervision, and the procedures and criteria for selecting cadres.[121] Similar themes appeared in the speeches of Members of the other parties, accompanied by broad hints from all sides that the bill required amendments to give assurances on at least some of these matters.[122]

A sharp note was struck early by the leader of the Opposition, who termed the bill a "monstrosity" which his party would reject "from the start." [123] This led to a taunting intervention by Adenauer, who, to a chorus of angry interruptions, said that he "had hoped that it would be possible to win over the SPD to collaboration on the basis of democracy." [124] Ollenhauer's sharp rejection of the bill was the stronger, perhaps, for the division within his party on whether or not to participate at all in committee deliberations on defense legislation. Adenauer's response, dictated by his ready willingness to underscore the negative approach of the Opposition, embittered the atmosphere throughout the remainder of the debate, as majority and Opposition Members mutually charged each other with unwillingness to cooperate. Erler's delicate task of expressing his party's basic opposition to rearmament and to the bill, while hoping nevertheless to influence its terms, became increasingly difficult as the surface tension of the debate led to a lengthening series of speeches and rejoinders which neither side had planned or desired.

The debate did little to promote the possibility of compromise among the parties. It exaggerated the differences between them, obscuring the areas of potential agreement. It did, however, indicate the

---

[121] *Ibid.*, pp. 5286–7.   [122] *Ibid.*, pp. 5272–3.   [123] *Ibid.*, pp. 5231–2.
[124] *Ibid.*, p. 5236.

breadth of criticism of the measure. Such spontaneity as the debate had was offset by the length of the average speeches, many of which were read verbatim. Although no detailed account of the debate appeared in the press, the customary summaries conveyed to the public the absence of support for the bill as it stood.[125] This corresponded with the editorial comment of most newspapers.

There was no agreement among the parties about committee referral of the measure. The coalition parties moved reference to the Committee on European Security, which was to be in charge of reporting, and also to the Committee on Civil Service Law and the Judiciary Committee. The SPD announced that it would vote against any reference to committee, but that in case its position did not prevail it wanted to see the Interior and Appropriations committees, which were chaired by its members, consider the bill also. Both of these SPD proposals were voted down, and the bill went to the three committees indicated in the motion of the coalition.[126] However, after a half-hour adjournment for a caucus, the CDU/CSU accepted an SPD motion that the meetings of the Committee on European Security be open to all Members of the Bundestag, although this was ordinarily one of a number of closed committees whose deliberations are not only closed to the public but secret within the House.[127]

The Federal Requisitions Bill

When the Government submitted the Federal Requisitions Bill—which had passed the Bundesrat with voluminous recommendations for changes—to the Bundestag, it accompanied the measure with a detailed response to the Bundesrat recommendations.[128] The bill had by this time also aroused a considerable amount of press criticism, especially from newspapers close to business interests, which claimed that it contained inadequate protection of property rights.[129] Because of the legal complexity of the bill, and the prospect that any amendments to it would be designed to protect individual rights, legal experts belonging to the Bundestag Judiciary Committee took the

[125] See, for example, *FAZ*, June 29, 1955.

[126] *Dt. Btag.*, 2. W.P., 93. Sitz., June 28, 1955, p. 5302.

[127] *Geschäftsordnung des Deutschen Bundestages*, par. 73, as implemented by *Dt. Btag.*, 2. W.P., Drs. 54.

[128] *Dt. Btag.*, 2. W.P., Drs. 1804, pp. 56–63.

[129] *Handelsblatt*, June 8, 1955; *Weser–Kurier*, June 10, 1955; *Industrie Kurier*, June 11, 1955; *DZ*, June 11, 1955; *Die Welt*, June 23, 1955.

initiative in examining the bill in the two largest parties; in the FDP, a leading member of the Economic Affairs Committee was placed in charge. The economic interests affected by the bill were well represented among Members of the CDU/CSU and the FDP, and both parties therefore approached it cautiously, unwilling to commit themselves in detail and anxious to leave room for committee alterations.

The first reading debate took about an hour. The bill was very briefly introduced by the State Secretary of the Ministry of the Interior. He was followed by only three speakers, from the CDU/CSU, SPD, and FDP respectively. The CDU/CSU spokesman welcomed the bill as an effort to replace the wartime requisitions law, with which, as a local government official, he had had experience. He was quite noncommittal about the details of the draft before the House, saying that the bill was unquestionably necessary and that it would be "the task of the legislature, that is, of this . . . House, to create it." [130] Later, the FDP speaker likewise accepted the necessity of the bill, but said that his party could not accept most of the points of the present draft.[131] The SPD took a much more generally critical position, condemning the Government bill for exceeding constitutional limits on federal powers, for threatening property rights, for inadequately providing citizens with legal redress, and for being so similar to the wartime measure as to be in every sense comparable. Quoting prominently from the Bundesrat's criticism of the bill, the party speaker savored the fact that its position placed the SPD in the forefront of the defense of property rights.[132] He expressed the hope that the bill could be adequately changed in the committee stage.

Although the initial discussion had been led by the legal experts of the parties, the Bundestag Interior Committee felt that the bill properly belonged in its jurisdiction, since it had been drafted by the Ministry of the Interior. The agreement on committee referral among the parties was therefore changed at the last moment, and the bill was unanimously placed in the charge of the Interior Committee, with only a secondary reference to the Judiciary Committee. Efforts made by Members, through motions from the floor, to send it to four other committees—European Security, Economic Affairs, Agriculture, and Local Government—were defeated.[133] In the brief and general terms in which the first reading debate had been held, no possible

---

[130] *Dt. Btag.*, 2. W.P., 112. Sitz., Nov. 11, 1955, p. 6052.
[131] *Ibid.*, p. 6057.   [132] *Ibid.*, p. 6054.   [133] *Ibid.*, p. 6057.

amendments of the measure in committee were foreclosed, although the governing parties had made it clear that they meant to pass the bill.

The Bill on Lawyers' Fees

The bill revising the Federal Schedule of Fees for Lawyers, having passed the Bundesrat on May 6, 1960, was submitted to the Bundestag on May 31. The Members of the Bundestag Judiciary Committee in all parties regarded it as a measure which did not raise partisan issues, and none wanted a first reading debate. There was no discussion of it in party caucuses. It appeared on the agenda of the first meeting of the House after the summer recess for a first reading and was referred to the Judiciary Committee without discussion.[134]

The Travel Bill

The bill on travel into and out of the Federal Republic received its fullest discussion in the period before the first reading, and by the time the first reading debate was over, it was all but dead. Taken unaware by the bill, a group of Members in the governing party began to consider ways of altering it almost immediately upon its publication.

The draft caused the greatest dismay in Berlin, because it empowered the Government to restrict travel between that city and the Federal Republic on the same basis as travel to and from the Soviet Zone. The dependence of Berlin on the freedom of its citizens to travel back and forth to the Federal Republic, the role of the city as a free point of exit for refugees from the Soviet Zone, the fear in Berlin that any restrictions which the Federal Republic placed on travel between East and West Germany might bring Soviet retaliation against the city, all motivated apprehension over the bill in Berlin.

While SPD Members from Berlin took the initiative in obtaining their party's complete rejection of the measure, the Berlin Representatives belonging to the CDU were in a more delicate position. One of their number, Ernst Lemmer, was a member of the Government as Minister for All-German Questions and had concurred in Cabinet approval of the bill. Another, Heinrich Krone, was chairman of the CDU/CSU parliamentary party, and still another, Josef Stingl, was a member of its executive committee. The others, backbenchers, began meeting *ad hoc* soon after the submission of the bill to the Bundesrat

[134] *Dt. Btag.*, 3. W.P., 124. Sitz., Sept. 28, 1960, p. 7228.

in late November, 1960, together with leaders of the CDU party organization in Berlin, to consider what they could do. The only lawyer among them, Ernst Benda, in his first term in the Bundestag, undertook to do research on the constitutionality of the bill. He concluded, that on at least four points it violated Article 11 of the Basic Law, which guaranteed freedom of movement to *all* Germans within the territory of the Federal Republic, permitting exceptions only to prevent criminal actions.

The press reaction to the bill had revealed sympathy with its objectives, but criticism of its broad delegation of powers to the Federal Government and fears of its effects on German unity. The *ad hoc* group in Berlin determined that it could not limit itself to a negative rejection of the Government draft. To gain party support outside of Berlin for their position, its members decided that they would have to develop a carefully restricted counterproposal which could be presented as fulfilling the Government's objectives while avoiding the shortcomings of the Government's bill with respect to constitutionality and German unity. In order to avoid dividing the party, they sought the cooperation of Krone and Lemmer, hoping through the intervention of these most prominent Berlin CDU Members to negotiate a compromise with the Minister of the Interior before the bill came to a first reading. On December 21, the day before the bill passed the Bundesrat, Benda presented an outline of a counterproposal to a full meeting of the CDU Representatives from Berlin as well as CDU members of the Berlin Government.[135] Krone suggested that the group send a formal letter to him, as chairman of the CDU/CSU parliamentary party, setting out its objections to the Government measure and its substitute proposals. At the same time, an approach would be made to the Ministry of the Interior. Contacts with the SPD were studiously avoided, as were appeals to the public, in order to facilitate an intraparty compromise.

The passage of the bill through the Bundesrat the following day, on a strict party vote, despite the criticism accompanying it, reinforced Minister Schröder's conviction that he would get his bill through the Bundestag, in an acceptable form, without making concessions before introducing it there. An official CDU statement issued after Bundesrat passage greeted the decision of the second chamber and announced

---

[135] *Die Welt*, Dec. 23, 1960, p. 2.

that "the opportunity now exists to deliberate carefully on the bill in the competent committees of the Bundestag since the Federal Government has indicated that it will be receptive to proposals from the Bundestag and from the *Länder*." [136] The first confrontation between the minister and two representatives of the Berlin group brought no results. Schröder intended to press for a first reading before discussing the bill further.

On January 2, the Berlin group sent Krone the letter he had solicited, with copies going to the chairman of the CSU group in the Bundestag, to Ministers Schröder and Lemmer, and to the head of the Chancellor's Office. It bore the signature of three CDU members of the Berlin Government, in addition to those of five CDU Bundestag Members from that city.

We are of the opinion [the letter stated] that the bill should not, under any circumstances, be submitted to the Bundestag by the Cabinet for a first reading until an agreement has been reached in our party. . . . Otherwise it may well happen that an open controversy would occur in the first reading, not between Government and Opposition alone.

The letter accepted the purpose of the Government bill, but pointed to the widespread press criticism of its methods and its threat to the cause of German unity.

Without at first mentioning the particular situation of Berlin, the letter said that the bill would in effect end the efforts of the Federal Republic to keep the doors open to the Soviet Zone of Germany, creating a national boundary between east and west. Furthermore, the bill would give unrestricted discretion to the Government to determine who might enter and who might not, raising doubts about its constitutionality. The letter indicated the abuse of travel between east and west could better be met by informal efforts and the strengthening of police powers against communist infiltration. Finally, the letter stressed the special effect of the bill on the relationship between the Federal Republic and Berlin, and warned of the dangers of an East German reprisal and the particular problems this would create in an election year. The pertinence of this warning seven months before the erection of the wall in Berlin could not of course have been appreciated.

Benda meanwhile pressed on with his efforts to draft a full-blown

[136] *Deutschland Union Dienst,* XIV, no. 243, Dec. 23, 1960.

bill as a counterproposal, either as a basis for negotiation with the Ministry of the Interior before it formally submitted its own bill to the Bundestag or, as a last resort, as a bill which he could introduce in the House himself, in competition with the Government bill. In either case, a draft representing the views of the Berlin group was a necessary instrument in its efforts. For the difficult task of bill drafting, Benda solicited the aid of the CDU Minister of Justice in the Berlin Government. Together with other CDU officials in Berlin, a bill was drawn up during the first week of January, discussed among and revised by the Berlin Members, signed by six of them, and duplicated.

Meanwhile, Schröder pressed for a first reading on the Government bill. Despite the efforts of the Berlin group, in a confrontation with Schröder at a meeting of the CDU/CSU parliamentary executive committee, to achieve a delay, pending completion of their own counterproposal and of negotiations, the Government submitted its bill to the Bundestag on January 10.[137] At a CDU/CSU caucus the same day, Schröder told the parliamentary party that he regarded the bill as "must" legislation and asked that the party approach it without too much controversy.[138] A Berlin Member advanced the doubts which his group had about the bill, but Krone, the chairman, expressed the hope that a common approach to it could be found within the party. The bill was placed on the Bundestag agenda of January 20 for a first reading. The SPD had no objections, depending by now on the division within the governing party to reinforce its own opposition.

The week of the debate opened on Monday afternoon with a meeting, attended by Schröder, of the executive committee of the CDU/CSU parliamentary party. At this meeting Stingl, one of the Berlin group on the executive, reiterated the group's objections to the bill. The executive committee decided to refer the bill for consideration to the party's working group on legal questions. It recommended that in the first reading debate the party's position be expressed by Walter Kühltau, a member of the Bundestag Interior Committee, to which the bill was to be referred by the House. The executive committee suggested that he should stress the Government's willingness to consider amendments at the committee stage. A member of the Berlin

[137] *Dt. Btag.*, 3. W.P., Drs. 2372. Cf. *Die Welt*, Jan. 10, 1961, p. 1.
[138] *Die Welt*, Jan. 11, 1961, p. 1.

group should then be given a chance to express his view. Chairman Krone urged the minister to be conciliatory and the Berlin group to avoid taking an extreme position.[139]

The working group, which considered the bill the following morning, had an agenda of five other items to be disposed of in a three-and-a-quarter-hour session before the party caucus which would take place the same afternoon. Minister Schröder was present, and recommended the creation of a subcommittee on the bill. In the discussion which followed, only one Member, Karl Kanka, spoke in support of the Government bill. He said that he felt the party should defend it in the first reading debate. The discussion was otherwise dominated by the Berlin Members, Benda and Johann Gradl, who reviewed all the objections to the bill and hinted that their view was shared by a large section of the parliamentary party. Kühltau, who was to be the official party speaker in the first reading, indicated that he shared many of Benda's views. Gradl, who was appointed to report to the caucus that afternoon, urged the minister to indicate publicly his receptivity to counterproposals.

The caucus received Gradl's report without discussion. It was agreed that Schröder's presentation of the bill would be followed by Kühltau, who would stress the Government's willingness to accept amendments in committee, and that Benda would then present the view of the Berlin group. Schröder confirmed that he was open to all suggestions.[140]

In the last days before the debate, the Berlin group had made a final effort to negotiate with Schröder directly.[141] In a second meeting with him, they suggested a postponement of the first reading, pending negotiation of a compromise bill. They threatened that they would otherwise introduce their own bill. Schröder rejected the proposal. The group thereupon met to discuss its tactics. Although some were in favor of introducing the bill which they had drafted and for which they felt they could easily obtain the necessary fifteen signatures, the dominant view was that this would be disloyal to the party. Instead, the bill would be presented in the committee discussions as a series of counterproposals. Benda was charged with presenting the group's

---

[139] *Die Welt*, Jan. 17, 1961, p. 2.
[140] *Bonner Rundschau, FAZ*, both of Jan. 18, 1961.
[141] *Die Welt*, Jan. 18, 1961; *Spandauer Volksblatt*, Jan. 18, 1961.

views as forcefully as possible in the first reading debate. When Benda drew up his remarks a day before the debate, he had already seen the text of the speech which the official party spokesman would make.

The first reading took place on January 20 as planned. Schröder's presentation of the bill was largely defensive. He concluded that although he had rejected "prefabricated compromises" he was prepared to discuss "further proposals without prejudice." [142] Kühltau, who followed, stressed his party's support of the objectives of the bill, but indicated its questions about methods and expressed satisfaction with the Government's willingness to consider alternatives in committee deliberations. The speaker of the SPD came next with a declaration of rejection of the bill, but willingness to consider alternatives to it in committee. He received applause from CDU/CSU Representatives as well as from Members of his own party. Then it was Benda's turn to present, as he put it, the views "not of the whole CDU/CSU, but certainly for a part of this party and particularly for my Berlin colleagues in the party." [143] He referred at once to concrete counterproposals which his group had worked out, and, addressing himself directly to Schröder, suggested that they be tested not merely by their practicality, as the minister had suggested, but also by their constitutionality. This received applause from Members of all parties, and Benda had the House with him thereafter. Mentioning Berlin only peripherally, he outlined the main points of his own bill without formally introducing it. The FDP speaker followed. Also strongly opposed to the bill, he objected particularly that it had not been discussed with the Opposition before its introduction.

When a second CDU Berlin Member was recognized next, the parliamentary whip of the SPD objected that "it had been agreed that it would now be the turn of a member of my party," [144] and the presiding officer agreed. Thereupon a Berlin Member of the SPD spoke, followed by the second Berlin Representative of the CDU, and by this time the planned length of the debate had been exceeded. Not to be outdone, an FDP Member from Berlin followed. Since none of the seven speakers after Schröder had really defended the bill, the only CDU Member to have spoken for it in the CDU working group spontaneously made the attempt.

Schröder spoke again in conclusion. He thanked the last speaker,

[142] *Dt. Btag.*, 3. W.P., 139. Sitz., Jan. 20, 1961, p. 7908.
[143] *Ibid.*, pp. 7913 ff.   [144] *Ibid.*, p. 7920.

but he was obviously upset at the tenor of the debate. In a reply to his critics which was longer than his original presentation, he ignored the problem of Berlin altogether, declaring that the counterproposals offered could not attain the objective commonly supported and expressing hope that "a more positive atmosphere" would exist in the committee than had been apparent in the debate.[145]

After nearly four hours, the bill was referred, without dissent, to the Interior Committee and secondarily to the Committee on All-German and Berlin Questions. The debate had clearly indicated the lack of parliamentary support for the Government measure, not only in the Opposition, but, to Schröder's surprise and distress, in the CDU/CSU as well.

The press reaction to the debate was to consider the bill, at least in the Government version, as finished.[146] Schröder, severely critical of the lack of support which his own party had given him, was now prepared to negotiate with the dissident faction. At its first meeting after the debate, the CDU working group created a committee, including two of the Berlin Members, to carry on preliminary discussions with the ministry on a compromise draft before the start of the deliberations on the bill in the Bundestag committee. But at this point, with time running out for the third Bundestag, the opponents of the Government bill were in no rush to negotiate. Subsequent meetings of the working group merely recorded the continuation of discussions with the ministry. By the end of April, the special committee of Members and officials of the Ministry of the Interior was close to agreeing on a compromise draft. But by then Schröder had lost the hope that any bill could still be passed before the final adjournment of the House at the end of June.

Although it had been placed on the agenda of the Interior Committee, the SPD was no more anxious to press it than was the CDU. Neither wanted to have it come up before an acceptable version had been drafted. Under a new SPD chairman, the Committee marked time on the bill, until time ran out.[147]

On August 13, the erection of the wall in Berlin finished the matter. Fortuitously, the defeat of the bill had saved the Federal Government from the onus of initiating measures to restrict east-west travel, leaving

[145] *Ibid.*, p. 7933.
[146] *Die Welt*, Jan. 21, 1961, p. 1.
[147] *Tagesspiegel*, March 1, 1961.

it free to express its abhorrence, not only of the brutality of that particular form of restriction, but of restriction itself in principle.

The unusual defeat of a Government bill at the hands of its own party in Parliament was due to a special combination of circumstances. Both the failure of the minister to clear the draft in advance with leaders of his party in the Bundestag and his failure to recognize until after the first reading debate that he did not have adequate parliamentary support greatly weakened his bargaining position. Once the bill had been published, the almost universally negative criticism of it in the press [148] made it difficult for him to accept a negotiated compromise without embarrassment. Once the measure had been debated in the Bundestag, the demonstrated lack of support for it within the majority party greatly diminished Schröder's power and prestige on the issue. The combination of the bill's special effect on Berlin, which caused organized opposition to it there, and its general implication for German unity, which made it a national issue, produced the ingredients of effectively led and widely supported rebellion against it. CDU chairman Krone, himself a Berliner, facilitated the opponents' work by his tolerance toward dissent. The opposition of the other parties backstopped the rebels in the CDU. Finally, the approach of the end of the parliamentary term placed time at the side of the dissidents.

While this combination of circumstances was of course unique, and few Government bills give rise to an *ad hoc* opposition of this type, the existence of opposition to Government bills within the CDU/CSU, based on the heterogeneity of the party, is not at all uncommon. Furthermore, the organization and procedure of the CDU/CSU in the Bundestag permits an internal opposition to be effective. It is the Government's knowledge that it cannot depend on automatic parliamentary support which inspires its practice of clearing legislation in advance with its followers in the Bundestag. This advance clearance often hides the distribution of power between Government and Parliament. In the unusual case when clearance fails and support disintegrates that relationship is more clearly illuminated.

The Child Benefits Bill

The bill on child benefits came to the Bundestag only after an arduous process of negotiation between the Government, the major interests, and the majority party in the Bundestag. In comparison with

[148] See the *Rhein Neckar Zeitung,* Jan. 18, 1961, for a particularly extensive critique.

the social reform program which had originally been discussed, the bill was a limited measure designed for quick passage before the end of the parliamentary term and, incidentally, for the electoral advantage of the CDU/CSU. It therefore encountered the strenuous criticism of the SPD, which was not, of course, opposed to child payments, but found the provisions of the particular measure too stingy, the reforms in administration inadequate, and the timing of the bill obviously to its own electoral disadvantage. Both sides clearly wanted a first reading debate, to publicize their respective positions. The bill had passed the Bundesrat on March 29, 1961, was promptly submitted to the Bundestag by the Government on April 6,[149] received the usual initial consideration in the parties in the following two weeks, and came up for first reading debate in the session of April 19.

The debate took more than two hours. Minister Blank led off with a defense of those portions of the bill which had been criticized by the Opposition. To do this, he found it necessary to explain the compromises which had been made in the process of drafting the bill. The next speaker came from the Opposition. An SPD Representative, by profession a trade unionist specializing in social welfare questions, she was a member of the Bundestag Committee on Social Policy, to which it had been agreed the bill would be referred. She criticized the bill's inadequacies, particularly its application only to families earning less than DM 550 monthly ($137.50), and tried, without apparent success, to exploit the divisions which had existed on the measure within the Government. The FDP had not chosen its speaker from among its two Members on the Committee on Social Policy, a teacher and a farmer, but selected a young businessman instead. He stressed the party's opposition to the principle of financing child benefits from employers' contributions, welcomed the departure from that system in the present bill, but objected that the bill did not revise the old system entirely. The CDU/CSU speaker came last. A member of the appropriate committee, and a prominent representative of the labor group within the party, he expressed his party's full support of the measure, and the hope that it could be passed quickly. A short epilogue followed, as the minister sought to answer his critics, and SPD and FDP speakers offered a rejoinder. The bill was referred without dissent to the Committee on Social Policy and, secondarily, to the Appropriations Committee.[150]

[149] *Dt. Btag.*, 3. W.P., Drs. 2646.
[150] *Dt. Btag.*, 3. W.P., 154. Sitz., April 19, 1961, pp. 8882–98.

COMMITTEE STAGE IN THE BUNDESTAG

Confrontation of the Chief Actors

In the specialized legislative committees of the Bundestag, the interested groups which have previously influenced the proposed legislation separately, now confront each other. The officials of the initiating ministry, as representatives of the Government, have privileged access; they must be heard at any time. Because of the Government's endeavor to have its ablest specialist on hand in the committee deliberations at all times, and the frequently indifferent committee attendance of Members of the Bundestag, officials sometimes outnumber Representatives in the committee sessions, despite repeated efforts of both Government and Bundestag to avoid this appearance of Government domination. The Bundesrat may also send its representatives to the committees, and they too must be heard at any time.[151] If the representatives of the *Länder* have a substantial interest in a measure, one or more of the members of the Bundesrat committee which considered the bill, who are usually officials of *Länder* Governments, are present. Government and Bundesrat representatives of course have no vote in committee.

The parliamentary parties are represented in proportion to their strengths in the House, and the chairmanships are also proportionately divided among all of the parties, depriving the governing majority of organizational control of the committees. The representation of interest groups varies with the committees, from those in which the Members of at least some parties are outright interest representatives, notably the committees concerned with economic and social policy, to those, like the Foreign Affairs Committee, where interest representation is remote. Interests which do not have committee members to represent them make themselves heard by submitting statements of their position in writing, or by requesting the right to appear for testimony.

Hearings

For interest groups which have not been heard or satisfied in the ministerial stage of the legislative process, particularly those too small to have effective ministerial contacts, the best chance to make them-

[151] *Basic Law,* art. 43(2).

selves felt is in the committee stage. But the task of those wishing to influence the committees from the outside is difficult. The practice of hearing or receiving testimony from interested groups is quite common but it has nowhere near the significance of Congressional hearings in the United States. An unsuccessful effort was made to introduce public hearings, American style, into German parliamentary life at the time of the adoption of the Rules of Procedure.[152] Compared to Congressional committees, the committees of the Bundestag receive legislation at a relatively late stage in the lawmaking process, and they do not see the need at that point to canvass the positions of the interests systematically. Furthermore, the hearings procedure, derived from American court practice, is unfamiliar in Germany.[153] Finally, the value of communicating the views of contending groups to a wide public audience through hearings, thereby compelling the interest representatives to justify their demands by the standards of a public interest, is not generally recognized. The fear is rather that public hearings would destroy the "objectivity" of the testimony offered. Undoubtedly, some interest groups realize well enough that public hearings would inhibit their ability to press their demands frankly and clearly.

The committees almost universally excuse their failure to employ the hearings provision of the Rules with practical arguments referring to lack of time and space for such a procedure. The idea of checking the influence of interest groups by compelling them to testify publicly is still alive, however, especially among some civic groups. Furthermore, some Members of the Opposition see the possibility of publicizing the committee work done under their supervision through the hearings procedure. Only half a dozen hearings have been held in the history of the Bundestag, none of them on really contentious political issues. But five of them occurred during the fourth term, and four of these were held by a single committee, that on Interior Affairs, which is chaired by a Member of the SPD.[154] The provision of the Rules

[152] *Geschäftsordnung des Deutschen Bundestages,* par. 73(2); Dt. Btag., 1. W.P., 179. Sitz., Dec. 6, 1951, p. 7412.

[153] Ernst Fraenkel, *Das amerikanische Regierungssystem, Eine politologische Analyse* (Cologne and Opladen: Westdeutscher Verlag, 1960), p. 307.

[154] With one exception, no public record of the hearings exists. Hearings have been held by the Committee on Transport, to hear expert testimony on road safety, and by the Committee on Cultural Policy, on the state of the film industry (see *DZ,* March 25, 1960, and *Die Welt,* May 15, 1962). During the fourth Bundestag, the Committee on Interior Affairs held hearings on the Hamburg flood disaster of

which permits hearings, at first virtually a dead letter, may yet come to life as Members recognize the potential uses of hearings, as the postwar pressure of legislation declines, and as the accommodations for committee meetings improve. But judging by past experience, hearings are likely to consist of testimony rather than cross-examination, and to be limited to subjects which all parties judge suitable for this form of publicity.

Privacy

The privacy of committee deliberations has been jealously guarded, without distinction among the various stages of the committee process. Except for the committees on Defense, Foreign Affairs, All-German Questions, and, on matters of internal security, Interior, committee meetings are not "secret." This means that they are open to all Members of the House, whether or not they are committee members, and to representatives of the Government and the Bundesrat. It also means that participants may report what has happened at committee meetings to interested outsiders, including the press. Furthermore, the minutes of the meetings are available to all those entitled to attend, and, with their permission, to outsiders, including scholars. The Judiciary Committee keeps a stenographic transcript of its deliberations, which is available to law schools; other committees, too, offer their records, which vary widely in their detail, as relevant material for the subsequent interpretation of a law. But the committee meetings are not open to the public or the press. Newspapers give little prominence to the secondhand reports which they receive. Interest groups, on the other hand, follow the committee deliberations which concern them as closely as their contacts permit. The committees meet in the intimate atmosphere of chambers just large enough to accommodate their members and the appropriate officials. The confrontation between the ministry and the committee, and the reconciliation of the views of the Government, the *Länder*, the interests, and the parties, therefore takes place in relative privacy.

1962, and three hearings on various aspects of civil defense. The record of one of the latter was published (see *Dt. Btag.*, 4. W.P., Protokoll Nr. 118 [6. Ausschuss]; Protokoll Nr. 63 [9. Ausschuss]). For the proposal of a study group on parliamentary reforms that the use of hearings be expanded, see SZ, July 30, 1963; *Der Spiegel*, XX, no. 10 (Feb. 28, 1966), 21–2. The fifth Bundestag took up consideration of such a proposal (see *Dt. Btag.*, 5. W.P., 48. Sitz., June 16, 1966, p. 2326; Drs. 125).

Party Teamwork

The committee members of each party operate as a team. They are led by a "foreman," who assigns responsibility for each bill to a particular member of his party, and they meet regularly as a subcommittee of one of the working groups of the parliamentary party. This is liable to be the same group of Members which has taken the initiative in formulating the party's position before the first reading. Throughout the committee stage, this group has charge of developing a unified party viewpoint, if possible, on each aspect of the bill as the committee considers it. Depending on their influence within the party generally, and on the relationship between the issues a particular bill raises and the general party line, the committee members stay in touch with the rest of the parliamentary party, whose support they eventually require. They may report back to the working group, or even to the executive committee and the caucus, and occasionally they may seek further instructions. The situation is complicated by the practice of referring bills to a multiplicity of committees, requiring the party's teams on the various committees to stay in close touch with each other.

Ministerial Officials

The Government is represented in the committees by the officials and department heads who have initiated the bill, and occasionally by the minister. They are officially present to explain and defend the Government draft, and to report the actions of the committee to the Government. They may provide a committee with the services of the legislative counsel of their departments, in order to help it to draft amendments to a bill. But their willingness to cooperate is dictated by calculations of the Government's tactical advantage in each case.[155] Ministries whose views on a particular bill have been overruled in the legislative process within the Government, may, through the informal contacts between officials and Members, seek to restore their views in the legislative text during the committee stage, just as interest groups and the representatives of the Bundesrat do. Latent divisions between ministries within the Government afford committee members the chance to arbitrate among the experts. Such differences, like the criti-

---

[155] *Geschäftsordnung der Bundesregierung*, par. 28; *Gemeinsame Geschäftsordnung der Bundesministerien*, Besonderer Teil (GGO II), pars. 41, 49. See also pp. 269, 271, *supra*.

cism of Government bills by the Bundesrat and the demands of interest groups, are the raw materials from which committees fashion revisions of Government legislation.

The Negotiating Process

Informal consultations among participants in the work of the committee surround its deliberations. Not only do the teams of Members of each party meet regularly to plot their course, but the representatives of the Government meet together, Bundesrat representatives may consult with other members of the second chamber or with their *Land* Governments, and Members report to the interest groups with which they are associated. For the development of compromises among contending viewpoints, two kinds of extracommittee consultations are particularly important: those among Members of various parties and those between Members of the governing parties and the ministerial officials. Despite the intimacy of the committee atmosphere, the most important bargains are struck outside the committee rooms by *ad hoc* groups. For purposes of bargaining the committee meeting has two disadvantages: its composition, in that it includes members of all parties as well as Government officials at all times; and its lack of secrecy, in that minutes are kept.

The committee meetings themselves are important for their painstaking scrutiny of the proposed legislation, article by article, usually in two readings. In this process of close examination, every point which is in dispute among the participants, or their principals, is registered, considered, and finally decided by a vote of the Members. In this careful analysis of the bill, the leading roles are played by the committee chairman and deputy chairman, the experts on the bill in each party, the Government officials of the responsible ministry, the committee reporter, and the committee's staff assistant.

The Role of the Chairman

The chairman has considerable organizational powers, which he exercises in close consultation with the deputy chairman. He may determine the schedule of committee meetings and the order of priority of the items on the agenda. Except with the special permission of the President, rarely accorded any but the Appropriations Committee, committees may meet only when the House is not in session and, of course, when the parties and their working groups are not meeting. In the normal month, during the third and fourth Bundestage, four days of one week were set aside entirely for committee meetings and two other weeks allowed one additional meeting each. The availability of only six days a month placed the most active committees under considerable pressure of time. During the last year of the fourth term, a new schedule confined them even further, leaving only two half-days a week for committees. This schedule was retained by the fifth Bundestag.

The power to establish the schedule and the agenda can be very important under these circumstances. In exercising this power, the chairman cannot affront the committee. Except with its general approval, he cannot pigeonhole legislation by refusing to place it on the agenda. But he can delay and drag out deliberations, as well as advance and facilitate them. His conduct of the meetings contributes to the pace of the discussions and the points which are emphasized, since committees operate quite informally without their own rules of procedure.

The chairman appoints the reporter for each bill under consideration. It is the reporter's task to prepare a written report on the committee deliberations for the House and an explanation of the textual changes which the committee recommends. He must take account of all views in the committee and make his presentation in a fair and nonpartisan manner. The reports attain a high level of objectivity. Reporters on Government legislation are chosen without regard for party, but with some consideration of subject matter competence among committee members, and for rotation. Reporters for bills introduced by Members of the House are generally selected from a party other than that of the initiators. For highly complicated bills, two reporters may be appointed. The chairman chooses a reporter with the tacit consent of the committee, generally after consultation with the deputy chairman. Despite the reporter's obligation to impartiality, the choice in a particular case may advance or retard the cause of the bill.

The committee staff, which works under the chairman's supervision, consists in most cases of an administrative assistant and two secretaries. This staff has charge of keeping the minutes and the committee correspondence, of summarizing and systematically arranging the viewpoints which interest groups submit in writing, of keeping track of the textual changes which the committee makes in the legislation under consideration, and of drafting the committee reports. During the second and third readings, the relevant committee assistants sit at a table to the left of the President's chair to give the presiding officer explanations of substantive problems which may arise, and to advise him in advance of the major issues which are likely to occur in debate, of prospective amendments, and of the likely outcome of the vote.[156]

Committee Cohesion

To some extent, each committee develops a corporate personality. Among its members, including those Government officials attending with regularity, a sense of shared subject matter competence diminishes partisan differences.[157] The Judiciary Committee acts as general legal adviser to the other committees, giving legal and constitutional interpretations, and examining technical legal aspects of other bills, as well as having primary responsibility for a large body of proposed legislation. During the third Bundestag, the committee had charge of fifty-four bills and participated in the consideration of fifty-two other bills and resolutions. In 188 sessions, it left as unfinished business four major pieces of legislation referred to it.[158] Occasionally the committee is a bottleneck in the Bundestag's legislative process. But efforts to facilitate its work by the formation of additional subcommittees, or a special committee on constitutional questions,[159] have failed because of the lack of qualified lawyers to compose them. The Judiciary Committee possesses a quasi monopoly of judicial talent in the Bundestag, giving it an unusual importance, and a sense of professional solidarity.

The Defense Committee was distinguished for a time by the importance of its jurisdiction, particularly during the period of rearmament. Considered as the parliamentary watchdog over the remilitarization which was widely viewed with apprehension, the committee was given special constitutional powers to constitute itself as an investigating committee on the demand of a minority of one-fourth of its members.[160] It receives the report of the Bundestag's Defense Commissioner, and oversees defense appropriations and expenditures. Each

[156] *Pflichten und Aufgaben der wissenschaftlichen Assistenten beim Deutschen Bundestag* (mimeographed, 1950/51; revised, 1957), *passim.*

[157] This is particularly true of the Appropriations Committee (see pp. 374–7, *infra*).

[158] *Die Welt,* July 22, 1961.   [159] *Die Welt,* May 3, 1961.

[160] *Basic Law,* art. 45a(2).

member has a specialty corresponding to the jurisdiction of a subdivision of the Defense Department. As one of three committees whose sessions are secret, its members, like those of the Foreign Affairs Committee, enjoy a special prestige.

The committee's supervision of the defense establishment has not, however, been exercised with the same success as its earlier influence on basic defense legislation in the first stages of rearmament. In the late 1950's, the committee exercised such extensive control over defense administration that the Defense Department could not make important decisions on the procurement of military hardware without clearing them first with the committee. But after a number of committee members were caught in serious cases of conflict of interest between their committee work and their employment as representatives of military suppliers, the committee restrained its effort to control procurement policy. Its prestige suffered subsequently from its inability to hold its own in a series of encounters with Defense Minister Strauss and from its failure to use the office of the Defense Commissioner to full advantage. At first composed of party leaders, especially of the Opposition parties, it gradually attracted mainly second-rank Members. In the hierarchy of committee prestige, the Foreign Affairs Committee stands higher, though its influence on Government policy may be no greater. Composed largely of party leaders, it is privy to at least some of the Government's foreign policy considerations, and for that reason alone retains a very special prestige.

Because of its jurisdiction over civil service law and internal security, the Interior Committee ranks high in importance, having influence on questions of government personnel, and on the exercise of police powers. Those committees which are composed primarily of interest representatives, notably the committees on Economic Affairs, Agriculture, and Transport, are united by the common interest of their members. But their influence suffers from the general realization that the recommendations of these committees have a special bias.

In the Committee on Social Policy, whose jurisdiction includes some of the most controversial items of postwar legislation, divisions between the parties and between the different interests within the CDU/CSU are particularly strong. For this reason, important legislative projects of the Ministry of Labor were stalemated there for two parliamentary terms. Although the ministry had been negotiating, throughout that time, with interest groups and party leaders on the committee on various important reforms of the social security system, it was unable to formulate drafts commanding sufficient support in the committee. During the fourth Bundestag, it largely gave up trying to introduce bills on these subjects. On one occasion, the Minister of Labor even took the unprecedented step of refusing to answer an interpellation in the House.[161]

Although on every committee the governing parties possess a majority proportionate to their strength in the House, their view does not necessarily prevail. The corporate sense within committees softens party differences and substitutes others. The privacy of committee meetings furthermore permits voting across party lines. On social and labor policy for example, Members from the labor group of the CDU may join SPD Members to create a majority; on church-state issues, SPD and FDP Members may vote together. If the SPD associates itself with a criticism previously advanced by the Bundesrat—a criticism which may, in fact, have been shaped by SPD *Land* Governments in the Bundesrat—even a united majority of Members of the governing parties may hesitate to outvote it, knowing that the Bundesrat may exercise its veto powers. The same hesitation to employ the powers of the majority exists if the Opposition can convincingly threaten to take a measure to the Constitutional Court to obtain a ruling on its constitutionality, since as few as one-third of the Members of the Bundestag have the power to petition the Court. On constitutional amendments, the need for a two-thirds majority on the floor also makes it futile for the majority to insist on its view in committee. Finally, committee work depends on a modicum of cooperation among the parties, especially if the chairman belongs to the Opposition; the deputy chairman will most likely belong to it, even if the chairman does not. For all these reasons, Members of the Opposition play a part in the committee stage which cannot be measured by their numbers, and committee decisions do not simply reflect party strengths, or predetermined party alignments. On the contrary, party positions are themselves influenced by committee deliberations.

When the painstaking task of examining a bill has been completed in the committee and the views of other committees to whom the bill has been referred have been heard, the reporter of the committee in charge draws up a report to the House, summarizing the committee's

[161] *Dt. Btag.*, 4. W.P., 16. Sitz., Feb. 22, 1962, pp. 479–91.

deliberations and the major differences of opinion. The report is usually presented in printed form, together with a committee motion that
the bill, as altered in committee, be adopted. The committee report
contains the original bill and the committee version in juxtaposition,
unless the original has been so thoroughly revised that it can no longer
be compared. In any case, the committee version becomes the basis of
the second reading debate. The chances that it will prevail are very
high, except in the rare cases when party caucuses have repudiated
their committee delegations. Four of the five legislative cases we have
been following passed the committee stage (the Travel Bill having
died in committee) and all four were enacted substantially as the
committees formulated them.

The Volunteers Bill

By the time the Volunteers Bill came up before the Committee on
European Security, one week after its first reading, the governing
parties, in negotiations among themselves and with the Chancellor,
had agreed on an extensive set of amendments to it.[162] These were
designed to limit to 6,000 the number of volunteers to be recruited, to
restrict them to staff duties and prevent their organization into military
units, to give the Security and Appropriations committees a veto
power over the creation of government jobs in the Ministry of Defense, to require the Government to set up a Personnel Commission to
screen officer candidates, and to assure that the permanent organization of the Ministry of Defense would be the subject of further
legislation, rather than being determined unilaterally by the Government under its power over the organization of executive departments.
Erler, deputy chairman of and SPD leader in the Security Committee,
found that these substantial amendments indicated the willingness of
the majority to review the bill critically, thereby justifying the participation of the Opposition in the committee stage, despite its general
aversion to the measure.[163] A meeting of the SPD caucus supported his
position, although there was criticism.[164] With the secrecy of its deliberations lifted, the work of the committee was reported in the press in
unusual detail, and this publicity, in turn, influenced the behavior of
the parties in the committee. It heightened the coatition parties' desire

[162] *Die Welt* and *FAZ*, both of July 4 and 5, 1955; *Die Welt* and *SZ*, both of
July 6, 1955.
[163] *FAZ* and *Die Welt*, July 7, 1955.   [164] *FAZ* and *SZ*, July 8, 1955.

to amend an unpopular bill and the Opposition's willingness to participate responsibly in the discussions.

The Security Committee deliberated on the bill for five days. In
view of the importance of the matter, attendance was particularly
high, including not only committee members but, especially on the
side of the SPD, their alternates as well. On the first day, those present
in what was normally a twenty-nine-member committee included
twenty-one members and alternates belonging to the CDU/CSU plus
one other member of that party, thirteen members and alternates of
the SPD plus one outsider, all three members of the FDP, and one of
each of the small parties—forty-one Members in all. The representatives of the Government included the Minister of Defense, who attended every session, and fourteen other officials from the Defense,
Justice, Finance, and Labor ministries, and from the Office of the
Chancellor. The Bundesrat was represented by seven members. Most
of the participants, however, were silent throughout the meetings. The
discussion was carried by the chairman, the party specialists, the
Minister, and one spokesman for the Bundesrat. Between the first and
the last sessions, Erler stayed away from the committee altogether,
leaving another Member to speak for the Opposition and confining
himself to negotiations behind the scenes.

The committee devoted its first morning to a general discussion of
the bill, in which the minister made a conciliatory statement, indicating that the Government regarded it as the task of the committee to
offer appropriate revisions of the bill. A consideration of the individual
paragraphs of the brief measure followed, led by FDP Member
Mende, who had been appointed as reporter. The amendments which
the governing parties had agreed on were offered by four of their
members in succession.

The second day began with a statement by an official of North
Rhine–Westphalia, representing the Bundesrat. He expressed the second chamber's opposition to the application of civil service regulations
to the recruits. Further, he proposed that the executive orders establishing salary grades and ranks for the recruits be subject to Bundesrat
approval, and that the Government's Personnel Commission include
three members appointed by the Bundesrat. He justified the Bundesrat's participation in the committee stage by the need for speed on the
bill, and implied that the second chamber could drag out the proceed-

ings by rejecting the bill and calling for negotiations through the Mediation Committee if its demands were not now met.[165]

On the afternoon of the second day, in first reading, voting began on individual paragraphs. Amendments were advanced not only by Members in the coalition parties, but by those in the SPD as well.[166] Voting tended to cut across party lines. The discussion soon turned to the Personnel Commission, which the SPD wanted to see permanently established by means of a separate law. To that end, it proposed a bill which would provide for Bundestag confirmation of the commission's members, require that the commission act by two-thirds vote, and determine that the commission would review the appointment of all officers from commanders of battalions on up. Although the Government felt that this would place too many appointments under the commission's review, a compromise whereby low-level appointments would be governed by general criteria to be established by the commission seemed possible. Support for the principle of such a commission came from Members of all but the German party.[167] It was regarded as much as a protection for the reputations of the officers to be recruited, as a protection against the recruitment of officers with unacceptable World War II records. An SPD leader indicated for the first time that if this commission were made the subject of a separate law, the SPD might vote for it, thereby giving its assent for the first time to a bill concerning rearmament. Attracted by this possibility, Jaeger and Erler undertook to negotiate privately on the matter. Meanwhile, the Defense Minister, having consulted the Cabinet, expressed the Government's opposition to a separate law on the Personnel Commission, regarding such a law as an infringement on the Government's prerogatives over executive organization. But the Security Committee was in no mood to be stopped by a Government opinion. Instead, on the motion of an SPD and a CSU Member, it created a subcommittee to consider the matter further.

The Defense Minister also expressed the Government's objection, for the same reasons, to the amendment which had been moved by committee chairman Jaeger, subjecting the final organization of the defense establishment to future legislation. The Government's implication that such an amendment was unconstitutional, and would give the

[165] *FAZ*, July 8, 1955.   [166] *Die Welt*, July 8, 1955.
[167] *SZ*, July 11, 1955; *FAZ*, July 12, 1955.

SPD a chance to take the bill to court, was repudiated by SPD speakers.[168] A rousing speech by Hellmuth Heye of the CDU, who had been a prominent officer in the Second World War, asserted the crucial importance of civilian control over military affairs and the consequent need to approach the organization of the Defense Department, and its relation to the rest of the Government, with the greatest deliberation.[169] Again the committee expressed a clear sentiment against the Government's position, adopting the Jaeger amendment, in a clarified form, unanimously.

Deliberations turned next to a report from the Committee on Civil Service Law, which had recommendations to make on salary scales for recruits, designed to protect the superiority of civil over military scales. The committee rejected these recommendations, which had the support of the Finance Ministry, and instead maintained the provisions of the Government bill substantially intact, as preferred by the Ministry of Defense.[170] The chairman then reported that an agreement had been reached with the SPD whereby the Personnel Commission would be established by a separate law, to be introduced by Members of all parties except the German party and considered by the Bundestag before the Volunteers Bill was given its final reading. With only the German party Representative opposed, the committee thereupon decided to include a reference to such a commission in the Volunteers Bill. This completed the first reading.

The chief issue with respect to the Personnel Commission was the method of its appointment. The SPD insisted on Bundestag approval of the appointments; the Government found this an unconstitutional interference with its appointment power. But the Opposition could not be dissuaded by offers from the leaders of the governing party that the appointments be informally cleared with all the parliamentary parties. In the Judiciary Committee, which met simultaneously with the Security Committee to consider the constitutional aspects of the Volunteers Bill, an SPD leader declared that the Opposition was not content with participation behind the scenes, but wanted to share responsibility in public for the membership of the commission.[171]

[168] *FAZ* and *SZ*, July 9, 1955.
[169] His committee remarks were subsequently quoted in the Bundestag debate (see *Dt. Btag.*, 2. W.P., 99. Sitz, July 15, 1955, pp. 5541–2).
[170] *SZ*, July 11, 1955.
[171] Protokoll des Ausschusses für Rechtswesen und Verfassungsrecht, 2. W.P., no. 70, p. 34.

Nevertheless, while accepting the creation of a Personnel Commission by means of a separate law, the Judiciary Committee determined, by a vote of all but one of its CDU members, against all of its SPD and FDP members, that Bundestag participation in the appointment of the Commission would be unconstitutional.[172]

At the same time, it decided that the Volunteers Bill, as amended, with the provision subjecting the organization of the Defense Ministry to legislative determination, was consistent with the constitution. Unconvinced, the Government held a special Cabinet meeting, which the chairman of the Judiciary Committee was invited to attend, but no consensus developed between the view of the ministers and that of their parliamentary followers on the question of constitutionality.[173]

The method of appointing the Personnel Commission had become the critical issue between the majority parties and the Opposition in the Bundestag. Negotiations between Erler and Jaeger, and within the subcommittee of the Security Committee, without the participation of representatives of the Government, produced the necessary compromise. The parties agreed on the membership of the Personnel Commission, agreed that the Bundestag would openly vote to confirm the appointments, and decided that the commission would not require a two-thirds vote to act. This agreement cleared the way for the approval, in a brief second reading in the Security Committee, of the Volunteers Bill, and the introduction, in the Bundestag, of a bill creating the Personnel Commission. The latter bill was given a hasty first reading, referred to the Security Committee—which, of course, saw no reason to discuss the bill further—and reported out simultaneously with the Volunteers Bill.[174]

In the heated sessions of the CDU/CSU parliamentary executive committee and the caucus, in which both bills were considered, Chancellor Adenauer warned that the SPD might take the measures to the Court to challenge their constitutionality if they contained the provisions which the Government found objectionable. But the caucus was assured by the committee chairman, Jaeger, that Erler had disclaimed any such intention on behalf of the SPD.[175] While the CDU/CSU

---

[172] *FAZ* and *SZ*, July 9, 1955.   [173] *Bulletin*, July 13, 1955.
[174] *Dt. Btag.*, 2. W.P., Drs. 1620.
[175] *FAZ*, *SZ*, *Die Welt*, and *Neue Züricher Zeitung*, all of July 14, 1955. Cf. *Frankfurter Rundschau*, July 15, 1955. See also *FAZ*, July 12, 13, 1955; *SZ*, July 11, 1955.

thereupon approved both bills in the versions which the committees had brought forth, an SPD caucus decided that the party would vote against the Volunteers Bill, despite its improvement in committee, because the party opposed its objectives. However, the SPD decided that it would vote for the bill on the Personnel Commission. Party leaders belonging to the Security and Judiciary committees were persuasive in recommending this unprecedented support for a rearmament measure. Only sixteen Members voted against the decision in the caucus, and two abstained.[176]

The Volunteers Bill which was reported out of committee after a week of deliberation, with the approval of every party, was an entirely different measure from the one the Government had presented. In unusually severe language, the committee report indicated that the committee had been obliged "not only to change the bill in form, and substantially to expand its scope, but also to amend its substance in such a way that it now presents a useable legal basis for preparing the establishment of armed forces." The reporter noted that this was the result of "the participation of all elements in the Security Committee and the other committees" and that "the representatives of the governing coalition as well as of the Opposition presented proposals which made possible the formulation of the text of the bill in its present form." [177] Except for the introductory and concluding paragraphs, no section of the Government bill had remained untouched. In the remaining paragraphs, only sixty-nine of the original words remained; running to around six hundred words, the committee draft was four times the length of the original. In substance, it had far greater precision and was far more restrictive in the powers it made available to the Government. The results of the committee's deliberations furthermore included an entirely new bill, creating the Personnel Commission. Finally, the committee had compelled the Government to specify its defense plans in detail.

Unquestionably, the role of the committees of the Bundestag in the formulation of the Volunteers Bill was unusual; to this day it marks a high point in parliamentary influence on Government legislation. The measure initiated a new and sensitive policy, German rearmament. Public interest was high. A large number of Members felt qualified to deal with the issue. The Government was severely weakened by its

[176] *Neue Züricher Zeitung*, July 14, 1955.
[177] *Dt. Btag.*, 2. W.P., Drs. 1600, p. 9.

haste, having failed to clear its bill with *Land* or parliamentary leaders in advance. It wanted legislative authorization to undertake the creation of armed forces, in order to give an international demonstration of its intent. From its point of view, any bill would do so long as it was passed promptly. The Parliament was strengthened because some of its defense specialists had a personal interest in the development of a defense establishment, as well as their own policy objectives. The CSU acted in support of its leader's hope for the position of Defense Minister. SPD leaders were interested in some participation in the development of the defense program, in spite of the party's basic opposition to rearmament. The parliamentary leaders of the CDU and the FDP were anxious for some cooperation from the Opposition, whose votes were eventually needed to pass the requisite constitutional amendments and whose participation was necessary to assure broad public support for the new armed forces. A few Members saw defense policy as a specialty on which they could build their parliamentary careers. The members of the Security Committee were, as a group, anxious to establish the committee's influence over the Defense Ministry. *Land* Governments wanted to assure their influence on defense administration. This combination of factors, which contributed to the unusual influence which Parliament had on the Volunteers Bill, was undoubtedly unique. At the same time, it demonstrates the range of sources on which parliamentary influence in the legislative process depends.

The Federal Requisitions Bill

The Federal Requisitions Bill, by comparison, although extensively altered in the committee stage, remained basically intact. The Interior Committee considered the complex measure in no less than fifteen sessions, beginning on January 18, 1956, nine weeks after the first reading, and ending on June 7. Of the committee's dozen CDU/CSU members, seven attended at least two-thirds of these sessions, as did four of its seven SPD members. On the average, fifteen Members, thirteen representatives of the Government, and one representative of the Bundesrat attended all or part of each meeting. The bill was also considered in five sessions of the Judiciary Committee and, at its request, by the Committee on Economic Affairs in one session. On March 19, Minister Schröder wrote to the chairman of the Interior Committee, an SPD Member, urgently requesting the conclusion of the committee's work. Although the chairman responded that it was the Judiciary Committee which was holding up the bill, the Interior Committee did not finish with it until two and a half months later and found itself at the end under considerable pressure of time.

Since the bill was highly technical, and the questions raised by it numerous and complex, little consultation between committee members and their party leaders was required in the course of committee deliberations; nevertheless committee sessions were recessed twice so that CDU/CSU Members could consult with their working group.

An SPD Member, Hermann Schmitt-Vockenhausen, a publisher in his first term in the House who had already been very active in the committee and had previously had charge of a similar measure, was appointed reporter for the bill. In the detailed consideration of every article, through two readings, the reporter took the initiative in proposing amendments whose general purpose was to restrict Government power under the measure. This had been the party's announced intent, expressed in the first reading debate.

In proposing changes, Schmitt drew on the criticisms of the bill advanced by the Bundesrat and on twenty detailed proposals submitted in writing by interest groups. These ranged all the way from proposals of the German Language Association, which suggested grammatical improvements in the bill, to the German Conservation Group, anxious about the damage to nature which army maneuvers might cause, and to proposals made by individuals, none of whom had, of course, been consulted by the ministry in preparing its bill. They also included demands of major interest groups, including the Federation of German Industry, the German Bar Association, and the German Farmers Association, which had been consulted by the drafting ministry, but which had not been fully satisfied. The usual technique, employed by Schmitt, but also by Members of the governing parties, was to attempt to persuade the committee to accept a change in the bill in principle, and then to request officials of the Interior Ministry to formulate the appropriate legal text. The officials served in this capacity, but they also played an active part in the deliberations, defending the Government draft against proposed changes.

The Judiciary Committee called a professor of law to submit an expert opinion on the provisions of the bill regarding compensation for damages to property; he convinced the committee that the Government draft was adequate in this respect.

In general, interest groups were anxious to protect their members by restricting or precluding the Government's power to requisition the type of property which they owned, or by obtaining a guarantee of adequate compensation. The narrow demands of small groups were less successful than more general demands of national associations. The Hotel Association, for example, was unsuccessful in excluding hotels from the scope of the bill, although the Bundesrat had supported this demand and the Government had, by an oversight, accepted the Bundesrat's formulation. Now the Government's argument prevailed, that the right to requisition hotels might avoid the need to requisition private dwellings.[178] On the other hand, the committee accepted the demand of the Federation of German Industry to insert a clause prohibiting the requisition of property which was indispensable to the running of a business. It partially followed the recommendation of the Bar Association that a requisition order should be limited in time and should lapse after one month; the committee settled for a three-month period. The request of the Conservation Association produced a clause protecting certain conservation areas from maneuvers. On the other hand, efforts of the Association of Insurance Companies to preclude the liability of private insurance companies for damages incidental to requisitions were rejected, as was the request of the Merchant Shipping Association that the law take account of the international obligations of shipping companies and therefore limit the Government's powers over them.

Schmitt-Vockenhausen successfully moved one change which was inspired by the Ministry of the Interior, whose view on the matter had lost out in the Cabinet decision on the bill.[179] As it stood, the bill provided that compensation for damages would be set by Government agencies to be determined by executive order. The Finance Ministry favored this version, expecting that it would be assigned the task of assessing damages. It defended the proposition that compensation should not be determined by the requisitioning ministry. The Interior Ministry, on the other hand, wanted the task assigned to itself, for the sake of unified administration, and wanted the bill to state this specifically. A CDU spokesman supported the Finance Ministry's view, while the position of the Interior Ministry had the support of the Federation of German Industry, which had constant and close dealings with that

[178] Protokoll des Ausschusses für Angelegenheiten der inneren Verwaltung, 2. W.P., no. 83.

[179] Ibid., no. 83.

ministry. The Interior Ministry's representative in the committee declared, according to the record of the committee, that

he did not want to arouse the impression that he was not willing to defend the Government bill. On the other hand, if the one-sided view of one Ministry were presented to defend the Government bill, he had to represent the contrary views of another ministry. The position of the Finance Ministry had been supported with arguments which the Ministry of the Interior had conceded only under pressure of time. It had contented itself, during the deliberations on the Federal Requisitions Bill (within the Government) . . . with not carrying the controversy any further, since it felt that Cabinet approval of the bill was more important than the settlement of a dispute among the ministries. But one could not say that the Ministry of the Interior had therefore lost some kind of vote.[180]

In another case, Schmitt-Vockenhausen, with the support of the FDP Members, successfully moved the elimination of a clause which the Defense Ministry had insisted upon, but which the Agriculture Department opposed, giving the Government the power to order agricultural enterprises to produce or store particular products.[181] He failed, however, to eliminate a similar clause applying to businesses in the field of transportation, meeting opposition from Members of all parties, including his own.[182]

Regarding the Bundesrat's proposal designed to assure that the *Länder* would administer the bill, the committee formulated a compromise whereby federal administration was limited to a few areas, with the remaining areas left to *Land* administration, though subject to federal control. It added a clause requiring all administration of the bill to be in the hands of civilian agencies. All told, the committee was strongly inclined to accept those revisions proposed by the Bundesrat to protect private property. Some of these corresponded to recommendations made by interest groups. Among the fourteen major recommendations of this kind made by the second chamber, to which the Government had objected, the committee followed ten entirely and four in part; it rejected none of them.

The general purposes for which requisitions might be made under the bill had been formulated in such sweeping terms that the Bundesrat had found them unconstitutional. They encountered the same opposition from the members of the Judiciary Committee of the Bundestag, regardless of their party. The opening provisions of the bill

[180] *Ibid.,* no. 84, pp. 18–19.   [181] *Ibid.,* no. 58.   [182] *Ibid.,* no. 69.

were therefore sharply qualified in the committee version. Further-more, on the proposal of the committee reporter, a provision was added to exempt political parties and labor unions from the organiza-tions subject to requisition.

Altogether, only twenty-five of the eighty-eight paragraphs in the bill reported out by the committee corresponded exactly to the Gov-ernment's draft. A multitude of major and minor changes, some among them the result of further review on the part of the Government itself, left the general purpose and structure of the Government bill intact, but greatly restricted the powers it provided and substantially strengthened the rights of the citizen under its provisions. In effect, the committee had arbitrated among the demands of special interests, tending to reject the most specific and to accept the more general, had restored those Bundesrat proposals which the Government opposed, had abitrated in three instances among the views of different minis-tries in the Government, and had added one or two proposals ad-vanced by one or more of the parliamentary parties. The process had required the painstaking work of the committee reporter, whose gener-ally conscientious committee work earned him the chairmanship when it fell vacant four years later. The work of specialists on the bill belonging to the other parties, and the cooperation of the Govern-ment's officials, also contributed significantly to the result.

The Bill on Lawyers' Fees

The bill to revise the Federal Schedule of Lawyers' Fees, which had received no debate at the first reading after the parliamentary parties had decided that it was a technical measure which did not raise partisan issues, received professional attention in the Judiciary Com-mittee, to which it was referred. More than half the members of the committee were practicing attorneys, and one of these was appointed reporter for the bill. The committee also included the vice-president of the German Bar Association.

The association, in a formal resolution officially communicated to the committee, had protested the scale of fees which the Government bill provided and had proposed one which would have required doubling the annual appropriation for this purpose in the budgets of the *Land* Governments, which bear the main cost.[183] The committee

[183] *Anwaltsblatt*, 1960, p. 154. Protokoll des Rechtsausschusses, 3. W.P., no. 140, app. 1 and 2.

immediately determined that it would have to negotiate a compromise between the demands of the lawyers' associations for a higher schedule of fees, and the position adopted by the Bundesrat, reflecting the scale of fees agreed on by the ministers of Justice of the *Länder*. Meeting for the first time on the bill in November, 1960, the committee decided to invite representatives of the Bundesrat to discuss the matter. They, in turn, had to consult the ministers of Finance of the *Länder*, and were not able to appear in the committee as authorized negotiators on behalf of the *Land* Governments until March of the following year. In a single all-day committee session at that time, the necessary compromise between the *Land* Governments and the legal profession was worked out. The chief participants in the discussion were four members of the Judiciary Committee of the Bundesrat, a representative of the Federal Ministry of Justice, and five members of the Judiciary Committee of the Bundestag, all five being attorneys and all supporting the views of the Bar Association regardless of their party affiliation. Altogether, sixteen Members of the Bundestag, six representatives of the Bundesrat, and twenty-two officials of the Federal Ministry of Justice were present at one time or another during the session.

The *Land* representatives implied that if the Bundestag committee decided on too high a scale, the second chamber would reject it and call for negotiations through the Mediation Committee, possibly making any settlement impossible within the four months remaining in the parliamentary term. After several hours of intense bargaining, and a close vote, a settlement was reached with technical assistance provided by the representative of the Federal Ministry of Justice.[184] A scale approximately 50 per cent higher than that in the Government draft was written into the bill, roughly splitting the difference between the original version and the demands of the Bar Association.[185]

The Child Benefits Bill

The bill on child benefits was a partisan measure. The Government had solicited the approval of the CDU/CSU caucus in advance of its introduction. It had been drafted in close consultation with party specialists on social policy. Accordingly, the majority party kept it under close control throughout the committee stage. There was fre-

---

[184] Protokoll des Rechtsausschusses, 3. W.P., no. 140.
[185] *Dt. Btag.*, 3. W.P., Drs. 2616.

quent consultation between CDU/CSU committee members and the parliamentary party's working group on social policy. The Opposition in the committee, consisting of its SPD and FDP members, was regularly outvoted. The majority accepted proposed changes only when it was convinced that they improved the measure technically. Members' attendance was high throughout the six sessions of the committee. On the average, twenty-three Members, nine representatives of the Government, and one representative of the Bundesrat attended all or part of each meeting.

Two issues dominated the deliberations. First, the Government bill provided payments for second children only for families with incomes below DM 6600 ($1,650) annually. The argument was that families with higher incomes were receiving comparable government assistance through income tax deductions for dependents. The Opposition wanted the income limit eliminated. Second, the Government bill provided that these payments would be administered by the Federal Employment Office instead of by the Family Equalization Payment agencies which, under previous legislation, administered payments for third and subsequent children. The labor unions and the SPD opposed using the Federal Employment Office for a task alien to it, fearing that its original functions might suffer. The FDP wanted a unified administration of the whole child payments program, in the hands of *Land* Finance agencies. The Government argued that its proposal was strictly transitional, pending a unified administrative solution, and that it was economical since the Federal Employment Office had, under conditions of full employment, little else to do.

Six days after the bill had received its first reading on April 19, the Committee on Social Policy met to hear expert testimony from representatives of the Family Equalization Payment agencies and of the Federal Employment Office. The former testified briefly that the agencies could not possibly handle the great additional burden of payments to second children. The latter spoke at length of the administrative problems involved. The office had at first resisted the efforts of the Ministry of Labor to assign it this new task, and negotiations between the two had been carried on at arm's length.[186] Convinced now that it would not be able to avoid its new responsibilities, the staff

---

[186] Letter from the executive committee of the Federal Employment Office to Minister of Labor Blank, dated February 14, 1961, and Blank's reply of April 13, 1961, Protokoll des Ausschusses für Sozialpolitik, 3. W.P., no. 106.

director of the office made a series of ten detailed recommendations for changes in the law from the point of view of rational administration. Nine of them were accepted by the CDU/CSU members of the committee, who moved the necessary amendments. The federal office which would administer the provisions of the bill was playing the role of reviewing its administrative provisions which the Bundesrat often plays on measures to be administered by the *Länder*. On this bill, the Bundesrat's recommendations—except for those technical ones accepted by the Government—were not followed by the Bundestag committee.

After hearing testimony, the committee did not meet again until June 7; but it then completed its consideration of the bill, giving it two readings in five meetings within two weeks. Although an SPD Member was chairman of the committee, it was clear at once that the CDU was in control. A CDU reporter was appointed on a motion by the CDU deputy chairman of the committee. The motion of an FDP Member that his party's proposed bill on child payments be taken as the basis of discussion was defeated. When the chairman suggested that a general discussion of the bill should precede any votes on it, and that two readings should then follow, he was overruled by the CDU deputy chairman who stressed the urgency of passing the bill before the end of the parliamentary term.

Seventeen interest groups had submitted proposed changes in the bill. These ranged from a number of Catholic family associations, to taxpayers associations, the German Trade Union Federation, the German Farmers Association, and the Federation of German Employers' Associations. Since the Government had carried on extensive negotiations with interest groups at the drafting stage, the CDU majority was unwilling to reopen consideration of any of their demands at this stage, and in only one or two minor instances was the bill altered to meet a request by one of them.

The number of changes made by the committee, on the initiative of its CDU majority, was high, affecting twenty-seven of the bill's forty-six paragraphs, but most of them were administrative improvements proposed by the representatives of the Federal Employment Office. One of the two most important substantive changes raised the income limit, above which families were not entitled to benefits, by DM 600 ($150) annually, mainly for technical reasons of taxation.[187] The other,

---

[187] *DZ*, June 7, 1961.

moved by the CDU to meet an SPD criticism on a sensitive point, assured orphans receiving public support of benefit payments. Together, these changes added DM 116 million ($29 million) to the DM 500 million ($125 million) estimated annual cost of the program. The Appropriations Committee, which had previously included the lower sum in its budget, met once more after the Committee on Social Policy had completed its work, to approve the increase. SPD criticisms of details of the bill were implemented by the majority in four or five other instances, by textual changes or authoritative interpretations included in the committee report. Additional technical changes were made at the request of the Government, resulting from its further study of the measure and, in one case, at the suggestion of the Bundestag Labor Committee, which the Social Policy Committee had consulted.[188]

But on the whole, the bill passed through the committee stage without any important policy changes. This was the result of effective leadership and discipline by the majority party, admittedly on a matter of immediate interest to itself. Passage of the bill would bring benefit payments to nearly two million families, beginning with a substantial retroactive payment just before the elections.

SECOND AND THIRD READINGS IN THE BUNDESTAG

The Influence of Committee Experts on their Parties

When the committee has completed its deliberations, and prepared its report, the parliamentary parties make a final determination of the stand they will take during the second and third readings in the House. The party members who have participated in the committee work take the initiative in recommending a position to the working group, which in turn makes a recommendation to the executive committee of the parliamentary party and, upon executive approval, to the party caucus. If the committee members have stayed in effective touch with their party leaders, or if influential leaders are included among them, they have, as the party's specialists on the subject, every chance of obtaining party support for their position.

But lack of communication between committee members and the rest of the party can produce a division of opinion between them. This is a particular peril in committees, notably the Defense Committee,

[188] Protokoll des Ausschusses für Sozialpolitik, 3. W.P., no. 106.

whose sessions are secret. Basic differences of opinion during the 1950's between the SPD's defense specialists, like Erler, Hans Merten, and Helmut Schmidt, and a group of pacifists opposed to German rearmament, whose chief support came from some of the constituency parties, was exacerbated by the presence of the defense specialists on the Defense Committee and the absence of the pacifist group from it. A dramatic example of the perils of poor communication between committee members and outsiders in both major parties occurred in 1962 over a provision in an amendment of the draft law, permitting the Defense Ministry to allow draftees to retain weapons upon their discharge from the armed forces. The provision appears to have been designed to create the potential for a civilian militia, Swiss style. It was originated by both CDU/CSU and SPD Members on the Defense Committee, and received the approval of the entire committee, except for three CDU/CSU Members. These dissidents took the issue to the CDU/CSU caucus, which voted against the provision; the SPD caucus reached the same conclusion. In neither party were the defense experts able to overcome their colleagues' fears that the provision threatened a dangerous proliferation of weapons among the population. A joint CDU/CSU–SPD motion to reverse the committee decision came before the House and was passed after a brief debate, in which two Defense Committee members, Fritz-Rudolf Schultz of the FDP and Paul Bausch of the CDU/CSU, once more defended the committee version, and one, Erler, explained why he now supported the position of the SPD caucus. The vote largely followed committee rather than party lines. But the case was unusual. As Schultz pointed out in the debate, "this . . . House generally follows the decisions of its experts." [189]

The failure of the parliamentary parties to support their committee members occurs more frequently when several committees have participated in the examination of a bill, and have come to different conclusions. In such cases, two sets of experts may contend with each other within a party, or two different interest groups may be in conflict. In the deliberation on the law on peaceful application of atomic energy, for example, SPD members of the Judiciary Committee took a different position on an important paragraph from that of their colleagues on the Atomic Energy Committee. When, after negotiations between them, the view of the latter group finally prevailed, a party

[189] *Dt. Btag.,* 4. W.P., 16. Sitz., Feb. 22, 1962, pp. 491–4.

leader in the Judiciary Committee declared during the third reading debate, in answer to a charge that the party was being inconsistent, that

one should be in the position to accept the better argument. We just happened to hear these better arguments afterwards. Now we believe— and the lawyers of the SPD believe it also—that the version presented by the Atomic Energy Committee offers a better solution [than that which we defended in the Judiciary Committee]. That is why we are giving up our previous position.[190]

In the CDU, this kind of intraparty compromise is usually more difficult to achieve.

The expertise of certain committees is respected, within their juris- diction, in all parties: the Appropriations Committee on expenditure, for example, and the Judiciary Committee on legal and constitutional questions. On the other hand, the recommendations of committees largely composed of Members representing special interests, such as the Agriculture Committee or, until its abolition in the third Bundes- tag, the Committee on Civil Service Law, may be suspect. This is true particularly when these committees have had only a secondary share in the consideration of a bill, and have come up with a recommen- dation different from that reached by the party's Members on the committee having the primary assignment. Furthermore, if the party's team on a committee is one-sidedly composed of interest representa- tives, or if it merely develops a narrow committee viewpoint, it may fail to carry the caucus with it. Because of indifferent participation in committee work by large numbers of Members who give the Bundes- tag only a part of their time, and the strong desire of interest repre- sentatives to be in the right committee at the right time to press their demands, unofficial substitutions of Members for each other occur on a large scale. As a result, the composition of the party team on almost any committee can vary with the subject matter under consideration, and is often less representative of the party than it appears to be from the official list of committee assignments. Even without substitutions of this kind, absenteeism often leaves committee work in the effective control of those Members with a special interest in the subject.[191]

But only in extreme cases can the parliamentary parties afford to repudiate the recommendations of their committee members. Ordinar-

---

[190] Dt. Btag., 3. W.P., 92. Sitz., Dec. 3, 1959, p. 5040.
[191] SZ, July 9, 1957; Der Spiegel, XIII, (June 17, 1959). See also p. 200, supra.

ily they are hesitant to challenge their experts, and particularly reluctant to vote down in public what these have negotiated in private. The parties cannot readily escape specialist leadership, which is frequently the leadership not even of all party Members belonging to a committee, but of a smaller, more narrowly specialized group which has actively participated in committee work in the particular case. The specialized committee system of the Bundestag has thus produced its counterpart within the parliamentary parties, greatly restricting their ability to function as agencies for the integration of special interests. The heterogeneous composition of the CDU/CSU makes that party especially vulnerable to interest-group influence, although its position as a governing party has so far provided an integrating counterbalance to its fissiparous tendencies.

Second Reading Procedure

The second and third reading debates receive the same amount of party planning, and the same degree of arrangement among the parties' parliamentary whips, as does the first reading. The parties may forego a debate at this point, though this is less likely than at first reading. Procedurally, the committee report and the committee version of the bill are before the House. The committee report is usually presented in writing; but the reporter, having the right to speak at any time, may add some oral remarks. If a bill has been referred to several committees, the one which was placed in charge reports, after having heard the recommendations of the others.[192] When bills entail expenditures, however, the Appropriations Committee gives its own report on them separately.

The second reading debate is devoted to the discussion of the individual paragraphs of the bill although it is often prefaced by a general debate. At this stage, any Member may introduce amendments to any section. The discussion of each section is followed by a vote, generally taken by a show of hands.[193] If a presiding officer and the two Secretaries do not unanimously agree on the result, the House is counted, all Members leaving the chamber and being tallied as they re-enter through doors marked "Yes," "No," or "Abstain." [194] During a second reading, votes are frequent on the detailed issues posed by the various paragraphs of a bill. In the front rows of each party's block of seats in the chamber, its experts on the subject follow the proceedings

---

[192] *Geschäftsordnung des Deutschen Bundestages,* pars. 33(2), 74.
[193] *Ibid.,* pars. 80, 81.   [194] *Ibid.,* pars. 54, 56.

carefully, and signal the party vote to their followers on the back-benches.

The amendments to bills offered during the second reading have many sources. Groups outvoted in committee may wish to publicize their stand on aspects of the measure by means of amendments, even if these have no hope of success. Divergent views within a party may find expression in the introduction of various amendments which test the support which the contending views attract. Occasionally, the majority may introduce amendments to overrule decisions taken by its Members in committees, to right committee decisions which went against the majority because of absences among its Members, or to take account of a change of mind in the Government. In the course of the second reading, the bill may therefore undergo changes, which, drawn up in print, form the basis of the third reading.[195]

Third Reading Procedure

If a bill has passed the second reading unchanged, the third follows immediately. Otherwise, the Rules provide an interval of one full day following the distribution of the printed version of the second reading changes. To avoid this delay, the majority sometimes saves its amendments for the third reading. But this interval may be skipped in any case unless ten or more Members object, and frequently the parliamentary whips, for the sake of convenience, arrange to skip it.[196] A final opportunity to amend a bill exists in third reading, but amendments at that point require the signature of as many Members as are needed to make up an officially recognized parliamentary caucus—at present fifteen.[197] The chief purpose of the third reading is to perfect the bill and to permit the parties to express their general view on it in its final form. But since a general debate may occur in the second reading and amendments may be saved for the third, the distinction between a stage for making detailed changes and one for taking a general view of the entire measure has been lost—another victim of "managed procedure."

Voting

Upon completion of the third reading, the final vote on the bill takes place. It is a rising vote.[198] A vote by ballot may take place at any stage

[195] *Ibid.*, par. 84.   [196] *Ibid.*, pars. 85, 93. See also p. 212, *supra.*
[197] *Ibid.*, par. 86.   [198] *Ibid.*, par. 54.

in the legislative process, if fifty Members demand it.[199] Under this procedure, each Member deposits in the ballot box a voting card bearing his name and "Yes," "No," or "I Abstain." The recorded vote is printed in the stenographic report of the session. The "management" of procedure, however, has tended to produce agreements to avoid recorded votes which would publicize divisions or abstentions within parties, or which for other reasons would embarrass the Members and, incidentally, complicate the task of the whips. Only when a party hopes for political gain by exposing the contrast between its position and that of the others, or hopes to win allies in other parties by compelling Members to honor election promises or interest-group commitments, does it demand a recorded vote. In the first Bundestag, during the year and a half following the introduction of the present rules on voting, 130 votes were taken by ballot; in the four-year period of the second Bundestag, there were 167; in the third term, there were only 46; and in the fourth, only 38.

Party Discipline

The emphasis on party discipline in the expression of opinion in debate and in voting varies somewhat among the different parties. But the feeling that a self-respecting party must appear united in public is strong in all of them. Conspicuous voting discipline already existed in the Imperial Reichstag, particularly on the left.[200] Less united, the lib-

[199] *Ibid.*, par. 57.

[200] A summary of 21 recorded votes between November 28, 1905, and May 18, 1906, indicates the number of times each of the parties exhibited perfect voting discipline, and the number of times they experienced division:

Party	Number of votes indicating perfect discipline	division
SPD	21	0
Deutsche Volkspartei	20	1
Polen	20	1
Freisinnige Vereinigung	19	2
Reformpartei	18	3
Freisinnige Volkspartei	18	3
Reichspartei	15	6
Nationalliberale	9	12
Wirtschaftliche Vereinigung	9	12
Deutschkonservative	9	12
Zentrum	2	19

Cited by Hellmuth von Gerlach, *Das Parlament* (Frankfurt: Rütten und Loening, 1907), pp. 34–40.

erals and the right-wing parties expressed pride that they lacked what they regarded as the coerced discipline of their competitors. The major parties today attempt to combine a high degree of unity in the speaking and voting of their Members with the denial that sanctions are employed. In the defense debate on the motion to reject the committee recommendation on arms for discharged draftees, a CDU Member opened his remarks with the assertion that he was "very glad to belong to a parliamentary party, which knows no party discipline (*Fraktionszwang*)." An SPD speaker countered immediately that "we are all proud to belong to a Bundestag, in which no party exercises compulsion over the convictions (*Gesinnungszwang*) of its Members."[201] Nevertheless, each parliamentary party has formal rules of procedure which suggest that it attempts to discipline the expression of its Members' views. The rules of the CDU/CSU in the Bundestag include the provision that

Members who have misgivings about accepting the decision of the majority [of the parliamentary party] are in every case obliged to express their divergent viewpoint promptly to the caucus and its chairman.[202]

The rules of the SPD state that

the party appoints the speakers who are to support its position in the plenary sessions [of the Bundestag].

If a member of the party wishes to participate in a debate, he must clear it with (*so verständigt er sich darüber mit*) the party foreman of the relevant committee, and the parliamentary whip.[203]

In attempting to obtain a unified position among its Members, each party employs a variety of organizational and ideological instruments. On most legislative questions, the role of the party members on the relevant Bundestag committees is crucial. If they are not agreed among themselves, or if their view is so out of touch with the party that the caucus will repudiate it altogether, the ability of the parliamentary party to find a position which all of its Members are willing to support is seriously impaired. Otherwise, the view of the experts commands general support. In the FDP, with its background of traditional liberal disunity, and in the CDU/CSU, with its complex sub-

---

[201] *Dt. Btag.*, 4. W.P., 16. Sitz., Feb. 22, 1962, pp. 493–4.
[202] *Arbeitsordnung der CDU/CSU Bundestagsfraktion*, 2. Bundestag (mimeographed, n.d.), par. 10(2).
[203] *Geschäftsordnung der Fraktion der SPD im Bundestag* (n.d.), pars. 2, 3.

structure of religious, social, and economic groups, some party division is frequently expressed in the second and third reading debates, and in the final vote. In the SPD, with its background of ideological commitment and loyalty to class, a unified position is more often achieved, if necessary by negotiation between working groups and the executive committee. If division persists nevertheless, as it did for many years on defense issues, Members unwilling to accept the majority view in the party may either absent themselves from the session of the House in which the issue comes up, or abstain in the vote; only rarely will an SPD Member go so far as to vote against his party's position, and the inhibition about speaking against it in debate is even stronger.[204]

Because of the sparse use of recorded votes, statistical analysis of the voting records of Members of the Bundestag is of only limited significance as an index of party cohesion. The high degree of voting unity which the statistics reveal undoubtedly exaggerates party cohesion, since the parties are most anxious to appear united when they go on record. Moreover, on a high proportion of bills passed by the House, though not usually the most important ones from the point of view of policy making, a compromise has been achieved among the parties, and they are therefore not partisan issues in the vote on enactment.[205] Nevertheless, the contrast in the degree of voting unity among the parties, in cases where ballots are taken, probably indicates at least their relative cohesion. (See Table 33.)

During the first three parliamentary terms, voting unity in the SPD approached perfection. Subsequently, there was some relaxation of the effort to cast the party's vote en bloc, in part because the most

[204] On the sources of party cohesion, see also pp. 170–75, 184–8, 190–91, *supra*.

[205] In an analysis of 546 votes in the first Bundestag on the final enactment of bills, Neunreither found that the SPD voted in opposition only 14.1 per cent of the time, abstained 2.0 per cent, and voted for passage in 83.9 per cent of the cases. However, in distinguishing among four categories of bills according to their importance, he found the SPD voted against 57.8 per cent of the most important bills, and 37.4 per cent of those in the next category of importance. But these two categories accounted for only 72 of the 546 bills studied (Kralewski und Neunreither, *op. cit.*, pp. 80–93). The tendency of the SPD to vote affirmatively on the final passage of bills grew even stronger in subsequent years. A count of laws published in part 1 of the *Federal Statutes* (*BGBl.*), which contains all the more important enactments, shows the SPD voting "yes" on 89 per cent of the 208 measures passed in 1960–61, and on 91 per cent of the 149 measures passed in 1962–63. The enumeration is given in the party yearbooks, *Jahrbuch der Sozialdemokratischen Partei Deutschlands, 1960/61* (Bonn: Neuer Vorwärts Verlag, 1962), pp. 191–200; *ibid., 1962/63*, pp. 180–89.

dangerously divisive issue for the party, that of rearmament, had passed; and in part because the party wished to appeal to a greater variety of interests by demonstrating that it had room for diversity. In 1962, for example, the SPD caucus permitted its members to vote their local interests in a vote on automobile tariffs.[206] For the SPD, this was a new departure, and some old-timers regarded it as another sign of the party's s'embourgeoisement.

Table 33. Party unity in Bundestag voting (per cent of Members voting with the plurality of the Members of their parliamentary party in recorded votes)

Party	1st Bundestag 1949–1953, 130 votes	2nd Bundestag 1953–1957, 155 votes	3rd Bundestag 1957–1961, 46 votes
CDU/CSU	93.6	95.0	97.0
SPD	99.9	99.7	99.8
FDP	91.3	89.5	96.3
DP	89.8	90.2	94.0

Sources: Information on voting during the 1st Bundestag taken from Heinz Markmann, Das Abstimmungsverhalten der Parteifraktionen in deutschen Parlamenten (Meisenheim am Glan: Anton Hain Verlag, 1955), pp. 142–45. Voting information for the 2nd Bundestag taken from So haben sie Abgestimmt, Register und Tabellen der namentlichen Abstimmungen im Bundestag (2. Wahlperiode) 1953–1957 (Bonn: Vorstand der SPD, 1957). The final twelve roll call votes taken during this term are not included. Voting information on the 3rd Bundestag taken from the official stenographic reports of the Bundestag. Only Members serving during the entire term are included.

In the CDU/CSU, on the other hand, voting discipline has gradually increased. The divisive tendencies in a party composed of such diverse interests made the achievement of voting unity a matter of serious importance, even while the party boasted about the freedom it permitted its Members. Patterns of voting deviation in the CDU/CSU have clearly reflected its regional, occupational, and religious differences. Voting deviation by groups within the party tends to vary inversely with their influence. The dominant groups show loyalty to the positions which they are obviously influential in determining; the

[206] Dt. Btag., 4. W.P., 32. Sitz., May 22, 1962, pp. 1351–2.

Table 34. CDU/CSU voting deviation, 1957–1961 [a]

	Per cent of CDU/CSU Bundestag Members in categories at left		
	No deviations from party majority shown in voting	*1–3 deviations from party majority shown in voting*	*4 or more deviations from party majority shown in voting*
A. *By issues (all CDU/CSU Members)*			
Foreign policy (7 votes)	98.9	1.1	
Civil Service salaries (2 votes)	98.2	1.8	
Foreign trade (2 votes)	96.0	4.0	
Social expenditure (9 votes)	90.2	9.8	
Agricultural policy (4 votes)	88.8	13.2	
Social policy (12 votes)	82.3	17.3	0.4
B. *By Parliamentary Position of Members*			
All CDU/CSU members (*n* = 278)	46.7	46.8	6.5
CDU only (*n* = 223)	48.9	45.7	5.4
CSU only (*n* = 55)	38.2	50.9	10.9
Committee chairmen or deputy chairmen (*n* = 26)	57.8	42.2	
Leaders in parliamentary party [b] (*n* = 41)	58.6	39.0	2.4
Members of Cabinet (*n* = 16)	93.9	6.1	
C. *By Background*			
Members holding local elective office (*n* = 83)	37.3	56.7	6.0
Members according to present private occupations			
Business (*n* = 55)	49.1	49.1	1.8
Agriculture (*n* = 40)	30.0	67.5	2.5
Skilled worker (*n* = 7)	28.6	57.1	14.3
Professional (*n* = 50)	52.0	40.0	8.0
Members according to present public occupations			
Party employees (*n* = 14)	57.2	35.6	7.2
Interest group employees (*n* = 39)	46.2	48.8	5.0
Government employees (*n* = 28)	35.7	46.4	17.9

Table 34 (continued).

	Per cent of CDU/CSU Bundestag Members in categories at left		
	No deviations from party majority shown in voting	*1–3 deviations from party majority shown in voting*	*4 or more deviations from party majority shown in voting*
Members according to position in party outside Bundestag			
Member, Fed. Executive Committee (n = 32)	78.1	18.7	3.2
Member, *Land* Executive Committee (n = 29)	41.4	51.8	6.8
Member, other party committee (n = 40)	52.5	45.0	2.5
Members according to interest group membership			
Business (n = 32)	53.0	43.7	3.3
Agriculture (n = 32)	35.4	64.6	
Trade union (n = 20)	50.0	40.0	10.0
Church (n = 14)	35.7	64.3	
Members according to religious affiliation			
Catholic (n = 169)	52.1	41.4	6.5
Protestant (n = 108)	38.9	54.6	6.5

[a] On the basis of the 46 recorded votes taken during the 3rd Bundestag. For source, see Table 33.

[b] For definition, see Table 18.

smaller groups show the highest tendency to deviate. Occupationally, Members with business and professional backgrounds vote the party line more regularly than those with backgrounds in agriculture or skilled trades; the same pattern exists when voting records are examined by interest-group membership. Regionally, members of the Bavarian wing of the party, the CSU, show above-average voting deviation, as do Protestant Members, when comparison is made by the religious affiliation of Representatives. Party leaders in the Bundestag, and, to an even greater extent, the members of the Government, show a higher allegiance to the party position than do backbenchers. Members holding local elective office, with responsibilities to their local constituencies, deviate more frequently than the average; local party leaders depart from the party line to a greater extent than national party leaders. The evidence for these generalizations from the Bundestag of 1957–1961 is extremely limited (see Table 34, secs. B, C), but it bears out the pattern established in previous sessions.[207]

Although its voting unity is very high on the average, the CDU/CSU cannot carry all of its Members with it when the issues affect their group interests. On foreign policy, the party was entirely united throughout the Adenauer era. On social policy, it regularly suffered its greatest divisions. (See Table 34, sec. A.) As a result, social policy was the area in which it became increasingly difficult to pass legislation. On these matters, there was always the peril that the party's labor group would vote with the SPD, and that its Protestant Members would vote with the FDP. The divisions within the major governing party thus set limits to Government legislation on a major domestic subject.

The voting cohesion of the Members of the Bundestag is partly the product of German party history, of the class basis of the parties, the ideological content of their original programs, their interest-group composition, and their voters' expectations of clear positions. The persistence of a high level of party unity, into a time when old ideological and class ties are weakening and multiple-interest parties are the rule, is above all a consequence of the high degree of party organization, which permits the parties to negotiate their internal differences in private and to reach a caucus decision which its Members are willing to support solidly in public. If the voting pattern is analyzed by types of Members, the professional politicians show by far the highest party unity, the interest representatives the lowest. (See Table 35.) The task of the professionals, who make up a large part of the parliamentary leadership and whose chief interest is in the party, is to serve as brokers among Members with a variety of private interests, in order to negotiate compromises on which they can all unite. The record testifies to their success. The outcome of the vote is nearly always a foregone conclusion, the result, like much of the rest of the public phase of the legislative process, of those of its phases which

[207] For a study of CDU voting in the Bundestag between 1953 and 1957, see G. L. Rueckert and Wilder Crane, "CDU Deviance in the German Bundestag," *The Journal of Politics*, XXIV (1962), 477–88.

Table 35. *Voting deviations by types of Members, 1957–1961* [a]

	Per cent of Bundestag Members in categories at left		
Types	No deviations from party majority shown in voting	1–3 deviations from party majority shown in voting	4 or more deviations from party majority shown in voting
Interest representatives (n = 158)	54.5	42.4	3.1
Members with part-time private occupations (n = 166)	57.7	39.2	3.1
Public employees (n = 49)	59.1	30.7	6.2
Professional politicians (n = 118)	72.9	24.6	2.5

[a] On the basis of the 46 recorded votes taken during the 3rd Bundestag. For explanation of types of Members, see pp. 121-8, *supra*. For source, see Table 33.

take place in private. The case studies illustrate how the second and third readings are primarily stages, not of decision, but of exposition, and sometimes not even that.

The Volunteers Bill

Just before the Volunteers Bill came before the Bundestag for a second and third reading, the special bill creating a Personnel Commission passed these stages, in accordance with the agreement which had been reached in the Security Committee. An effort to keep the debate on this bill brief failed when a speaker of the German party explained his opposition to the measure in some detail. The overtones of militarism in his speech provoked speakers of the other parties to rebuttal, especially the Free Democrats, who were particularly sensitive to indications that the party to their immediate right might try to outbid them in appeals to national traditions. The bill passed both readings unchanged, with CDU/CSU, FDP, and SPD support, in a rising vote. The composition of the commission, previously agreed on by all parties, received formal parliamentary approval, as the bill required, immediately thereafter.[208]

The debate, which lasted nearly two hours, was the overture to the

[208] *Dt. Btag.*, 2. W.P., 99. Sitz., July 15, 1955, pp. 5528-40.

second reading debate on the Volunteers Bill. To a considerable extent, the earlier debate had discharged the atmosphere. Furthermore, the committee work on the Volunteers Bill, which had taken place relatively openly, and had just been completed, had already made it possible to articulate the major viewpoints adequately. The second reading of the bill was therefore an anticlimax. With one exception, the speakers were the same Members who had actively participated in the committee stage. Conspicuously, no member of the Government spoke. The arguments, familiar through newspaper reports of the committee deliberations, had been amply heard in the previous weeks. The divisions on the bill now followed party lines. Whatever differences there had been among the members of the CDU/CSU were subordinated to support for the measure before the House. Each paragraph was considered in turn and adopted unchanged, in most cases against SPD opposition.[209]

The third reading took place the following day, in the last session of the Bundestag before its summer recess. In a four-hour series of long speeches, leading speakers of the parties justified their positions on the bill before its final passage. But the debate went beyond the bill at issue, to consider the general questions of defense and foreign policy which had been the background for the deliberations all along. The Minister of Defense addressed himself to the results of the most recent NATO maneuvers, and was subjected to a long reply from an SPD Member most strongly identified with the opposition to rearmament. Thereupon, Strauss, then minister in charge of questions of atomic energy, joined the debate with the longest speech of the day, in which Germany's participation in the defense of Europe received its most persuasive justification. The minister, whose personal ambitions had been among the factors determining the fate of the Volunteers Bill, received an immediate rejoinder from Erler, who taunted him on his participation in a debate outside his formal ministerial jurisdiction. In this way, the third reading debate gave a preview of both the issues and the men who were to dominate German defense and foreign policy in the immediate future. The bill was passed by a standing vote. The conspicuous part which the Bundestag played in the passage of the legislation which initiated German rearmament attracted further public interest to parliamentary deliberations on the major defense legislation which followed in the next session. Throughout the next

[209] *Ibid.*, pp. 5540–59.

year, Bundestag debates enjoyed greater public attention than they did for a decade thereafter.

The Federal Requisitions Bill

The Federal Requisitions Bill received its second and third readings on the same day, just short of a month after the final committee meeting on it. Despite the length of the committee's deliberations, the reporter opened the second reading debate with a set of amendments, supported by all parties, which he said were clarifications required by the committee draft, in view of the speed with which it had been completed. One of them answered objections which had been registered by the Economic Affairs Committee of the Bundestag, which was considering a related bill; one further limited the time for which living quarters could be requisitioned; others dealt with the position of Allied armed forces in Germany.

A group of farm-bloc Members belonging to the CDU/CSU and the FDP moved an amendment slightly improving the provisions for compensation applicable to losses incurred indirectly through the withdrawal of farm land for Government use; it passed without debate. A terminological amendment proposed by members of the Judiciary Committee of all parties led to some debate between the mover of the change and the reporter of the bill, who opposed the alteration. It also was adopted. The SPD withdrew an amendment restricting the requisitioning of living quarters, because it corresponded substantially to an amendment already passed.

There was no further debate as every paragraph of the bill was called by number, and votes were taken on each major section of the measure. Despite the changes made in second reading, the third reading followed immediately, by general agreement. A group of CDU/CSU Members, led by a former church official, proposed an amendment to clarify the meaning of the reference in the bill to church organizations, but withdrew most of it on reassurance from all parties that it was unnecessary. The reporter thereupon offered brief remarks, in his capacity as speaker for the SPD, thanking all parties for their cooperation in improving the bill during the committee stage and explaining that the SPD would nevertheless vote against it, because of its opposition to the policy of rearmament to which the bill related. No other general party statements were made. The bill passed by a standing vote. The second and third readings on this complicated and lengthy measure had together taken less than an hour; the committee stage had spanned five months.[210]

The Bill on Lawyers' Fees

The bill on the Federal Schedule of Lawyers' Fees came up for second and third reading six weeks after the decisive committee meeting. There had been no debate in first reading, nor discussion in the party caucuses at any stage. It was regarded as a technical measure to be disposed of by the Judiciary Committee, and so it was. When the presiding officer asked the reporter of the bill whether he had any oral remarks to add to his written report, it turned out that the reporter was not present in the chamber. No one spoke except the presiding officer, who called up the bill's five paragraphs, determined that no amendments were proposed, asked for a show of hands, announced the third reading, saw that there were no requests for recognition, called for a standing vote, and declared that the bill had passed unanimously. The procedure took less than a minute. The Bundestag gave the measure its approval without ever speaking a substantive word on it in public.[211]

The Child Benefits Bill

The bill on child benefits also received its second and third readings, successively, in the same session—it was one of those mammoth sessions shortly before the summer recess. This particular meeting of the House lasted from 9:00 A.M. until 11:10 P.M., and was the third-to-the-last session before the end of the parliamentary term. The bill occupied the House for nearly three hours. The party differences over it had been clear in the committee stage, as had the dominance of the governing party. The same was true in the second and third readings, as the parties endeavored to make their positions public.

In a series of amendments, the SPD and the FDP moved to revise the bill to eliminate the income limit on those eligible for benefits, to assure that the entire child benefits program would eventually be financed by taxation, and to prevent the creation of a separate administration for the payment of benefits for second children. These had been the major issues in the committee discussion. They were rehearsed again in the second reading, in an active interchange among

[210] *Dt. Btag.*, 2. W.P., 158. Sitz., July 5, 1956, pp. 8725–9.
[211] *Dt. Btag.*, 3. W.P., 154. Sitz., April 19, 1961, p. 8882.

the committee members of the various parties. As before, the CDU/CSU majority held firm, rejecting all amendments.

In the third reading, the parties took their final positions on the bill, with even the opposition parties, the FDP and the SPD, explaining why they would support it, in spite of what they regarded as its shortcomings. Ten weeks before the elections no party could afford to vote against a social welfare measure. A single FDP Member explained that he and a colleague (both of them, incidentally, well placed for re-election) felt compelled to vote against the bill. It was adopted in a rising vote, with only four negative votes and two abstentions. Immediately thereafter, the FDP moved a resolution asking the Government to submit a reform of the entire child benefits program by April 1 of the following year; it was defeated.[212]

FINAL PASSAGE IN THE BUNDESRAT AND PROMULGATION

Second Passage Through the Bundesrat

When a bill has passed the Bundestag, whether initiated there or by the Government, it goes to the Bundesrat. For bills initiated in the Bundestag, this is the first and only look which the second chamber gets at the measure; for Government bills, as for bills initiated by the Bundesrat, it is a second passage. In either case, the Bundesrat may approve the measure as passed by the Bundestag, or it may, within two weeks of receiving it, ask for a meeting of the joint Bundestag-Bundesrat Mediation Committee to seek a more acceptable version.[213] On those bills which require Bundesrat approval—about 60 per cent of important measures—the second chamber has an absolute veto. Whether or not it has asked for a meeting of the Mediation Committee, the measure cannot be enacted without Bundesrat approval.[214] On

---

[212] *Dt. Btag.*, 3. W.P., 165. Sitz., June 29, 1961, pp. 9584–9608.

[213] *Basic Law*, art. 77.

[214] The provisions of the Basic Law which determine the subjects on which legislation requires Bundesrat approval are scattered over many sections of the document. Primarily they are subjects affecting the interests of the *Länder*. They include bills altering the territorial boundaries of the *Länder* (art. 29, sec. 7); amendments to the Basic Law, which require a two-thirds vote of the members of both Houses (art. 79, sec. 2); bills passed under conditions of "emergency" (art. 81, secs. 1, 2); bills containing provisions for their administration by *Land* agencies (art. 84, sec. 1); bills permitting the Federal Government to issue administrative orders to the *Länder* (art. 84, sec. 5, and art. 85, sec. 1); bills creating new Federal administrative agencies, at intermediate and subordinate

all others, it may enter a suspensive veto, but only after an effort at compromise through the Mediation Committee has been made. In that case, it must act within one week of Bundestag action on the compromise, or, if no new compromise is proposed by the committee, within one week of the completion of its work. If the Bundesrat enters its objection by a vote of a majority of its members, then the Bundestag can override it by the same majority; if the Bundesrat has entered its objections by a vote of two-thirds of its members, it can only be overridden in the Bundestag by a vote of two-thirds of the Members present, but these two-thirds must also constitute at least a majority of the total membership. If the Bundesrat fails to act within the prescribed time limits, bills which do not specifically require its approval are ready for promulgation.

The decision of the Bundesrat on bills it is considering a second time is largely influenced by its initial position.[215] To the extent that this position has been respected by the Bundestag, the measure is likely to pass the second chamber without question. Where the initial recommendations of the Bundesrat have been ignored, the Bundesrat is likely to press its point at this stage. The influence of the Bundesrat on the Bundestag in the legislative process is strengthened—especially on Government bills—by this ability of the second chamber to take a stand before the bill reaches the Bundestag, and subsequently to press that stand. Its chief instrument at the latter stage in the legislative process is the Mediation Committee, a postwar innovation in Germany which has attained very great importance.

The Mediation Committee

Modeled on the Conference Committee of the United States Congress, the German counterpart is a joint standing committee composed

---

levels, and agencies in certain fields of defense administration (art. 87, sec. 3, and art. 87b, secs. 1 and 2); and, finally, tax laws on tax sources constitutionally assigned to the *Länder,* laws affecting the distribution of the major sources of taxation between the Federation and the *Länder,* laws redistributing tax resources between rich and poor *Länder,* and laws affecting *Land* tax administration (art. 105, sec. 3, art. 106, secs. 4 and 5, art. 107, and art. 108, sec. 3). Half of all laws passed, and 60 per cent of the more important measures, have, under these provisions, been susceptible to Bundesrat veto, three-quarters of them falling into this category because of the provisions of art. 84, sec. 1, which has been responsible for the expansion of the applicability of this absolute veto power far beyond the intention of the framers of the Basic Law (see Neunreither, *op. cit.,* pp. 64–72.)

[215] *Ibid.,* pp. 74–85.

equally of Members of both Houses; its membership does not change with the bill before it, as is the case in Congress. It consists of eleven Members of the Bundesrat, one from each *Land*, and eleven Members of the Bundestag, divided among the parties in proportion to their numbers in the House. Each Member has one alternate. To assure some stability in the Committee's composition, and to avoid its becoming an *ad hoc* committee of specialists on the subject matter before it, each House may recall and exchange one of its Members or alternates on the Committee only four times during a parliamentary term.[216] Bundesrat Members are ministers of *Land* Governments; Bundestag Members tend to be party leaders and important committee chairmen, possessing the authority to persuade their followers to accept the committee's proposals.

The committee meets in secret, usually on the formal request of the Bundesrat. In addition to its members, only ministers of the Federal Government and, rarely, their state secretaries, may attend. In two particularly complex cases, it set up a subcommittee which recruited a few outside experts, but this is very unusual and offends against the basic conception that this is to be a group of generalists rather than specialists. The technical points at issue are usually clarified in advance of the meeting of the committee. On bills over which the second chamber has an absolute veto, the Bundestag and the Federal Government may also call for a meeting of the committee.

The specific provisions of the bill on which a compromise is sought are indicated in the formal call, limiting the committee's jurisdiction. In practice, it addresses itself only to points of dispute between the two Houses, and makes its proposal within the limits of the positions taken by them. Its recommendation is presented first to the Bundestag, by one of the committee members acting as reporter. It must be approved or defeated without amendment or debate, although Members may give explanations of their vote.[217] If voted down, the Bundestag, in effect, insists on its version of the bill. The Bundesrat must then act within a week.

The availability of such a committee of mediation has caused the Bundesrat to refrain from exercising its veto power to block legislation. On the other hand, it has called the committee without regard to

[216] Gemeinsame Geschäftsordnung des Bundestages und des Bundesrates für den Ausschuss nach Artikel 77 des Grundgesetzes (Vermittlungsausschuss) vom 19. April 1951, *BGBl.* II, p. 103, par. 4.

[217] *Ibid.*, par. 10.

whether it has an absolute or a suspensive veto in a particular case, or to whether its objections to a Bundestag bill are based on distinct *Land* interests. During the first four terms of the Bundestag, the committee was called 226 times, 207 of them at the request of the Bundesrat. Over 90 per cent of the bills with which it dealt were ultimately enacted. (See Table 36.) The committee's high rate of success in mediation is due not only to its composition and to the skill of its members, but to the circumstances in which it meets. That it functions at the end of the legislative process and makes recommendations which are not subject to change gives its proposals a compelling character: their rejection by either House is likely to mean the bill's failure.

Beyond its success in achieving compromise, the committee has proven to be an effective instrument of the Bundesrat. The threat of Bundesrat veto hangs over its deliberations, influencing its Bundestag members to compromise in order to produce a measure acceptable to the second chamber. A detailed study of the proposals made by the committee during the first six years of its existence indicates that in one-third of all legislation, it recommended acceptance of the Bundesrat viewpoint; in most other instances, it produced a proposal that lay somewhere between the positions of the two Houses; rarely did it support the Bundestag view.[218] The technical skill available to the Bundesrat members of the committee, who are ministers in their *Land* Government and command ministerial bureaucracies, also contributes to Bundesrat influence within the committee. This influence, plus the delay which the Bundesrat can cause in the legislative process merely by submitting a bill to the committee, strengthens the position of the second chamber even in the earlier stages of legislation. When Bundesrat representatives speak in the committees of the Bundestag, their views are therefore heard with respect.

The Appropriations Veto

When a bill has passed the final parliamentary hurdle in the legislative process, it is presented to the Government. Under Article 113 of the Basic Law, it requires specific Cabinet approval if it entails expenditures in addition to or exceeding those appropriations which the Government has proposed. If the Finance Minister opposes it, the Cabinet can overrule him only if an absolute majority of its members,

[218] Neunreither, *op. cit.*, p. 81.

Table 36. *The legislative decisions of the Bundesrat*

Action on bills	Parliamentary term				Total	Per cent of total
	1949–1953	1953–1957	1957–1961	1961–1965		
No. of bills passed by Bundestag and submitted to Bundesrat	559	518	428	429	1934	100.0
No. accepted by Bundesrat without change	484	456	377	392	1706	88.3
No. defeated because of failure of Bundesrat to approve bills requiring its assent	4	0	2	1	7	0.4
No. on which Mediation Committee was called	71	62	49	36	218	
By Bundesrat [a]	69	59	46	33	207	
By Bundestag [a]	2	3	0	2	7	
By Cabinet [a]	3	3	3	3	12	
Subsequent action on bills on which Mediation Committee was called						
Enacted	62	56	47	34	199	10.3
Withdrawn by Bundestag	4	2	0	0	6	0.3
Subjected to suspensive veto by Bundesrat	1	1	3	0	5	
Veto overridden by Bundestag	0	1	1	0	2	
Suspensive veto sustained	1	0	2	0	3	0.2
Absolute veto by Bundesrat	4	4	0	2	10	0.5
Total no. of bills passed by both Bundestag and Bundesrat	546	512	424	426	1908 [b]	98.6
Total no. of bills defeated by Bundesrat	9	4	4	3	20	1.1
Total no. of bills withdrawn by Bundestag	4	2	0	0	6	0.3

[a] Since the same bill may be submitted to the Mediation Committee more than once, the number of times the Committee was called exceeds the number of bills submitted to it.

[b] Four of these bills were ultimately not promulgated.

Source: Sekretariat des Bundesrates, *16 Jahre Bundesgesetzgebung* (Bonn: Bonner Universitätsbuchdruckerei, 1965).

including the Chancellor, insist.[219] Actually, this provision, designed to give the Government control over the initiation of expenditures, has been employed in only one minor case to veto legislation. In view of the close relationship between Cabinet and parliamentary majority, it is rare that an appropriation passes the Bundestag without at least the tacit assent of the relevant ministers. Should this nevertheless occur, the veto power is a crude instrument, capable of killing a measure at the end of the legislative process, but not of producing a satisfactory compromise during it. Because its use would reveal divisions within the governing majority, and would leave important interests dissatisfied, it has proved to be an unacceptable instrument politically. In practice, the provision is therefore a dead letter, expressing the constitutional theory of a separation of powers which does not correspond with political reality. Its existence encourages those who believe in the superior fiscal responsibility of the Cabinet compared to the Parliament, but their repeated demand that it be used has had no effect except to help obscure the Cabinet's part in the appropriations enacted by the Bundestag.[220]

Promulgation

Except for this provision, a bill which has passed all parliamentary stages requires only formal promulgation by the Government. It is signed by the minister within whose jurisdiction the bill falls, and by the Chancellor, to indicate that the measure has been properly enacted. It then goes to the Federal President for his signature, and is published in the Federal Statutes, completing promulgation. Whether either the Government or the President may refuse to sign a bill which has been properly enacted, because they doubt its constitutionality, is a latent issue which has arisen in only one or two cases of any importance.[221]

The Mediation Committee was called to act on one of the four bills which we have traced through to enactment as case studies, and its recommendation was typically successful. The other three bills passed the final stages unchanged.

[219] *Geschäftsordnung der Bundesregierung*, par. 26.

[220] For a discussion of the adoption of this provision, and early experience with it, see Wilhelm Henrichs, *Artikel 113 des Grundgesetzes* (Schriftenreihe des Instituts "Finanzen und Steuern," no. 55, Bonn, 1958). For more recent experience with it, see n. 23, *supra*.

[221] See p. 275, *supra*.

The Volunteers Bill

In its second consideration of the Volunteers Bill, the Bundesrat decided that its original objections had been substantially met by the revisions of the bill in the Bundestag. The reporter referred to the active participation of representatives of the Bundesrat in the Security Committee of the Bundestag and concluded that "a gratifying understanding between Bundestag and Bundesrat has taken place." [222] The second chamber accepted the bill, against the expressed objection of the representatives of Hesse, whose government was led by the SPD. It next considered the bill on the Personnel Commission, which had originated in the Bundestag and had not previously been discussed in the Bundesrat. Regretting that the bill had not provided for Bundesrat participation in the selection of the commission, and that the Bundestag did not consider the bill itself as requiring Bundesrat approval, the reporter proposed that it should nevertheless receive the approval of the second chamber. [223] Both bills were promulgated on July 23, exactly eight weeks after the Volunteers Bill had first been submitted to the Bundesrat. The bill on the Personnel Commission was promulgated in the form which acknowledged that it required Bundesrat approval, as the second chamber had requested. [224]

The Federal Requisitions Bill

When the Federal Requisitions Bill came before the Bundesrat on July 20, two weeks after its passage in the Bundestag, the second chamber decided, on the urging of its Judiciary and Finance committees, to call the Mediation Committee, although many of the original recommendations of the second chamber had been implemented by the Bundestag. The remaining issue, as stated explicitly in the call, was the provision for the administration of the bill. The Bundesrat preferred the version it had originally proposed, by which administration was placed essentially into the hands of the *Länder* governments, to the compromise version passed by the Bundestag. [225] Since the bill required Bundesrat approval, the position of the second chamber was strong. The Mediation Committee issued its report on Septem-

[222] Bundesrat, *Sitzungsbericht*, 145. Sitz., July 22, 1955, p. 227.
[223] *Ibid.*, pp. 228–9.
[224] *BGBl.* I, pp. 449–51.
[225] *Dt. Btag.*, 2. W.P., Drs. 2639.

ber 14,[226] and it was considered in the Bundestag on September 27. The reporter, a CDU/CSU Member, explained that the committee regarded the Bundesrat proposal as impractical, since it would lead to the creation of eleven different administrations of what was really a national matter. However, the committee proposed an addition to the paragraph in the Bundestag version, providing that the federal executive orders governing the administration of the bill required Bundesrat approval. The reporter regarded this addition as merely a clarification. There was no debate, as the Bundestag approved the committee's recommendation by the same party vote by which it had passed the bill the previous summer.[227] The Bundesrat approved the new version the following week,[228] and the law was promulgated on October 19, sixteen and one-half months after its introduction and nearly four years after the first ministerial draft had been completed.[229]

The Bill on Lawyers' Fees

The bill on the Federal Schedule of Lawyers' Fees passed the Bundesrat two weeks after its undebated acceptance in the Bundestag. Once again, the second chamber insisted that the bill required its approval, not because of its content, but because it was a revision of a measure whose content did subject it to Bundesrat approval.[230] Both the Government and the Bundestag had rejected this argument, and the bill was promulgated in the form used for measures on which the Bundesrat has only a suspensive veto.[231] The bill had taken fourteen months to pass the various stages of the legislative process.

The Child Benefits Bill

The Child Benefits Bill, rushed through by the Bundestag under the influence of the approaching election, received the approval of the second chamber although many of its original recommendations had not been met and its enactment required Bundesrat approval.[232] But partisan considerations were predominant in the second chamber also. The bill was promulgated on July 18, 1961, four months after its

---

[226] *Dt. Btag.*, 2. W.P., Drs. 2686.
[227] *Dt. Btag.*, 2. W.P., 160. Sitz., Sept. 27, 1956, pp. 8900–1.
[228] Bundesrat, *Sitzungsbericht*, 163. Sitz., Oct. 5, 1956, p. 296.
[229] *BGBl.* I, p. 815.
[230] Bundesrat, *Sitzungsbericht*, 232. Sitz., May 5, 1961, p. 106.
[231] *BGBl.* I, p. 769.
[232] Bundesrat, *Sitzungsbericht*, 236. Sitz., July 14, 1961, p. 185.

introduction and less than two months before the parliamentary elections.[233] The first checks of DM 150 ($37.50), covering a retroactive six months' payment, went out in the following months and by election time 600,000 payments had been made; [234] by the end of the year, 1.6 million applications were on hand, and 1.4 million of them had been paid.[235] A year later, rising income levels had already taken 250,000 to 300,000 families out of the eligible group, and a reform of the program was again urgent.[236]

THE APPROPRIATIONS PROCESS

The appropriations for the Federal Government are annually enacted by Parliament in the form of a law. The procedure is entirely parallel to that employed in the enactment of ordinary Government legislation, but the influence which the Bundestag has over expenditure is restricted by the traditional prerogatives which the Government continues to enjoy in this field. Even the appropriations bill, in all other Western democracies regarded as within the special province of the popular House, is submitted first to the Bundesrat, depriving "budget day" in the Bundestag of all drama. Although appropriations are made on an annual basis, the Government is constitutionally empowered to continue those expenditures which are authorized by existing legislation, even if the budget has not been approved by Parliament. It may also exceed authorized appropriations in exceptional cases, subject to retroactive parliamentary approval.[237] In practice, the budget is never enacted before the start of the fiscal year, because its parliamentary passage requires more time than the timetable established by law makes available, and because the Government has frequently submitted the budget past the legal deadline.[238]

[233] BGBl. I, p. 1001.

[234] Die Welt, Sept. 11, 1961.

[235] Bulletin, Dec. 21, 1961.

[236] Die Welt, July 31, 1962.

[237] Basic Law, arts. 110–12.

[238] Through 1960, the fiscal year began April 1, and the Government was obliged to submit its budget to the Bundesrat by November 5 of the previous year, and to the Bundestag by January 5 of the same year (see Reichshaushaltsordnung vom 31. Dez., 1922, RGBl. II [1923], p. 17, par. 22). After the dislocations of the first post-war years, the Government met this deadline successfully from 1953 through 1957 and in 1959 and 1960. Beginning in 1961, however, the fiscal year began on January 1, with budget submission to the Bundesrat due July 1 the

As a result, parliamentary decisions on the budget come after a considerable proportion of the expenditures has already been made.

Under this pressure of time, the Bundestag has adopted shortcuts. It has followed the practice of empowering its Appropriations Committee to authorize transfers within the budget as enacted, or new expenditures and deficiency appropriations in advance, or in place of, the action of the House.[239] Or, it has adopted the budgets, as in 1963 and 1964, before the Appropriations Committee had even considered, let alone reported on, any part of the personnel titles.[240] The second and third reading debates on appropriations, traditionally the occasion for a detailed scrutiny of Government policy, led by the Opposition, have taken place under severe limitations of time. The minimum, reached in 1964, was two days, for a document exceeding 2,500 pages.[241]

The Appropriations Committee

The appropriations power of the House is therefore largely exercised by its Appropriations Committee, whose recommendations deci-

---

previous year, and submission to the Bundestag by October 5 (see Gesetz zur Anpassung des Rechnungsjahres an das Kalendarjahr vom 29. Dezember 1959, *BGBl.* I, 832). The Government met these deadlines for the first time with the presentation of the budget for 1965 (see *Die Welt,* June 17–18, 1964).

The enactment of the budget has normally come several months after the beginning of the fiscal year, the situation having become worse since the fiscal year was moved up to begin on January 1. The recent dates have been as follows:

Enactment of the budget	Start of fiscal year
July 24, 1958	April 1, 1958
July 6, 1959	April 1, 1959
June 2, 1960	April 1, 1960
April 10, 1961	January 1, 1961
May 23, 1962	January 1, 1962
June 24, 1963	January 1, 1963
May 13, 1964	January 1, 1964
March 18, 1965	January 1, 1965

[239] See, for example, Gesetz über die Feststellung des Bundeshaushaltsplans für das Rechnungsjahr 1965, *BGBl.* II, p. 193, par. 2(2), 3(7), 11(10), 13(1), 14, 15(3), 17(2), 28(3), and 32. For the constitutional justification of this delegation of power from the House to one of its committees, see the authoritative commentary of the State Secretary in the Finance Ministry, Friedrich Karl Vialon, *Haushaltsrecht,* 2nd ed. (Berlin-Frankfurt: Verlag Franz Vahlen, 1959), p. 56.

[240] See *Die Welt,* April 17, 1964; *Die Zeit* (U.S. ed.), May 1, 1964.

[241] *Dt. Btag.,* 4. W.P., 122. and 123. Sitz., April 15 and 16, 1964.

sively determine the action of the Bundestag on the budget, and whose year-round work entails frequent actions on behalf of the entire body. The resulting autonomy of the committee has given it an unusually high sense of corporate identity, and an orientation toward budgetary questions which is usually inspired neither by partisanship nor by opposition to the executive departments, but by professionalism and expertise. Within the limits of the energies and abilities of its thirty-one members, it gives careful scrutiny to the Government's budgetary proposals and to the post-audit on expenditures presented by the Federal Audit Office. Charged with the consideration of every bill entailing expenditures, as well as the annual budget, it is the busiest committee in the House. It alone may regularly meet even while the Bundestag is in session, and it makes considerable use of subcommittees and specialization among its members. A group of two to four Members, representing both governing and opposition parties, is in charge of the budget for each ministry. The group hears the recommendation of the Bundestag committee within whose jurisdiction that ministry falls. It is likely to negotiate directly with ministry officials in advance of committee deliberations. Its members may also consult their party colleagues who are specialists in the relevant area. When the committee meets, its subcommittees are ready to present proposals which have been cleared with ministry officials and party experts, and which are therefore liable to carry great weight.[242]

More significant than the fact that the chairmanship of the committee has always been in the hands of the SPD (presumably on the theory that the Opposition has a primary role in the control of expenditure) is the uninterrupted tenure of Erwin Schoettle as chairman since the committee was first constituted in 1949. The membership of the committee has likewise been unusually stable. The autonomy and expertise of the committee place it in a relationship to other committees which is similar to the relationship between the Ministry of Finance and other Government departments. In fact, the Appropriations Committee has developed a strong kinship with the Finance Ministry, sharing its financial orthodoxy, specifically its desire to maintain a balanced budget, and its tendency to resist demands for larger

[242] For an account of the organization and procedure of the Appropriations Committee, see Friedrich Schäfer, "Aufgabe und Arbeitsweise des Haushaltsausschusses des Deutschen Bundestages," in F. Schäfer, ed. *Finanzwissenschaft und Finanzpolitik* (Tübingen: Mohr, 1964), pp. 251–67.

appropriations from whatever source. An official of the Ministry of Finance observed with obvious satisfaction that

the work of the [Appropriations] committee was, all told, carried on in a remarkably objective fashion. An atmosphere of confidence existed among Members of all parties, which made it possible to forget party membership. This expressed itself particularly in voting . . . [which] usually cut across party lines. A remarkable relationship of confidence also developed between the committee and the regular representatives of the Government.[243]

And in a similar vein, the committee assistant has written that

the members of the committee, in their decisions, which very frequently went against the wishes of their own party colleagues on other committees, were guided only by objective considerations, and by the thought that the maintenance of financial stability should have priority over the fulfillment of special demands.[244]

In 1962, with a budgetary deficit in prospect which the Minister of Finance sought to avoid by an across-the-board cut of 12 per cent in all expenditures, the Appropriations Committee undertook to propose selective cuts instead. In a number of decisions affecting Government policy, notably in the field of transportation, the committee proposed some sharp reductions of individual items, which the Government accepted as an alternative to its across-the-board cut. Its action represented collaboration between the Appropriations Committee and the Finance Ministry to limit expenditures in some departments of the Government, under the duress of a budget deficit which both wished to avoid.[245] At other times, the Appropriations Committee has arbitrated among different demands for increases in the budget, without affecting total expenditures. It has not attempted to alter the net size of the budget.

The committee has not tried to influence Government fiscal policy specifically. Parallel to an appropriations procedure reflecting the nineteenth-century division of power between Government and Parliament, a similarly outdated orthodoxy prevails in the theory of Government finances. The emphasis of both ministry and committee is almost

[243] W. Charlet, "Die Arbeit des Haushaltsausschusses des Deutschen Bundestages in der zweiten Wahlperiode," *Bulletin*, no. 135, July 26, 1957, p. 1290.
[244] Paul Stolla, "Die Aufgaben des Haushaltsausschusses," *Bulletin*, no. 222, Nov. 30, 1957, p. 2056.
[245] *Dt. Btag.*, 4. W.P., 26. Sitz., April 12, 1962, p. 1142. Cf. *Die Welt*, Jan. 25, March 2, 9, 10, and 31, and April 13, 1962.

exclusively on budget balance, with no systematic distinction made between capital and current expenditures, and no attention to the policy options available in using the government budget to affect the national economy.

The practices of the Bundestag on appropriations have attracted wide criticism, not least from those who have played a leading role in the procedure. The chairman of the Appropriations Committee, speaking critically of the existing practice at the end of the two-day budget debate in 1964, acknowledged that "our current appropriations procedure was designed for other times." He demanded reforms in the schedule of submitting the budget, elimination of the delegation of authority to the Appropriations Committee by the House, distinction among types of expenditure and lengths of authorization, and attention to fiscal policy.[246] This appeal for reform, although particularly comprehensive, echoes those perennially heard in the budget debates of the Bundestag.[247] But the practices of the House show little sign of changing, rooted as they are in traditional relationships between Government and Parliament on questions of expenditure, and affected by the tendency toward specialization and expertise which influences the legislative process generally.

THE LEGISLATIVE ROLE OF THE BUNDESTAG

The Bundestag is the source of a relatively small proportion of the bills which are ultimately enacted into law. Those introduced by its Members have a much higher rate of failure than those submitted by the Government, and among those apparently presented by Members of the House, a considerable proportion have actually been drafted in a ministry. But if bills tend to originate in the offices of legislative counsels of the ministries, the Bundestag subjects them to a deliberate process and to a majority decision without which they cannot be enacted into law. Few bills remain unchanged as they traverse the legislative stages in the Bundestag, and fewer still would have had the same text in the first place had not the Government anticipated parliamentary reaction in advance.

[246] *Dt. Btag.*, 4. W.P., 123. Sitz., April 16, 1964, pp. 5906–16.
[247] The fifth Bundestag took up two proposals to reform its appropriations procedure (see *Dt. Btag.*, 5. W.P., 46. Sitz., June 15, 1966, pp. 2283–96; Drs. 69, neu, 114).

Indirect Influences

Some influences on legislation which would exist in any case are strengthened by the need for passage through the Bundestag. Although many reasons motivate the Government to consult interest groups in the drafting of bills, the influence which such groups have within the parliamentary parties reinforces the demands which they can make on the ministry. Likewise, although *Land* administration of federal laws and the role of the Bundesrat in the legislative process leads the Government to consult the relevant *Land* ministries in drafting legislation, the respect which Bundestag committees have for the administrative expertise of the Bundesrat compels the Government to anticipate with particular care the initial reaction of the second chamber to its legislative proposals. Finally, the close ties which many ministries have with their committee counterparts in the Bundestag oblige a ministry sponsoring a bill to obtain a consensus on it within the Government, rather than the approval of a mere Cabinet majority, to discourage ministries who are outvoted in the Cabinet from taking recourse to parliamentay committees in order to secure their legislative objectives.

Direct Influences

Some important influences on legislation, furthermore, are largely or entirely the result of the role which the Bundestag plays in the legislative process. The smaller interest groups not normally consulted at the ministerial drafting stage find the parliamentary committee their only point of access to the legislative process. The privacy of committee deliberations makes it difficult for outside groups to exercise influence unless they have spokesmen among the committee members. Otherwise they are dependent on the persuasiveness of their written statements, or, occasionally, their oral testimony. But the extent of interest-group representation in the composition of the Bundestag, the subject specialization of committees, and the important place of the committee stage in the legislative process, all enhance the influence of organized interests on the content of legislation. If a bill is of sufficiently narrow concern, it can in effect be written entirely within a Bundestag committee in negotiation between the representatives of the relevant interest group and the appropriate ministerial officials, as was the case with the bill on lawyers' fees. If a bill touches a wide variety of interests, the deliberations within the committee are merely a part of a broader series of negotiations between interested organizations and the Government, as the case of the Federal Requisitions Bill indicates.

The influence of the parliamentary parties on legislation is a direct result of the need for Bundestag approval. This influence is not limited to the parties comprising the governing majority, nor does the majority serve as the mere instrument of its ministers. One reason for this lies in the persistence of a pattern of organization which leaves the leadership of the parliamentary parties of the majority entirely separate from the leadership of the Government. Originating in the political system in which ministers were not recruited from Parliament, and in which there was no stable distinction between governing and opposition parties, this pattern gives the parliamentary parties considerable autonomy. They have their own leadership, their own executive committees, their own specialized subject-matter committees, and their own procedures. Rarely do parliamentary leaders participate in Cabinet decisions and, in turn, ministers participate in the parliamentary party as influential outsiders rather than as its accepted leaders. Both sides still cherish their traditional independence of each other. This organizational separation imposes obstacles to the Government's ability to mobilize its parliamentary majority. The negotiation between ministers and Members of the Bundestag is carried on *ad hoc,* with far less regularity than the negotiations between ministers and interest groups or *Land* governments.

Ironically, the provisions of the Basic Law designed to assure Cabinet stability weaken the Government in its negotiations with its parliamentary followers. For since the Government's tenure in office is constitutionally independent of its ability to enact its program, parliamentary alteration or even defeat of its measures does not raise a question of confidence.

The inability of the Government to count on the support of its parliamentary followers is also due to the differences between the interests shaping policy at the ministerial level, and those affecting Members of the Bundestag. In some areas of legislation, notably in social policy, the Government was for long periods quite unable to obtain any consensus within its parliamentary majority, and was consequently limited to those narrow enactments, like the Child Benefits Act, which served the direct and immediate self-interest of the party.

In other areas, sharp differences within the parliamentary majority resulted in defeats or substantial alterations of Government legislation, as in the case of the bill on travel between the Federal Republic and the Soviet Zone, and the Volunteers Law. Occasionally, as in the last case, the ministerial ambitions of parliamentary leaders sharpen the policy conflict. Particularly when parliamentary debate takes place in an atmosphere of broad public concern, as in both of these cases, the parliamentary parties become responsive to unorganized interests and electoral considerations to which individual ministers may not be nearly so sensitive.

The Government cannot organize Opposition support for its measures in place of the support of its normal majority, since its organizational ties to the Opposition are still far looser and lack the bond of common party interest. When the Government needs the approval of the Opposition, as for amendments to the Basic Law, which require a two-thirds vote, the bargaining process is long, difficult, and sometimes, as in the case of the proposals for new constitutional emergency provisions, unsuccessful for long periods of time.

The parliamentary Opposition also has sources of influence over legislation not limited to its veto on constitutional change. To some extent it may work with or through the Bundesrat. Within the Bundestag it has its share of positions of power in the committee chairmanships, the Council of Elders, the Mediation Committee, and the presidium. As the minority, the Rules of the House offer it extensive rights, which at the least give it bargaining power in the negotiations, constantly taking place among the parliamentary whips, to secure the procedural consensus which all parties prefer to procedural disputes. Within the privacy of the committee room, the differences between the parties are often overshadowed by other lines of division, occasionally putting the Opposition on the prevailing side. Interests which overlap party lines can produce shifting majorities, depending on the legislative issues. Church-state questions may produce an SPD-FDP majority, and social policy questions can bring about a majority composed of the SPD and the labor faction of the CDU. Furthermore, the common interest of all Members in restricting administrative discretion produces regular confrontations between entire committees and ministerial officials.

The legislative functions which the Bundestag performs permit it to exercise substantial influence over many areas of Government policy.

Although the five illustrative cases do not, of course, constitute a random sample of the 2866 bills which the House considered during its four terms between 1949 and 1965, each one details some of the influences which are brought to bear on legislation as a result of the Bundestag's role in lawmaking. Among the major functions which it performs in the political system, this is the one most closely related to its institutional origins in Germany and most generally accepted in the political culture. But so large a part of the legislative process in the Bundestag takes place in private that its details are not closely followed by the public. While this permits the Bundestag to work with a certain efficiency, manifested in high legislative output, it restricts public insight into legislative decisions, public awareness of the issues and interests involved, and, potentially, public acceptance of the results. The conclusion that the public has insufficient insight into legislative decisions in Parliament relates to the conclusion of the previous chapter, that the public does not adequately perceive the extent to which the Bundestag influences the selection of the Cabinet. Together, these conclusions suggest the difficulties which the German Parliament confronts in the performance of representative functions in the political system, and it is to these that we now turn our attention.

VII

Representation

PARLIAMENT stands in a distinctive relationship to the
public, both because of the elective process by which its members
are chosen and the relative openness with which it works. Both parties
to this relationship may derive expectations from it: the public expects
from parliament a particular responsiveness to its demands; parliament expects from the public a special respect for its words and deeds.
The fulfillment of both expectations depends on communication between parliament and public.

The performance of a communications function by parliament has
significance for the entire political system. Parliament can communicate public demands to the policy makers, and policy options and
decisions to the interested public. It can exhibit the conflicts of viewpoint among political groups and the perimeters within which these
conflicts can be reconciled. The information transmitted may promote
the responsiveness of government to the demands of its various publics. Parliamentary discourse may inform public participation in politics. The very process of communication can impart to the interested
public a sense of access to government, and thereby contribute to
public acceptance of governmental decisions. Especially where political institutions and symbols are undergoing change, as in postwar
Germany, the relationship between parliament and public may be an
important determinant of attitudes toward the legitimacy of the entire
political system.[1]

These forms of communication, and their political consequences,
constitute the representative function of parliament. The Cabinet

[1] On "crises of legitimacy", see, for example, Seymour Martin Lipset, *Political
Man* (New York: Doubleday, 1960), pp. 77–90. For an interesting discussion of
the relationship between social communication and legitimacy beliefs, see Karl W.
Deutsch, *The Nerves of Government* (New York: The Free Press, 1963), pp.
151–4.

forming and lawmaking functions, which we have so far examined, are derived from this representative function. For it was the demand for representation by the major social groups in the medieval political systems of Europe which originally shaped the institution of parliament. Its representativeness justified parliament's claim to participate in the more tangible functions of government: the selection of executives and the making of policy. In turning to an analysis of the representative function of the Bundestag, we therefore address ourselves to an aspect of the work of parliament which is fundamental to it as a political institution.

However, the relationships between the functions of parliaments developed differently in different political cultures. A century ago, Walter Bagehot observed that "a great and open council of considerable men cannot be placed in the middle of a society without altering that society." He attributed to what he called the expressive, the teaching, and the informing functions of the House of Commons of his day a significance greater than that of its lawmaking functions.[2] But this priority, which still applies to the role of parliament in Great Britain, never applied in Germany.

FORMATIVE EXPERIENCES

Representation Without Authority

When Bagehot wrote, German unification had not yet occurred, no national political audience yet existed to listen and learn and attempt to exert influence. A generation later this had changed, and the debates of the Reichstag had become a focal point of political attention for the interested public. Press coverage of the Reichstag's deliberations reached an all-time high in the first decade of this century, when the serious newspapers regularly included extensive paraphrases of the debates in their reporting. But even then the prominence of the Reichstag's debates greatly exceeded their political influence. Severe criticism of Government policy, from most sides of the House, as in the debates on the *Daily Telegraph* affair in 1908 and on the Zabern affair in 1913, did not seriously impair the Government's authority. Government actions still did not generally require parliamentary legitimation. That the Reichstag was representative gave it, as yet, no special

---

[2] Walter Bagehot, *The English Constitution* (London: Kegan Paul, Trench, Trubner, 1922), Ch. V, esp. pp. 133–5.

authority. The legitimacy of the monarchical Government, operating through a highly competent and well-established bureaucracy, and governing in accordance with the venerated principles of the *Rechts-staat*, or rule of law, remained intact until the final year of the First World War. The debates of an assembly which constitutionally could not affect the composition of the Government, nor influence its policy except when new legislation or appropriations were required, had a futile quality which contributed to the derogation of the Reichstag as a "twaddle shop."

The Style of Public Deliberation

These circumstances affected the style of public deliberation. The old ruling elites, accustomed to equating their own interests with the national interest, were contemptuous of those who advanced contrary views. But universal suffrage assured the representation of the great diversity of viewpoints which existed in a nation experiencing the social tensions of unification and industrialization. The new elites, anxious to press their interests in the only governing institution to which they had access, expressed themselves with a militancy unsoftened by the incentive to compromise which responsibility for government might have given them. Anxious to impress the public with their cohesion, and possessing the *élan* of new and embattled political organizations, they used their debating time to present official party viewpoints, creating that rigid succession of prepared, and therefore poorly related, statements which has marked the German parliamentary style.

The contrast between the sharpness of parliamentary speech and the absence of its effect on government gradually diminished the attention given to the Reichstag's public deliberations. Even during the Empire, a strong tendency developed among the parliamentary parties to turn their attention to lawmaking, in the privacy of committees, which offered influence on policy as public debate did not. When Parliament won greatly increased constitutional powers in the Weimar Republic, its debates were overshadowed not only by committee work on legislation, but by the decisions of the party groups which could now affect the tenure of Cabinets and administrative policy. Only when sensational verbal clashes with the radical, antiparliamentary parties made good newspaper copy, was parliamentary debate prominently reported.[3] The abuse of parliamentary debate to destroy the parliamentary system was far more clearly demonstrated in the Weimar Republic than its use to legitimate and integrate.

In the inheritance of the Bundestag, therefore, as Ernst Fraenkel has observed, "the tradition of the great parliamentary debates, in which victory or defeat for the Government is at stake, is missing." Nor is there a "parliamentary style which arises from an *espirit de corps* among members of the various parliamentary groups."[4] The House performs its public functions under these historically conditioned handicaps. They are evident in the neglect of public-speaking skill as a criterion for the selection of candidates, in party control over the content of speeches, in the absence of a clear confrontation between Government and Opposition in debate, in the lack of resonance which parliamentary deliberation receives in the press, and in the relatively small proportion of parliamentary business transacted in public. But if these characteristics are derivatives of a history which has discouraged debate, they have also been reinforced by recent influences.

Obstacles to Extemporaneous Speech

The German educational system offers little training in extemporaneous public speaking, in the development of a capacity for quick thrust and parry in argumentation, which a lively debating style requires, or in the ability to advance controversial views within procedural limits assuring courtesy and good order. The process of candidate recruitment places little emphasis on these consequently rare skills. While party selection committees in Great Britain, for example, impose on all prospective candidates the requirement that they give a sample political speech,[5] the ability of the prospective candidate as a public speaker hardly figures in Germany. All the other traditional criteria of selection are more important. To be sure, persuasiveness in

[3] On the development of newspaper coverage of parliamentary debates, see Helga Haftendorn, "Die politische Funktion der Parlamentsberichterstattung," *Publizistik*, VI, nos. 5 and 6 (1961).

[4] Ernst Fraenkel, "Historische Vorbelastungen des deutschen Parlamentarismus," *Vierteljahreshefte für Zeitgeschichte*, VIII (1960), p. 333.

[5] Peter G. Richards, *Honourable Members* (London: Faber & Faber, 1959), pp. 18–19; Austin Ranney, *Pathways to Parliament* (Madison: The University of Wisconsin Press, 1965), pp. 60, 172–3, 278–9.

private party meetings is an obvious advantage for the parliamentary politician, both in his constituency and in many conclaves in the House, but the capacity to sway a private audience of party colleagues is not the same as the ability to engage in public deliberation. The Rule of the House that "speakers must, fundamentally, speak extemporaneously," [6] is unenforceable, because so few of the Members could conform to it.

Furthermore, other factors encourage lengthy, prepared speeches, rather than many-sided, extemporaneous debates. The party groups insist on the presentation of official positions, which must necessarily be carefully prepared in advance. The complexity of much of the subject matter and the influence of committee specialization also promote the use of prepared texts. The control which the parliamentary party whips exercise over the agenda and the order of speakers deters the average Member from speaking, and contributes to a debating monopoly held by the official party spokesmen and the committee reporters. Even second-string experts sometimes have a hard time getting to speak under this degree of party domination. The complaint of an SPD Member, deputy chairman of the Defense Committee, that "I have recently been the victim of the arrangements among the parliamentary parties at least two or three times," was rare only as an open expression of a frequently felt frustration.[7] Party organization of debate has induced a degree of collegiality among the speakers which has contributed to courtesy and good order. The invective overtones produced by ideological convictions and feelings of class solidarity

---

[6] Par. 37.

[7] *Dt. Btag*, 4. W.P., 153. Sitz., Dec. 11, 1964, p. 7603. On another rare occasion, a CDU/CSU Member gave the following description in the Bundestag of how management of debate struck one backbencher:

"First of all the debate runs at great length, with speeches which occasionally exceed a full hour. At a given point, Members, who may have asked for recognition hours earlier, hear that the list of speakers is exhausted. From this they shrewdly conclude that they have been struck from the list of speakers, and etiquette in the Bundestag at that point demands that a gentleman remain silent."

To this SPD whip Mommer gave the revealing reply that the CDU/CSU Member had apparently been mistreated by his party the previous week. "We do these things differently," Mommer added. On the same occasion, he said, "we also had speakers left who had asked for recognition, but we agreed among ourselves that our speakers would relinquish the right to speak, since the debate had reached a point where it was no longer worthwhile to continue" (*Dt. Btag.*, 5. W.P., 21. Sitz., Feb. 16, 1966, p. 854).

sound only rarely now,[8] but the more temperamental discussions of the Weimar Reichstag or even the first Bundestag, while occasionally disruptive, had a spice which the new orderliness sorely lacks.

Participation

A statistical analysis indicates the narrowness of participation in debate. In the third Bundestag, which sat from 1957 to 1961, three-fifths of the Members spoke ten times or less; eighty-four Members never spoke at all, seventy of these serving the full four-year term.[9] In purely quantitative terms, taking no account of the length or importance of contributions, fewer than one-fifth of the Members made over two-thirds of the speeches. These active speakers were predominantly members of the Cabinet, two-thirds of whom spoke more than thirty times each, and parliamentary leaders, nearly one-third of whom spoke this often. Only 11 per cent of the backbenchers, on the other hand, participated in debate with this degree of frequency, while nearly 70 per cent of them spoke only ten times or less in four years. (See Table 37.)

Narrowness of participation is demonstrated in another sense, by the extent to which speakers specialize on a single topic. Of 128 Members who were active enough in debate to have participated more than twenty times during the four-year term, 37 per cent spoke on a single subject over two-thirds of the time, and another 46 per cent concentrated on one subject in one-third to two-thirds of their speeches. Only 17 per cent of this active group had a greater versatility than this in the subjects to which they addressed themselves, and they prominently included the parliamentary party leaders. Public deliberation is not only carried on by a small minority of the membership, but largely by a group of subject specialists, each of whom is conversant in only a narrow area and whose approach to his subject is correspondingly technical, even when he is raising a politically important point.

[8] For an amusing account of the types of remarks for which Members have been called to order, see Arnulf Kriedner, "Ordnungsrufe im deutschen Bundestag," *Der Monat*, XVI (1963), 87–94.

[9] In contrast, during a single year in the House of Commons, according to a recent example, only 28 out of 629 Members did not speak at all, and 545 spoke at least ten times (see Kurt Peschel, "Die Verhandlungen im britischen Unterhaus," *Das Parlament*, July 10, 1963, p. 11).

Table 37. *Debating frequency in the Bundestag, 1957–1961*
(*in per cent of categories indicated at top of each column*)

Number of times recognized to speak	All Members (n = 519)	Members of Cabinet (n = 18)	Parliamentary leaders [a] (n = 141)	Back-benchers [a] (n = 360)
0	16	0	9	20
1	8	0	5	10
2	6	0	1	8
3–5	14	0	12	15
6–10	15	0	11	17
11–20	15	11	21	13
21–30	7	22	8	6
31–50	10	17	13	8
51–75	3	0	8	2
76–100	2	11	4	1
101–150	3	22	6	0
Over 150	1	17	2	0

[a] For the definition of Parliamentary leaders and backbenchers, see Table 18.

Party Influence on Debate

The narrowness of participation in debate, both quantitatively and qualitatively, is in part a consequence of the large size and high degree of internal organization of today's parliamentary parties, compared to their predecessors in the Reichstag. Even among the three parties remaining in the Bundestag, it is clear that subject specialization among speakers increases with party size, being greatest in the CDU/CSU and least in the FDP. The proportion of Members actively drawn into debate, on the other hand, declines with party size. It is largest in the FDP and smallest in the CDU/CSU. (See Table 38.)

Party control over what is said in the House robs the discussion of many themes and views which individual Members might want to discuss but which fall victim to strategic partisan considerations. After some highly emotional foreign policy debates in the 1950's, foreign policy was all but eliminated from the agenda of the House between 1958 and 1962 in the wake of a newly developed bipartisanship in this area between the SPD and the CDU/CSU, and their conviction that the national interest would not be served by an open discussion of the

Table 38. Participation in debate by party, 1957–1961 (in per cent of party members, excluding Cabinet members)

Number of times recognized to speak	CDU/CSU (n = 262)	SPD (n = 181)	FDP (n = 43)
0	20	15	7
1	11	8	2
2	8	5	2
3–5	15	14	9
6–10	17	16	9
11–20	14	15	19
21–50	12	18	35
51–100	3	4	12
101–150	0	4	5
Over 150	0	1	0
Of those speaking over 5 times			
"Generalists" [a]	10	11	15
"Concentrators" [b]	1	3	9
"Specialists" [c]	47	53	50
"Experts" [d]	42	33	26

[a] Members who did not speak on any one subject as much as one-third of the time.

[b] Members who did not speak on any one subject as much as one-third of the time, but who spoke on only two subjects between one-half and two-thirds of the time.

[c] Members who spoke on any one subject between one-third and two-thirds of the time.

[d] Members who spoke on any one subject over two-thirds of the time.

subject. At other times the discussion of the sensitive issue of restitution was avoided, even when legislation on the subject was being enacted. Although all political communities have their taboos which are beyond discussion, fear of facing the Nazi past and the consequences of unconditional surrender, as well as fear of a public whose capacity to give daemonic political responses is still fresh in the memory of parliamentary leaders, placed an unusually large proportion of important German political issues into this category for many years. By contrast, the debate in 1965 on the extension of the statute of limitations for war crimes was a bold departure from party timidity, with the CDU/CSU and the SPD favoring the extension which the FDP and 57 per cent of the public opposed.[10] "It is one of the consequences of the burden of history which has been imposed on us, that we could only rarely discuss questions of great political significance in public debates," President Gerstenmaier told the opening session of the fifth Bundestag. But while admitting that "a nation in our situation must show consideration of many kinds," he declared that "it now seems justifiable to permit more spontaneous discussion in this House of important questions of German existence than heretofore."[11] More than presidential encouragement is probably required, however, to persuade the parties to overcome their hesitation to debate the great issues.

Party influence on speaking has failed to produce a clear, two-sided confrontation of views in compensation for what it suppresses in the way of individuality of expression. In the past, the multiplicity of parties assured that a wide variety of viewpoints would be articulated in German parliaments, even if party, rather than individual positions were heard. The decline of the number of parties represented in Parliament to three has reduced variety, but has not replaced it with a simple contrast between Government and Opposition.

Cabinet Influence on Debate

In part, this is due to the after-effect of the traditional political system in which the Government was present in Parliament, but was not composed of Members of Parliament. Although today the Cabinet is recruited nearly exclusively from Members of the coalition parties in the Bundestag, the traditional prestige, emoluments, and long tenure of ministerial office separate Cabinet members from their colleagues in their own parliamentary parties. Symbolic, in a title-conscious society, is the distinction which Bundestag Members observe between their ordinary fellow parliamentarians, whom they address as "Mr. Representative" (*Herr Abgeordneter*) or "Mr. Colleague" (*Herr Kollege*), and members of the Cabinet, whom they address as "Mr. Minister" or "Mr. Federal Chancellor." Symbolic also are the two seats reserved in the chamber for each Cabinet member: one, on the Government bench, facing the House and looking down upon it,

[10] *Dt. Btag.*, 4. W.P., 170. Sitz., March 10, 1965, pp. 8516–71; *Die Welt*, March 16, 1965.
[11] *Dt. Btag.*, 5. W.P., 1. Sitz., October 19, 1965, pp. 3–4.

which he normally occupies, together with his senior officials; and one on the floor, with his party colleagues, which he uses mainly for purposes of voting or conferring with the party leaders.

The aloofness of the members of the Cabinet keeps them from regarding the Bundestag as their natural political audience. Neither the Chancellor nor his ministers feel an obligation to inform the House first of important events or policies. The selection of the audience is determined by other considerations. In any case, Government bills and the budget must, for constitutional reasons, be presented first to the Bundesrat. The need to exert party leadership creates the tendency to give priority to the executive committee and, to a lesser extent, to the caucus of the parliamentary party, in making policy proposals or reporting on developments. The need to persuade interest groups may inspire a policy address to a major professional or economic organization. The technology of modern communications indicates the use of press conferences or television addresses to the nation. Unrestrained by any tradition of courtesy toward the House or a sense of common membership in it, and oblivious, therefore, to any claims it might have as a public audience of first priority, ministers address themselves first to the sources of their power: their parliamentary party, the major interest groups, and the electorate. To the extent that the Bundestag is thereby bypassed as the point of contact between Government and public, the plebiscitary elements in the German constitutional tradition, as Fraenkel has referred to them, have reappeared, despite constitutional efforts to avoid them.[12] The tendency toward a "Chancellor democracy," observed under Adenauer, and, even more, Erhard's ambition to rule as a "people's Chancellor," manifest this development.

Influence of the Opposition on Debate

The leadership of the Opposition has also failed to concentrate on the parliamentary forum. Kurt Schumacher, the first postwar leader of the SPD, was schooled in the dogmatic politics of the Weimar Republic. Isolated from political developments between 1933 and 1945 by his incarceration in a concentration camp, and committed to the ideology of socialism, he was a political hero not given readily to compromise. Far more than his successors at the head of the largest Opposition

[12] Ernst Fraenkel, *Die repräsentative und die plebiszitäre Komponente im demokratischen Verfassungsstaat* (Recht und Staat in Geschichte und Gegenwart, Vol. CCXIX–CCXX [Tübingen: Mohr, 1958]), esp. pp. 48–58.

party, he sought to distinguish his position from that of the Government with the aim of eventually winning a governing majority for the SPD.[13] "As the Opposition, one cannot be a substitute party for the Government, taking responsibility for things from which some governing parties shrink," he declared in an early Bundestag debate in which he appeared to reject parliamentary compromises. "We want to conduct our Opposition," he continued, "with the aim of obtaining a majority in this House one day for the policy of Social Democracy." [14] Accordingly, he, like Adenauer, appealed directly to the electorate, in press conferences and speeches which frequently stole the thunder from Bundestag debates.

Although even under his leadership the party in the Bundestag negotiated a steady stream of legislative compromises with the majority, the departure from an opposition of principle accelerated under his successors. Unsuccessful in obtaining the national majority Schumacher had counted on, the party sought to exercise influence on politics wherever the political system permitted it, at the *Land* and local level, in interest groups, on the electorate, and in the committees of the Bundestag. This blurred the distinction between the positions of majority and minority on the floor of the Bundestag. It also multiplied the foci of the political contest. Prominent party leaders established themselves in the *Land* Governments and in 1960 the SPD named the most conspicuous of these, Willy Brandt, its "candidate" for the Federal Chancellorship. As a result, Brandt conducted the parliamentary elections of 1961 and 1965 from his position as mayor of Berlin. Although he was a candidate for the Bundestag in both elections, he resigned his seat in 1961 soon after speaking for the Opposition in the Bundestag on the new Government's policy declaration, and declined to accept his seat in 1965—both times in order to retain the Berlin mayoralty. Other *Land* leaders, whose prominent names had headed the party's list of candidates in their respective sections of the country, likewise resigned their seats as soon as it was clear that the SPD would serve another four years in Opposition.[15] After Ollenhauer's death in

[13] Lewis J. Edinger, *Kurt Schumacher, A Study in Personality and Political Behavior* (Stanford: Stanford University Press, 1965), esp. Ch. 8.

[14] *Dt. Btag.*, 1. W.P., 6. Sitz., Sept. 21, 1949, pp. 32, 42.

[15] Those resigning their seats after the election of 1961 were, in addition to Brandt, Wilhelm Hoegner, former Minister-President of Bavaria, who had headed the SPD's list of candidates in that *Land*, and G. A. Zinn, Minister-President of Hesse, who headed the party's list there.

1963, Brandt became chairman of the Opposition party although he did not have a seat in the Bundestag. From time to time leading SPD members in the Bundestag resigned their seats in order to accept positions in the cabinets of the *Länder*.[16] Executive office at the *Land* level has thus exerted a particular attraction for the Opposition, taking some of its major leaders from the Bundestag.

The Influence of Private Negotiation on Debate

Debate in the Bundestag lacks the drama of clear confrontation between Government and Opposition not only because of the alternative audiences which command the attention of the leaders of both sides, but also because of the attraction of bargaining and compromise between the two sides in the privacy of parliamentary committees. Both the organization and the functions of the committees rest on the assumption of a separation of power between Government and Parliament, not between Government and Opposition in Parliament. Composed and chaired proportionately by Members of all parliamentary parties, the Government cannot fully control them and the Opposition does not necessarily face a united front of the Government and its parliamentary supporters in these bodies. Because the fate of the Government's legislation does not constitutionally raise a question of confidence in the Cabinet, the way is open for an active participation of the Opposition in the legislative process. For this purpose, the SPD commands impressive sources of quiet influence, in addition to the well-known procedural rights of the parliamentary minority. It can rely on the legislative expertise of its Members; its ability on some issues to divide the governing parties; its influence with major interest groups which are able to apply pressure behind the scenes; its voice in the Bundesrat, expressed by SPD-controlled *Land* Governments; and since 1957, when it gained more than one-third of the seats in the Bundestag, its ability to block constitutional amendments and to appeal questionable legislation directly to the Federal Constitutional

---

[16] Within the first half year after the 1961 election, three other prominent SPD Members resigned their seats in order to accept positions in the Governments of the *Länder*: Irma Keilhack, Helmut Schmidt, and Klaus Schütz. In the course of the parliamentary term these other SPD Members resigned their seats to accept executive positions in local government: Willi Birkelbach, Kurt Neubauer, and Karl Wittrock; Heinz Kühn resigned to take over the party's leadership in the North-Rhine–Westphalian Landtag. On a slightly smaller scale, a similar exodus took place among Bundestag Members in the governing parties.

Court. Even Schumacher, in the Bundestag speech in which he announced an Opposition based on principle, added that

the Opposition cannot exhaust itself in mere rejection of the Government's proposals. The essence of Opposition is the continuing attempt, to force the positive constructive will of the Opposition on the Government and its parties with concrete proposals for concrete situations.[17]

In the first term of the Bundestag, such important measures as those creating the Federal Constitutional Court, setting up the federal police force, providing for codetermination in the iron and steel industry, and establishing a federal housing program received the support of both CDU/CSU and SPD after being negotiated between them. Altogether, the SPD voted in favor of 84 per cent of all bills passed during this first term. To be sure, those which it opposed included important and conspicuous measures, including appropriations bills, traditionally rejected by the Opposition, and, above all, foreign policy measures.[18] For it was in the foreign policy field that Schumacher led his party into the sharpest opposition to the Government. While participating in a process of committee revision of legislation which associated it with the Government on major domestic policies, Schumacher chose to confront Government policy most clearly in the area in which party differences are most difficult to explain to the public. But after Schumacher's death, and particularly after the SPD's devastating defeat of 1953, the party endeavored to disengage itself from its fundamental opposition to the Government in this area also.

The longer it failed to win a national majority and the more strongly it felt the need to expand its electoral appeal and to abandon its traditional ideology, the more the SPD felt impelled to participate in the legislative compromises which alone permitted it to exercise influence on national policy. Its participation in the revision of the Volunteers Bill represented a move toward support of the Government's defense and foreign policy—a move that culminated in Vice-Chairman Wehner's 1960 speech in which the party associated itself with the

[17] *Dt. Btag.*, 1. W.P., 6. Sitz., Sept. 21, 1949, p. 32.
[18] Wolfgang Kralewski and Karlheinz Neunreither, *Oppositionelles Verhalten im ersten Deutschen Bundestag, 1949–1953* (Cologne and Opladen: Westdeutscher Verlag, 1963), pp. 84–93; Klaus Schütz, "Die Sozialdemokratie im Nachkriegsdeutschland," in M. G. Lange, Gerhard Schulz, Klaus Schütz, et. al., *Parteien in der Bundesrepublik* (Stuttgart and Düsseldorf: Ring Verlag, 1955), pp. 222–60.

Government's foreign policy generally.[19] On domestic policy, the SPD participated in the enactment of an ever-growing proportion of the bills before the Bundestag, voting in favor of 90 per cent of those passed between 1960 and 1963.[20] During the reorganization of the Government after the *Spiegel* crisis in 1962, it went one step further still, by seriously and publicly considering participation in a coalition government together with the CDU/CSU, a possibility entertained by a growing portion of the party's leaders as the only realistic avenue to national office.[21]

In availing itself of the opportunity to exercise parliamentary influence through private negotiation with the majority, the Opposition to some extent sacrificed the possibility of mobilizing public support by expressing a distinctive position in parliamentary debate.[22] The possibility of private negotiation inhibits public discourse: before the negotiations, it enjoins restraint; after the negotiations, it permits only the justification of the agreements reached, or of the failure to reach agreements; and differences within the party must be so far as possible concealed. Increasingly, major public criticism of the Government was left to the press, with the SPD acting as a somewhat reluctant agent of an outraged public when the critics struck home. This occurred in the

[19] *Dt. Btag.*, 3. W.P., 122. Sitz., June 30, 1960, pp. 7052 ff.

[20] See p. 356 and n., *supra*.

[21] *Die Welt*, Dec. 6 and 7, 1962. For a discussion of the considerations generally impelling opposition parties today to seek participation in the exercise of governmental power, see Otto Kirchheimer, "The Waning of Opposition in Parliamentary Regimes," *Social Research*, XXIV (1957), 147–56. A systematic analysis of the transformation of the SPD's program and tactics, leading it to what the author calls a "pluralist-plus public-relations" approach, is offered by Douglas A. Chalmers, *The Social Democratic Party of Germany* (New Haven: Yale University Press, 1964), esp. Chs. 2–4, 8. See also Otto Kirchheimer, "Germany: The Vanishing Opposition," in Robert A. Dahl, *Political Oppositions in Western Democracies* (New Haven: Yale University Press, 1966), pp. 237–59, which appeared after this chapter was written.

[22] For a discussion of the history and recent development of the relationship between Government and Opposition in Germany, see Waldemar Besson, "Regierung und Opposition in der deutschen Politik," *Politische Vierteljahresschrift*, III (1962), 225–241, esp. 235. There was criticism of the SPD for its tactics in Opposition right along, both within the party and outside. At the 1958 party conference, a motion was made calling on the parliamentary leadership to abandon its emphasis on deliberations in parliamentary committees and to concentrate on appeals to the public (see Kralewski and Neunreither, *op. cit.*, p. 206). For an example of public criticism, see Hans Robinsohn, "Haben wir eine Opposition?" and a rejoinder by Theodor Eschenburg, "Opposition muss nicht Selbstmord sein," *Die Zeit*, May 25, 1962, and June 8, 1962.

"Fibag" affair in which the Minister of Defense was accused of favoritism in assigning contracts for public housing and the SPD moved to instigate a parliamentary investigation after months of newspaper exposé. In the *"Spiegel* affair," the SPD moved in with a series of questions in the House, after the Government had arrested the editors of the nation's major news magazine on charges of treason. In the "wire tapping affair," in which the Government was accused by the influential weekly, *Die Zeit,* of abusing the rights of the occupation powers to tap telephone lines in the interests of national security, the SPD likewise followed through with a motion for an investigation. But the party did not take the initiative in any of these instances. It preferred to exercise its political influence in the quiet of legislative committees and thereby restricted the possibilities for open parliamentary discourse.[23]

After its fifth straight electoral defeat in 1965, and the disappointment of its hopes of entering a "Great Coalition," there were signs that the SPD was prepared to reconsider its tactics, and to explore the possibility of making better use of the public forum of Parliament to criticize the Government. The immediate result was the most vigorous debate in twelve years on the general declaration of policy with which the Government traditionally opens a parliamentary term. A month later, on the request of the SPD, a report by the Foreign Minister on recent foreign policy developments, which had been scheduled for the privacy of the Foreign Affairs Committee, was transferred to an open session of the House, and was followed by an informative debate. Soon thereafter, a sharp defense policy debate was initiated by the Opposition. The effect of a change of Opposition tactics on the state of parliamentary discourse could not have been more obvious. But the further development of active opposition in parliamentary debate depends on whether this tactic brings an electoral response which the

[23] On the initiation of the "Fibag" affair, see *Der Spiegel,* XVI, no. 5–14 (Jan. 31-April 4, 1962). For a case study of the *"Spiegel* affair", see Otto Kirchheimer, "A Free Press in a Democratic State? The *Spiegel* Case", in Gwendolen M. Carter and Alan Westin, *Politics in Europe: 5   Case Studies in Euopean Government* (New York: Harcourt, Brace & World, 1965), pp. 87–138. For the initiation of the investigation of wire-tapping, see *Die Zeit* (U.S. ed.), Sept. 6, 13, Oct. 18, and Nov. 15, 1963. For the relationship between newspaper criticism and parliamentary opposition generally, as it developed in Germany in the early 1960's, see Günter Gaus, "Die parlamentarische Opposition" and "Die lästige Presse", SZ, Jan. 26 and March 23, 1963.

tactics of private bargaining have failed to produce. The image of parliamentary debate which the public receives is the product, however, of other factors in addition to Opposition tactics.[24]

Traditional Concepts of Organizing Debate

The traditional concept of a separation between the Government, on the one hand, and the entire Parliament, on the other, still influences the way in which parliamentary debate is organized, and presents its own obstacle to a confrontation between Government and Opposition. It may, for example, affect the distribution of speaking time. Not only do members of the Cabinet have an absolute constitutional right to speak at any time,[25] but the Rules require the President of the Bundestag to take account of the strengths of the parties in recognizing the order of speakers and in distributing speaking time. When the CDU/CSU insists, therefore, its speaker may directly follow a speech by a member of the Government, a sequence which the SPD sought to alter by a Rules change at the beginning of the fifth Bundestag—an attempt in line with its renewed efforts to engage in a vigorous debate with the Government.[26] Meanwhile, whatever gain the CDU/CSU derives from speaking first in a debate opened by a Government spokesman is won at the expense of a clear confrontation between Government and Opposition.

The Rules furthermore provide that the time taken by a minister in debate cannot be charged against the time available to the largest party, even though that party already can claim its proportionately large share of speaking time. In practice, with one exception, it has not been necessary to make such a formal allocation of time since 1953, because of the success of informal agreements among the parties, on the basis of equal shares for all.

But the old theory still lurks in the background, effective whenever interparty agreements fail, as the exception in 1958 demonstrated. At that time, in a foreign affairs debate which the majority found to be

[24] For the four-day debate on the declaration of Government policy, see *Dt. Btag.*, 5. W.P., 7–10. Sitz., Nov. 29, 30, and Dec. 1, 2, 1965, pp. 82–127, 139–227, 231–334, 353–386. For the foreign affairs debate, see *Dt. Btag.*, 5. W.P., 13. Sitz., Jan. 12, 1966, pp. 498–516. For the defense debate, see *Dt. Btag.*, 5. W.P., 33. Sitz., March 24, 1966, pp. 1510–1597.

[25] *Basic Law*, art. 43(2).

[26] *Die Welt*, March 9, 1966. See also the debate on this proposal, *Dt. Btag.*, 48. Sitz., June 16, 1966, pp. 2318–2323; Drs. 396.

going against it, CDU/CSU whip Rasner moved to limit the debate to an additional eight hours, to be shared by the parties in proportion to their size, in accordance with the existing but rarely employed Rule of the House. The SPD protested, and subsequently appealed to the Federal Constitutional Court, asserting that to leave the members of the Cabinet unrestricted when allotting debating time among the parties gave the majority an unjustifiable advantage in principle. But the Court ruled in favor of the majority, clearly basing its opinion on the theory of the separation of powers between Government and Parliament. "In the speeches of Members of the Government," its opinion stated, "it is primarily the view of the Government which is expressed, which need not coincide with that of the parliamentary majority." [27]

Since the Government is not fully identified, either legally or popularly, or even by its members, with the parliamentary majority, the parliamentary minority is not clearly regarded, either by those belonging to it or by the public, as the Opposition to the party in office. Until 1961, the minority always consisted of more than one party, and made very little concerted effort to act as a single Opposition.[28] The SPD, the largest, most continuous, and, after 1961, the only party in opposition, still suffered, despite its moderate course, from the traditional accusation that it stood in opposition to the state rather than merely to the political majority. CDU/CSU leaders in the Cabinet, particularly

[27] *BVerfGE* 10, 4, at p. 19. The Rule of the House employed in this instance was par. 39.

[28] One index of the division among the opposition parties can be found in the sponsorship of parliamentary motions. During the first Bundestag, out of 153 motions sponsored by Members belonging to the SPD as well as other parties, only 3 motions were advanced entirely by Members of the Opposition, not including a single interpellation or written question (see Kralewski and Neunreither, *op. cit.*, pp. 47, 52, 63, 70–71, 75). In the second Bundestag, the situation did not change despite the disappearance of extremist parties from the ranks of the Opposition. Of 1421 motions designed to exercise some sort of control over the Government, including interpellations, written and oral questions, and resolutions requesting Government action, only 4 were moved entirely by Members of more than one opposition party. Each party was apparently anxious to demonstrate its independence in its public actions in the House. Likewise, in the third Bundestag, with only the FDP remaining with the SPD in Opposition, their cooperation in the sponsorship of motions was extremely rare. For the statistics on the second Bundestag, I am indebted to Jürgen Fijalkowski, who made available to me an unpublished study he directed at the Institute for Political Science of the Free University of Berlin entitled "Die Interpellation als parlamentarisches Kontrollinstrument" (May, 1961).

Adenauer, frequently played on this Bismarckian image of the SPD. Furthermore, to the extent that these Government leaders remained aloof from parliamentary politics, they reinforced the traditional distinction between a Government which stood above politics, and a Parliament enmeshed in it.[29] Occasional CDU/CSU criticism of the Government contributed to this image. Traditional conceptions of the political system, therefore, reinforced by the self-interest of the parties throughout most of the first four terms of the Bundestag, prevented the appearance of a two-sided parliamentary alignment which, in its simplicity, could add greatly to the attraction of the parliamentary debate.

Press Coverage of Debate

Inadequate press coverage of parliamentary debate is another obstacle to its ability to perform the function of political communication. The mass circulation boulevard press, of which the *Bild Zeitung* is the leading example, gives no serious attention to parliamentary news at all, although it occasionally panders to popular prejudices about Parliament. Television news is undoubtedly the widest source of parliamentary news for the general public, but although the presentation is done in an accomplished documentary style, and quite naturally focuses on the debates, the reports are necessarily very brief. The dramatic capacity of television to communicate parliamentary debates to the public has been evident whenever live telecasts of entire debates have been permitted, but the policy of the House in allowing such telecasts has varied, as we shall see, and they are in any case limited to exceptional occasions. The politically interested public must normally depend on the serious national dailies, such as the *Frankfurter Allgemeine Zeitung, Die Welt,* and the *Süddeutsche Zeitung,* all of which give fairly extensive coverage to parliamentary developments.

On the occasions of major debates, these newspapers offer substantial summaries of the most important speeches. Their normal emphasis, however, is on decisions taken rather than the procedures by which they have been reached, relegating the parliamentary process, including debate, to a subordinate position. Whether a bill has re-

[29] See Adolf Arndt's discussion of the consequent dilemma facing the SPD, in "Die Entmachtung des Bundestages," *Die Neue Gesellschaft,* VI (1959), 435.

ceived Cabinet or Bundestag approval, or whether a policy has been announced in a press conference or in answer to a parliamentary question, receives little attention in the press. How successfully the Opposition defended its position receives far less notice than its inevitable defeat in the vote. Caucus and committee meetings, where parliamentary decisions usually hatch, receive coverage only in those newspapers which happen to have special access to these closed meetings. Newspapers with an affinity for a particular party may gain admittance to its caucus, but not to the caucuses of the other parties. The organ of an interest group may have special sources of information among the members of a particular committee and may report its work in some detail; but general coverage of caucus and committee meetings is not to be found in any single newspaper.

Most reporting in the serious newspapers is nonpartisan to a fault. The partisan content of parliamentary decisions is frequently ignored, and actions taken, in effect, by party leaders or party majorities are attributed to "the Bundestag," with the implication that the institution is accountable for them. This tendency to overlook partisanship is in part the consequence of the structure of the postwar press. While over half the daily newspapers in the Weimar Republic were bound to political parties, and reported with corresponding political color, this is true of only one-eighth of the press today as a result of the licensing policies of the Allied occupation. Two-thirds of the papers, including all the best-known national dailies, aspire to nonpartisan independence, leading them to revert to those legalistic interpretations of events which are second nature to German political observers.[30]

Interpretive news analysis suffers from the unfamiliarity of most capital correspondents with the complexities of parliamentary procedure. Elegant portrayals of parliamentary atmosphere in *feuilleton* style are their *forte*, but effective analysis which explains the background of parliamentary decisions is rare. In this respect, the press reflects the ignorance of parliamentary politics of a generation of reporters and readers which did not grow up familiar with them, a generation whose politically interested members are concerned with the results of parliamentary politics but indifferent to its methods.

The lack of sophistication in parliamentary reporting is also in part a

[30] Helga Haftendorn, *op. cit., passim.*

consequence of technical problems. The location of the capital in a provincial university town, separated from the major publishing centers, insulates both politicians and newspapers from the immediacy of events. Even the largest dailies depend for their parliamentary reporting on a small staff of capital correspondents whose field is the entire Federal Government. None regularly assign correspondents to the press gallery of the Bundestag. Only the press associations, which supply most of the smaller papers in the country, have representatives on the scene in the House. The large newspapers have conveniently arranged loudspeaker transmission of debates to their offices in Bonn, and their reporting has a corresponding secondhand quality. The delay of the appearance of the previous day's stenographic transcript until mid-day, out of a desire for a "corrected text" checked by the speakers, indexed, and with bold-faced emphases and official pagination,[31] further handicaps coverage of debate.

The spartan amenities offered in Bonn inhibit the social contact between correspondents and politicians on which reporting in depth depends. The weekend exodus reduces the chance for leisurely contacts. Few practicing journalists have sat in the House, although two prominent members of the profession were elected in 1965, and few Members have turned to parliamentary reporting.

Some parliamentarians do cultivate contact with the press. The President of the House has a press secretary, appears frequently on national television news and feature programs, and devotes considerable energy to explaining the Parliament to the public in newspaper and magazine interviews. The same is true of the parliamentary party leaders and, to a somewhat lesser extent, to the vice-presidents of the House. Many backbenchers use their local newspapers to publicize their activities and explain their actions. But this attention to publicity on the part of Members is no substitute for informed newspaper reporting of parliamentary developments.

The success of two periodicals, the newsmagazine *Der Spiegel* and the weekly newspaper *Die Zeit*, demonstrates that a demand exists for more penetrating political reporting than the daily newspapers supply. But the critical, inside-dopester reporting of the first, and the didactic

[31] For a discussion of the process of preparing the official stenographic report, see the article by the chief of the stenographic division, L. Krieger, in *Das Parlament*, Jan. 14, 1953, p. 8.

discussions of political institutions in the second, while valuable in many respects, supplement the informing function of Parliament, rather than facilitate it.

The news coverage which Parliament receives therefore offers little reward for the Member who is able to turn in a brilliant solo performance in a debate, who can make a telling attack on the position of the other side, or a particularly effective defense of his own. It places a premium on the carefully prepared speech expressing the official party position, on the well-planned parliamentary timetable, on the effectively marshalled party vote. Genuine parliamentary debate, extemporaneous speech, or spontaneous procedural developments are not effectively transmitted to the public. The coverage of what is said in Parliament and of how decisions are made is sparse and dull, creating a vicious circle in which the quality of the parliamentary discourse and of the parliamentary style, the report of it, and public interest in it, depress one another.

The Functions of Debate

In the chamber of the Bundestag, itself more appropriate for lecture than for debate, the public discourse can perform few of the political functions which Bagehot regarded as among Parliament's most important. Given the limits of the skills of its Members, the insistence of each of the parliamentary parties upon speaking with one voice, the absence of a clear confrontation between Government and Opposition, and the disinterest of the press, public speaking in the Bundestag is dominated by a succession of party statements hopefully addressed to the electorate. Speaking is therefore the special province of the party leaders and, on technical issues, the party specialists. It cannot affect the tenure of the Government in office, which can be replaced only by the very unlikely formation of a new majority capable of electing a new Chancellor. It cannot change votes on the floor in the face of strict party discipline. It does not permit many Members to make individual reputations with their constituents, because there is little room for the expression of individual views. Because it lacks spontaneity, clarity of viewpoints, and variety of styles, it does not readily reach the large general public to which it is addressed. Other forums provide political leaders with more efficient means of reaching specialized audiences. Debate is not employed as a means of communication between Members of the House, because the private channels available within the caucuses and the committees are preferred for this purpose. In short, debate is not an integral part of the process of negotiation and bargaining which takes place within the Bundestag, but rather a cover for this process. What it has to communicate is hence of very limited interest.

Public vs. Private Deliberation

The time available for public debate is therefore under severe pressure from the caucuses and committees which must carry on in private the deliberations which do not take place in public. These organs of Parliament, while dating back to the Empire and earlier, have in the postwar period developed a greater structural complexity and a more time-consuming deliberative process which has eaten heavily into the time allotted to the public sessions of the House. The creation of working groups within the parliamentary parties—in effect, committees of the caucus covering the entire range of policy subjects— and the growth of a salaried staff of research assistants for these groups have produced an arduous deliberative process within the party caucuses. The committees of the Bundestag, in turn, have multiplied since the time of the Reichstag in a desire to match the complexity of political issues with the necessary parliamentary division of labor and expertise. Equipped with staff, keeping records of their deliberations, they too occupy a larger proportion of the time of Members than during the Weimar Republic. In view of the proportion of the deliberative process which takes place in private, the public sessions of the Bundestag take on a staged appearance, registering what the parties and the committees have worked out, and are often regarded as a chore to be dispensed with as efficiently as possible. Their number has declined not only in comparison with the Imperial and Weimar Reichstage, but quite steadily throughout the postwar period, until a major reform effort in the final year of the fourth Bundestag reversed the long-term trend. (See Table 39.)

During the third and most of the fourth parliamentary term, the public business of the House was performed in a relatively few, long sessions, concentrated in two weeks per month and in three days of each of these weeks. The schedule, designed to reserve ample time for the committees and the parties, produced sessions which were tiring

Table 39. Frequency and duration of public sessions of parliaments

Parliament and time period	Sitting days (annual average)	Length of sitting (daily average in hours and minutes)	Length of sitting (annual average in hours)
Imperial Reichstag, 1903–1911	104 [a]	– [b]	–
Weimar Reichstag, 1920–24;			
1925–30	108.2	4:24	475
1st Bundestag, 1949–1953	68.5	6:19	433
2nd Bundestag, 1953–1957	55.8	7:37	425
3rd Bundestag, 1957–1961	41.8	6:45	281
4th Bundestag, 1961–1965	49.0	5:33	273
U.K. House of Commons,			
1954–1958	161.6	7:54	1280
U.S. House of Representatives,			
1954–1958	125.8	4:13	532
French National Assembly,			
1954	132	6:02	796

[a] For the Imperial Reichstage the figure represents number of sessions rather than days of sitting; in view of the possibility of having more than one session on a single day, the average number of sitting days might be slightly lower.

[b] Dash indicates no information available.

Sources: Based on Karl Gutzler, "Wie die Parlamente tagen," *Das Parlament,* December 7, 1960.

for participants and tiresome for observers, beginning generally at 9 A.M. and often lasting well into the evening. A weekly agenda commonly contained twenty to thirty items, including half a dozen pieces of legislation, with twice as many points during the pre-vacation rush. In the endeavor to make the public sessions more attractive, a new schedule adopted in 1964–1965 provided half-day sittings on the last three days of the three weeks a month when the House was in session, with the fourth week in each month free of all parliamentary meetings. This was a compromise between the committee chairmen and party leaders, who fought tenaciously to reserve three days a week entirely for their meetings, and the reformers, led by the President of the House, who pressed for four sitting days a week. In the last months of the parliamentary term, full-day meetings again proved unavoidable, but in its final year the fourth Bundestag held sixty-three public sessions while its predecessor had held only forty-five. A long trend away from public sessions was, for the moment, halted by a determined effort to re-emphasize the public performance of the House and concern about the atrophy of this aspect of its work.

Parliamentary debate depends not only on the ability and propensity of Members to discuss their political differences in the public sessions of the House, but upon the procedural framework within which deliberation is possible. The traditional procedures for debate have each exhibited important shortcomings in the experience of the Bundestag, leading to significant innovations.

Declarations of Policy

Among the conventional formats, debates on general declarations of Government policy have become particularly stiff and formal. In the nature of broad-ranging state-of-the-union addresses, such policy statements are expected of the Chancellor following his election, and, during the fourth Bundestag, they took place annually. Because the parties have required substantial time to prepare their responses, discussion of these statements has usually been delayed until a week after their presentation and has consisted of a succession of similarly broad, hour-long speeches read by the party leaders. No longer timely when they are presented, these speeches have produced no real debate. While in the first two parliamentary terms the discussion of the statement of Government policy occupied several days and was marked by a variety of contributions and responses, in 1957 it was completed in a single session lasting eight hours. On that occasion speeches by five party leaders were followed by some debate, including rejoinders from members of the Government.[32] Four years later the Government refused to be drawn into a debate, and after nine and one-half hours of speeches by nine party leaders, the Opposition abruptly announced that it saw no point in carrying the discussion further.[33] The ultimate in formality was achieved upon Erhard's accession in 1963, when the whole debate, consisting of a speech by each of

[32] Dt. Btag., 3. W.P., 4. Sitz., Nov. 5, 1957, pp. 31–98. Cf. FAZ, Nov. 6, 1957.
[33] Dt. Btag., 4. W.P., 6. Sitz., Dec. 6, 1961, p. 123. Cf. FAZ, Dec. 7, 8, 1961.

the three leaders of the parliamentary parties and a brief response by the new Chancellor, lasted only four and three-quarter hours.[34] The four-day debate on Government policy at the beginning of the Bundestag's fifth term, which was a product of the SPD's renewed interest in vigorous opposition, indicated that this parliamentary occasion had been unduly neglected, although even in this case the debate suffered from long, prepared speeches, and from a two-week interval between the Chancellor's statement and the parliamentary rejoinder.

Budget Debates

Budget debates, in earlier times a high point of parliamentary discussion, have also declined in importance as occasions for public deliberation. The presentation of the budget to the Bundestag by the Finance Minister has none of the drama of budget day in Great Britain, since the budget, like all legislation, is first submitted to the Bundesrat. The first reading debate has the stiff and formal character of the debates on general declarations of Government policy; in 1964 the budget debate was actually combined with a debate on a general policy declaration with which the Chancellor followed the Finance Minister.[35] Theoretically, the second reading of the budget, when amendments are in order, offers an excellent opportunity to the Opposition to raise questions of administrative policy. However, this stage of the passage of the budget has always taken place under intense pressure of time, coming well after the beginning of the fiscal year, with the whole House anxious to achieve the budget's enactment. Furthermore, since the Appropriations Committee has considered the budget in detail, giving all parties the opportunity to negotiate changes, the public debate can merely repeat the committee deliberation and there is hence no genuine possibility of making further changes. As a result, the Opposition limits itself to a few specific aspects of administrative policy for public criticism during the second and third readings. Since 1957, this stage of the budget debate has occupied between four and eight sittings annually, although a speed record of 2 days was set in 1964.[36]

[34] *Dt. Btag.*, 4. W.P., 92 Sitz., Oct. 24, 1963, pp. 4244–87.

[35] *Dt. Btag.*, 4. W.P., 136., 137., 138., and 139. Sitz., Oct. 13, 15, 16, and 21, 1964.

[36] *Dt. Btag.*, 4. W.P., 122. and 123. Sitz., April 15 and 16, 1964. Cf. *Die Welt*, April 16 and 17, 1964; *Die Zeit* (U.S. ed.), May 1, 1964. See also p. 374, *supra.*

Debates on Legislation

By far the most frequent opportunity for debate is given in the course of the legislative process, but this too has severe limitations. A large part of the discussion of a bill has been completed before it ever reaches the Bundestag. More than half of all bills are enacted without any public discussion in the House. These tend to be technical measures of little interest to the parties, or instruments ratifying international treaties or agreements. Major legislation may be discussed in three readings, but the first reading debate has become increasingly rare, as the parties are reticent about making public commitments prior to the committee stage. The second and third readings are generally telescoped, since, although they are technically distinct under the Rules, they each offer equally good opportunities for advancing amendments. The debate at this stage is therefore largely addressed to specific changes being offered to the texts. Conducted by the subject-matter specialists of the parties against the background of exhaustive committee deliberations, the main legislative debate thus centers on technicalities.[37] At the same time it is often the most spontaneous debate which the House ever hears, and offers examples of experts persuading each other on various details at the last moment, in brief, genuine interchanges. "I don't deny that the remarks of the gentleman of the SPD have made some impression on us," a CDU Member declared during a debate on a defense measure in 1962 for example.[38] He thereupon proposed that a motion for higher army severance pay be referred back to committee for further consideration, achieving a mutually satisfactory compromise of the type occasionally possible on the floor of the House. The necessarily complicated and fragmented discussions of this type are, however, of only very limited general interest.

[37] The tendency in this direction was already discernible in the first Bundestag (see Kralewski and Neunreither, *op. cit.*, p. 78). In a recent article, a parliamentary whip of the SPD wrote that in the legislative process "the Bundestag no longer regards itself as the place where political opinion is decisively formed, but merely as the technical instrument for the enactment of bills," because, as he charges, "the political discussion takes place outside the Bundestag." Friedrich Schäfer, "Aufgaben einer Parlamentsreform," *Die Neue Gesellschaft*, XII (1965), 690.

[38] *Dt. Btag.*, 4. W.P., 16. Sitz., Feb. 22, 1962, p. 504.

Interpellations

All three of these procedural devices fail to provide an opportunity to discuss major current issues independently of the timetable of legislation, appropriations, and the formation of Cabinets. The classic instruments for this purpose in continental parliaments has been the interpellation (*Grosse Anfrage*). In existence in the rules of procedure of German parliaments for over a century, its strengthening in 1912 was one of the major achievements in the development of parliamentarism during the Empire. Its use and abuse thereafter typified the problems of debate in the German Parliament. During the Weimar Republic, interpellations were moved with such frequency that they could be considered only in groups, or in connection with substantive questions, often in the context of appropriations debates, and frequently with much delay. In the four-year term of the Reichstag elected in 1924, a high point was reached with the introduction of 231 interpellations, three-fourths of them by the opposition parties. Of the total number of interpellations, 189 were actually dealt with, but only 3 of them were treated as individual items on the agenda, and only 14 were not combined with other substantive motions. Under these circumstances, the interpellation was largely destroyed as a device for debating Government policy on a major current issue.[39]

During the first term of the Bundestag, the interpellation was employed at something near its prewar rate, but great efforts were made to debate these interpellations as separate agenda points. Although only three parties possessed the minimum strength of thirty Members required to advance an interpellation under the Rules, 160 interpellations were submitted during the four year-term, resulting in 104 interpellation debates. Sixty per cent were introduced by the opposition parties, and most of these by the SPD, but the governing parties employed them also to permit the Government to take the initiative in debating policy questions, and some were advanced by the joint efforts of various parties.[40] The number of interpellations has declined ever since. There were 97 introduced in the second Bundestag, with 71 interpellation debates; 49 during the third Bundestag, resulting in 42

---

[39] P. Thamm, "Die gegenwärtige Handhabung der Interpellation im Deutschen Reichstag" (unpublished doctoral dissertation, University of Kiel, 1930).

[40] Kralewski and Neunreither, *op. cit.*, pp. 60–61.

debates; and 34 during the fourth Bundestag, discussed in 33 debates.[41]

The decline in the number of interpellations is due in part to their cumbersomeness. Although the Rules enable the Bundestag to debate an interpellation even if the Government does not answer after two weeks, the House, restrained by the governing majority, has always contented itself to wait at least a month for the Government's reply. This limits the usefulness of the interpellation to general policy issues which do not have great timely interest. For the major governing party, the interpellation has proved awkward, for the order of speeches in this procedure is out of keeping with the political relationship between Government and Opposition. Under the Rules, the interpellant must first justify his questions, and must be followed by a minister as respondent; other Members can be recognized only in the subsequent debate. This places the Opposition third, after two speakers for the viewpoint of the majority, in cases where a member of the governing coalition initiates the interpellation. During the third and fourth terms of the Bundestag, the CDU/CSU all but abandoned interpellations, leaving them to be used by the Opposition and by the smaller coalition parties, which employed them to demonstrate their individuality.

As the sessions of the House became fewer, the number of interpellations also declined, but the average interpellation took five times as long in the third Bundestag as it did in the first. The proportion of the total debating time of the House spent on 49 interpellations between 1957 and 1961 was more than three times as great as that spent on 160 interpellations between 1949 and 1953. The questions raised in each interpellation have become ever more numerous and complex, requiring longer and more ponderous substantiations and replies. Both require detailed preparation, but since the interpellant and the minister prepare their statements in ignorance of each other's remarks, it is a matter of chance if they end up responding to each other instead of merely following one another in the debate. As a result, an instrument designed to call the Government to account promptly for a specific act of policy has become merely a device on which to hang an occasional discussion of a major policy theme.

[41] Statistics for the second, third, and fourth Bundestage were supplied by the Bundestag secretariat.

Question Hour

All of these traditional procedural forms of debate fail to provide the opportunity for the lively, timely discussions which are most likely to attract the public interest. Two new procedures have been introduced to fulfill this objective. The first is the question hour, modeled after British practice, with which nearly every sitting of the Bundestag has been opened since the fall of 1960. The right of Members to ask oral questions during a special hour, set aside at least monthly for the purpose, was included in the Rules of Procedure adopted in 1951, with the hope that it would "enliven the relationship between legislature and executive" and would give the individual Representative a means of obtaining information from the Government efficiently and rapidly.[42] Precedents existed, since oral questions without debate had been introduced in the Imperial Reichstag in 1912 and had been in use early in the Weimar Republic. Their abuse by the antiparliamentary parties, however, led to their transformation in 1922 into written questions with written replies, depriving them of most of their publicity value.[43]

Those who first employed oral questions in the early years of the Bundestag therefore lacked all experience with the procedure, and the results were awkward. Long questions, painfully read from the podium, prompted exhaustive prepared replies, read by ministers or their senior officials.[44] Supplementaries could be asked only by the original questioner. Few Members possessed the skill to follow up a prepared question with further extemporaneous ones. Few ministers, and even fewer civil servants, were willing to depart from their prepared responses. Although the Chancellor is constitutionally responsible for determining the general policy of the Government, Adenauer refused to submit himself to questioning and Erhard has answered only once or twice. Instead, the Chancellor's office distributes the questions to the various ministries for response.[45] Since the question hour took

[42] *Dt. Btag.,* 1. W.P., 179. Sitz., Dec. 6, 1951, p. 7449; *Geschäftsordnung des Deutschen Bundestages,* par. 111.

[43] For the earlier history of oral questions, see pp. 18, 22, *supra.*

[44] See for example, the reprimand administered by Bundestag President Ehlers to Economics Minister Erhard for having given an eight minute answer (*Dt. Btag.,* 2. W.P., 35. Sitz., June 24, 1954, p. 1642).

[45] See *Gemeinsame Geschäftsordnung der Bundesministerien,* Besonderer Teil (GGO II), par. 9, which foresees, however, that the Chancellor might answer important questions.

place only once or twice a month, considerable delay could occur between the posing of a question and the reply.

Under these circumstances, questions tended to be of a parochial nature, designed mainly to obtain information on matters of local concern to constituents. More than half of them were directed to the ministries of Finance, Transport, and the Interior, in that order of frequency. The attention which ministers gave to the questions varied considerably. More than half the answers from the Finance Ministry were given by its senior official during the second Bundestag, while the Minister of the Interior answered three-fourths of his Department's questions himself, and the Minister of Transport personally answered four-fifths of his. During the first full term that questions were allowed, more than a third of them were answered by senior officials.[46] Occasionally, questions had to be passed over because neither the minister nor his official was present to answer them.[47]

The question hour survived its early growing pains, however, and has gained an important place as an instrument of lively discussion in the Bundestag, although it has developed characteristics which distinguish it from its namesake in the House of Commons.[48] The question-and-answer procedure improved through experience, as the reading of the question was abandoned, in favor of placing its text on the agenda; [49] ministers were permitted to respond from their place on the Government bench; [50] and questioners were allowed to ask supplementaries from microphones on the floor.[51] In 1960 the Bundestag undertook a major reform of the procedure, designed to encourage the use of questions to raise current political issues.[52] Thereafter, nearly every

[46] For the statistics on oral questions in the second Bundestag, I am indebted to Bernhard Vogel, research assistant at the Institute for Political Science at the University of Heidelberg, and, since 1965, a member of the Bundestag, who is engaged in an extensive study of the question hour.

[47] For an extreme example, see Dt. Btag., 2. W.P., 103. Sitz., Sept. 29, 1955, pp. 5676, 5679, 5680, 5681.

[48] For the definitive study of questions in the House of Commons, see D. N. Chester and Nona Bowring, Questions in Parliament (Oxford: Clarendon Press, 1962). See also the analysis now available of questions in the French Parliament by Michel Ameller, Les Questions-Instrument du Contrôle Parlementaire (Paris: Librairie Générale de Droit et de Jurisprudence, 1964).

[49] Dt. Btag., 2. W.P., 7. Sitz., Dec. 3, 1953, p. 129; 8. Sitz., Dec. 10, 1953, p. 176; 10. Sitz., Jan. 21, 1954, p. 278; 116. Sitz., Dec. 7, 1955, p. 6192.

[50] DZ, Nov. 4, 1959.

[51] SZ, March 6, 1954.

[52] Dt. Btag., 3. W.P., 121. Sitz., June 29, 1960, pp. 6960, 7031–2.

session of the House was opened by a question hour, supplementaries could be asked by Members other than the questioner, and questions admitted as "urgent" by the President could be put as late as noon on the day before they were to be answered. Normally an interval of two to three working days was required, and each Member could submit up to three questions per week. To facilitate the presence of ministers when questions addressed to them arose, a system of grouping questions by ministries was adopted which enabled the President of the House, in consultation with ministers, to arrange the order in which the various ministries would answer.[53]

With these changes, oral questions have assumed a greater and a more varied importance in the public sessions of the House. The rate with which Members have submitted them has increased sharply, from 200 annually in the first years, to over 1,200 per year during the fourth term of the Bundestag. By far the largest proportion continue to be parochial in nature, directed heavily, as before, to the ministries of Transport, Finance, and the Interior, with the first named now leading all others.[54] Although the departments of Defense and Foreign Affairs continue to attract only a small proportion of all questions, some of these have been politically very important. In 1962, almost by accident, the SPD discovered that a series of closely related questions permitted a systematic examination of a major Government policy. Near the parliamentary recess that year, with time inadequate to initiate the interpellation on foreign policy which the Opposition wanted, SPD leaders submitted ten questions on the Government's European policy. Skillfully followed up with supplementaries, the questions produced a forty-five-minute interpellation in abbreviated form, without the usual preparation and delay. A genuine and spontaneous debate, though marked by extremely brief contributions, enabled the minister to explain and justify the Government's policy, and the Opposition to illuminate its misgivings and to prod the Government. Public interest in the exchange was strong. The press gallery,

[53] See "Richtlinien für die Fragestunde," *Geschäftsordnung des Deutschen Bundestages,* Anlage 1.

[54] An analysis of the 649 questions answered orally in the 31 question hours held between the end of the summer recess on October 9, 1963, and the start of the Easter recess on March 19, 1964, indicates that the greatest number of questions are addressed to the following Ministries (with percentages of the total in parentheses): Transport (22%), Finance (11%), Interior (11%), Foreign Affairs (9%), Agriculture (8%), Defense (7%), Labor (6%).

usually all but empty during the question hour, was crowded with eighty newsmen for the occasion, and newspaper coverage was correspondingly extensive.[55]

Encouraged by the possibilities of this new dimension of the question hour, the Opposition employed systematic questioning again, with more spectacular effect, the following autumn, with eighteen questions on the "*Spiegel* affair." The issue became so heated, the supplementaries so numerous, that three days elapsed before all the questions had been answered. At the conclusion of the first day's questioning, the Chancellor intervened with a policy statement which produced rejoinders and an unruly debate. By the time the questions had been disposed of, Defense Minister Strauss had been severely damaged in the cross-examination, and other ministers substantially implicated. This public exposure directly produced the FDP's withdrawal from the coalition and the subsequent reorganization of the Cabinet without Strauss. In the process, however, the question hour, in the words of the President, had been "distorted into a not very successful debate," and its limitations became a matter of concern.[56] Nevertheless, the Opposition continued to make occasional use of this type of systematic questioning, using it in 1964 to question the Minister of the Interior about wire tapping, in a question hour during which a record seventy-seven questions and supplementaries were answered.[57] Later in the same year, the SPD used it to obtain a foreign policy debate, at which time, as a rare exception, the Chancellor himself answered a question.[58] The occasional use of oral questions as a major instrument of the Opposition was undoubtedly due both to the versatility of the procedure and to the absence of a satisfactory alternative for a debate on a current issue.

Apart from the great variety of forms which oral questions take, the sheer rise in their volume, the regularity with which they appear on the agenda, the speed with which responses must be prepared, and the greater chance for supplementaries from the floor have all increased

---

[55] The occasion is described in detail in the general article by Nevil Johnson, "Questions in the Bundestag," *Parliamentary Affairs*, XVI (1962–63), 22–34, esp. 29–31.

[56] *Dt. Btag.*, 4. W.P., 45., 46., and 47. Sitz., Nov. 7, 8, and 9, 1962, pp. 1949–63, 1980–2010, 2013–26, 2075–90.

[57] *Dt. Btag.*, 4. W.P., 112. Sitz., Feb. 7, 1964, pp. 5141–52.

[58] *Dt. Btag.*, 4. W.P., 145. and 147. Sitz., Nov. 11 and 13, 1964, pp. 7156–7, 7227–40.

their importance for the ministries. Although a minister may evade questions by sending his senior official, there is a considerable political incentive for him to appear personally. The proportion of all questions answered by ministers has increased from two-thirds ten years ago to over three-quarters today.

The backbencher has not used the question hour as widely as has his counterpart in Great Britain.[59] Not counting the Cabinet, only one-third of the Members of the House ask questions in an average year, a proportion only slightly higher than it was ten years ago. Furthermore, 10 per cent of the Members ask over 60 per cent of all questions, indicating that there are question specialists in each party. In part this is undoubtedly due to the general reticence about participation in debate, and in part it is due to the influence of party control and specialization, which affects oral questions as it does every other procedure of the House. As in Britain, the propensity to ask questions is stronger in the Opposition than in the main governing party. Among CDU/CSU Members, with their superior direct access to ministers and their reluctance to embarrass them publicly, the rate of questions per member was one-fourth as high as in the SPD during the early years and, though significantly higher now, is still less than half of what it is in the Opposition. But the SPD, which supplies the large majority of all queries, subjects the questioning activity of its Members to party control, as no party does in Britain. Members must submit their draft questions to the party's parliamentary whip for clearance on form, consistency with party policy, and tactics. Furthermore, the party plans questions and question series, as well as supplementaries, to develop policy points, and frequently engages its research assistants in drafting the questions. In important cases, as in the foreign policy and *Spiegel* series, questioning is done by the top leaders. In general, the party relies on Members who have specialized in the use of oral questions. Supplementaries are sometimes as carefully written out as the questions themselves.

The CDU/CSU permits its Members to submit their questions directly to the clerks' office. A smaller proportion of its Members partici-

[59] Although in a typical five week period in 1958–59 there were 260 Members who did not ask any questions in the House of Commons, and 12 Members asked one-fifth of all the 2418 questions which were put down for oral reply, in the course of the whole year, only 60 Members failed to ask any questions at all (Chester and Bowring, *op. cit.*, pp. 192–6). The statistics for the Bundestag in the following paragraph are based on the sample referred to in n. 54, *supra.*

pate than in the SPD, and those who do so employ questions mainly for constituency purposes. In the relationship which exists between the parliamentary majority and the ministries, informal persuasion can be employed, if necessary, to obtain the withdrawal of a question, so that indirect party control suffices.

Opposition specialization in asking questions confronts Government specialization in answering. Within ministries, replies to questions are generally drafted by the appropriate technical specialists and frequently have a correspondingly detailed thoroughness. This, plus the care with which the questions tend to be drafted in the first place, produces lengthier and stiffer exchanges on the floor of the Bundestag than in the House of Commons. In addition, the popularity of supplementaries, since the new rules liberalized their use, and the reluctance of the presiding officers to cut them off with the same discretion exercised by Mr. Speaker, has added to the time spent on each question. In an average hour, the Bundestag covers somewhat less than half the number of questions which the House of Commons dispatches in fifty minutes.[60] As a result, the 167 question hours held during the 198 sittings of the fourth Bundestag could not dispose of all of the 4,758 questions submitted, and about one-fourth of the questions had to be answered in writing.[61]

The versatility of the oral question, which explains its quantitative

[60] In the House of Commons during an average sitting in 1964, 40 questions, which were accompanied by 60 supplementaries, were answered in about 50 minutes (see Second Report from the Select Committee on Procedure, Session 1964–65, p. 9). The average in the Bundestag during 1963–64 was 21 questions, accompanied by 38 supplementaries (a greater proportion than in Great Britain) answered in a full hour.

[61] Questions are answered in writing, and published in the stenographic reports, if the questioner agrees to this procedure in advance, is not present in the House and has not named a substitute when the question comes up, or when the question has not been reached during the question hours of the week for which it was submitted; oral questions put during the summer recess of the House are also answered in writing, within 14 days of their submission. In addition, the procedure of the Bundestag permits a minimum of 15 Members to submit written questions (Kleine Anfragen) to the Government for written reply (Rules, par. 110). This is a vestigal remainder of the oral questions of the Weimar period and is still actively used on subjects requiring detailed responses. Written questions receive less publicity than oral questions, since the responses are published in the printed papers of the Bundestag. The overwhelming majority of them is submitted by the SPD. Their number has remained high despite the rapid rise in the number of oral questions, totaling 355 for the 1st Bundestag, 377 for the second, 411 for the third, and 306 for the fourth.

success, also suggests its liabilities as a deliberative procedure. Because of the great variety of subjects which come up in the question hour, because ministers need not answer and ministerial reputations do not necessarily depend on this type of parliamentary performance, and because the questioning often comes at an inconveniently early morning hour, neither the House nor the press pays as careful attention to it in the Bundestag as it does in Great Britain. The diffident attitude of Members toward the question hour is apparent most mornings as, with only an average attendance and with the usual hum of conversation and turning of newspaper pages, the exchanges between minister and Member take place across the vast reaches of the chamber, unattended by the press. Since local papers, lacking their own correspondents or alert representation through the national agencies, are poorly equipped to report on answers of interest in their area, only the questions of general concern receive that newspaper prominence which gives the question period in the House of Commons its exceptional resonance.

So far there are few rules or conventions governing the questioning. The reform of the procedure in 1960 was accomplished by an agreement upon "guidelines," rather than a revision of Rules, because party leaders wanted to experiment and were reluctant to make commitments. The guidelines state that questions must pertain to the policy of the Federal Government or to administrative matters for which it is responsible—but without further definition this covers an extremely broad area.[62] Although the President has occasionally decided that a question is inadmissible, his approach has been permissive, and, being reluctant to issue rulings, he has relied on persuasion through the Council of Elders to obtain a withdrawal. Together with his colleagues in the chair, he has been liberal in accepting supplementaries from the floor, employing occasional sarcasm rather than rules to achieve brevity in the interrogation.[63] In the atmosphere of easy cooperation among the parliamentary parties, there has been little incentive to develop precedents which would protect the practice of oral questioning against misuse, and all efforts have concentrated on stimulating the use of the procedure.

[62] *Richtlinien,* par. 5. In addition, subjects on the agenda for the week's sittings are, by agreement reached in the Council of Elders, ineligible.

[63] The usual practice is to permit all other Members up to two supplementary questions after the original questioner has had two.

The resulting flexibility has permitted the question hour to be used for everything from the constituency business of a backbencher to official Opposition criticism of major Government policies or ministers; from rapid exchanges to substantial debates; from obtaining narrow technical information to extracting major political confessions. Its vitality and development indicate the need for various procedures permitting the prompt discussion of current issues, while its lack of form leaves it open to abuse and ridicule.

Hour Debates on Current Subjects

To preserve the question hour as a means of publicizing a wide variety of points in short compass and to provide a more suitable framework for brief debates on current subjects, the Bundestag in 1965 began to experiment with a type of adjournment debate. Deciding once again not to alter its formal Rules, but merely to agree provisionally on some regulations, the House determined that on application of fifteen Members, a debate on "a definite subject of general current interest" could be placed on the agenda, either by agreement within the Council of Elders or, failing that, by a vote of the Bundestag. Alternatively, such a debate could occur if at least thirty Members demanded it immediately after a question hour, to discuss the Government's reply to a question of general current interest.[64]

Between February and July, 1965, each method was employed once, the first to conduct a foreign policy debate on a press conference which General DeGaulle had recently held, the second to discuss matters of educational policy which had come up in questions that day. That only two such debates were held in six months, despite the simple requirements for initiating them, indicated the unwillingness of Members to make use of the new technique without their party's consent, and the reluctance of the parties to employ the format of unrehearsed discussion. The provisional rules limited the debate to one hour, and each speaker to five minutes, and required extemporaneous speaking; members of the Cabinet and the Bundesrat voluntarily agreed to abide by the five-minute limit.

The unfamiliar perils of this type of unrehearsed debate limited participation to the party leaders. The thirteen speakers in the foreign

[64] "Vorläufige Bestimmungen über Aussprachen zu Fragen von allgemeinem aktuellen Interesse," *Geschäftsordnung des Deutschen Bundestages*, Anlage 6. *Dt. Btag.*, 4. W.P., 159. Sitz., Jan. 27, 1965, p. 7821.

policy debate included the Chancellor (twice), the Foreign Minister, the parliamentary party chairmen of the SPD and the CDU/CSU (twice each), the vice-chairman of the FDP, and the chairman and six prominent members of the Bundestag Committee on Foreign Affairs. All but two of the speakers were members of the executive committees of their caucuses. Some of the old habits of debate planning manifested themselves in the party proportions among the speakers: two ministers and four other Bundestag Members of the CDU/CSU (one of these belonging to the CSU), four SPD and three FDP Members. Before the hour was up, there were no further hands requesting recognition.[65]

The pattern was similar in the second debate of this type, three months later. It was initiated, without warning, when the SPD's expert on educational policy decided that his oral questions on this subject had been inadequately answered by the Minister of the Interior. With the support of party leaders, he demanded a debate which took place immediately after the question hour. Participation was once again limited to party leaders and experts on the subject, with only five speakers other than the minister and the initiator, and the debate was exhausted in three-quarters of an hour.[66] Party control and the dominance of experts has thus inhibited the early development of these hour debates on current issues, demonstrating the limited effect which procedural changes can have on the style of public debate in the Bundestag.

PUBLIC INVESTIGATION

Investigating Committees

Apart from debate (and the election of its officers and the Chancellor), the only other activity of the Bundestag which regularly takes place in public is the work of its special investigating committees. The place of such committees in the parliamentary system is, however, ambivalent. Conceived during the Imperial political system by the advocates of increased powers for Parliament, they do not readily fit into a political system in which the Cabinet consists of the leadership of the parliamentary majority. In anticipation of this difficulty, the framers of the Weimar Constitution, which first provided for such

---

[65] *Dt. Btag.*, 4. W.P., 161. Sitz., Feb. 10, 1965, pp. 7918–29.
[66] *Dt. Btag.*, 4. W.P., 181. Sitz., May 12, 1965, pp. 9092, 9094–9103.

committees, gave minorities the right to set them up. In the badly divided Reichstag of the time, this right was gravely abused by extremist parties of right and left.[67]

Nevertheless, the Basic Law contains an only slightly attenuated version of the Weimar provisions, enabling a minority of one-fourth of the Members of the Bundestag to create an investigating committee, which ordinarily is to take testimony in public sessions.[68] With the regular standing committees exercising varying degrees of continuous control over the ministries corresponding to their jurisdictions, and obtaining the necessary information for lawmaking, the distinctive function of the special investigating committees has been public exposure of government wrongdoing. Their use for this purpose strongly tempted parliamentary minorities in the first Bundestag, and nine investigations were set up during the first four years.

However, the development of a stable governing majority, capable of controlling the course of investigations, if not of blocking their establishment, dampened the interest of the opposition parties in this procedure. For while one-fourth of the House can create the committee, the majority determines its size, will hold a majority of its seats, and control the course of its deliberations. Once set up, the committee therefore escapes the minority's control. Three committees were created in the second Bundestag, none in the third.[69]

The first investigation established in six years, set up in 1962 to inquire into a building contract let by the Defense Ministry, demonstrated the difficulty of investigating a highly partisan issue. The investigation, hesitantly initiated by the SPD after an extensive magazine exposé and directed primarily at the Minister of Defense, was effectively controlled by the CDU chairman, who was anxious to protect the Government. "We stand united behind the Federal Defense Minister," he declared in the House.[70] The balance of power in the committee, as in the House, was held by the FDP, which exploited

[67] Winfried Steffani, "Funktion und Kompetenz parlamentarischer Untersuchungsausschüsse," *Politische Vierteljahresschrift*, I (1960), 153–77.

[68] *Basic Law*, art. 44.

[69] The most complete treatment of investigating committees in postwar Germany is Karl Josef Partsch, "Empfiehlt es sich, Funktion, Struktur, und Verfahren der palamentarischen Untersuchungsausschüsse grundlegend zu ändern?" Gutachten, *Verhandlungen des 45. Deutschen Juristentages*, Vol. I, Pt. III (Munich and Berlin: C. H. Beck'sche Verlagsbuchhandlung, 1964).

[70] *Dt. Btag.*, 4. W.P., 37. Sitz., June 28, 1962, p. 1584.

its position by dramatically joining the SPD in rejecting the committee's first report when it was presented to the House, and referring it back to committee.[71] A second report, finally accepted four months later, was still inconclusive, and was in any case accompanied by a minority report from the SPD Members.[72] The experience in this case persuaded the leaders to restrict the use of investigating committees to subjects in which interest crossed party lines. A year later, the second and last investigation established during the fourth Bundestag, to inquire into Government wiretapping, was more successful precisely because the impetus to it was less partisan. The committee reached a unanimous conclusion on the main points, supported by all parties in the House, and induced the Government to agree to submit regulatory legislation.[73]

The Defense Commissioner

In the specially sensitive area of defense, the investigating function of the Bundestag has taken some special forms. The Defense Committee of the House may constitute itself as an investigating committee, on the request of at least one-fourth of its members.[74] Its experience in the performance of this function has been similar to that of the investigating committees generally.

More distinctive is the institution of a parliamentary Defense Commissioner, elected by the House to act as an auxiliary agent of Parliament in the control of the defense establishment. The commissioner is to act on behalf of the Bundestag or its Defense Committee as an investigator, with the right to initiate inquiries on his own authority, and to receive complaints directly from members of the armed forces who feel that their legal rights have been violated.[75]

From the start, however, the office was placed at the mercy of the parliamentary majority. After considerable controversy, the Bundestag, against SPD opposition, decided on simple majority election—and recall—of the commissioner, and limited his powers of investigation. From the start also, the commissioner had to contend with hostility from the Ministry of Defense, as well as from the CDU/CSU majority

[71] *Ibid.*, pp. 1581–4.
[72] *Dt. Btag.*, 4. W.P., 43. Sitz., Oct. 25, 1962, pp. 1874–1920; Anlage 2, p. 1921.
[73] *Dt. Btag.*, 4. W.P., 124. Sitz., April 29, 1964, pp. 5991–6035.
[74] *Basic Law*, art. 45 a(2).
[75] *Basic Law*, art. 45 b; *BGBl.* I, p. 652.

on the Bundestag Defense Committee, to any criticism he expressed of the defense administration.[76] His first annual report[77] drew heavy criticism from Defense Minister Strauss and from the committee majority, when the Defense Committee considered it. In its conclusions on the report, the committee declared that it had reached an agreement with the Defense Commissioner that "in carrying out his assignment, [he] does not take positions on the political decisions of Parliament and the Government."[78] The commissioner took the hint, and subsequent reports concentrated on the individual complaints he was receiving from members of the armed forces at the rate of 3,500 to 5,500 annually.[79] Neither House nor committee made specific use of his investigatory services.

Parliamentary debates of his annual reports did not take place until the sensational trial and conviction, early in 1964, of nine army officers on charges of the mistreatment of soldiers. This event brought the organization of the armed forces back into the limelight. The debate then hurriedly arranged dealt with the commissioner's last annual report—by then ten months old and having nothing to do with the incident—and took place in the absence of the commissioner, whose right to participate in the discussion had been questioned by the Council of Elders.[80]

Four months later, the long-slumbering question of the function of the institution was clearly presented by the commissioner himself. Rebelling against the limited potential his office offered him to advance public criticism based on his investigations, he published a series of sharply critical articles in a popular magazine, simultaneously with the appearance of his annual report to the Bundestag.[81] His chief theme, initially raised in the first annual report of his predecessor in office, and since then continuously discernible beneath the surface, was that the Government was paying insufficient attention to the democratization of the organization and leadership of the armed

[76] H. P. Secher, "Controlling the New German Military Elite: The Political Role of the Parliamentary Defense Commissioner in the Federal Republic," *Proceedings of the American Philosophical Society*, CIX (April, 1965), 63–84.

[77] Dt. Btag., 3. W.P., Drs. 1796.

[78] Dt. Btag., 3. W.P., Drs. 2666, p. 4.

[79] Dt. Btag., 4. W.P., Drs. 371, 1183.

[80] Dt. Btag., 4. W.P., 117. Sitz., Feb. 21, 1964, pp. 5359–77. See esp. p. 5364.

[81] Helmuth Heye, "In Sorge um die Bundeswehr," *Quick*, XVII, June 21 and 28, and July 5, 1964. Dt. Btag., 4. W.P., Drs. 2305.

forces. The theme itself was largely obscured by the ensuing controversy over the right of the commissioner to appeal to the public in this way. Leaders of the governing parties saw the possibility of an affront to the House.[82] The commissioner maintained that the House had not given him adequate opportunity to make his views public.

But the weakness of his position vis-a-vis a Government backed by a parliamentary majority was soon apparent. Against the votes of its SPD members, the Defense Committee adopted a recommendation to the Bundestag accepting the commissioner's report, but regretting the publication of his magazine articles and declaring that the individual shortcomings he had unearthed did not warrant his general critique of the methods of leadership and organization of the armed forces.[83] In the midst of the controversy, the commissioner asked to be relieved of his post for reasons of health.[84] His resignation enabled the majority to choose a successor more acceptable to it. In nominating Matthias Hoogen, it chose the then chairman of the Bundestag Judiciary Committee, a member of the CDU/CSU who had also chaired the Fibag investigation. For the first time in the history of the institution, there was no consensus on the choice, the SPD voting against the candidate.[85] At the same time, the outgoing commissioner's report became the subject of an unprecedentedly prompt and thorough Bundestag debate.[86] Furthermore, the Bundestag voted to change its Rules to permit the commissioner to speak before the House. Over the objection of the chairman of the Defense Committee, the new Rule gives as few as thirty Members the right to demand that the commissioner be heard.[87]

The office of the Defense Commissioner, like other agencies of parliamentary investigation, has therefore proven to be subject to control by a Bundestag majority, which is likely to act in support of the Government. The experience of the last three parliamentary terms demonstrates that with stable, governing majorities, parliamentary

---

[82] *Dt. Btag.*, 4. W.P., 133. Sitz., June 25, 1964, pp. 6547–50.

[83] *Dt. Btag.*, 4. W.P., Drs. 2795.

[84] *Die Welt*, Nov. 11, 1964.

[85] *Dt. Btag.*, 4. W.P., 153. Sitz., Dec. 11, 1964, pp. 7584–5. *Die Welt*, Dec. 12, 1964.

[86] *Dt. Btag.*, 4. W.P., 153., 156., 157. Sitz., Dec. 11, 1964, Jan. 20 and 21, 1965, pp. 7586–7603; 7667–7716; 7737–59.

[87] *Dt. Btag.*, 4. W.P., 159. Sitz., Jan. 27, 1965, pp. 7844–6. *Geschäftsordnung des Deutschen Bundestages*, par. 116c.

investigation cannot normally serve as an instrument for control of the Government in the manner expected in a system of legislative-executive separation. The significance of the investigatory agencies of the Bundestag, therefore, lies in the use which the Opposition can make of them to inform and stimulate parliamentary debate.

PUBLIC RELATIONS

Ambivalence Toward the Public

The role which the public deliberations of the Bundestag may play in the political system depends, of course, on the extent to which they receive public attention. But the attitude toward the general public on the part of most Members is ambivalent. In much of their work, Members seek to escape public scrutiny. They lack talent in reaching the public and confidence in public judgment. In the pursuit of specialization and party cohesion, they sacrifice open communication with each other. Their desire to reach the public is, by comparison, occasional, and does not grow out of the requirements of their day-to-day work. It is the desire of party leaders to appeal to the electorate, or of the officers of the House to improve its image, or of the average Member to make a contribution to civic education. But these are weak motives compared to those which constantly impel Members to take refuge from the public in closed committee chambers. And the general public, for its part, hardly clamors for access to those deliberations which take place privately, as long as interest groups within it have adequate information on decisions concerning them. Public interest in the work of the Bundestag suffers from the anti-parliamentary attitudes of past generations, from the unfamiliarity of present institutions of government, and from a general affluence which, ironically, has made the political system uninteresting just because its results have been so satisfactory.

Education

Aware of its dependence on public interest, yet anxious to preserve ample privacy, the Bundestag has sought to escape its dilemma by a program of public relations designed to improve its rapport with the public without requiring it to change its habits of work. A steady stream of visitors, a large proportion of them students on class excursions, passes through the public galleries of the House in organized shifts. The total during the first four parliamentary terms was five million persons, but nine-tenths of the visitors saw the House empty, because of the infrequency of public sessions. Individual Members, when they are present, meet with groups of visitors to answer questions, and the staff of the Bundestag conducts guided tours or question-and-answer sessions after the visit. An annual budget of DM 250,000 ($62,500) for "the introduction of educational and youth groups into the work of Parliament" helps to defray travel costs of student groups.[88] In many cases, hospitality extends to an invitation to lunch or refreshments in the parliamentary restaurant.

For teachers, a program of week-long seminars is offered in the Bundeshaus in Bonn, under the sponsorship of the Federal Office for Political Education, a government organization supported by the Ministry of the Interior which conducts a great variety of citizenship training programs.[89] Its weekly documentary newspaper, *Das Parlament*, contains extensive excerpts of the parliamentary debates, and is by far the most important medium of their dissemination. With a weekly circulation of nearly 100,000 copies, most of them sent without charge to schools, church and youth organizations, and military units, it largely displaces the official stenographic transcript as a documentary source of the debates for the general public.[90] Less than 1,000 copies of the official debates are purchased by private subscribers, the press run of 4,000 being reserved largely for Members of the Bundestag, each of whom receives one copy, and for Government offices and university libraries.

Radio and Television

The difficulty of a public relations program for a publicity-shy subject is demonstrated by the vacillation of the Bundestag regarding live radio and television transmission of its sittings. Marking the initial decision to broadcast or telecast major debates, Bundestag President Ehlers explained in 1952 that "we must bring the people directly into

---

[88] *Bundeshaushaltsplan für das Rechnungsjahr 1965*, Einzelplan 02, Tit. 308. Quadrennially, the House appropriates funds—the sum was DM 335,000 ($83,750) in 1965—to distribute the Official Handbook of Parliament (*Amtliches Handbuch des Deutschen Bundestages*) to public libraries, schools, and youth organizations (see *ibid.*, Tit. 874).

[89] *Das Parlament*, Oct. 14, 1964, p. 4.

[90] *Ibid.*, Oct. 25, 1961, pp. 8–9.

contact with the work of its Parliament, into contact with its debates, its differences of opinion, and the motives of the various decisions." [91] But the result, especially in some of the heated foreign policy and defense debates of the following years, was not entirely what had been sought. In a public unfamilar with parliamentary procedure and behavior, observing for the first time a Parliament whose public sessions constituted only a small part of its work, there were some extremely critical responses. The special objects of dismay were the sparse attendance and conspicuous inattention of Members of the House, and the sharp partisanship of the speeches. The institution of Parliament did not clearly and unquestionably benefit, as had been expected. Furthermore, each party became anxious to gain the best television audience for its speaker, introducing an extraneous factor into the organization of the debate. Finally, and most effectively, the governing party found that the televising of debates subjected it to a new, and unwelcome, source of criticism. The Council of Elders therefore determined, at the beginning of the third parliamentary term in 1958, that live radio and television broadcasts of debates would be abandoned except on those ceremonial occasions "which do not serve parliamentary discussion, but which document the unity of the House."

But growing concern about public disinterest in Parliament led to a new decision five years later: with Presidential approval, now always given, radio and television may record the sessions of the House for later broadcast, in excerpts, in news and feature programs. In addition, on subjects of major public importance, such as the extension of the statute of limitations on war-crimes trials, and on major occasions, such as debates on declarations of Government policy, live transmission is permitted. During 1965, debates were telecast live on six days, four of them in succession devoted to the discussion of Government policy after the opening of the fifth term of the Bundestag. The SPD, having decided to conduct a more vigorous opposition in debate, favored a general rule allowing live transmission of Bundestag proceedings at the discretion of the broadcast networks. Simultaneously, new efforts were made to explain to visitors, and to the public, the role which public debate has in the total work of the House.

[91] Hermann Ehlers, "Die Demokratie im neuen Deutschland," in Friedrich Schramm ed., *Um dem Vaterland zu Dienen* (Cologne: O. Schmidt, 1955), pp. 39–40.

The Public Image of the Bundestag

These massive efforts to reach the public, and the passage of time, may have contributed to the measurable growth in public awareness of the identity of Parliament, and a decline in the original cynicism toward its work. More than half the population can today distinguish the Bundestag from the other major institutions of government, and nearly half can correctly identify the Member from their constituency.[92] In the decade after 1951, the proportion of the population believing that a Member of the Bundestag needs great competence rose from 39 to 61 per cent, and those believing that the public interest was the primary concern of Members rose from 25 to 41 per cent of the population.[93] Finally, those who held a fair or better opinion of the Bundestag rose, between 1951 and 1965, from 66 to 86 per cent of the population, and within this group, those who found it good or better increased from 35 to 52 per cent of the total.[94]

Formal knowledge about the institution correlates closely with the educational level of the respondents,[95] suggesting that it will continue to rise with rising educational levels and with special efforts in the field of civic education. But the growing ability to give correct answers

[92] In answer to the question, "Does the Bundestag in Bonn represent the *Länder*, the people, or is it the Government?," the responses in 1951 and 1965 were as follows:

	1951	*1965*
representation of the people	48%	54%
representation of the *Länder*	8	4
the Government	24	28
no answer	20	14

The ambiguity of the concept of "the Government" (*die Regierung*) in a parliamentary system may be a source of some of the confusion (*EMNID Informationen* [Bielefeld: EMNID Institut, 1965], no. 9, pp. 2–3). A satisfactory identification of the Bundestag Member representing the respondent's constituency was given by 43 per cent of respondents in October, 1961. That proportion has risen steadily since 1951, when it was 22 per cent (see E. N. and E. P. Neumann, eds., *Jahrbuch der öffentlichen Meinung* [Allensbach: Institut für Demoskopie], I [1947–55], 161; II [1957], 174; III [1958–64], 262).

[93] *Ibid.*, I, 162–3; II, 176–7; III, 262–3.

[94] *EMNID Informationen*, 1965, no. 9, p. 4.

[95] While, on the average, 54 per cent of respondents could identify the Bundestag correctly (see n. 92, *supra*), 84 per cent of those who had completed a college preparatory curriculum (*Abitur*) could do so (*EMNID Informationen*, p. 3). A similar correlation exists with respect to other measures of formal knowledge of the Bundestag (see *Jahrbuch der öffentlichen Meinung*, III, 261–2).

to textbook questions about the Bundestag is not matched by a measurably growing interest in or understanding of the work of Parliament. Over 85 per cent of the population has not heard anything about the work of its Member in the Bundestag, a figure which has hardly changed from the beginning.[96] In a study comparing the political cultures of the United States, Great Britain, Italy, Mexico, and Germany, Germans alone displayed a greater sense of being able to affect administrative than legislative decisions.[97] Only 12 per cent of German respondents indicated that they would try to contact elected leaders (or the press) in an attempt to influence a national political decision, while 44 per cent of British and 57 per cent of American citizens said they would do so.[98]

Correspondingly, the mail which Members of the Bundestag receive from their constituents is small in quantity and consists mainly of special requests for intervention with ministries, or other kinds of assistance with personal problems. Members from rural areas, particularly those who hold or have held local office, may receive ten to twenty letters daily, and may, in addition, hold weekly or fortnightly office hours in their constituency, where they receive additional requests.[99] Many of them spend a large proportion of their energies on such constituency errands, which can contribute more than anything else to their renomination. On the other hand, Members elected in urban areas receive very little direct mail. In either case, mail expressing the correspondent's views on current issues is rare, and Members, poorly equipped to deal with correspondence, do nothing to encourage it. A steady flow of letters urging particular political decisions comes to the President of the Bundestag, who, in the eyes of the correspondents, is apparently the appropriate authority. The average German is inclined to look to local government officials rather than to his Member of Parliament for a redress of grievances. He is content to allow interest groups to act in his name in expressing demands on

[96] *Jahrbuch der öffentlichen Meinung*, I, 161; II, 174; III, 262.

[97] Gabriel A. Almond and Sidney Verba, *The Civic Culture, Political Attitudes and Democracy in Five Nations* (Princeton: Princeton University Press, 1963), pp. 218, 225–7.

[98] *Ibid.*, p. 203.

[99] For the experiences of two Members, see Heinrich Ritzel, *Einer von Vierhundertzwei* (Offenbach/Main: Bollwerk Verlag, 1953), pp. 55–60, 74; *Die Welt*, Jan. 12, 1963.

national issues.[100] The direct contact between the individual Member and his constituents is weak.[101]

The inadequacy of the Bundestag as an avenue of access to government for the citizen limits its capacity to serve as an instrument for legitimating the actions of government. The comparative study of political cultures reveals a general correlation between a citizen's sense of participation in affecting political decisions and his attachment to the political system. In Germany, not only is the sense of participation relatively low, but so is pride in the political system.[102]

The results of a survey of attitudes toward the Bundestag which has been conducted regularly since 1951 bear this out in several respects. They indicate substantial fluctuations in popular judgments of the institution, in spite of a long-term tendency toward a more positive attitude toward it. (See Table 40.) Furthermore, there is a strong correlation between the fluctuations in attitude toward the Bundestag, and changing attitudes toward the policy of the Chancellor and his Government.[103] Among respondents at any given point in time, attitudes toward the Bundestag vary with party identification. While 75 per cent of CDU/CSU adherents thought well of Parliament in the 1961 survey, this was true of only 64 per cent of FDP and 45 per cent of SPD supporters. Only 1 per cent of CDU/CSU respondents thought the Bundestag "poor," but 5 per cent of FDP and 11 per cent of SPD supporters did.[104] In the 1965 survey, in which, on the average, 38 per cent of respondents found the Bundestag "fair" or "poor," this was true of 52 per cent of SPD supporters.[105]

The attitude toward the institution of Parliament therefore appears

---

[100] Almond and Verba, *op. cit.*, pp. 314, 431–2, 435, 439.

[101] By contrast, a large number of citizens make use of the traditional right to address petitions to the Bundestag, which is guaranteed by article 17 of the Basic Law. Coming in at the rate of 7–10,000 annually, these petitions present a great variety of requests, mostly pertaining to personal affairs. A standing committee of the Bundestag deals with them or forwards them to the appropriate authority, reporting regularly to the House on its work and requesting its approval (see, for example, *Dt. Btag.*, 4. W.P., Drs. 459). But in this relationship, the Bundestag serves as one of many agencies providing remedies for personal problems, not as an avenue by which the citizen participates in political decisions.

[102] Almond and Verba, *op. cit.*, p. 103.

[103] Compare the responses between 1951 and 1963 to the question, "Are you by and large in agreement or in disagreement with the policy of Adenauer?" (*Jahrbuch der öffentlichen Meinung*, I, 172–3; II, 182–3; III, 298–305).

[104] *EMNID Informationen*, 1962, no. 8, pp. 3–5.

[105] *Ibid.*, 1965, no. 9, p. 4.

Table 40. Public attitudes toward the Bundestag (in per cent of respondents to the question: "What do you think of the Bundestag in Bonn as our representative assembly?" ª)

	Response			
Year	Excellent or basically good	Fair	Poor	No opinion
1951	35	31	9	25
1952	30	35	13	22
1953 (May)	46	31	10	13
1953 (November)	59	25	4	12
1954	49	37	10	4
1955	57	33	6	4
1956	46	37	12	5
1957 (September)	55	30	7	8
1958	37	41	16	6
1959	56	30	5	9
1960	52	35	6	7
1961 (December)	55	25	6	14
1963 (May)	46	36	7	11
1965 (January)	52	34	4	10

ª ("Wie denken Sie über den Bonner Bundestag als unsere Volksvertretung: ausgesprochen gut, im Grunde gut, mässig, oder schlecht?") From *EMNID Informationen* (Bielefeld: EMNID Institut, 1965), no. 9, p. 4.

to correlate with attitudes toward the party which has dominated that institution throughout its existence, and with satisfaction with Government policy. The "ins," who have a sense of better access to government and are more satisfied with its decisions, find the institution of Parliament more acceptable than the "outs." Furthermore, the complete party control of the Bundestag's public performance makes it difficult for it to attract support independent of party. For the compromises among parties which are negotiated in the Bundestag, and the procedures by which they are reached, are largely hidden from public view. But the failure of the Bundestag to gain general acceptance as a political institution impairs its capacity to legitimate the decisions of government. In this respect the attitude toward the Bundestag is part —perhaps a decisive part—of the general attitude toward the political system. The available evidence indicates that the support which the system enjoys depends on the specific accomplishments it has so far produced, and that it has failed to gain legitimacy independent of its concrete achievements.[106] Insofar as the Bundestag has been unable to supply substitutes for the symbols of legitimacy which the authoritarian political system possessed, its limits as an agency of legitimation may explain the conditional support given the present system generally.

Alternatives to Parliamentary Communication

As an avenue of communication between the Government and the public, Parliament has severe competition. The Government employs press conferences, interviews and planted articles. Interest groups address themselves to ministries and parliamentary committees directly and privately. But the channels of communication which thus compete with Parliament, whatever their advantages to those who employ them, cannot provide a forum in which conflicting opinions confront each other in the open. At best, they permit a flow of diverse demands and responses among specialized publics. They do not exhibit these conflicting opinions to the general public, do not permit an organized debate between opposing sides, and they leave the unorganized interests in society unheard. In short, to the extent that the chief actors in the political system bypass Parliament as a medium of communication, parliamentary debate cannot contribute to the reconciliation of conflicting demands and to public acceptance of the policy result. To that extent Parliament does not perform a representative function in the political system.

[106] Almond and Verba, *op. cit.*, pp. 103–5, 247–51; Lucien Pye and Sidney Verba, eds., *Political Culture and Political Development* (Princeton: Princeton University Press, 1965), pp. 141–5.

VIII

Parliament and German Politics

A NATIONAL Parliament has existed in Germany for as long as there has been national politics. From the moment that there were national political demands, there was a national representative assembly to express them. The establishment of the Bundestag in 1949 was therefore not a new beginning, but the continuation of an institutional tradition, however disrupted that tradition may have been.

Some of the most conspicuous characteristics of the German Parliament are consequently the hardened products of over a century of parliamentary experience. The arrangement of seats in the chamber, the separation between Cabinet and parliamentary leadership, the pattern of recruitment of Members from various occupational backgrounds, the formal Rules of Procedure, the importance of party and committee organization, the emphasis on lawmaking, are all the results of long development, and particularly of the formative period before the First World War. Many of these characteristics are related to the political system of constitutional monarchy, with its separation between Cabinet and Parliament, its multiplicity of ideological and class-based parties, and its acceptance of the legitimacy of the monarchy. In that system, the popularly elected chamber was limited to lawmaking and interest articulation, and its structure reflected these functions.

But despite the force of tradition, the comparatively brief and apparently uneventful years since 1949 have profoundly affected this institutional inheritance. The experience of totalitarianism caused a deep break in the continuity of political development. In a remarkable and, in some respects, distressing manner, it prompted a desire to escape from the heritage of the past, to blot out political habit and memory. It left the postwar political system exceptionally vulnerable to current political demands, to the styles of existing leaders, to the present alignment of forces—in short, to the influences of the moment.

So far as Parliament is concerned, some of these influences were constitutional. It was the intention of the framers of the Basic Law, reacting against the subordination of Parliament in the Weimar Republic, that the Bundestag should play a central part in the political system. Unlike the Weimar Constitution, the Basic Law provided for Bundestag election of the Chancellor and established a lawmaking process in which parliamentary approval was essential for all legislation, with no escape to presidential emergency government possible. These new aspects of its constitutional position encouraged changes in the party pattern in Parliament, providing new incentives for the formation of governing majorities. They also stimulated a rationalization of the legislative process, promoting committee specialization and new, informal procedures to permit the House to deal with the enormous volume of complex postwar legislation.

But the most important influences on Parliament since 1949 have undoubtedly been political. The consequences of war, the division of the nation, and the social changes accompanying the most recent stages of industrialization created a new pattern of political parties, issues, and interest groups. The outlines of this pattern have been apparent at least since the election of 1953. That election demonstrated that many traditional ideological and class appeals had lost their force, that a single political party could embrace a wide variety of interests, accept the leadership of a single national politician, and attract the support of a large plurality of the electorate. The dominance of the CDU/CSU since that election resulted in a consolidation throughout the party system, the reduction of the number of parties with national representation to three, and the convergence of party programs on a common denominator. It promoted the rise of a new type of professional politician in all parties, chiefly distinguished by his skills as a tactician and as a broker among diverse interests, rather than by the more traditional skills of agitation and advocacy.

The structure of Parliament has responded to these changes in the political system. The existing organization of the parliamentary parties broke down under the size of the new parties, the diversity of their composition, and the complexity of the issues they faced. In order to preserve their habitual cohesion and their role in policy making, the parties developed a far more intricate parliamentary organization, including working groups, interest groups (in the CDU/CSU), executive committees, and inner executives. Their success has permitted the parties of the governing coalition to extend their influence beyond the election of the Chancellor to the selection of his Cabinet. As a result, Parliament has become the nearly exclusive source of Cabinet personnel, and success within the parliamentary parties has become the prerequisite for ministerial appointment. The recruitment of Cabinet ministers from parliamentary politics, without recourse to leaders from local government or from public or private bureaucracies, is one of the most important innovations in the postwar political system, even while the traditional separation between parliamentary and Cabinet leadership has been maintained.

The procedural rules of Parliament have also responded to political change. The relationships between parties no longer divided by sharp ideological cleavages, but encouraged to collaborate in the formation of governing coalitions and legislative majorities, demanded flexible interpretations of existing rules and new folkways facilitating compromise. While the formal Rules were hardly altered, the necessary innovations were made informally, on the authority of the party whips. The reduction in the number of parliamentary parties greatly simplified the arrangements among them.

Finally, the roles of Members within Parliament have been shaped by political change. Although there seems to be considerable continuity in the pattern of recruitment to Parliament, so that the total composition of the House bears marked similarity to its prewar predecessors by all the major sociological criteria, leadership has increasingly been exercised by a small group of professional parliamentarians possessing the relevant tactical skills. In turn, the large numbers of Members who enter Parliament chiefly as interest-group representatives play subordinate roles as legislative experts in their particular fields of interest. The relationship between the professional parliamentarians and the interest representatives is one of broker to client.

The uncommon political stability which has existed in the postwar period has permitted the new pattern of parliamentary organization, procedure, and leadership to become quickly established. For this stability has provided a continuity of membership and leadership in Parliament which is unprecedented in German history. A group of Members has sat in Parliament through three, four, and even five terms, gaining influence with seniority. With every passing year, the chances have improved that their style will become the habit of their successors. The turnover in some of the most influential positions has been extremely small. Gerstenmaier's parliamentary presidency spans four of the Bundestag's five terms. Rasner and Mommer, the incumbent whips of the two major parties, are in large part the founders of their offices and the authors of the body of informal procedure which they practice. Seventy-one of the Members re-elected in 1965 have served continuously in the House from the beginning. The characteristics and skills of a single group of political leaders have therefore had an enormous influence in setting the norms of the institution.

The rapidity with which Parliament has adapted to a new political environment explains its capacity to perform major functions in the political system. Its recruitment processes have produced the personnel for both parliamentary and executive leadership; its party and committee organization has provided the framework for the aggregation of interests and for bargaining among them; its role in lawmaking is a major part of the process by which rules are made in the political system.

But the very ease with which the institution has responded to the political environment has also produced incongruities between public perceptions of Parliament and parliamentary performance. For the changes in the structure and function of Parliament have occurred largely informally and have been obscured by the traditional formal structure. The attitudes, emotions, and evaluations found in the political culture still bear the marks of the Imperial political system, while the reality of parliamentary performance is very different. The available evidence indicates that there is little public understanding of the functions performed by Parliament in the formation of the Cabinet, nor of the complex process by which the Bundestag influences legislation. There is little respect for the type of professional politician who conspicuously leads Parliament. The sense of public participation in politics through Parliament is not well developed, and parliamentary decisions do not carry any special legitimacy by virtue of being the decisions of a representative body. An administrative view of politics prevails which values expertise and efficiency, and disparages the influence of special interests and partisanship.

The Members of Parliament are themselves influenced by these culturally conditioned attitudes. They feel a far stronger incentive to develop their legislative specialties, for example, than to engage in political discourse with the general public. Parliamentary leaders and whips have concentrated on developing an informal body of procedural norms which facilitate their negotiations among themselves, but they have felt no obligation to formalize any aspect of the new arrangements to make them publicly visible. They have furthermore hidden their professional commitment to politics under a great variety of misleading occupational designations, among which "civil servant" is the most common. They have permitted the decision-making process which takes place in the convenient privacy of the committee room or the party caucus to displace the public deliberations of the House. In short, the Members regard their party leaders, or their interest-group patrons, as their chief constituents, and they treat the general public with the reserve and discretion more typical of the bureaucrat than the politician.

Only relatively weak influences are at work to diminish the incongruity between parliamentary performance and public perceptions of it. Some of the most conspicuous characteristics of the Bundestag are derived, as we have seen, from parliamentary experience in the time of the Empire, and these relatively obvious characteristics reinforce attitudes having a similar origin. The postwar political tranquility, so favorable to other aspects of institutional adaptation, has the effect of creating a political apathy which allows Parliament to keep the general public at arm's length. The system of proportional representation and candidate selection gives the individual Member considerable freedom from the general electorate and ties him the more closely to party and interest group. The mass communications media, themselves exhibiting many of the misconceptions and traditional political values characteristic of the culture, do little to change perceptions and attitudes.

The cultural gap which separates the Bundestag from the public seriously inhibits the performance of the function of representation. Furthermore, it permits some of the characteristics of bureaucracy to grow in the structure of Parliament. The hierarchy of influence among Members, the emphasis on specialization, the demand for staff, the preference for private channels of communication and deliberation, the concentration on policy-making processes, are all reminiscent of administrative organization. These tendencies, undoubtedly observable in other parliaments, are given a freer reign in the Bundestag because of the neglect of the representative function, which tends to encourage amateurism, common sense, publicity, and open competition for electoral support. But if the price of maintaining Parliament's influence is emulation of the bureaucratic institutions with which it competes for the performance of political functions, then the survival of Parliament makes little difference for the political system. For the distinctive characteristic of parliament is the relationship in which it can stand to the public, the contact it can supply between the expert in government and the society he governs.

That contact, more difficult to maintain in a modern technological society than ever before, is more crucial in Germany than anywhere else in the Western world. For twice in this century German political systems have encountered crises in the relationship between government and public, crises of legitimacy. These crises account for the failure of both the constitutional monarchy and of the Weimar Republic. Perhaps still more disturbing, only a totalitarian dictatorship has been able to mobilize the German people for politics.

Even if the present system faces no early crisis, the constant growth of executive power, and the prospect of the establishment of larger political units in Western Europe on a supranational level, steadily increase the urgency, and the difficulty, of representing government and public to each other. While, in the short run, the failure of Parliament adequately to perform a representative function is consistent with its institutional survival, in the long run it may be fatal.

Politicians are, however, motivated mainly by short-run considerations. Although the relationship between Parliament and public has by no means been ignored in Germany, it has been chiefly the province of civic groups and educators, who can at best deal with one side of the equation. Within the House, broad concern for the place of Parliament in the political system has been a luxury in which only its President, a few other officers, and the members of their staffs have seriously indulged. Although this concern among a few leaders of the institution has produced a steady flow of reform proposals, the limits on what can be accomplished are set by the interests of the party leaders and their clients on the backbenches. Most parliamentarians have either relegated the problem to occasional civic lectures or have tried to escape it by means of public relations programs which are only substitutes for a genuine contact between the House and its constituency.

To some extent, the shortcomings of Parliament as an agency of representation are being offset by the plebiscitary relationship which has developed between the Chancellor and the electorate. To some extent, the functions of political communication may be performed by a variety of special-interest groups, the parties, and the mass media.

But such performance of communications functions by other structures may still leave some of the need for representation unfulfilled. So far, at least, there is no evidence that these other structures have imparted to the public a sense of participation in government, or a commitment to the political system which goes beyond satisfaction with the day-to-day results it produces. The problem of legitimacy remains.

No balance can therefore be struck between the influence of the Bundestag in forming the Cabinet and in lawmaking, and its weaknesses as an agency of representation. For ultimately public support is Parliament's title to authority in all areas. Furthermore, in the performance of the function of representation, the stability of the entire political system is at stake.

Appendix I

Table 41. *Popular vote cast in elections to the Bundestag, 1949–1965 (per cent of valid votes cast for party lists)*

Parties	1949 [a]	1953	1957	1961	1965
Christian Democratic Union/Christian Social Union (CDU/CSU)	31.0	45.2	50.2	45.3	47.6
Social Democratic Party of Germany (SPD)	29.2	28.8	31.8	36.2	39.3
Free Democratic Party (FDP)	11.9	9.5	7.7	12.8	9.5
German Party (DP)	4.0	3.2	3.4		
All-German Party (GDP)				2.8 [b]	– [c]
All-German Bloc (Expellees) (GB/BHE)	–	5.9	4.6		
Bavarian Party (BP)	4.2	1.7			
Federal Union (FU)			0.9	–	–
Center Party (Z)	3.1	0.8			
Economic Reconstruction League (WAV)	2.9	–	–	–	–
Communist Party of Germany (KPD)	5.7	2.2	–	–	–
German Peace Union (DFU)	–	–	–	1.9	1.3
German Reich Party (DRP)	1.8	1.1	1.0	0.8	–
National Democratic Party of Germany (NPD)	–	–	–	–	2.0
Other parties	1.4	1.6	0.4	0.2	0.3
Independent candidates	4.8	–	–	–	–
	100.0	100.0	100.0	100.0	100.0
Participation (% of eligible voters)	78.5	86.0	87.8	87.7	86.8
Invalid votes (% of votes cast)					
On 1st vote (constituency candidates)	3.1	3.4	3.0	2.6	2.9
On 2nd vote (party lists)		3.3	3.8	4.0	2.4

[a] Figures for 1949 are in per cent of votes cast for constituency candidates, since there was no separate vote for *Land* lists.

[b] Braces denote merger of parties indicated.

[c] Dashes indicate no candidates presented.

Appendix II

Table 42. Seats won in elections to the Bundestag, 1949–1965

Parties	1949	1953	1957	1961	1965
CDU/CSU	144	250	277	251	251
In constituencies	115	172	194	156	153
On *Land* lists	24	72	76	86	92
In Berlin	5	6	7	9	6
SPD	140	162	181	203	217
In constituencies	96	45	46	91	95
On *Land* lists	35	106	123	99	107
In Berlin	9	11	12	13	15
FDP	57	53	43	67	50
In constituencies	12	14	1	0	0
On *Land* lists	40	34	40	67	49
In Berlin	5	5	2	0	1
DP	17	15	17	— ª	—
In constituencies	5	10	6		
On *Land* lists	12	5	11		
In Berlin	0	0	0		
GB/BHE	—	27	0	—	—
In constituencies		0	0		
On *Land* lists		27	0		
In Berlin		0	0		
BP	17	0	—	—	—
In constituencies	11	0			
On *Land* lists	6	0			
In Berlin	0	0			
Z	10	2	—	—	—
In constituencies	0	1			
On *Land* lists	10	1			
In Berlin	0	0			
WAV	12	—	—	—	—
In constituencies	0				
On *Land* lists	12				
In Berlin	0				

Appendix II

Table 42 (continued).

Parties	1949	1953	1957	1961	1965
KPD	15	0	–	–	–
In constituencies	0	0			
On *Land* lists	15	0			
In Berlin	0	0			
DRP	5	0	0	0	–
In constituencies	0	0	0	0	
On *Land* lists	5	0	0	0	
In Berlin	0	0	0	0	
Other Parties	1	0	1	0	0
In constituencies	0	0	0	0	0
On *Land* lists	1	0	0	0	0
In Berlin	0	0	1	0	0
Independents	3	0	0	0	0
In constituencies	3	0	0	0	0
Total	421	509	519	521	518
In constituencies	242	242	247	247	248
On *Land* lists	160	245 [b]	250 [c]	252 [d]	248
In Berlin	19	22	22	22	22

[a] Dash indicates no candidates presented

[b] Includes 3 superproportional victories (See Ch. III, n. 39)

[c] Includes 3 superproportional victories (See Ch. III, n. 39)

[d] Includes 5 superproportional victories (See Ch. III, n. 39)

Index

The index includes references, by author, to all works cited more than once in the footnotes. In cases of multiple authors, only the first is indexed.